Governance

Ralf-Eckhard Türke

Governance

Systemic Foundation and Framework

Physica-Verlag

A Springer Company

Dr. oek. HSG, Dipl. Wirtsch.-Ing. TUD
Ralf-Eckhard Türke
Wunderlistrasse 35
8037 Zürich
Switzerland
mail@ralf-eckhard.com

ISBN 978-3-7908-2079-9   e-ISBN 978-3-7908-2080-5

Contributions to Management Science ISSN 1431-1941

Library of Congress Control Number: 2008934295

© 2008 Physica-Verlag Heidelberg

Cover design: WMXDesign GmbH, Heidelberg

Printed on acid-free paper

9 8 7 6 5 4 3 2 1

springer.com

To my parents
Hildburg and Erhard Türke

Foreword

by Prof. Dr. Markus Schwaninger

Ralf-Eckhard Türke's book is the impressive result of high-quality basic research, and constitutes a very important contribution to the governance of social systems. It is written with verve and empathy.

Türke presents a holistic, integrative framework for governance based on an interactional perspective. Due to his extraordinary creativity and enormous commitment, he has succeeded in building a theory that is not only consistent but also potentially very powerful. The main emphasis of the book falls on organizational diagnosis and design, and the author presents a coherent system of propositions that is highly innovative. In principle, the foundation for a drastic improvement of the standard of organizational interventions is offered. That is revolutionary!

The theory presented here is no mere mental construction from the "ivory tower". On the contrary, it capitalizes on the author's substantial experience in the application field, while also benefiting from an empirical test documented in the opus.

This volume is full of valuable insights, and furnishes the conceptual basis for superior governance. Practitioners will gain a great deal from it.

I wish Türke's book the broad dissemination that it deserves.

St. Gallen, March 2008   Prof. Dr. Markus Schwaninger
                                          University of St. Gallen, Switzerland

Foreword

by Prof. Dr. Kuno Schedler

Public Governance has been ardently discussed for several years. It is an extremely well published field in the interface of political science, jurisprudence, and economics including business administration. Ever since the 90ies the debate around Governance has been considered as the "renaissance of the political aspects of administrative reforms" (Schedler 2003) helping to differentiate the narrow economical approaches of the New Public Management. The primary question of Public Governance is the steering of the public sphere, which increasingly shifts from hierarchic into network types of arrangements (Scherer / Schnell 2002, Mastronardi 2005). This creates new demands for the organisation and cooperation of public institutions. Public private partnerships (Zimmermann / Ehrensperger / Weber 2005), outsourcing (Proeller 2002), joint ventures (Knechtenhofer 2003), self-regulating organisations (Scherer / Grabherr / Walser 2001) – these are topics which are directly connected with Public Governance and which (as cited) have been at the research agenda of the University of St. Gallen for some time now.

The research methods applied in the field of Public Governance are diverse, yet in majority they are based on (qualitative) approaches of political science. Many derive from (neo-)institutionalism or the theory of social networks; usually they remain analytical and refrain from normative conclusions. Others as for example the World Bank explicitly develop a concept of "good governance" – which remains practically without theoretical foundations (World Bank 1989). The "e"-aspect of Governance, i.e. supporting system structures with modern information and communication technologies, has only recently begun to be researched (World Bank 2003).

This is the point where the research documented in this publication begins. The author develops a general conceptual framework for the examination of public governance arrangements, which may also be used for comprehensive structural audits. His concepts are primarily based on systemic and cybernetic approaches, yet these are supplemented with other theoretical approaches and further advanced. With his work, he positions himself within the synthetic approaches to governance, i.e. neither focusing solely on structural relationships or actors but taking a holistic perspective with a consistent systemic approach.

Ralf-Eckhard Türke works on the state of the art of governance research, yet at the same time he develops an independent terminology which he applies later on in his case studies. Türke defines his concepts with utmost precision, clearly using notions from the existing governance literature, while at the same time being firmly rooted within systemic and cybernetic models. When elaborating on abstract concepts and relations he moves with clear focus, absolute precision and full of relish. Almost he seems to spin a tale around the theory yet with deep analytical knowledge and understanding.

For somebody (like me) who is not accustomed to daily move within this realm it is no light reading. Captivating and consistent, yet demanding, Türke becomes part of the tradition of systemic theorists who create their own notions and concepts thus explaining things by using their own specific semantics. Even the special symbols used by him to distinguish between the ontology and epistemology of one and the same concept are characteristic for his work, for example *systems* are distinguished from °systems°.

Türke considerably advances the systemic and cybernetic foundations that have so far primarily been applied for business contexts. He does not stop at the limits of existing knowledge, but pushes them further, rethinks and rephrases until he achieves enough complexity to precisely grasp and describe the highly complicated structures of German communities. It is easy to imagine how much this challenges the abstractive abilities of the author himself as well as his readers. Türke, however, achieves this on a high level without loosing himself in the banality of overcomplexity. Türke's advancement of existing theories closely approximates the character of fundamental research and can be expected to be broadly received in the future.

Its empirical applications give the research a practical relevance, which provides substantial benefits for further research. In a case study of German communities in the state of Hesse Türke shows how the Governance framework applies to community life. He demonstrates how existing governing structures of a community can be evaluated and improved with respect to their viability and sustainability. Above and beyond, the consequences and benefits of the use of electronic media within communities are identified.

From my point of view, this research on Governance is extremely thorough, creative and theoretically as well as empirically well founded. It deserves highest attention and recognition from both systemic researchers and the public governance community. It is no surprise that Türke has already provided well-received contributions to international conferences thus receiving recognition from both sides.

St. Gallen, March 2008   Prof. Dr. Kuno Schedler
                                              University of St. Gallen, Switzerland

Preface

This book creates a mosaic of first principles of and fundamental insights into governance. It is less concerned with how these insights evolved and who discovered them – although it certainly touches on those facts. Rather, it strives to assemble these principles and insights into a synthetic frame which inter-relates them and, just as with a puzzle, makes them visible, accessible, tangible, and thus prepares them for their selective, purposeful application in any governing context.

Those who embark on a journey through this book in search of 'know-how' shall be forewarned: you might become a victim of your own expectations. You will not find a step-by-step procedure on how to attend to certain governing issues or problems that you might be contemplating. To simply read what has been written here will not produce any benefits. Although you may call what you read a "theory", you will find it of no value in applying it theoretically. The benefit of the synthetic frame has to be deployed; it is not in this book. To discover it you will have to use the frame as a pointer in some real life experience. Like a lense, you may look through it at any context around you, let's say, the company you work for, the community you live in, the bakery around the corner, your son's football team, your family, or whatever context is of interest to you. All of them are governed somehow by somebody. Upon focussing on one context, you will be confronted with its actual situation, as it is highly unique at that very moment. As you immerse yourself in that specific situation, your view of it immediately develops from the context. You realise that the specificty

---

[1] "Those who observe just inform themselves. If instead you do what you see, you learn to see what you do; you see while learning and learn while seeing; you thus cultivate yourself." Sprotte, Sigwart German painter.

of the context usually does not match with your previously acquired 'know-how' about how to resolve certain governing issues. To know how bakeries usually determine their market and the expected customer demand for the next month does not help to understand the specific problem and situation underlying the current conduct of that bakery around the corner. The common practice – although it might be adequate in a typical case – may be completely inadequate for the specific case one faces, e.g. because specific customers are addressed there and personnel expertise is lacking. What you need in all such cases is a synthetic frame, something that enables you to make sense of the current situation of a governing context in all its specificity. This 'theory' provides you with such a frame for referring to and reflecting on the actual situation faced. You will discover its benefits if you use it as a 'lens' for your eyes or a 'grammar' for your thoughts that sharpens your perspective on the governing context in focus, to understand its logic, to recognise its strength and deficiencies, to dismantle the root causes of its most current issues. Instead of 'know-how' to resolve certain governing issues the synthetic frame can enable you to acquire the capability to make sense of governing contexts, their specific issues and conditions, and using that as a basis, to assess the means established to attend to them and to compose and promote interventions that are truly suitable. The only way out of complexity is through it. This synthetic 'theory' is not a map for some path to be taken but a guide on how to make sense of a territory. Although it might lead you to create a map if that is adequate. Upon experiencing its benefits, it will cultivate your own day-to-day theory building and development. And that will give you the sense of cutting a Gordian knot.

Zürich, June 2008   Ralf-Eckhard Türke

Table of contents

1 Introduction   **1**

   1.1   Perspectives on governance   2
         1.1.1 The structure-oriented view   3
         1.1.2 The actor-oriented view   4
         1.1.3 Synthetic views   5
   1.2   Motivation, objectives and research questions   8
   1.3   Theories and research methodology   12
         1.3.1 Making explicit the underlying *Weltanschauung*   14
         1.3.2 Identifying and integrating relevant theories   15
         1.3.3 Deriving instruments and tools for practice   19
         1.3.4 Project experience and expert dialogue   19
         1.3.5 Conducting a case study   20
   1.4   Structure of the manuscript   21

2 Actors, images, and systems   **23**

   2.1   Actors   23
   2.2   Images   25
         2.2.1 Individual percepts   28
         2.2.2 Individual and social contexts   28
         2.2.3 Individual and social intentions   32
         2.2.4 Complexity of actor backgrounds   33
   2.3   Systems   37
         2.3.1 Boundaries   41
         2.3.2 Elements and relations   42

3 Interaction   **47**

   3.1   Mutual orientation   47
         3.1.1 Coupling   47
         3.1.2 Aspects of structure   62
   3.2   Change or transformation capacity   66

3.2.1 Meaning   68
3.2.2 Referencing situations and issues   71
3.2.3 Triggering change   83
3.2.4 Method   89

3.3   Channel capacity   92

3.3.1 Relationships, tasks, and responsibilities   93
3.3.2 Sequences and time lags   97
3.3.3 Shapes of representation   100
3.3.4 Physical settings   107
3.3.5 Channel capacity   108

3.4   Transduction capacity   110

3.4.1 °System° boundaries   112
3.4.2 Logical boundaries   116
3.4.3 Actor boundaries   119
3.4.4 Transduction   120

3.5   Sustainability of control   121

4   Viability   127

4.1   Structural characteristics of °systems°   129

4.1.1 Invariance   130
4.1.2 Recursion   131
4.1.3 Organisational entities and actor involvement   133
4.1.4 Autonomy   134
4.1.5 Viability   136

4.2   Invariant °system° topics   138

4.3   *One* issues – °sub-system° implementation   140

4.3.1 *One-One*   142

4.4   *Two* topics – coordination   143

4.4.1 *Two* arena   145
4.4.2 *Two-One*   146

4.5   *Three* topics – operative governing   146

4.5.1 *Three-Two*   148
4.5.2 *Three* arena   149
4.5.3 *Three-One*   150
4.5.4 *Three(*)-One*   153

4.6   *Four* topics – strategic governing   154

4.6.1 *Four* arena   155

4.6.2	*Four-Environment*	157
4.6.3	*Four-Three*	159
4.7	*Five* topics – normative governing	161
4.7.1	*Five* arena	163
4.7.2	*Five-Four* and *Five-Three*	168
4.7.3	*Five-(Four-Three)*	171
4.7.4	*Five-One*	172
4.8	Integrated framework	173
4.8.1	*One* issues	179
4.8.2	*Two* topics	180
4.8.3	*Three* topics	182
4.8.4	*Four* topics	185
4.8.5	*Five* topics	188

5   Case: Community   **193**

5.1	Purpose	193
5.2	Research methodology	194
5.2.1	Unit and focus of analysis	198
5.2.2	Sources of percepts	200
5.2.3	Structure of chapters	201

6   Governance of Hessian °communities°   **203**

6.1	Channel capacity: actor roles	209
6.1.1	Actors and settings	209
6.1.2	Systemic contributions	211
6.1.3	Compliance with systemic functions	225
6.1.4	Suggestions	237
6.2	Change or transformation capacity: methods	240
6.2.1	Systemic contributions	242
6.2.2	Compliance with systemic functions	251
6.2.3	Suggestions	270
6.3	Channel capacity: Sequences and time lags	273
6.3.1	Systemicity of budget reconciliation	274
6.3.2	Compliance with systemic functions	279
6.3.3	Suggestions	282
6.4	Excursus on Transduction	284
6.5	eGovernance with eMedia	285

7   Conclusion   **291**

Bibliography   **299**

Summary   **313**

About the Author   **315**

Table of figures

Figure 1. Governance as a process of interaction   7
Figure 2. eMedia – Media   9
Figure 3. Determinants of exploratory research   14
Figure 4. From disciplines to an integrated framework   16
Figure 5. Structure of the manuscript   21
Figure 6. Sources of distinction for image creation   27
Figure 7. Image creation and sources of distinction   37
Figure 8. Surface and inside views of social systems   40
Figure 9. Surface view of a social *system* notion and types of
           actor involvement   43
Figure 10. Surface and inside views on social systems   45
Figure 11. Autopoietic perceive-reflect-expose loop   48
Figure 12. Interaction as orientation towards representation   49
Figure 13. Contextual variety as a function of contextuality   54
Figure 14. Individual intentional variety as a function of
           intentionality   55
Figure 15. Three fundamental °system° spheres   57
Figure 16. Interaction stretching up a social °system° notion   58
Figure 17. Exemplary variety drivers of a °health° notion, e.g. a
           hospital   60
Figure 18. Exemplary amplifiers and attenuators of a °hospital°   61
Figure 19. Individual untuned actions versus concerted °system°
           implementation   62
Figure 20. Structures of °system° governance and implementation   63
Figure 21. Change, channel, and transduction capacity   65
Figure 22. Characteristic representations addressing governing
           elements   72
Figure 23. Four governing elements for addressing °system° issues   74
Figure 24. Logical spheres in a shared social °system° notion   83

Figure 25. Three fundamental change triggers   84

Figure 26. Algedonic concerns in representation   86

Figure 27. Method: a way to address an issue with a concern   90

Figure 28. Rationalities model (RM)   116

Figure 29. Logical levels of representation and their translation   118

Figure 30. Sustainability as a meta-criterion of structure   122

Figure 31. Aspects of structure (Organisational principles)   126

Figure 32. *One* interactions   141

Figure 33. *Two* interactions   145

Figure 34. *Three* interactions   147

Figure 35. *Four* interactions   154

Figure 36. *Five* interactions   162

Figure 37. Invariant systemic topics   174

Figure 38. Governance framework for viability of °system° notions   175

Figure 39. Invariant interactions required for °system° viability   177

Figure 40. *One* issues   179

Figure 41. *Two* topics   180

Figure 42. *Three* topics   182

Figure 43. *Four* topics   185

Figure 44. *Five* topics   188

Figure 45. Interdependencies between invariant systemic topics   191

Figure 46. Steps of governance case study on Hessian
            °communities°   201

Figure 47. Convention to qualify systemic compliance of methods   202

Figure 48. Common °sub-systems° of Hessian communities   208

Figure 49. Major actors of Hessian °community°   210

Figure 50. Community council   213

Figure 51. Boards (B)   214

Figure 52. Factions (F)   215

Figure 53. Magistrate (M)   217

Figure 54. Commissions (Co)   217

Figure 55. Administration (A)   221

Figure 56. °Super-° and °sub-system° actors   223

Figure 57. Commity Residents (CR)   224

Figure 58. °Federal°, °state° and °county° authorities   225

Figure 59. Current assignments of topic spheres to community
            councils   232
Figure 60. Proposed assignments of topic spheres to community
            councils   238
Figure 61. Compliance of methods with *Two* topics   254
Figure 62. Compliance of methods with *Three* topics   260
Figure 63. Compliance of methods with *Four* topics   266
Figure 64. Systemicity of the traditional process of budget
            reconciliation   275
Figure 65. Suggested conduct of °community° planning   284
Figure 66. Impact of eMedia on °system° structures   285
Figure 67. From a dispersed to an integrated °system° notion   292

Table of tables

Table 1.   Exponents of synthetic views on governance   6
Table 2.   Twelve fundamental boundary judgements of °system°
            notions   41
Table 3.   A classification of actor contributions in °system°
            interaction   51
Table 4.   Qualifications of representation   70
Table 5.   Logical levels of representation   77
Table 6.   Manifestations of governing elements on logical levels   81
Table 7.   Manifestations of algedonic concerns   87
Table 8.   Amplifying and attenuating concerns (exemplary)   88
Table 9.   Attributes of tacit and explicit representations   106
Table 10.   Typical boundary judgements of key °community° actors   114
Table 11.   Structural aspects of exemplary °system° notions   124
Table 12.   Invariances and variables within a °system° notion   131
Table 13.   Four invariant topic domains to solve *One* issues in
            °system° implementation   140
Table 14.   Capacity of research methodologies   196
Table 15.   Selection of governance aspects and topics focused   199
Table 16.   Convention to qualify compliance of systemic tasks and
            responsibilities   202
Table 17.   Typical °living spheres° for creating °community°   207
Table 18.   Systemic contributions of °community° actors   233
Table 19.   Methods and instruments for addressing *Two* topics   251
Table 20.   Methods and instruments for addressing *Three* topics   255
Table 21.   Methods and instruments for addressing *Four* topics   262
Table 22.   Structural contribution of common eMedia applications
            and services   286

1   Introduction

'Complexity', 'Dynamics', and 'Diversity' are omnipresent in today's discourse on governance. They refer to the fact that social conditions in modern societies are perceived as multi-layered and complicated. Social issues are being addressed by multiple actors; governments are not necessarily playing a primary role anymore. A multiplicity of actors is involved, expressing individual interests yet having unequal capacities to exert influence. Resolutions for governing issues are the result of various interacting factors that are rarely wholly known. Knowledge, experiences, and interests are dispersed over many actors constantly changing their roles and relationships. Actor dependencies and constellations increasingly differ from global to local and from sector to sector. Diversity cumulates as these processes gain speed as well as intensity. There have always been competing interests, e.g. countryside versus city, sacred versus secular, merchants versus manufacturers, employers versus workers, etc. However, there was, in earlier times, considerable cohesion within those groups as a consequence of their strong tribal and nationalistic frames. Today, the actors involved struggle hard to realise legitimate and effective governing but can rarely keep pace with changing trends and shifting roles.[2] It is difficult to have a truly representative government when actor and group identities are fragmented and pluralistic, while political parties are either 'big tents' with multiple, sometimes even conflicting, constituencies, or 'small tents' representing a variety of regional interests, or even small single issue parties.[3]

The aforementioned points to a most central question of our time, i.e. how can actors in social systems reach agreement and reconcile their varied interests in regard to the needs and limitations of their social contexts (such as community, company, or country)? Obviously, new arrangements are needed for addressing governance issues, arrangements which adequately involve actors and stimulate them to contribute as well as to respect the attendant community needs and limitations and to assume collective

---

[2] Kooiman, J.: Governing as Governance, London, Thousand Oaks, New Delhi, 2003

[3] Leonard, A.: Between Momentum and Control, 2004, Sunderland

responsibilities along with individual and separate ones. Such arrangements must be capable of relating actors to each other in a differentiated way that can be integrated permanently into their everyday life. They have to stimulate actors to interact in ways that constantly renew and harmonise their relationships. Discovering and implementing such governing arrangements of productive interactions is surely a major challenge of our time.[4]

This research was inspired by the emerging possibilities of new technologies for social systems.[5] They open up new ways to organise information exchange and to conduct interaction. With electronic media, social interactions can be supported in innumerable ways: visualising, categorising, discussing, generally reshaping social interactions and involving large numbers of actors at the same time. Interactions have become mouldable; actors themselves can shape and configure the media. Hence – as is undisputed in theory and practice – interesting possibilities for solving central governance problems arise. Thus, new technologies pave the way for integrating solutions that reflect the characteristics and necessities of the different actors constituting social systems.

1.1 Perspectives on governance

The concept of 'Governance' carries a wide range of different meanings and connotations and is used in multiple notations addressing different aspects of social life.[6] The research evolved here draws upon a synthetic concept of governance which is derived as a merged approach of formerly

---

[4]   Kooiman, J.: (Governing as Governance); Willke, H.: Systemtheorie I: Grundlagen, Stuttgart, 2000

[5]   This was reflected in the previously used working title of this book: "eGovernance – an integrated framework to promote Governance". eMedia as a starting point was essential because the "e" linked to the concept of (e)Media, which helped to clarify the required components of interaction for the integrative concept of governance. However, during the explorative research process it turned out, that the focus had to be shifted primarily to creating a solid theoretical foundation in order to be able to assemble an integrated framework which can capture the concept of governance and ground it in empirical application.

[6]   Contrary to the concept of 'Government', which refers to an entity. see Beer, S: Governance or Government?, in: Beer, S, Beyond dispute: the invention of team syntegrity, Chichester, 1994; Jann, W.: Der Wandel verwaltungspolitischer Leitbilder: vom Management zu Governance?, in: König, K., Deutsche Verwaltung an der Wende zum 21.Jahrhundert, Baden-Baden, 2002

opposing perspectives on governance. Below, a short introduction will be given to those opposing views of governance, each of which asserts the importance of a different aspect in social arrangements: structures on the one side and actor-constellations on the other. Subsequently, a merged approach will be presented which mainly builds upon the analytical frame Kooiman has provided and to which he has been adding since 1993.[7] His concept focuses on the notion of governance as a process of interaction between different social and political actors. It thus integrates structure- and actor-perspectives with the intention to extract a model that integrates both perspectives and thus is more appropriate as a basic analytic toolset to capture governance issues.

1.1.1 The structure-oriented view

In the structure-oriented view, social systems are independent objects. They basically govern themselves through circular, self-referential processes that constitute their identity (autopoiesis[8] of the social system). Autopoietic social systems are operationally closed and structurally determined: actions are conducted and the environment is perceived according to the system's internal configuration and skills. Social systems undertake structural coupling, as a consequence of which they coordinate their behaviours. Taking direct influence from outside is considered impossible; only indirect influence and coordination between systems is possible. Communication, not action, constitutes the basis of governing and the unit of analysis.[9] No other elements are considered relevant; actors are themselves not part of the social system.

This view focuses on the structural limitations of social systems. It almost completely relies on societal self-governing and takes a pessimistic stance on cooperative governing forms. The consequence is a fragmented

---

[7] Most notably: Kooiman, J.: Modern Governance, London, 1993; Kooiman, J.: (Governing as Governance)

[8] Αυτοποίησις, autopoiesis is Greek and stands for self-production. Autopoiesis is a specific characteristic of living systems in contrast to non-living and artificial systems. Maturana, H.: Erkennen: Die Organisation und Verkörperung von Wirklichkeiten – Ausgewählte Arbeiten zur biologischen Epistemologie, Braunschweig, 1982

[9] Luhmann, N.: Politische Steuerung: Ein Diskussionsbeitrag, Politische Vierteljahresschrift, 30, 1, 1989; Kikert, W.: Complexity, governance and dynamics, in: Kooiman, J., Modern Governance, London, 1993

system of governance in which actors find their energies sapped by having to engage with an increasingly diverse range of stakeholders. Niklas Luhmann is the most important exponent of this perspective on governance.[10]

1.1.2 The actor-oriented view

Here, social systems are characterised as "Gebilde", i.e. formations which are composed not only of communications but also of actors as empirical subunits.[11] Thus, processes of mutual stimulation between these actors lead to mutually reinforcing (or curbing) behaviour patterns. The dynamic consequences of situational factors which result from actor constellations, interest aggregations, organisational structures, etc. are seen as a necessary aspect for analysis which cannot be ignored. Human action and the intentions of actors within social systems are the focus of this view on governance.

Actors are the basic, autopoietic entities of social systems. Governance is about a diversity of such actors playing different roles within social systems and their capacity to act in organised ways towards a common purpose. Depending on the specific conditions under which actors organise themselves, governing is facilitated or hampered.[12] Therefore, the individual is the unit of analysis and modelled as an autopoietic entity, which means it is seen as operationally-closed and capable of maintaining its identity based upon self-referential processes.

---

[10] Luhmann, N.: Soziale Systeme. Grundriss einer allgemeinen Theorie., Frankfurt a.M., 1984; Luhmann, N.: Die Politik der Gesellschaft, Frankfurt a.M., 2002; Luhmann, N.: Die Gesellschaft der Gesellschaft, Frankfurt, 1997; Krause, Detlef: Luhmann-Lexikon, Stuttgart, 2001; Luhmann, N.: Interpenetrationen – Zum Verhältnis personaler und sozialer Systeme, Zeitschrift für Soziologie und Sozialpsychologie, 6, 1977; Luhmann, N.: Politische Planung, Opladen, 1971

[11] Mayntz, R.: Funktionale Teilsysteme in der Theorie sozialer Differenzierung, in: Rosewitz, Bernd, Schimank, Uwe, and Stichweh, Rudolf, Differenzierung und Verselbständigung – Zur Entwicklung gesellschaftlicher Teilsysteme, Frankfurt a.M.; New York, 1988

[12] Renate Mayntz and Fritz Scharpf are the most important exponents of this perspective on governance. Scharpf, F.: Politische Steuerung und politische Institutionen, Politische Vierteljahresschrift, 30, 1, 1989; Mayntz, R. and Edelmann, B.: Eigendynamische Soziale Prozesse, Kölner Zeitschrift für Soziologie und Sozialpsychologie, 39, 4, 1987; Mayntz, R. and Scharpf, F.: Gesellschaftliche Selbstregelung und Politische Steuerung, Frankfurt & New York, 1995; Mayntz, R.: Soziale Dynamik und Politische Steuerung, Frankfurt & New York, 1997

The concept of social system applied here builds upon Maturana's interpretation, which includes both actors and interactions.[13] This approach is analytically distinct from other interpretations limiting social systems to communications, as defined most notably by Luhmann.

1.1.3 Synthetic views

Each perspective has a specific contribution to make. In the autopoietic-view social systems are operationally closed entities, i.e. they develop and maintain their identities based upon self-referential processes. This means that social systems 'understand' and integrate external influences only if they can understand and accept those influences as part of their identity. Thus, the autopoietic view emphasises the aspect of autonomy of social systems.

The actor-oriented view, on the other hand, refers to the importance of actor-constellations in social systems. Social systems can organise actor activity and thus create powerful actor-constellations or networks which are hard to influence from outside. This self-governing capacity can be exploited for governance purposes; nevertheless, when governance endeavours are in conflict with the interest of those actor-constellations, these may well hamper governing purposes.[14] Thus, the actor-oriented view emphasises the effects emerging from constellations of actors.

As both perspectives seem to provide valuable contributions, several authors tried to merge them in order to come to an enriched concept that integrates the two aspects. These synthetic views in literature have been plotted on a continuum between total structure- or actor-focus. Further, they have been distinguished according to the unit of analysis that has been chosen as actors (individual, organisation, or subsystem). The following table assigns the major exponents to these dimensions. The differences among these concepts are discussed in detail in the literature cited below.

---

[13] Maturana, H.: Autopoiesis, Communication and Society, in: Benseler, F., Hejl, P. M., and Köck, W., Autopoiesis, Communication and Society: The Theory of Autopoietic System in the Social Sciences, Frankfurt a.M., New York, 1980; Maturana, H. and Varela, F.: El arbol del conocimiento: Las bases biológicas del conocimiento humano, Santiago, 1985; Beer, S.: The Heart of the Enterprise, Chichester, 1979

[14] Kooiman, J.: (Governing as Governance)

Table 1. Exponents of synthetic views on governance[15]

	Structure in focus	Actors in focus
Individuals as actors	Druwe[16], Görlitz[17]	Beyerle[18]
Organisations as actors	Ulrich[19]	Mayntz, Scharpf, Schimank
Larger entities	Willke[20]	

This research project was inspired by the work of Jan Kooiman, who claims that interaction is an adequate concept to use in merging the different views on governance. Interaction is a mutually influencing relation between two or more actors.[21] Governing is then considered as *"the totality of interactions, in which [...] actors participate".*[22] It is the sum of the interactive 'movements' a social system makes, or metaphorically expressed,

> *"Governing, compared with the steering of a ship, means navigating by continuously perceiving the movements of the subsystems, and, dependent on these movements, adjusting the course".*[23]

---

15 Adapted table, the original from: Lange, Stefan and Braun, Dietmar: Politische Steuerung zwischen System und Akteur, Opladen, 2000, p. 101
16 Druwe, U.: Rekonstruktion der 'Theorie der Autopoiese' als Gesellschafts- und Steuerungsmodell, in: Görlitz, A., Politische Steuerung sozialer Systeme. Mediales Recht als politisches Steuerungskonzept., Pfaffenweiler, 1989
17 Görlitz, A. and Burth, H. P.: Politische Steuerung – Ein Studienbuch, Opladen, 1998
18 Beyerle, M.: Staatstheorie und Autopoiesis – Über die Auflösung der modernen Staatsidee im nachmodernen Denken durch die Theorie autopoietischer Systeme und der Entwurf eines nachmodernen Staatskonzepts, Frankfurt a.M., 1994
19 Ulrich, G.: Politische Steuerung – Staatliche Intervention aus systemtheoretischer Sicht, Opladen, 1994
20 Willke, H.: (Systems theory One); Willke, H.: Systemtheorie III: Steuerungstheorie, Stuttgart, 2001; Willke, H.: Entzauberung des Staates – Überlegungen zu einer gesellschaftlichen Steuerungstheorie, Königstein / Ts., 1983; Willke, H.: Ironie des Staates, Frankfurt, 1992
21 Kooiman, J.: (Governing as Governance); Görlitz, A. and Burth, H. P.: (Political control)
22 Kooiman, J.: (Governing as Governance)
23 Kooiman, J. and van Vliet, M.: Self-Governance as a mode of Societal-Governance, Public Management, 2000

This means that any governing stimuli being expressed and processed in interaction re-affects its originators and thus system implementation. In Kooiman's integrative view, intentional (or action) and contextual (or structural) aspects stand vis-à-vis in interactions and thus merge the two perspectives. Intentions originate actors' impulse to act; they express in individual purposes, benefits sought and in goals being aspired to. Structures, on the other hand, determine social and cultural necessities and constraints that underlie actor activities. Any aligned purposeful actions originate from intentions and structures and each of these aspects influences the other: intentions influence (i.e. change or conserve) structures – while structures induce (i.e. enable or control) intentions of the actors involved.[24]

The research at hand builds on this integrative view and considers governance as a process of interaction. Figure 1 sums up the main conceptual elements applied.

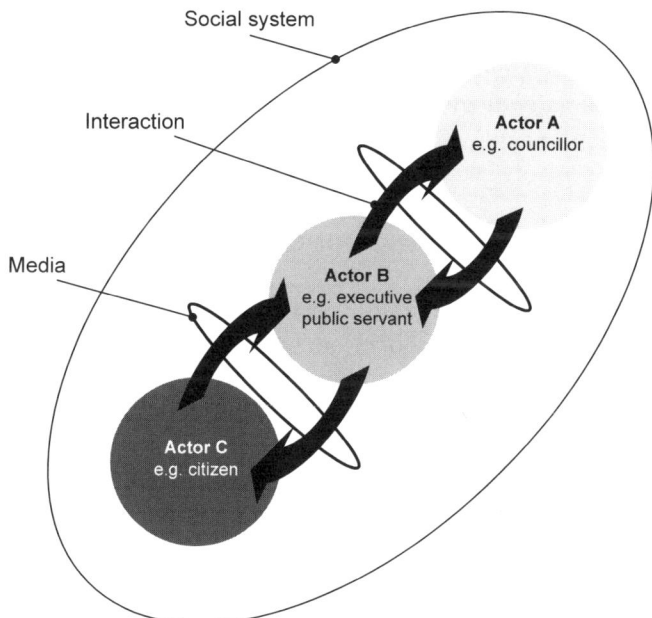

Figure 1. Governance as a process of interaction

---

[24] Kooiman, J.: (Governing as Governance), pp. 12-17

Thus, this research starts with the following assumptions: Interactions can adequately be used as key analytic elements of social systems. They unite the relevant aspects that define and form relationships between actors. Social systems evolve from the interactions between involved and affected actors. The key to understanding the governance of social systems therefore lies in distinguishing characteristic interactions and topics and in making explicit the conditions that enable effective reconciliations. Looking at the parameters of interaction as they are manifested in real-life situations, the diversity, complexity, and dynamics of the social context become perceivable, and adequate conceptual tools and instruments can be defined for dealing with them. Thus, it becomes apparent to what extent system actors are intertwined and cohesively implement the purposes aspired to in the social context addressed. At all times, interactions evolve from the underlying structures.

Defining interaction as the root concept of governance does not mean that other concepts, such as 'actor', 'system', 'function', 'hierarchy', 'recursion', 'participation', etc., are secondary. As the smallest basic entity where reconciliations actually take place, all macro phenomena are ultimately rooted in and emerge from micro agreements. Rather, taking the interaction perspective is considered useful for facilitating the understanding of each of these concepts in its contribution to governance and for facilitating the application of the framework in practical applications.

1.2   Motivation, objectives and research questions

The previous chapter outlined the scientific discussion that inspired this research. As mentioned the major motivation has been to discover the principles and rules of productive and effective governing arrangements. That has has been inspired in the light of the emerging possibilities of modern information and communication technologies. Characteristically, the literature and scientific discussion on the creation of structures and the use of media to support governance are found to be twofold and contradictory.[25] This has been reflected in the lively discussion on the use of (electronic) media. The effects of media are seen to be responsible for both redefining

---

[25]   Contradictions found in the selection of papers submitted to the 26th International Congress of Administrative Sciences held by the International Institute of Administrative Sciences – IIAS on July 14th – 18th, 2004 at the Coex Congress Center, Seoul, Republic of Korea. See also Türke, R. E.: eGovernance. Building blocks for theory., in: Suk-Kim, P. and Jho, W., Building e-Governance: Challenges and Opportunities for Democracy, Administration and Law, Seoul, 2005

and laying down processes and conventions in organisations; they are blamed for both involving and excluding actors in governing, for promoting coalescence as well as fragmentation, for both centralising and decentralising governing functions. To comment on these contradictions, it is important to note that the understanding of media applied here is not limited to 'information technology', usually understood as whatever enables the collection, processing, and distribution of data. Rather, media are understood in a general way, i.e. as whatever provides the ground for social structures to be established between actors. Electronic forms of media are a sub-group of media and are labelled 'eMedia' here (compare Figure 2). They provide new ways to shape communication and to constantly broaden the range of possible applications. Through eMedia, nearly any type and process of two-way mediated interaction is possible today.

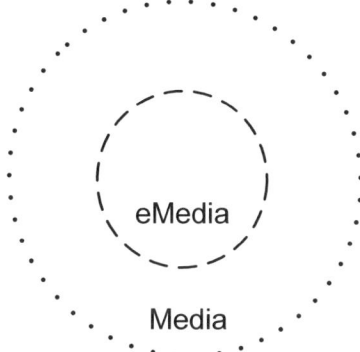

Figure 2. eMedia – Media

Thus, media themselves are 'per se' undefined and value free. They simply constitute a potential to create structures that overcome physical and temporal frontiers, actively involve actors and promote them in the reconciliation of their governing issues. Today in our society, eMedia such as television and the internet have come to exercise major impacts on the construction of social realities. The understanding of eMedia that support established codes of conduct, processes, and relationships is therefore necessarily insufficient. All Media have to be seen as having the potential to form and design structures according to specific governing needs. As expressed in the contradictions just mentioned, eMedia may be used to implement structures that both support or hinder our governing challenges. This is why it is argued here that the structures determining interaction of a social system have to be focused upon to enable Good Governance. Do we know yet,

what contributions eMedia offer and what effects they cause on our governing systems?[26] Such thoughts have lead to the following research questions:

1. How can the concept of governance be captured in a holistic, integrated, and context-independent framework?

2. What structures are required to establish a governance of social systems that is viable and sustainable in the sense of self-organising,
   self-learning, and self-adapting?

3. How can established system structures be designed to promote the
   viability of social systems? Consequently, what can eMedia contribute to promote governance (eGovernance[27])?[28]

Based on the potential of eMedia, their application is neither a necessary
nor a compulsory requirement. The focus of this work can therefore not be
restricted to developing or designing structures with eMedia. Rather, the
focus is to find a way to acquire an in-depth understanding of the governance of social systems based on real-life cases and to identify the existing
strengths and weaknesses of their structures. It must be understood what role
interactions play in a governing context and how they can be evaluated and
assessed. Only then will it be possible to identify how the governance in that
system can be improved and supported by eMedia. It is based on such an
understanding of specific social systems that the contribution of structures,
media, and eMedia should be appraised.[29] However, the framework to be

---

[26] Winograd, T. and Flores, F.: Understanding computers and cognition: a new
foundation for design, Reading, Massachusetts, 1987

[27] The term of 'eGovernance' is new in international scientific discussion. For
this reason there exists no common understanding and conceptual demarcation
as of yet. Nevertheless the following authors have engaged in this topic: 6, Perri:
eGovernance: Weber's revenge?, in: Dowding, K. M. and Margetts, H., Challenges to Democracy: Ideas, Involvement and Institutions, New York, 2003;
Reinermann, H. and Lucke, J.: Speyerer Definition von eGovernance, Forschung-
sprojekt Regieren und Verwalten im Informationszeitalter, 2001, Speyer

[28] The term 'governance media' is not to be equated with Luhmann's concept of
symbolically generalised control media. Nevertheless, notational similarity is
intended and should invite further exploration of common characteristics of the
concepts. See Willke, H.: (Systems theory One).

[29] Once the structure was right, including the new communication links, all people
in the virtual teams began to flow together rather than compete. The prototype
also showed that introducing technology is much easier if attention is paid first to
designing an appropriate structure. Espejo, R.: Giving Requisite Variety to Stra-

described shall facilitate the definition of requirements for configuring eMedia. The overall purpose of this work is to lay the foundation for a comprehensive theory of governance based on first principles; the framework derived from it will specify application of the theory in all kinds of social system contexts and allow linkage and embedment of existing research findings. Therefore, the objectives pursued are:

1. To take an interaction perspective on governance and derive logical consequences for the governance of social systems.

2. To assemble an integrated framework for the governance of social systems (a systemic governance frame) that describes the necessary and sufficient criteria for viability and to make it accessible for broad application in different governing contexts.

3. To enable a holistic, comprehensive understanding of social systems; therefore, to aid application by formalising the language and grammar used to describe system phenomena.[30]

4. To demonstrate and test the applicability and significance of the framework with a practical case study.

5. To show, how the framework can be applied for diagnosing and designing social system structures and how it can be used for deriving (and assembling) effective instruments for specific governing contexts and situations.

6. To show in what respect the framework provides clues for the development and implementation of improved media configurations.

7. To sketch what kind of practices an integrated approach to governance is likely to promote.[31]

---

tegic and Implementation Processes: Theory and Practice, http://bprc.warwick. ac.uk/LSEraul.html, 2000

[30] As Anderton states, the need for formal development "is one of the main reasons that [the theories underlying this research – primarily the Viable systems model (VSM) – have not yet; R.T.] entered the mainstream of contemporary thought.", in Anderton, R.: The need for formal development of the VSM, in: Espejo, R. and Harnden, R., The Viable Systems Model: Interpretations and Applications of Stafford Beer's VSM, Chichester, 1989, p. 40

[31] Ulrich, W.: The Quest for Competence in Systemic Research and Practise, Systems Research and Behavioural Science, 18, 2001

An essential step toward these objectives will be to acquire a sufficient degree of formalisation of governance. Only if the framework can be expressed in a way that is largely independent from any particular context, will it be comprehensible to different people with different backgrounds and attitudes, involved in different types of social systems and therefore engaged in highly diverse activities. And even more so, the framework is meant to be useful and accessible not only for scientists or philosophers but also for those engaged in governing and managing roles, whatever branch, culture, and age they may be. Beside the independent expression, such a formalisation is also likely to improve the validation of the framework. Since social systems manifest themselves in highly diverse settings, applications will usually not have much in common, unless the framework itself has been formulated in a context-independent way.[32]

1.3 Theories and research methodology

The motivation for this research arises primarily based on the practical needs identified in the consulting activities and the personal interests of the author. Unsatisfactory experiences gained with the application of contemporary main stream approaches such as Business Process Re-engineering, Balanced Scorecards, Cost Accounting, etc. on the one hand and New Public Management approaches around the concept of Results-Oriented Public Management (RoPM)[33] on the other hand initiated this research. However, project and conceptual experience showed that none of the approaches proved to be capable of coping with the complexity, diversity, and dynamics of the actual issues that met in governing settings. At the very start of this research, it became clear, that the multiplicity of faculties and disciplines involved in governance research such as for instance political science, public management, business administration, jurisprudence, social science, psychology, philosophy, and others does not facilitate the understanding of social systems. Rather, the approaches of the disciplines base their conclusions on differing incompatible assumptions and concepts which is why their pieces do not fit into one puzzle.[34] Further, with the interaction in focus and related concepts of 'actor', 'system', 'structure', 'image', 'action' attached to it, this research touches on several issues at the heart of

---

[32] Heylighen, F.: Advantages and limitations of formal expression, Foundations of Science, 4, 1, 1999

[33] From German "Wirkungsorientierte Verwaltungsführung"

[34] See Table 1 for an example with the different synthetic views on governance.

cognitive science. Assembling a sound and consistent framework of governance will therefore require that the underlying cognitive assumptions are made explicit and are dismantled for scientific dialogue. The research adopts a strong self-reflective character as 'interactions', the primary object of interest to be examined, is an inherent part not only of the research 'object' but of the research process itself. In consequence, it can be expected to come across paradoxes which cannot be solved within the limits of the individual disciplines.

These conditions make clear that this research has a clear transdisciplinary character; it seeks to interlink the various faculties in an adequate way. It will therefore require an explorative and pragmatic research approach if it is to explore the broad field of theories and to gain insights with valuable contributions for practical application. The applied research methodology has to reflect the explorative and pragmatic character pursued.[35] With the given research focus, the research object has a broad character and is not yet specific. Rather, its definition is part of the research process itself, which is guided by the research question. With the concepts of interaction and governance, only a broad direction has been given from which to start from. The details of what can usefully be done and fruitfully analysed will depend on the findings and assumptions acquired in the research process. Furthermore, it is also clear that the research object as defined is not yet accessible to any kind of quantitative analysis.[36] Consequently, the research method applied must reflect the investigative character set up. That means that it should involve different perspectives on and experiences with the research object, thus allowing it to be elucidated from different angles. A qualitative explorative heuristic, dedicated to an exploration of untrodden ground is appropriate. This applies in particular to the interaction perspective on governance, which has not yet been examined in a systematic and transdisciplinary way. That allows the development of the framework following a hermeneutic, circular procedure within which the underlying basic assumptions and definitions – in this case the primary *Weltanschauung* and concepts – are refined according to the insights gained throughout the ongoing research process. This approach emphasises the collection and interpretation of qualitative data. It is thus well-suited to a design-oriented and diagnostic research endeavour which assembles a theory, draws from practice and

---

[35] Schwaninger, M.: Rückgekoppelte Exploration in der Forschung – Arbeitspapier 2.Fassung, 1996

[36] Ulrich, H.: Die Betriebswirtschaftslehre als anwendungsorientierte Sozialwissenschaft, Bern, Stuttgart, Wien, 2001

validates the findings. However, as a consequence of the broadness of the topic, it is also clear that the findings cannot be expected to be definite; rather, they are to be continuously refined. Figure 3 illustrates the determining steps that were taken to assemble the Governance framework, each of which is described as follows:

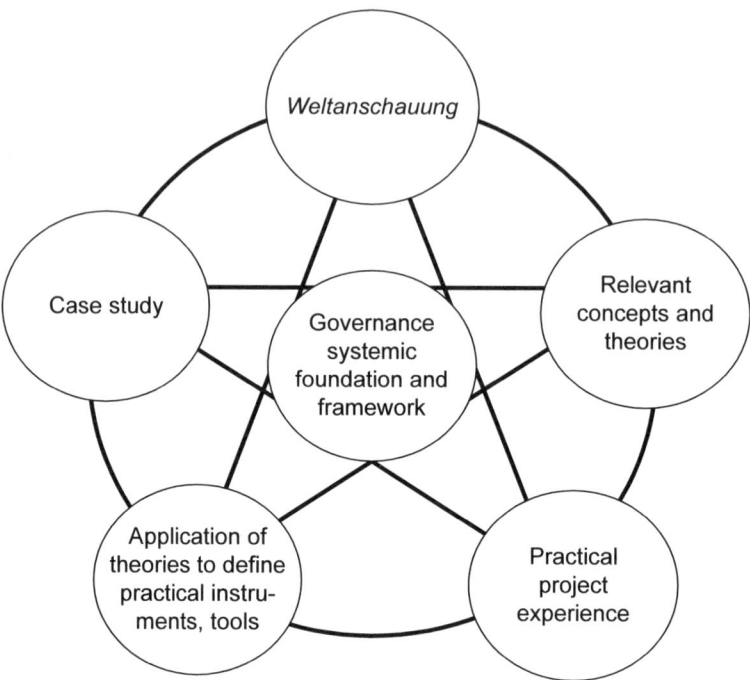

Figure 3. Determinants of exploratory research

1.3.1 Making explicit the underlying *Weltanschauung*

Before the concept of governance can be addressed as a topic, the underlying premises and the adopted *Weltanschauung* must be delineated.[37] Therefore, the primary, fundamental concepts constitutive for a perspective on governance will have to be made explicit: actor, image and system. It is the understanding of these concepts that determines how actors are seen to

---

[37] "We must declare in advance the framework in terms of which research lessons will be expressed. (Technically, we must define the epistemology which is defined as 'knowledge' in this experience).", in Checkland, P.: Information, Systems, Information Systems, 1999, p. 24

create their lifeworlds, how they create their knowledge of the world, i.e. their epistemology[38] and how they achieve a perception of their world, i.e. their ontology[39]. Only based on such an understanding of "how actors are seen to create their lifeworld", can conclusions be drawn on how they engage and accommodate common intentions and contexts, i.e. how they govern themselves. The concptualisation of the *Weltanschauung* will have to establish a language and methodology that enables the understanding and expression of how cohesion can be achieved between actors following common endeavors. Thus, chapter 2 depicts the *Weltanschauung* upon which the subsequent foundations and the framework build. Obviously, making explicit the *Weltanschauung* in the case of this research topic not only states the fundamental assumptions applied for theory development but also serves for making explicit and discussable the underlying research notion, i.e. how the research object can be addressed.

1.3.2   Identifying and integrating relevant theories

This section is concerned with the identification and integration of relevant theoretical concepts. What are conceptual building blocks that can cope with the derived concept of governance and how can they provide valuable contributions for answering the research question? To answer these questions, we employ a kind of "yo-yo technique"[40] which allows identifying invariances in governance by the constant repetition of the following steps:

---

[38]   Epistemology refers to the study of the nature, origin, and limits of human knowledge. The name is derived from the Greek epistēmē ("knowledge") and logos ("reason"); accordingly, the field is sometimes referred to as the theory of knowledge. Epistemology has had a long history, spanning the time from the pre-Socratic Greeks to the present.

[39]   Ontology is the theory or study of being as such; i.e. of the basic characteristics of all reality. […] ontology is synonymous with metaphysics or "first philosophy" as defined by Aristotle. […] Because metaphysics came to include other studies (e.g., philosophical cosmology and psychology), ontology has become the preferred term for the study of being. […] It was brought into prominence in the 18th century by Christian Wolff, a German rationalist, for whom it was a deductive discipline leading to necessary truths about the essences of beings. His great successor, Immanuel Kant, however, presented influential refutations of ontology as a deductive system and of the ontological argument for God's necessary existence (as supreme and perfect being).

[40]   With the "yo-yo technique", Beer referred to his account of scientific modelling, which consists of a three-step procedure identifying invariances and ex-

1. Perceiving and conceptualising phenomena in the world (case study).

2. Recognizing existing theories on the phenomena.

3. Identifying analogies between conceptions and existing theories of the world.

4. Rigorously formalising properties of the identified analogies through homomorphic mappings.

5. Identifying invariances in mappings.

6. Generalising identified invariances in an integrated framework.

The yo-yo technique allows us to start from a set of existing, more or less unrelated disciplines, and leads to the recognition of invariances in the research object. Based on these invariances, intersections between the disciplines can be recognised and disciplinary concepts (Con-X_i) can be merged into integrated concepts (Con-I_i). Finally, these can be subsumed in a comprehensive integrative framework (compare Figure 4).

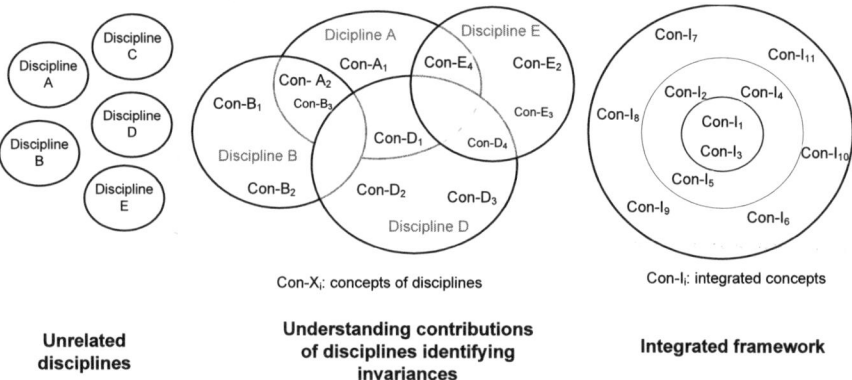

Figure 4. From disciplines to an integrated framework

---

pressing them in a model by identifying a) similes, b) analogies, and c) homomorphs of actors' real-world perceptions and constantly repeating these steps in a yo-yo process until an isomorphic model has been formulated. Beer, S.: The Viable System Model: Its provenance, development, methodology and pathology, Journal of the Operational Research Society, 35, 1984, pp. 10-11

Related faculties and disciplines relevant for governance as they are indicated above are described in depth elsewhere.[41] The transdisciplinary and context-independent character underlying the research question clearly points to a systems theory as adequate to address the research question. Whenever an integrated, holistic perspective is chosen, system- oriented theories are appropriate. They bridge disciplines and allow the examination of corresponding or correlating phenomena in systems. They provide a consistent and interdisciplinary language that is sufficiently abstract to be applicable in different fields and thus helps to diminish the subjectivity of the individual faculties. System theory is a multiperspectual body of theories that studies the structure and behaviour of systems. It is adequate wherever relevant aspects and variables from multiple economic, sociologic and technological viewpoints have to be integrated. However, the body of literature on theories is not easily assessable as it entails a multiplicity of different concepts and approaches.[42] Based on the research question and an in-depth examination of the literature in the systems field and related disciplines, the following subject areas and transdisciplinary system theories have been most influential for this research:

1. Socio-cybernetic view on 'Governing as Governance', Jan Kooiman;

2. New Public Management, Kuno Schedler, et al.;

3. Second order cybernetics, Heinz v. Foerster, Warren McCulloch, et al.;

---

[41]   Pierre, Jon and Peters, B. Guy: Governance, Politics and the State, New York, 2000; 6, Perri: Towards Holistic Governance, New York, 2002; Schedler, K. and Proeller, I.: New Public Management, Bern, 2000; Barzelay, M.: How to argue about New Public Management, International Public Management Journal, 2, 2(A), 1999

[42]   The following statement illustrates the difficulties people have faced with some of the theories used here: "In spite of the extensive and brilliantly written publications, a large, diverse, and enthusiastic following, and a significant number of attempts, often very successful, at application, it remains true that many people, including highly intelligent ones, attracted by the ideas, find them most difficult to grasp; they understand them superficially and find them cogent but when it comes to the point of detailed practical use they seem to slip away. The work has failed thus far to enter the mainstream of intellectual development, whether in the social sciences of administration or management, or in those theoretical parts of sociology or biology to which it has relevance.", see Anderton, R.: (Formal development), pp. 40-41

4. Constructivism, Paul Watzlawick, Ernst v. Glasersfeld, Jean Piaget;

5. Laws of Form, George Spencer-Brown;

6. Autopoiesis, Humberto Maturana, Francisco Varela;

7. Neuro-Linguistic Programming, Gregory Bateson, Richard Bandler, John Grinder;

8. Managerial Cybernetics and the Viable Systems Model (VSM), Stafford Beer;

9. Critical System Heuristic, Werner Ulrich;

10. Soft-System Methodology, Peter Checkland;

However, this list is not complete. It is expected that further research in the future will provide other valuable contributions.[43] The selection of theories draws from the typical characteristics of social systems: a diversity of actors, a complexity of interrelations, and extensive dynamics of general conditions. These characteristics require social systems to adapt their structural and functional configuration to a constantly and rapidly changing environment. But how can all these factors be captured in a single framework? Kooiman's socio-cybernetic approach to governance initiated the research process and provided the first set of concepts (as described in chapter 1.1). With the *Viable Systems Model (VSM)*, Beer provides a mature theory of viable systems that provides a holistic structure which can be used for describing the preconditions for social systems to maintain a separate existence on a sustained basis. Within the the frame of the Viable Systems Model, the theories of *2nd order cybernetics*, *Autopoiesis* and *Neuro-Linguistic Programming (NLP)* facilitate understanding actors and interactions; *Critical System Heuristic (CSH)* delimits the normative underpinnings of system notions and *Soft-system methodology (SSM)* supports process modelling in

---

[43] Further related theories touched in the research process have been: Spencer Brown´s Laws of form, Luhmanns' Social System Theory, Frederic Vesters' Sensitivity Analysis, Haken's Synergetics and Schiepeks Synergetics in Psychology; Habermas' Theory of Communicative Action, Maurice Yolles' Viable Systems Theory. See Spencer-Brown, G.: Laws of Form, London, 1969; Haken, H.: Synergetik, Berlin, 1982; Haken, H. and Schiepek, G.: Synergetik in der Psychologie: Selbstorganisation verstehen und gestalten, Göttingen, 2006; Luhmann, N.: (Social Systems); Vester, Frederic: Die Kunst vernetzt zu denken – Ideen und Werkzeuge für einen neuen Umgang mit Komplexität, Stuttgart, 1999; Habermas, J.: Theorie des kommunikativen Handelns, Volume 1, Frankfurt a.M., 1981; Yolles, M.: Management Systems – a viable approach, London, 1999

systems, which can be used for general problem solving when managing change processes. This step engages in merging these theories into the integrated framework of governance. The results are elaborated in chapters 3 and 4.

1.3.3   Deriving instruments and tools for practice

A framework is useful only in the light of the added-value it delivers for coping with practical issues. In the case of governance, the framework should allow the creation and customisation of instruments and tools that facilitate the understanding of social systems and enable their diagnosis and structural re-configuration. The derived instruments and tools for practice are described in chapters 4 and 5.

1.3.4   Project experience and expert dialogue

Practical projects that were conducted throughout this research comprise the following:

1. Development of a comprehensive cross-sectoral controlling in a large public administration and implementation of a result-oriented controlling software.

2. A requirements review with regard to new instruments for the German chancellery.

3. A feasibility study on the implications of new media for administrative reform and governance; examination of the impact of modern controlling instruments and communication technologies on governance with the 92 city governments involved.

4. Three audit assessments of the conduct of local city governments in comparative analysis for the Hessian Audit Court.

5. Numerous consulting projects on the topics of organisational structure in German and international companies.

6. A diagnosis of organisational structures and an ongoing project to anchor viable structures in rural municipalities as a part of development aid, province of Sofala, Mozambique.

Further, expert dialogues took place at the following conferences, where papers were presented:

1. Public Law and the Modernizing State, European Group of Public Administration (EGPA), Oeiras, Portugal, 2003;

2. Society for Economic and Social Cybernetics (GWS), Lüneburg, Germany, 2004;

3. Governance and Cybernetics, Metaphorum, Sunderland, United Kingdom, 2004;

4. 26th International Congress of Administrative Sciences held by the International Institute of Administrative Sciences (IIAS), Seoul, Korea, 2004;

5. Designing Governance, Metaphorum, Dublin, Ireland, 2005;

6. World Organisation of Systems and Cybernetics (WOSC), 13th international congress, Maribor, Slovenia, 2005 and

7. Enterprise Tools and Approaches, Metaphorum, Liverpool, United Kingdom, 2006.[44]

1.3.5 Conducting a case study

For sound empirical substantiation and validation of the explorative research endeavour undertaken here, the governance framework will be applied in diagnostic mode to test, assess, and improve its application. Thus, the framework will be prepared for application in a real-life setting. In the process, the central aspects of interaction in community will be sketched and evaluated in the light of adequate criteria. Small Hessian communities of up to 5,000 inhabitants were chosen for the diagnosis. Through an intensive literature review and expert interviews a general outline of the governing system will be depicted and typical strengths and weaknesses defined. Im-

---

[44] Türke, R. E.: Research proposal on eGovernance, European Group for Public Administration Conference, Public Law and the Modernising State, Research Workshop 2: Governance: What Do We Know?, Lisbon, Portugal 3-6 September, 2003; Türke, R. E.: eGovernance – Aspekte zur Steuerung sozialer Systeme, in: Kahle, E. and Wilms, F. E. P., Effektivität und Effizienz durch Netzwerke, Berlin, 2005; Türke, R. E.: eGovernance – an integrated framework to promote Governance, Metaphorum Colloquium, Application of Cybernetics in Government, University of Sunderland, April 30th and May 1st, United Kingdom, 2005; Türke, R. E.: (Building blocks); Türke, R. E.: Towards productive and sustainable forms of interaction in Governance, Kybernetes, Volume 35, Number 1 / 2, 2006

plications and suggestions for the improvement of community governance in Hesse will be derived. The detailed set-up and conduct of the case study is described in chapters 4 and 5.

1.4 Structure of the manuscript

This manuscript explicates the determinants of exploratory research as they have been identified above (chapter 1.3, Figure 3). In chapter 2, the fundamental *Weltanschauung* underlying this research is made explicit and with it, the conceptual elements of any *Weltanschauung* are identified (Actors, images, and systems). Chapter 3 specifies the concept of interaction based on the defined *Weltanschauung* as a mutual orientation of actors that depends on three structural capacities (Change / transformation, channel and transduction capacities). Chapter 4 formulates the necessary and sufficient

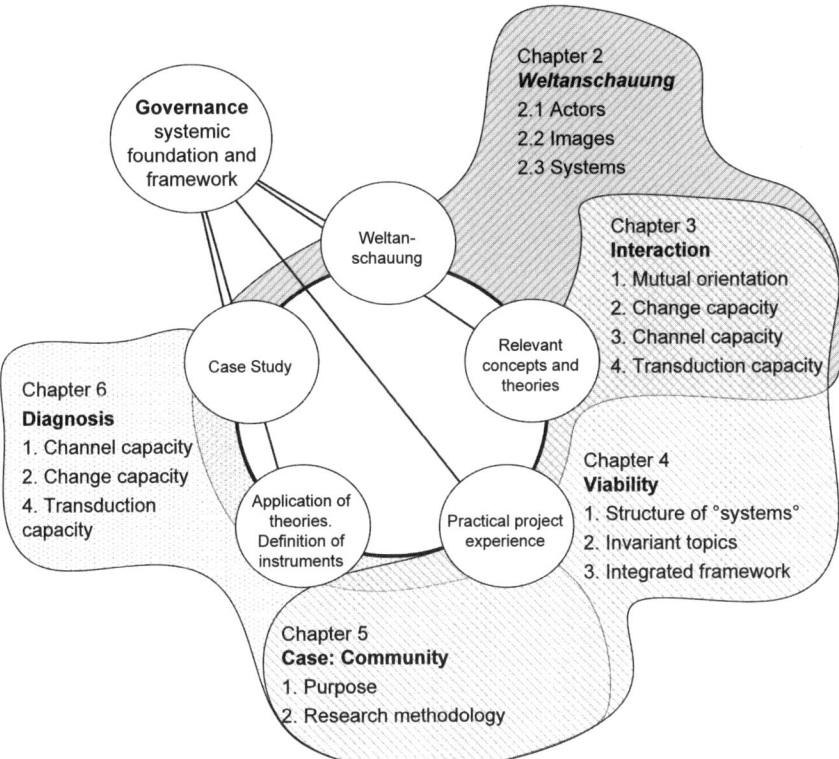

Figure 5. Structure of the manuscript

requirements for the viability of a social system based on the perspective and concepts established and merges them into an integrated framework. Chapter 5 formulates the purpose and defines the methodology of the practi-cal case study. That study, which examines the three structural capacities in the context of Hessian communities, is discussed in chapter 6. Finally, chapter 7 provides the conclusion of this research, sums up the main findings and indicates the potential for further research. Figure 5 depicts the structure of this manuscript; the intersections between the chapter topics indicate the contribution of each chapter to the identified determinants of exploratory research (Figure 3).

2 Actors, images, and systems

This chapter defines how a *Weltanschauung* evolves and thereby implicitely describes the *Weltanschauung* underlying this research. Therefore, it introduces the three basic concepts of actor, image, and system and thus describes how actors are seen to create their common lifeworld. The definitions and intrepretations presented are not the only possible variants. There have been and constantly are major struggles going on in the scientific discussion. However, whatevever *Weltanschauung* is adopted, it will always entail assumptions on how actors create their images on the world and how they commonly create contexts, i.e. systems. Therefore, actors, images and systems are invariant determinants of any evolving *Weltanschauung*.

2.1 Actors

Actor refers to a living, human system.[45] Living systems perceive their environment according to their internal configuration and act with the specific skills provided by their structure.[46] Their main characteristic is a continuing production and re-production of their constituting elements and the relations between them. This is a self-referential, recursive and autopoietic process[47] that

---

[45] Actors may be male or female, the masculine form is used as genus neutralis in this text.

[46] Maturana, H.: (Autopoiesis and society); Maturana, H.: Everything said is said by an observer, in: Thompson, W., Gaia: A way of knowing, Hudson, NY, 1987

[47] According to Humberto Maturana and Francisco Varela, autopoiesis is the process within which a system produces itself. An autopoietic system is an autonomous and self-maintaining entity. By way of interaction, its components (re-)produce recursively the network of processes which generated them. An autopoietic system is operationally closed and structurally determined without apparent inputs and outputs. Cells or organisms are examples of autopoietic systems. Here its application to social systems is described. See Maturana, H. and Varela, F.: Autopoiesis and Cognition – The Realization of Living, Dordrecht, London, Boston, 1973; Maturana, H.: (Autopoiesis and society)

"continuously generates and specifies its own organisation through its operation as a system of production of its own components, and does this in an endless turnover of components under conditions of continuous perturbations and compensation of perturbations." [48]

Actors perceive their world based upon their imprint, i.e. their internal (pre-) condition and the rationality evolving from it.[49] External stimuli of any kind cannot determine actor behaviour; rather, depending on the (pre-) condition established actors perceive stimuli and act based upon their reflections and interpretations.[50] As actors are in principle autonomous units, it is impossible to effectuate determinative influence on them. Whether they perceive stimuli and how they interpret them once perceived, depends exclusively on their conditioning: language, identity, rationality, etc. Action taking place as a response to a certain stimulus does not occur determinatively; rather, it happens with a certain probability.

Thus, human actors continuously evolve their images in an autopoietic process. Images are the constitutive elements of their existence. Image creation takes place autonomously and cannot be determined from outside. Rather, actors do perceive external stimuli through their own eyes based on their backgrounds. By way of distinction, they perform selection, projection, and subjective interpretation and they assign meaning and create their images based upon their *Weltanschauung*.[51] Making distinctions[52] is

---

[48] Maturana, H. and Varela, F.: (Autopoiesis and Cognition), p. 79

[49] Görlitz, A. and Burth, H. P.: (Political control). See also Maturana's remarks on dominance-relations as a consequence of interactions between animals, in: Maturana, H. and Varela, F.: (Tree of knowledge), p. 205f

[50] Görlitz, A. and Burth, H. P.: (Political control)

[51] Görlitz, A. and Burth, H. P.: (Political control), pp. 223-227; To illustrate this, Maturana and Varela use the analogy of a submarine driver who is being congratulated via radio by a spectator standing on the beach for a perfect manoeuvre. The driver is confused when he receives compliments for avoiding reefs, beaches, etc. All he perceived himself doing was reading certain dials and maintaining correlations between indicators within the limits of the submarine equipment. The dynamics of the submarine's operation with its driver are structure determined. They do not concur with representations of the outside world. Beaches and reefs "are valid only for an outside observer, not for the submarine or for the navigator who functions as a component of it", Maturana, H. and Varela, F.: (Tree of knowledge), p. 137

[52] Spencer-Brown, G.: (Laws of Form); Ashby, W. R.: An Introduction to Cybernetics, London, 1964; Espejo, R.: Giving Requisite Variety to Strategic and

the primary operation of image creation. As a consequence of their autonomy, individual actors do not have to conform to generally adopted beliefs,
despite any social pressure to do so. But as a consequence of the social
contexts they adopt, they are both gregarious and heteronymous at the
same time.[53] Obviously, such actors have limited capacity to perceive their
environment.[54] They cannot identify it as an objective reality. They can
grasp only a definite part of the indefinite characteristics of their environment. To cope with this, they have to reduce somehow the plurality of their
percepts. They do this by continuous reproduction of images.[55]

2.2 Images

Images are an actor's constitutive elements, actor behaviour manifests itself in them. They allow an actor to respond to the issues he faces. By creating images, an actor applies and recognises distinctions that constitute
his view of the situations he confronts. Images are the assembled momentary responses or judgements an actor forms continuously in the light of
the situations he faces. In them, the distinctions evolve that an actor requires for undertaking actions.[56] In fact, creating images and taking action
cannot be separated properly. All action reflects emergent images, but not
all images created necessarily result in action.

Images do not emerge from a void, but rather tie up to an actor's percepts,
intentions, and contexts.[57] Perceiving, recognising, conceiving, judging, and
reasoning are all processes of image creation that confront and somehow

---

Implementation Processes: Theory and Practice, http://bprc.warwick.ac.uk/
LSEraul.html

[53] Vickers, G: The Art of Judgement, London, 1965 as referred to in Checkland,
P.: (Information Systems)

[54] Beer, S.: (Heart)

[55] See also McCoulloch, W.: What is a number that a man may know it, and a
man that he may know a number?, Embodiments of Mind, Cambridge, 1961;
McCoulloch, W.: A logical calculus of the ideas immanent in nervous activity,
Embodiments of mind, Cambridge, 1943

[56] Espejo, R.: What is Systemic Thinking?, System Dynamics Review, June, 1994

[57] When 'context' is used in this work, it relates to the underlying claims, i.e. the
specific circumstances and conditions that provide reference for image creation
to individual actors and determine the meaning of ideas, propositions, decisions, theories or concepts emerging at a certain point in time.

process percepts based on existing intentions and contexts. Image creation
is continuously unfolding thus providing a perspective or a mental picture
of the world, i.e. the things and relationships at a certain point of time. Images evolve by associating and judging perceptions in the light of prevailing
assumptions (compare Figure 6).[58] Intents and claims are such prevailing
assumptions, i.e. existing distinctions that co-determine image creation. New
images may reproduce distinctions based on established claims as well as
create new distinctions, adding to or changing existing claims.[59] Percepts
are related to some claims and distinguished from others. Finally, they are
recognised through some concept, e.g. a 'car' distinguished from 'no car',
'good' versus 'bad', 'important' versus 'insignificant'. This process is self-
referential: adopted claims cause subsequent perceptions and attributions
of meaning to differ from those which would have been made in the absence of those claims. Contexts entail the stocks of claims adopted
throughout the previous image creation. They change and accumulate over
time as new experiences are made.[60]

Thus, image creation draws conclusions upon percepts based upon individual intentions and contexts.[61] This understanding is in line with the
findings of the Swiss psychologist Jean Piaget, who examined and described the logic, process, and background of small children's image creation. He referred to assimilation and accommodation as the two basic
processes of cognitive adaptation. With 'assimilation' he described the
process of actors interpreting reality in terms of their internal models of the
world based on previous experience. Further, with accommodation he la-
bels the process of changing existing models by adapting to changing circumstances.[62] Consequently, "reasoning" and also "feeling", "sensing",
"wishing", etc. refer to processes of drawing inferences on intentions and

---

[58] Arthur, Brian: Cognition: The Black Box of Economics, in: Colander, D., The
      Complexity Vision and the Teaching of Economics, Northampton, Mass.,
      2000

[59] Compare the notion of "appreciative systems" as invented by Vickers, G:
      (Judgement) as cited in Checkland, P.: (Information Systems)

[60] Vickers, G: (Judgement) as referred to in Checkland, P.: (Information Sys-
      tems)

[61] Kooiman, J.: (Governing as Governance)

[62] Piaget, J.: Abriss der genetischen Epistemologie, Stuttgart, 1970; Piaget, J.:
      Biologie und Erkenntnis, Frankfurt, 1967; Piaget, J.: Der Aufbau der Wirk-
      lichkeit beim Kinde, Stuttgart, 1936

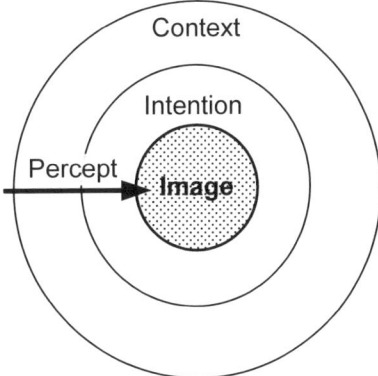

Figure 6. Sources of distinction for image creation

contexts manifested in images.[63] By drawing logical inferences on their percepts, intentions and claims, the actor applies and reveals his rationality.[64] Cognition refers to an actor creating a fit between images and the situation, therefore continuously adopting and eliminating claims.

The distinctions captured in an actor's intentions and context do not simply reflect his *Weltanschauung* but, more so, constitute it. The process of image creation itself is predominantly unconscious.[65] It underlies neurological constraints and evolves based on individual and social intentions and contexts.[66] Intentions and contexts entail the entire set of conditions

---

[63] Compare the respective Merriam-Webster's authors: Article on 'Reason', Encyclopaedia Britannica Ultimate Reference Suite DVD, 2005; according to the German philosopher Immanuel Kant, pure reason is the power of synthesising into unity, by means of comprehensive principles, the concepts that are provided by the intellect. Pure reason is to be distinguished from practical reason, which is especially concerned with the performance of actions.

[64] 'Rationality' is "1: the quality or state of being rational; 2: the quality or state of being agreeable to reason : reasonableness; 3: a rational opinion, belief, or practice – usually used in plural", Merriam-Webster's authors: Article on 'Rationality', Merriam-Webster's Collegiate Dictionary, 2005

[65] "Thinking about the world and having experiences in it cannot properly be separated.", Checkland, P.: (Information Systems)

[66] "We have no choice but to hold in our heads low-variety models of high variety realities. We also have no choice but to attenuate the variety of new states of the system, since this is proliferating too fast for anyone to accommodate. Then obviously, we shall make terrible mistakes in our judgements.", Beer, S.: (Heart)

which determine image creation.[67] In the following, these constraining parameters are described briefly.[68]

2.2.1 Individual percepts

Percepts of the external world are always mediated by an actor's sensory organs and nerves. Many physical phenomena of the outside world lie beyond an actor's sensory capacity. For instance, sound waves below 20 cycles or above 20,000 cycles per second are not recognised by humans. The human eye can detect optical waves between 380 and 680 milli-microns only. These neurological limitations dramatically reduce the range of possible percepts and restrict the actor's ability to perceive the outside world.[69] Percepts do not convey outside phenomena; the images that are created based on them cannot mirror outside phenomena. Further, the image creation of the human mind is limited to handling approximately seven (plus or minus two) distinctions at any given time.[70] It is therefore capable of introducing only a limited number of distinctions in image creation. Thus, neurological constraints constitute a first determining set of filters which distinguishes the world – the territory – from the images created by any individual actor.

2.2.2 Individual and social contexts

Nothing has meaning,

> *"as long as it is not seen in a context. This [...] is a general phenomenon of human relationship. It is a universal characteristic of any interaction between persons, because finally what happens between you and me yesterday takes effect upon, how we react today towards one another. [...] Without context there is no meaning at all to words and actions".[71]*

---

[67] Bateson, G.: Geist und Natur. Eine notwendige Einheit., Frankfurt/Main, 1979

[68] For an analoguous definition of the constraints in image creation see Bandler, R. and Grinder, J.: The Structure of Magic Volume I, Palo Alto, 1980

[69] Bateson, G.: (Mind and Nature); Bandler, R. and Grinder, J.: (Structure of Magic I)

[70] Miller, G. A.: The Magical Number Seven, Plus or Minus Two: Some Limits on our Capacity for Processing Information, Psychological Review, 63, 1956

[71] Author's translation from Bateson, G.: (Mind and Nature)

Literally, context is a paradoxical concept, because it cannot be defined properly. Any definition itself evolves from a context and is thus inherently flawed. As the properties of real world phenomena are infinite, they cannot be made explicit. On the other hand, defining a context is a way of sharply clarifying the boundaries it is pointing towards, which is a necessary requirement to share meaning. Meaning is implicit in any context and its boundaries. The boundaries of a context must therefore be addressed explicitly. A defined context or consensual domain[72] enables actors to consider only those phenomena relevant to their specific situation and perspective. And doing so obscures other phenomena at the same time.[73]

Claims are the basic units of contexts. They are the smallest entity of belief capturing an actor's adopted assumptions and judgements about the world.[74] They express an actor's understanding of "how things are". Some claims are unconscious, e.g. those supporting the essential life-sustaining functions like reflex movements. Others are consciously adopted throughout the ongoing interactions. An actor can actively (re-) formulate them and learn to use more than one set of claims to organise his experience and to create his images of the world, e.g. in languages or cultures.[75] Claims may refer to all kinds of belief systems such as convictions, memories, knowledge, facts, metaphors, presuppositions, hypotheses, models, theories, etc.[76] A percept triggering a claim leads an actor to recognise a thing, object, topic, actor-constellation, time, language, culture, purpose, etc.[77] Thus, contexts are evolutionary products, i.e., they evolve from the previous history of an actor.

---

[72] As used in Harnden, R.: Outside and then: an interpretative approach to the VSM, in: Espejo, R. and Harden, R., The Viable Systems Model – Interpretations and Applications of Stafford Beer's VSM, Chichester, 1989

[73] "How shall we ever conceive however express a new idea if we are bound by the categorization that delivered our problem to us in the first place?", in Beer, S.: Beyond Dispute: The Invention of Team Syntegrity, Chichester, 1994, p. 8

[74] Beer, S.: Diagnosing the System for Organisations – Companion Volume to Brain of the Firm and The Heart of Enterprise- Brain of the Firm, Chichester, 1985a

[75] Bandler, R. and Grinder, J.: (Structure of Magic I)

[76] Kooiman, J.: (Governing as Governance)

[77] "Circumstances and conditions can be spatial, temporal, situational, personal, social, cultural, ecological, etc.", Gershenson, C.: Contextuality: A Philosophical Paradigm, with Applications to Philosophy of Cognitive Science, School of Cognitive and Computer Sciences,University of Sussex, 2004

Since different actors hold different belief systems, they refer to different claims while evolving their images, and consequently they experience different ways of perceiving, experiencing, and interpreting the outside world. Obviously, without having any compatible claims, individual actors would never be in a position to develop compatible concepts of objects, of space and time, of ego and consciousness.[78] Although an individual actor's reality is always subject-dependent, it is not arbitrary, since claims constantly evolve from and are shaped through social interaction. Primarily, claims are adopted because they have been experienced as useful or successful in attending certain issues. Only a record of failures could lead an actor to discard them.[79] As human actors are social animals, to experience success in most of the cases means adopting compatible claims. Social reconciliation is the major source of claims. By adopting compatible claims, actors are setting themselves common domains of reference and mutually influence their image creation. Usually, an actor operates in multiple shared contexts such as family, company, community, etc. By sharing a common context with others, he ties in with what he perceives as shared, i.e. the sphere of claims he has individually developed for that context. Some of those will be shared claims.[80] These are both social enablers and constraints which do not concur for all actors but only for members of the same lifeworld.[81] Sharing claims does not mean that these are identical. Rather, they have proved to be compatible. For instance, an 'elephant trunk' is usually considered to be a 'nose' only due to a shared claim reconciled before. It is the context of the 'elephant' which identifies 'the trunk' as a

---

[78] Schmidt, S. J.: Medien, Kommunikation und das 18. Kamel, in: Merten, K., Schmidt, S. J., and Weischenberg, S., Funkkolleg „Medien Kommunikation. Konstruktion von Wirklichkeit – Einführungsbrief, Winheim; Basel, 1990

[79] "A hypothesis or association or belief model is clung to not because it is 'correct' – there is no way to know this – but rather because it has worked in the past and must cumulate a record of failure before it is worth discarding.", in Arthur, Brian: (Cognition)

[80] Espejo, R.: Giving Requisite Variety to Strategic and Implementation Processes: Theory and Practice, http://bprc.warwick.ac.uk/LSEraul.html

[81] "People […] have free will. Yes, maybe; but people also have constraints laid upon their variety by upbringing, or by the roles that they agree to play in a social unit like a firm. It is true that, for example, the liver cannot resign and be replaced by one less gnarled, but what about it?", Beer, S.: (Provenance), p. 20; Lifeworld is the "culturally transmitted and linguistically organised stock of interpretative patterns" actors refer to. Habermas, J.: (Communicative action One), p. 124

'nose', communicating that whatever lies between two eyes and above a mouth is a 'nose'.[82] This applies, although actors always draw from different references in regard to the nose.

Husserl refers to these imaginary shared contexts of reference as the lifeworld.[83] The lifeworld holds patterns of meaning for an actor. It is the huge imaginary stock of generally acknowledged shared claims, which actors use as a common reference system. Culture and language[84] manifest themselves in the lifeworld.[85] These are an actor's inter-subjectively shared and compatible claims. Through them a context specifies meaning. Lifeworld forms the fundamental context for the conception and interpretation of outside world experiences. It can be described as

> *"the unquestioned ground of everything given in my experience and the unquestionable frame in which all the problems I have to deal with are located".*[86]

---

[82] Example adapted from Bateson, G.: (Mind and Nature)

[83] Husserl, E.: Erfahrung und Urteil. Untersuchungen zur Genealogie der Logik., Hamburg, 1948, pp. 38, §10

[84] An example of the contribution of language as a stock of validity claims is the distinction of colours by English and Maidu- speakers (Maidu are a group of Native Americans who lived in northern California). The people who are native speakers of Maidu habitually group their experience into three categories supplied by their language. These three categories cover the same range of real-world sensation which the eight (specific) colour terms of English language do. A person who speaks Maidu is characteristically conscious only of the three categories of colour experience while the English speaker has more categories and, therefore, more habitual perceptual distinctions. This means that, while English speakers will describe their experience of two objects as different, speakers of Maidu will typically describe their experience of the identical real-world situation as being the same (two tulak books). Bandler, R. and Grinder, J.: (Structure of Magic I)

[85] Culture refers to the customary beliefs, social forms, and material traits of a racial, religious, or social group. It is the set of shared attitudes, values, goals, and practices that characterises a company or corporation, in Merriam-Webster's authors: Article on 'Culture', Merriam-Webster's Collegiate Dictionary, 2005

[86] As cited in Yolles, M.: Viable Systems Theory, Anticipation and Logical Levels of Management, Conference proceedings for International Conference on Creativity and Complexity, 2003, London, p. 5

Lifeworld is the backdrop of interaction and the sphere of reference for creating understanding between actors.[87] It is the origin of the actor's self-interpretation, i.e. upon which he create his images.

2.2.3 Individual and social intentions

Actors do have the capacity to actively influence their own image creation. They do this firstly through conscious selection of claims and secondly through unconscious constraint. When selecting distinctions from claims in the light of percepts, they are guided by their intentions. An intention is referred to as the act of will whereby an actor adheres to an end.[88] Intentions point to the capacity of an actor to direct image creation towards certain desired intentional[89], i.e. affective or algedonic, states[90]: a feeling of pain or pleasure originating from wishes, fears, purposes, goals, interests, and purposes.[91] Intentions can appear in different intensities determining the intentional state of an actor. Different degrees of attention or concentration manifest in the obliviousness or retentiveness of an actor. The basic unit of intentions are intents.

---

[87] Habermas, J.: Theorie des kommunikativen Handelns, Volume 2, Frankfurt a.M., 1981

[88] As cited from Aristotle in Frank, W. A.: Authority as Nurse of Freedom and the Common Good, Faith and Reason, 4, 1990; For an understanding of intention as goal-orientation in conscious and unconscious behaviour see: Scherer, K. R.: Kommunikation, in: Scherer, K. R. and Wallbott, H. G., Nonverbale Kommunikation: Forschungsberichte zum Interaktions-verhalten, Weinheim; Basel, 1984

[89] Searle defines intention as a characteristic of mental states to be directed towards certain objects or issues within the world, see Searle, J.: Intentionality: An Essay in the Philosophy of Mind., New York, 1983

[90] Algedonic from αλγος, algos = pain, ηδος, hedos = pleasure. Beer, S.: National government: disseminated regulation in real time, or "How to run a country", in: Espejo, R. and Harnden, R., The Viable System Model – Interpretations and Applications of Stafford Beer's VSM, Chichester, New York, Brisbane, Toronto, Singapore, 1989

[91] Kooiman, J.: (Governing as Governance); "This quality is known as teleological, goal-seeking behaviour.", in Waelchli, F.: The VSM and Ashby's Law as illuminants of historical management thought, in: Espejo, R. and Harnden, R., The Viable System Model: Interpretations and Applications of Stafford Beer's VSM, Chichester, 1989

Intents give impulse to generating or absorbing distinctions in image creation. They motivate an actor to enrich or restrict his repertoire of claims as needed for pursuing personal goals, interests, and purposes. Intents may initiate the enlargement of the stock of claims, i.e. underlying beliefs, models, theories, etc. Or they may restrict the set of claims consulted in image creation by defining selection criteria. For example, let us imagine Paul has lost his key. Focusing image creation on an imaginary 'lost key' and the actor's recent history facilitates finding the real lost key.

Intentions direct image creation to specific claims, either individual ones such as their personal history, backgrounds, or socially shared ones referring to their family, firm, or nation. Intentions can arise consciously, which distinguishes human actors from animal instinct or the automatism of machines. As soon as actors agree to share intents, they become social intentions with impacts for all actors involved.

The ambivalent character of these conversions makes clear that the constraints enabling actors to reach the most extraordinary achievements may be restricting their further development when the adopted perspective is confused with reality.[92] Image creation highly depends on the actors intentional states. In an indifferent mood ("That is no concern of mine"), actors will casually select distinctions to reinforce their prevailing backgrounds; in a worried mood ("I am concerned about…"), they will actively search without bias for those relevant aspects (distinctions evolving from percepts) which assess or question their prevailing intentions and contexts. Whereas the former mode generalises on existing distinctions, the latter distorts percepts, and thus challenges an actors' prevailing background.[93] As a consequence, image creation can never be objective or completed. Actors have to be suspicious and sustain the awareness that their beliefs, models, and theories are not exogenous but rather constructed with agendas from other times.[94]

2.2.4 Complexity of actor backgrounds

Actors always find themselves in situations facing issues to be resolved. Situation refers to the fact that each individual actor is always exposed to a combination of circumstances. As a consequence of an actor's autopoiesis

---

[92] Bandler, R. and Grinder, J.: (Structure of Magic I)

[93] Beer, S.: (Heart)

[94] Arthur, Brian: (Cognition)

(chapter 2.1), what a situation 'is', i.e. its 'is-ness', is always determined individually. One situation cannot be perceived in the same way by two different actors. In other words, the 'is-ness' of a situation always evolves from the distinctions that are being made individually, and is thus based on the actor's background. "Background" refers to the general conditioning of the actor, i.e. his genetic, cultural, and individual imprints from which he evolves his images. As a convention an actor's adopted intents (I) and claims (C) referring to a specific image, e.g. an

(I) Image (C) is abbreviated here as °image°. The superscripted circles (°community°) are introduced to indicate a pre-conditioning that has been adopted by an actor or is shared by a group of actors. Thus, an actor's repertoire is determined by the total set of distinctions (°images°, °instruments°, °actions°, and °actors°, etc.) he can choose from out of his background. His background is the whole set of imprinted distinctions accessible to image creation. The number of alternative distinctions at choice derives from it. The stock of distinctions of the background thus attenuates the complexity of the actor's environment (i.e. his perceived lifeworld) to a degree that the actor can handle.[95]

Now, the measure for describing the actor's repertoire to act is termed variety. It is a general measure of complexity defined by Ashby as

> *"the number of possible states of whatever it is, whose complexity we want to measure."* [96]

An issue refers to a certain variety an actor faces, which has to be resolved (or rather dissolved). The number of possible answers (or states) that can be adopted when confronted with an issue defines the actor's variety or repertoire to respond to it.

Now, the law of requisite variety expresses a fundamental cybernetic insight:

> *"Only variety can absorb variety"*.[97]

---

[95]   It "just happens. The brain [...] will filter out what variety is left-in beyond the capacity to assimilate", Beer, S.: (Diagnosing), p. 24

[96]   Beer, S.: (Heart); Beer, S.: (Provenance)

[97]   Ashby, W. R.: (Introduction); Beer, S.: (Heart); "I consider that this law stands in the same relation to management as the law of gravity to Newtonian physics.", in Beer, S.: (Heart), p. 89; Beer, S.: National government: disseminated regulation in real time, or `How to run a country´, in: Espejo, R. and Harnden, R., The

This means that an actor can resolve (or eliminate) issues only if he is capable of providing solutions to all states that may emerge from the situation. The background determines to what extent the actor is able to cope with an issue.[98] Actor variety manifests itself in the prevailing imprinted distinctions determining the actor's image creation with respect to an issue. It is a function of the actor's knowledge, competence, trust, and also of his interests. A background provides requisite variety if it enables the actor to cope with the state of the issues being faced. This requires that the prevailing intentions and contexts produce images which respond adequately to the disturbances likely to occur.[99] Therefore, the background can provide models, theories, beliefs, etc. which allow the actor to understand what happens in a situation and to identify the relevant problematic part of it (i.e. to comprehend the variety inherent). The actor may acquire a topic[100] competence which enables him to cope with all issues belonging to the topic that evolve. With an adequate topic background, the actor can cope with numerous specific issues.[101] However, it is always the actor himself who constitutes the varieties based on his individual predisposition to solve an issue faced.

Viable System Model – Interpretations and Applications of Stafford Beer's VSM, Chichester, New York, Brisbane, Toronto, Singapore, 1989

[98] Both intentional and contextual varieties refer to the involved actor's predisposition to attend to an issue.

[99] "To say that management controls the company does not mean that the varieties of both are the same, but that the residual variety that is left unattended by the processes of self-organisation and self-regulation in the company has to be absorbed, equated by management.", in Espejo, R.: The VSM revisited, in: Espejo, R. and Harden, R., The Viable System Model: Interpretations and Applications of Stafford Beer's VSM, Chichester, New York, Brisbane, Toronto, Singapore, 1989

[100] A topic is a distinction that delimits other distinctions as belonging to or not to. With a topic a category is established that distinguishes a certain field of ontological *system* phenomena or issues from others. Thus, topics can be used to demarcate issues and to subsume experiences gained with them.

[101] It is important to notice that any selection of action taking place starts with some intentions and contextual premises that cannot be questioned nor justified further. Every chain of actions (i.e. images created) in a situation inevitably starts and ends with some claims. Therefore, image creation does not per se follow a normative or ethical grounding. Ulrich, W.: Critical heuristics of social systems design, European Journal of Operational Research, 31, North-Holland, 1987

And as will be seen below, assigning a certain variety is always an active imposition of an actor (the observer) based on the distinctions selected.

In short it can be concluded as follows regarding the perspective taken on actors and their recognition: Image creation is described as an autopoietic process constituting actor behaviour, i.e. perceiving, attributing meaning, making judgements upon percepts, and forming intentions, thus inventing an individual actor's world. Image creation and action cannot reasonably be separated. Percepts, intentions, and contexts are an actor's sources of distinction for evolving images. These define how he perceives and experiences his *Wirklichkeit*[102] and which alternative options he sees for his life. The autopoietic character of image creation protects actors from being overwhelmed or confused by the indefinite character of their environment. Through deletion and generalisation, the majority of largely useless and irrelevant phenomena are ignored, distinctions are created only for that selection of phenomena which is likely to be practically useful.[103] Consequently, there is a difference between reality and any individual image created by an actor. Different actors create different images of the same reality. The

> *"facts about the nature and purpose of a system are not objective realities".*[104]

Thus, an actor's unfolding rationality, his internal logic or way of thinking, is determined through his background, i.e. the total set of his intents and claims. Whether an observer attributes 'rational' to the actor's behaviour evolving from his background is a different question.[105] Figure 7 summarises the process of image creation based upon the sources of distinction identified. Individual percepts pass contexts – with the prevailing claims (C) – and intentions – with the prevailing intents (I) -, thus acquire meaning and emerge into the image.

---

[102] The German word for reality as it is perceived by a human actor. The German language clearly distinguishes it from "Realität" which refers to the reality of the outside world that is ultimately not perceivable by a human actor.

[103] Huxley, A.: The Doors of Perception, New York, 1954

[104] Beer, S.: (Heart)

[105] Rationality is "1 : the quality or state of being rational, 2 : the quality or state of being agreeable to reason : reasonableness, 3 : a rational opinion, belief, or practice – usually used in plural", see Merriam-Webster's authors: Article on 'Rationality', Merriam-Webster's Collegiate Dictionary

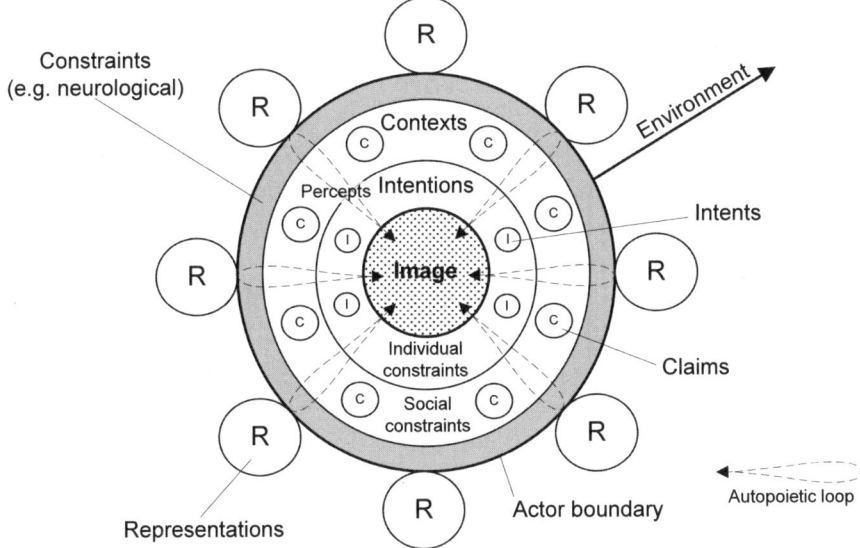

Figure 7. Image creation and sources of distinction

2.3 Systems

A system is understood here as a perceived or inferred notion of purpose which stems from a set of presumptions defining its boundary. Actors who adopt a common system notion align their backgrounds to that notion and derive their images based on it. The establishment of an organised or formalised social °system° notion proves that there are some common ideas about what kind of purpose should be implemented in what way. As a consequence of the autopoietic character of image creation, there may not be consensus between actors on the notion of a system as each actor draws from individual intentions and contexts concerning the system.

A system notion evolves whenever actors create or recognise a shared intention and thus decide to make some joint effort. In so doing, they actively compose and adopt a notion of a system based upon a subjective nature and purpose.[106] As soon as an intentional statement of purpose ex-

---

[106] Beer gives the example of a lighting system, in Beer, S.: (Heart); "Social systems are constituted in the operational domain by peoples' interactions. This constitution is languaged by the participants.", in Espejo, R.: Giving Requisite Variety to Strategy and Information Systems, in: Stowell, F. A. and Howell, J. G., Systems Science – Adressing Global Issues, New York, 1993

pressing "what should be" turns into "what is", the notion of the system is transformed into a claim. Actors who have adopted a °system° notion can now refer to the distinctions that derive from it. The adopted intents and claims referred to as the °system° have now become a shared reference against which actors can align their perspectives. Actors are enabled to create their images based upon those parts of their background which reflects the °system° notion. They can now align and realign their image creation based on it.

As a consequence of the autopoietic character of image creation, systems are not ontological but epistemological entities, i.e. they evolve from the purposeful agreements actors settle on concurrently in their interactions. Any actor not aware of the autopoietic character of image creation may tend to assume the °system° to be "out there" with all properties of being able to act, think, decide, etc.

> *"We say 'Shell has decided to build a refinery in Singapore', and everyone accepts without question that this is a meaningful statement".* [107]

But social °systems°, whether they manifest themselves as organisations, institutions, firms, communities, or families, are abstract ideas which do not act.[108] They are reified aggregated claims with no objective existence 'out there'. It is the set of shared distinctions actors refer to in image creation which constitutes the °system°. Ontology evolves from epistemology. Sharing the notion of a °system° enables actors to make sense of their world.[109] Only in a shared context, can °systems° such as the refinery in Singapore be meaningfully considered to perform certain functions or activities. And

> *"these things can never in practise be finally defined or isolated. Does a hospital cure the sick, or promote iatrogenic order?"*[110]

---

[107] Checkland, P.: (Information Systems)

[108] Hoebeke, L.: Identity: the paradoxical nature of Organizational Closure, Kybernetes, Volume 35, Number 1/2, 2006

[109] Jackson, M. C.: Evaluating the managerial significance of the VSM, in: Espejo, R. and Harnden, R., The Viable Systems Model: Interpretations and Applications of Stafford Beer's VSM, Chichester, 1989 with reference to Dachler, 1984; Checkland, P.: (Information Systems)

[110] Harnden, R.: (Outside and then)

A common social °system° such as an 'elementary school' refers to a set of coherent judgements, enabling actors to reconcile compatible conventions (intents and claims) to commonly produce the purpose aspired to, e.g. "to educate young children to cope with every day situations and to integrate them in society". Other °system° notions may refer to the island of Hawaii, the moon, etc. Thus, actors tailor their individual contexts to a purposeful, shared °system° notion. For instance, °family°, °community°, or °association° are all complex, purposive social °systems° that actors bring into being[111] for the purpose of creating some desired change in their lives. Any organisation is a °system° with a common purpose.[112]

Depending on the sort of claims assigned to a °system°, individual, social, biological, physical, and other types of systems may be distinguished. It is then a special feature of social °systems° in contrast to biological or mechanical °systems° that their boundaries cannot be assessed against a shared reference. To share a common view of a biological or physical °system°, actors can accommodate their views of certain aspects (relevant distinctions) representing perceived phenomena they intend to address. For instance, agreeing to identify a perceived phenomenon of an object as 'blue' establishes a distinction that can now be referenced to in different contexts. Thus, invariant characteristics of the world out there can be addressed. Mutual agreement about 'blue'-ness and reliability in the application of the concept 'blue' establishes it as a useful concept. However, while

> *"Copernicus and Ptolemy offer very different hypotheses about the basic structure of our solar system, we know that, irrespective of whether the sun or the earth is at the centre of the system, the actual structure is entirely unaffected by our having theories about it ..." (continues)*[113]

Thus, even based on percepts, final °system° boundaries and characteristics cannot be revealed as they always draw from underlying assumptions that have been settled before. In the case of biological °systems°, distinctions are supplied by a common point of reference that is experienced to be invariant. In the case of social °systems°, invariances depend on the coherence of the established boundaries and concepts. To accommodate differ-

---

[111] Waelchli, F.: (VSM and Ashby's Law)

[112] Morgan, G.: Images of Organization – The executive edition, San Francisco, 1998

[113] Zuboff (1988) as cited in Checkland, P.: (Information Systems)

ent views towards social °systems°, their boundaries must be reconciled first before actors can derive any compatible distinctions. Thus, in both cases, the constituting distinctions themselves depend on which individual and social, value-related distinctions have already been established. Depending on the definition of the °system° boundaries, there remains a scope, in which actors can struggle for purposes.[114] Some actors, when changing notions of the °system°, may provoke other actors to change their notions as a consequence of them experiencing improved competence in coping with their issues. Consequently, the whole notion of the social °system° as it is shared changes dynamically.

> *"...Whereas when Marx propounds a theory of history, this changes history!"*[115]

The following figure illustrates how the ontology of perceived phenomena (a *system*) evolves from an actor's prevailing epistemology (the °system°). That means "how actors perceive things" (a *System*) always evolves from "what they claim and intend" (the claims and intents that constitute an adopted °system° notion).

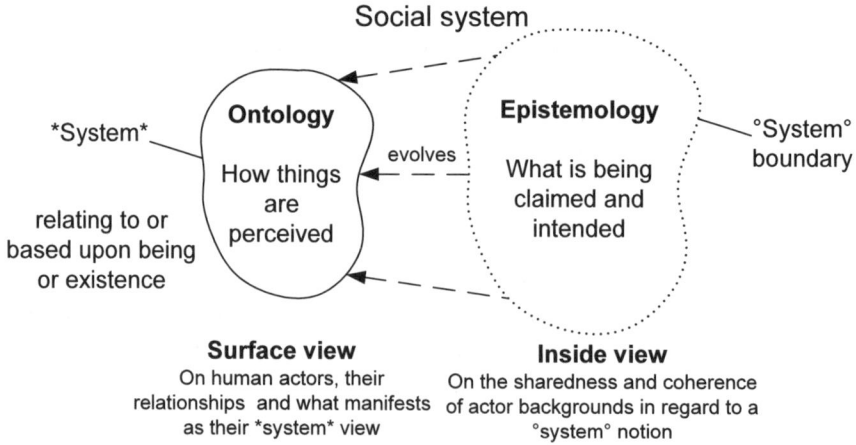

Figure 8. Surface and inside views of social systems[116]

---

[114] Remer, A.: Instrumente unternehmenspolitischer Steuerung: Unternehmens-verfassung, formale Organisation und personale Gestaltung, Berlin, New York, 1982

[115] Zuboff (1988) as cited in Checkland, P.: (Information Systems)

2.3.1 Boundaries

Thus, a system is not a given. Rather, its presumed boundary identifies and delineates a context which may be entailed in another, larger context. By separating the inside from the outside, the part of the context addressed with the system is captured and made accessible to individual actors.[117] Boundaries are subjective[118] and attributes of a system are imputed. For instance, a lighting system at home or in a borrowed office can be looked at from different perspectives, ascribing different boundaries. Is only the light bulb part of the whole defining two possible states (on and off), or should the context

Table 2. Twelve fundamental boundary judgements of °system° notions

Boundary judgement	Typical question
1. Affected actors	Who are the beneficiaries, clients, citizens?
2. Purpose	What is the purpose aspired to?
3. Measure of improvement	What is the measure of improvement?
4. Decision-maker	Who is the decision-maker?
5. Resources	What resources are controlled by the decision-maker?
6. Decision environment	What conditions lie outside a decision maker's control?
7. Professional	Who is considered a professional?
8. Expertise	What expertise is consulted?
9. Guarantor of success	What or who is assumed to be a guarantor of success?
10. Witness	Who is witness to the interests of those affected but not involved?
11. Emancipation	What secures the emancipation of those affected from the premises and promises of those involved?
12. Weltanschauung	What Weltanschauung is determining?

---

[116] Stars (such as in *system*) are used to indicate the ontological manifestation of a system notion, i.e. what actors see. Circles refer to the system notion's epistemological root (such as in °system°).

[117] "Whenever we apply the systems concept to some section of the real world, we must make very strong a priori assumptions about what is to belong to the system in question and what is to belong to its environment.", in Ulrich, W.: (Critical heuristics social systems), p. 278

[118] Beer, S.: (Heart)

attached to them be looked at, e.g. the fact that the electricity bill has not been paid, which would reflect another off state? [119] And so on. Thus, the °system° boundary sets the conditions for all °system° interactions and determines the varieties involved. Variety is a relative measure that can be meaningfully determined only in reference to a shared °system° boundary. When a °system° issue is faced, variety refers to the number of states that could potentially be adopted in the light of the chosen °system° boundary. For identifying social °system° boundaries, a critical system's heuristics identifies the following twelve central boundary judgements of any social °system° notion.[120]

2.3.2 Elements and relations

In a surface view, actors are the *system* elements. Through interactions these actors establish relations with each other. In so doing, it can be distinguished between actors

1. actively involved in °system° implementation,

2. involved *and* affected by °system° implementation,

3. *not* involved *but* affected by °system° implementation,

4. *not* involved and *not* affected by °system° implementation.

This is depicted in the following figure. Actors engaged in social *system* implementation are placed in the the inner circle; those affected through *system* implementation are situated within the boundaries of the *social *system* (outer circle) but do not contribute actively to implementation (inner circle). Some actors may do both: they are involved and affected and therefore part of both outer and inner circles. Other actors neither involved nor affected therefore have to be placed outside the outer circle.

Based upon a °system° boundary, actors evolve distinctions that continuously constitute and implement the *system*. The intents and claims upon which these distinctions evolve create the system's elements and relationships between those elements.[121] °System° elements are characteristic sets

---

[119] Beer, S.: (Heart)

[120] Ulrich, W.: (Critical heuristics social systems)

[121] Klaus, G.: Wörterbuch der Kybernetik, Berlin, 1968; Hill, W., Fehlbaum, R., and Ulrich, P.: Organisationslehre 1, Ziele, Instrumente und Bedingungen der Organisation sozialer Systeme, Bern-Stuttgart, 1994; Ulrich, H.: Die Unternehmung als produktives soziales System, Bern; Stuttgart, 1970

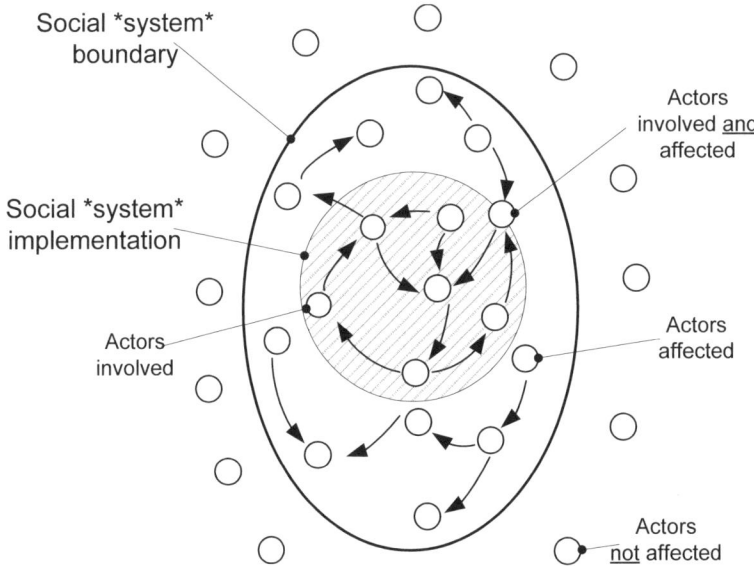

Figure 9. Surface view of a social *system* notion and types of actor involvement

of imprints, reconciliations which comprise what the °system° notion is about, its essence. Generally, four kinds of °system° elements can be distinguished:

1. °**Actors**° identify those involved or affected in °system° implementation.

2. °**Images**° are adopted views about a system or states of the system, how it is believed to be now, or how it ought to be in future. They indicate *"what governing is about"*[122], where and how possibilities, opportunities and limitations are in dealing with situations.[123] Based upon them, percepts are interpreted and considered as relevant with respect to a social °system° notion.

3. °**Instruments**° are means for implementation, i.e. how things are being done. They are the devices, utilities, means, resources, and *"crafts applied"* that actors use to *"reach what they want to accomplish"*.[124] Instruments create links between images and actions and describe what is needed for implementation of a system notion.

---

[122] Kooiman, J.: (Governing as Governance)
[123] Ibid.
[124] Ibid.

4. °**Actions**° identify the activities that actors undertake or intend to undertake at a certain point in time to bring °instruments° into place.[125] They identify the behaviour needed to apply °instruments°, e.g. quick, slow, thorough, attentive, sloppy, etc.

Nevertheless, these elements, even if they are shared, would not suffice to lead actors to coherent, contiguous behaviour. Further, there must be established relations between these elements indicating for instance, what °instruments° should be used to implement °images°. Only through the relations between elements, are actors enabled to implement and realise purposeful activities that together comply with their adopted °system° notion and evolve in *outcomes* and *results*.

For instance, let's think about a group of actors who have agreed 'to build a water fountain in the desert' (°image°). And let's suggest that these actors share a compatible boundary of that system °fountain°, i.e. they have a congruent understanding of the purpose, measure of improvement, etc. implied in that activity. The actors involved will then engage in specifying some common °image° of the fountain to be built. Obviously, this cannot just be any kind of fountain, but has to be one of a kind that is especially adequate for a desert and the special geographic and geologic conditions prevailing there. As soon as the actors have agreed upon some notion of the °fountain°, they will need to reconcile some shared understanding of helpful °instruments° that enable them to implement it. They might ask some known experts or buy a book describing how a fountain is to be built. Further, they will probably arrange for some tools, such as scoops, borers, tubes, cement, bricks, and a pump. As soon as the actors have prepared the °instruments°, they will start to actively implement the °fountain° based upon their °actions°. °Actions° are those characteristic backgrounds based upon which they move, i.e. to screw, dig, bring up walls, carry, climb, go, jump, push, remove, roll, split, stir, switch, take off, traverse, walk, withdraw. Throughout this process, they may agree to distribute the °actions° to the different °actors° about whom they share the impression that they are the most talented and competent.

This means that the manifestation of a °system° notion originating from some common boundary adopted, takes place through continuous reconciliation of the distinctions that form it, i.e. the °systems° elements and relations. Percepts of *elements* and *relations* are confronted with the existing distinctions, i.e. actors' respective °elements° and °relationships°.

---

[125] Ibid.

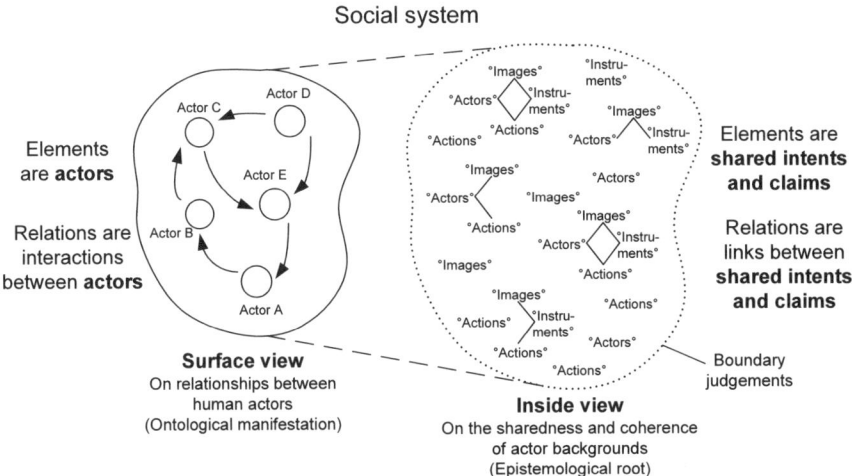

Figure 10. Surface and inside views on social systems

As a consequence, actors recognise their adopted °system° notion to be satisfied, accomplished, disturbed, changed, or spoiled.

Any °system° notion is not only subjective with respect to a single actor and conditioned by his constitution of its boundaries, but also a function of what is shared as a consequence of previous mutual reconciliations.[126] As long as actors entertain major differences in their notions of a °system°, they will necessarily identify different elements and assign different relations. Only under the condition that actors share the essential boundary judgements and a sufficiently large number of intents and claims, will they be able to derive and share some common °images°, °instruments° and °actions° in the light of that °system° notion. If they do so, they can reasonably characterise a condition or state of that °system° notion as a specific manifestation of °elements° and their °relations°. The situation of a °system° is its momentary condition as perceived individually or shared commonly at a specific point in time.[127] Thus, a °system° is understood as any correlated set of intents and claims adopted by an actor which are perceived as purposeful. All °systems°, their natures and purposes are subjective, as they emerge from an actor's active composition.[128]

---

[126] Beer, S.: (Heart)

[127] Waelchli, F.: (VSM and Ashby's Law)

[128] Beer, S.: (Heart)

3   Interaction

An individual actor's behaviour can have effects on others ranging from negligible to profound. Sometimes, beliefs are shared by many others. As has been defined above, social °system° notions are sets of agreements establishing some degree of commonality in the actions and behaviours of the actors involved and affected. It is through interaction that actors negotiate and renegotiate the conditionings underlying their image creation, thus continuously producing their shared lifeworld.[129] Interaction indicates how actors cope with complexity in a continuous, interdependent process of mutual variety attenuation and amplification. It is the fundamental regulative activity that evolves, maintains, changes, or dissolves °system° notions. The outcome of interaction depends not only on the actual situation, but strongly on the prevailing contexts and intentions, e.g. the established structures and cultures.

This chapter introduces the basic notion of interaction (3.1) and illustrates the three essential aspects of interaction (3.2, 3.3, and 3.4) and how they concur (3.5).

3.1 Mutual orientation

3.1.1 Coupling

As a consequence of the autopoietic nature of image creation (see chapter 2.2), changes in an actor's background may be induced but not determined from outside. Through coupling, changes can be triggered, but will be adopted only if the actor actively decides to do so.[130] Such coupling is an ongoing process running continuously at all times in a perceive-reflect-expose loop (Figure 11).

---

[129] Espejo, R. and Schwaninger, M.: Organizational Fitness – Corporate Effectiveness through Management Cybernetics, Frankfurt a.M., 1993

[130] Varela, F.: Two principles of Self-Organisation, in: Ulrich, H. and Probst, G. J. B., Self-Organisation and the Management of Social Systems, Berlin, 1984; Winograd, T. and Flores, F.: (Understanding computers)

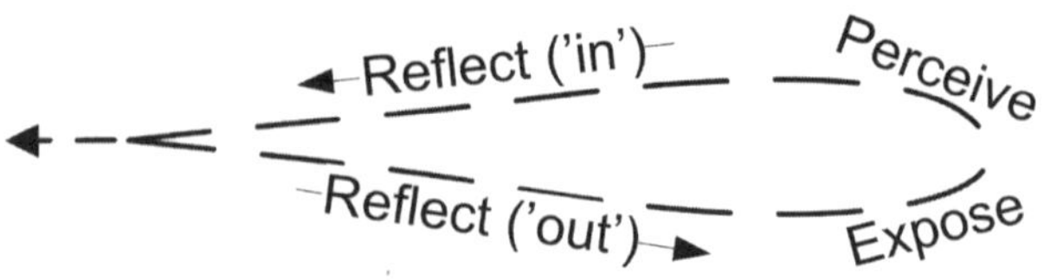

Figure 11. Autopoietic perceive-reflect-expose loop

Continuously following that loop enables actors to create and maintain shared °system° notions and thus to cope with their environment. But how does this happen?

Media are all materiality used for establishing couplings between actors.[131] Actors use media to expose and orientate each other towards representations. Media are a fundamental prerequisite of interaction defining how actors can share distinctions and how they can be distributed over space and time. They allow for structures to be established enabling actors to create and share representations that expose their distinctions. Representations make explicit a certain set of distinctions – a content – through which actors orientate each other towards a certain message. By exposing representations, actors mutually orient themselves towards their message.[132] A message or a statement is the set of distinctions actors' reference to attend to their °system° issues. As follows, wherever annotation is indicated in single quotation marks (e.g. 'element') it is emphasised that the marked term is a representation pointing to the respective concept: an unmarked – image – refers to an individual actor's model or construct of reality, whereas 'image' – refers to a representation that is used to point towards a concrete manifestation of an individual or shared image. Similarly, 'instruments' and 'actions' are expressions pointing at specific instruments or actions to be taken. Thus, a situation is being distinguished from a 'situation'. Whereas the former (situation) refers to the is-ness of a certain state of the °system° being focussed on, the latter ('situation') refers to a representation used between actors to express a message, i.e. some content about a situation. A 'situation' is thus a reflection on a situation and not to be confused with

---

[131] Schmidt defines media as "all materiality, which can be used systematically for establishing a regulated and socially relevant semiotic (resp. symbolic) coupling of living systems.", in Schmidt, S. J.: Medien: Die Kopplung von Kommunikation und Kognition, in: Krämer, S., Medien, Computer, Realität: Wirklichkeitsvorstellungen in neuen Medien, Frankfurt a.M., 1998

[132] Rusch, G.: Kommunikation und Verstehen, in: Merten, K., Schmidt, S. J., and Weischenberg, S., Die Wirklichkeit der Medien, 1994

the situation itself. It may be expressed by an individual actor referring to his relative position and his combination of circumstances at a certain moment, or it may be expressed by an observer expressing his individual references to that situation. In any case, it is a selection of distinctions derived from an individual actor's background. It is the ontological correlatives of the message an actor intends to communicate. The apostrophe is thus being used to indicate the difference between a perception of the world based on a set of distinctions applied (a situation) and the distinctions made explicit in a representation as to allow interaction between actors about the situation ('situation').

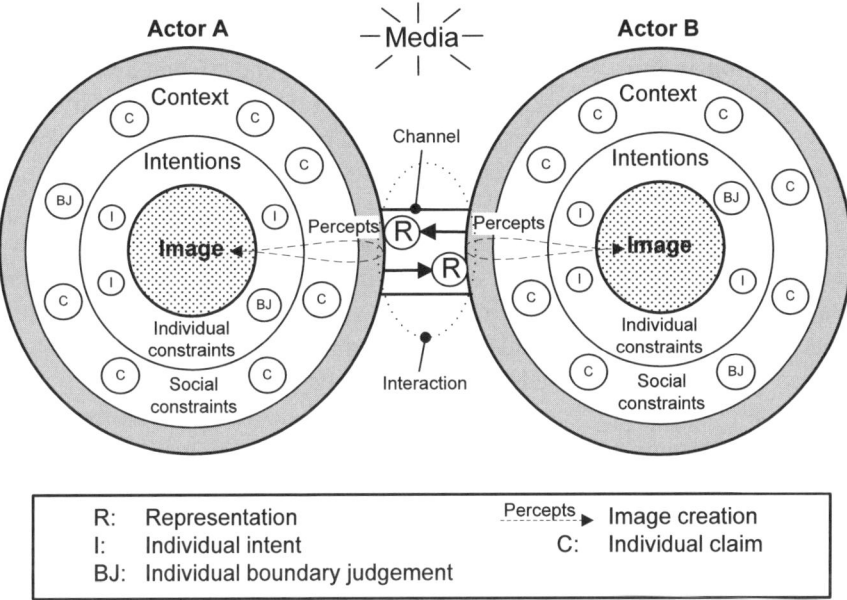

R:	Representation		Percepts ►	Image creation
I:	Individual intent		C:	Individual claim
BJ:	Individual boundary judgement			

Figure 12. Interaction as orientation towards representation

For instance, in a face-to-face setting of two actors (Figure 12), A orients B towards a message which he articulates in a representation (R). Any message between A and B has to be articulated in and interpreted from a representation. To create a representation, A draws on his background of verbal and / or non-verbal expressions, e.g. speech, sound, body language, script, etc., and assembles a representation reflecting his message. He does this based on his expectation towards the oriented actor's ensuing behaviour. Both expectations and actions towards his counterpart rely on the conventions and patterns expressed in his background. Both creation ('in') and exposition ('out') of representations are engaged in translating the intented message into the diction of the receiving actor.[133] To ensure compatibility, exposing representations ('out') relies on the shared claims adopted, e.g. the shared backgrounds. Thus, representation is translated into the defining logic of the counterpart. In ongoing interaction, a conversation may evolve in which the °system° issues and topics are discussed and negotiated and thus re-formulated, specified, resolved, etc.[134] Hence, actor A creates a representation reflecting his own assumptions of B's behaviour. After placing the representations at B's disposal, A observes the consequences in B's behaviour. Actor B perceives the representation presented, interprets it and confirms or rejects it based upon his background. To confirm or reject, he emits a response (e.g. 'Yes, I do agree'; 'No, I do not agree').

Interaction is thus a setting of logically independent perceive-reflect-expose loops (see Figure 11) the actors conduct individually and internally.[135] Each actor autonomously perceives his situation, reflects upon it based on his background, thereby evolving an image expressing distinctions and deciding in favour of a certain response. This mutual orientation of independent perceive-reflect-expose loops continues as long as the participating actors engage in interaction. Whenever one of the actors qualifies one of his percepts as "informative", "valuable", "interesting" to him, it may lead him to challenge his background accordingly and to undergo a process of re-conditioning, adopting new intents and claims.

Thus, a change of an actor's background is the consequence of multiple mutual adjustments taking place among actors adjusting in response to perceived representations. Change is always triggered and not determined. However, each actor's autopoiesis does not lead to a specific behaviour in coupling. It does not necessarily mean that they interact on an equal basis; they may well develop patterns of super- or subordination.

To align their intents and claims with respect to a °system° notion, actors perform reciprocal interactions. Thus, they continuously develop, shape and confirm their mutual conditionings towards a °system° notion. Orientation succeeds if actor B understands A's message. Any qualification

---

[133] Beer, S.: (Diagnosing); Ashby characterises transducers as "a machine with input (according to the convenience of the context)". The input covers all conditions of the environment. See Ashby, W. R.: (Introduction)

[134] Beer, S.: (Heart); Beer, S.: (Diagnosing)

[135] Espejo, R.: Giving Requisite Variety to Strategic and Implementation Processes: Theory and Practice, http://bprc.warwick.ac.uk/LSEraul.html

of an orientation as "understood" relies on A's approval of B's compliance with his expectation.[136] Thus, understanding is a subjective achievement actors commonly attain as a consequence of interaction.[137] It is always subjective and individual because autopoietic actors cannot objectively compare their evolving images. Interaction can therefore lead to accommodation between actors, but it cannot (and need not) lead to consensus.[138] Every interaction is an offer to the participating actors to challenge their underlying backgrounds. The contributions of individual actors in addressing and resolving an issue in °system° interaction can be classified according to their role within the reconciliation taking place (Table 3). Practically, actor contributions will often be seen to adopt multiple classifications.

Table 3. A classification of actor contributions in °system° interaction

1.	**Reference**, any neutral statement or background data that provides orientation or builds a frame for other statements.
2.	**Declaration**, any neutral statement that makes something known formally without the aim to initiate change.
3.	**Concern**, any statement of appeal, compromise, or imperative that implicitly or explicitly aims at initiating change in a °system°; a concern makes explicit an interest or regard expressed for a °system° issue in a certain situation.
4.	**Solution**, agreement that a °system° concern, i.e. an appeal or compromise, has been met.
5.	**Justification**, agreement that a concern, i.e. an imperative, has been met.

Minimally, orientation leads actors to consider the existence of a representation.[139] If it succeeds, actors share a relevant set of distinctions, align their individual backgrounds into a shared, compatible conditioning and thus cause an amplification or attenuation of °system° variety.

Although through their autopoiesis, actors do retain a potential selectivity to perceive and interpret the world in their own unique way, their image creation is always strongly conditioned through their backgrounds.[140] As

---

[136] Rusch, G.: (Kommunikation und Verstehen)

[137] As Rusch emphasises, "understanding is a means for the social control of individual cognition.", in Rusch, G.: (Kommunikation und Verstehen), p. 74

[138] Ulrich, W.: Reflective Practise in the Civil Society, Reflective Practice, Volume 1, Issue 2, 2000

[139] Rusch, G.: (Kommunikation und Verstehen)

[140] Vickers, G: (Judgement) as referred to in Checkland, P.: (Information Systems)

explained before (see 2.2, Figure 6), intentions and contexts are the two characteristic references or sources of distinction from which images emerge.[141] Intentions as well as contexts as sources mutually influence each other, i.e. shared intentions initiate the establishment of shared claims, or vice versa. Actors' shared conditionings of a °system° notion create the 'glue' that originates attuned images and actions in °system° implementation.[142]

3.1.1.1 Contextuality of actor backgrounds

Actor contexts essentially predetermine the conduct of interaction. Shared contexts consist of the shared claims established by actors. They create a *"mode of solidarity"* [143] between actors. Reference to them allows mutually attuning image creation and forming safe assumptions and expectations about their unfolding issues. Shared claims create stable and enduring patterns or conditions which ensure that shared °system° notions *"don't fall down and apart"*[144] and actors can successfully relate to each other. They settle on what is socially accepted and thus provide the constraints that have been established (see chapter 2.2.2).

Actors (re-)create their context individually. Interaction is the mechanism enabling them to establish shared claims and to reconcile their contexts. Through their interactions, actors create agreements and commitments which evolve their °system° notions.[145] With reference to these commitments, actors align their image creation and their behaviour. °Languages°, °Cultures°, °*Weltanschauung*° and °Paradigms° emerge from shared claims and allow actors to choose manifold behaviours within the frame (i.e. a high degree of variety remains between them).[146] °Systems°, °Norms°, °Organisations°, °Institutions° and °Rules° are much more concrete claims

---

[141] Espejo, R.: Organizational Transformation and Learning, A Cybernetic Approach to Management, Chichester, New York, Brisbane, Toronto, Singapore, 1996

[142] Beer, S.: (Heart), p. 336 for Beer's usage of 'glue' in regard of planning.

[143] Beer, S.: (Heart)

[144] Gordon, J. E.: Structures or, Why things don't fall down, New York, 1978 as cited in Kooiman, J.: (Governing as Governance)

[145] In distinction to this position, Winograd, T. and Flores, F. argue that "Organisations are constituted as networks of conversation in which commitments are generated.", in Winograd, T. and Flores, F.: (Understanding computers) as cited in Checkland, P.: (Information Systems)

[146] Espejo, R., Schuhmann, W., Schwaninger, M., and Bilello, U.: (Transformation and Learning)

restricting actors' behaviour (e.g. a much lower contextual variety remains for image creation).[147] A social °system° exists as soon as actors adopt some shared boundary. For instance, a shared claim of °Democracy° establishes but does not necessarily specify a shared understanding of actor coordination. It may be specified in a 'constitution' or in 'laws', what the understanding is, explicating the social norms, values and constraints being adopted.

Aligning claims results from reconciling definitions of concepts, hypotheses, theories, or abstractions.[148] Claims of individual relations between actors are to be distinguished from claims that specify °system°-wide relationships. Whereas individual relations are specific because they constitute the conditions (e.g. friendship, hostility, favourableness) that are realised between individuals, °system°-wide relationships constitute conditions independent from the individuals (e.g. roles, positions, jobs).[149] The structural similarities of both will be shown below (compare chapter 4.1.2 on recursion).

Actor contexts confronting one another in interaction give rise to a contextual variety, i.e. the total number of possible selections available to actors from their individual contexts in regard to an issue. It is a function of the coherence of the participating actor's contexts, i.e. his language, culture, *Weltanschauung*, Paradigm, etc. Coherence of backgrounds in regard of a °system° notion facilitates reconciliation. Processes of socialisation, formalisation, and organisation[150] refer to coherent contexts achieved through interaction. A set of claims, i.e. a belief or a theory, is adopted coherently when the actor's images that derive from it are mutually supportive and consistent with each other. The degree of contextual coherence prevailing between actors is referred to here as "contextuality". The degree to which their individual images, i.e. their actions and behaviours emerging from these backgrounds, are compatible is defined through actor cohesion. Hence, coherence refers to the individual backgrounds, whereas cohesion points to the resulting images and behaviour that evolve.[151] The following figure illustrates the relation between contextuality and the resulting contextual variety. Different types of actor agreements are roughly assigned to different degrees of contextual coherence.

---

[147] Yolles, M.: (Management Systems)

[148] Beer, S.: (Heart)

[149] Espejo, R., Schuhmann, W., Schwaninger, M., and Bilello, U.: (Transformation and Learning)

[150] Kooiman, J.: (Governing as Governance)

[151] Derived from the Merriam-Webster's authors: Articles on 'coherence' and 'cohesion', Merriam-Webster's Collegiate Dictionary, Online Version, 2005

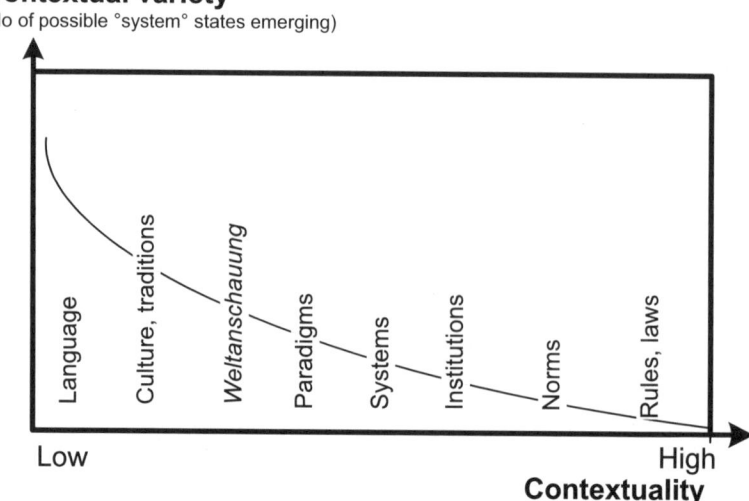

Figure 13. Contextual variety as a function of contextuality[152]

3.1.1.2 Intentionality of actor backgrounds

Before actors can identify and judge any claims, they delineate their situation of interest. Their intentions essentially predetermine the boundary judgements of whatever °system° is individually delimited, i.e.

"Whose interests are at stake? What different notions of improvement are there? What worldviews may be in conflict? What counts as relevant knowledge and expertise?"[153]

In interaction, actors always express conscious or unconscious choices to attain an end. By referencing these intentions in representation, they orientate each other towards common ends to be aspired to. Shared intentions turn individual actors into a purposive collectivity. Individual intents of actors converge into a social intentionality. Intentionality initiates the reconciliation of claims. It reflects the degree to which a group of actors is willing to align and to create common intentions.

---

[152] Contextual variety refers to the number of possible distinctions actors can refer to in the light of a °system° issue. It makes apparent the degree to which the adopted shared claims have accommodated their beliefs.

[153] Ulrich, W.: (Reflective Practice); Maturana, H. and Verden-Zöller, G.: Liebe und Spiel – Die vergessenen Grundlagen des Menschseins, Heidelberg, 2005

The intentional variety prevailing in interaction is a function of the specification and coherence acquired in actors' intentions. Low degrees of intentionality point to ambiguity and uncertainty between actors and leave open a huge variety to choose from. Higher degrees of intentionality are manifested in shared interests, goals, purposes, or agreements on specific roles for implementing common actions. These result in lower intentional varieties. By way of mutual orientation, actors align their intents and accord their individual backgrounds. Amplification and attenuation of possible individual states is the most important effect of shared intentions: agreed purposes, goals, or developing fears, etc. strongly constrain individual image creation. Some social intentions are prioritised over individual intents. Actors motivate each other to adapt their individual intentions in regard to the shared purposes aspired to. All kinds of personal conflicts, disputes and power plays originate from different intents confronting each other. What individual intents actors adopt also depends on the degree of autonomy settled on in the adopted °system° boundary as a consequence of the power relations that prevail. The level of intentionality defines a certain inten-

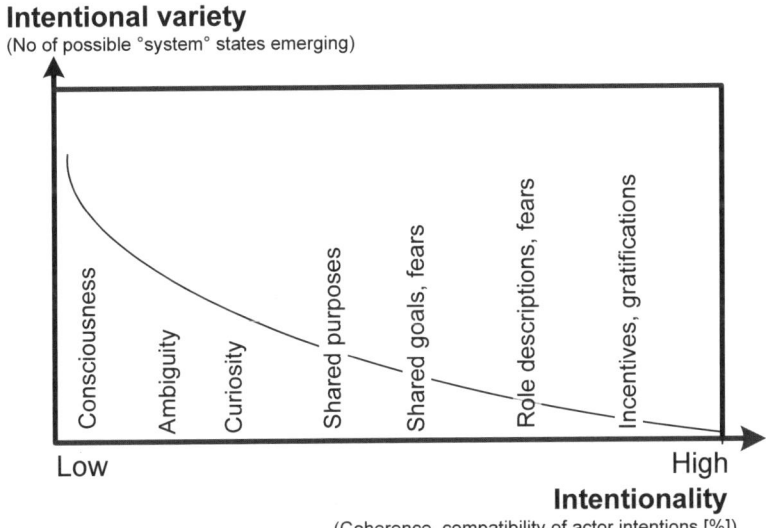

Figure 14. Individual intentional variety as a function of intentionality[154]

---

[154] Intentional variety refers to the number of states actors can adopt in their mutual orientation in the light of a °system° notion. It makes apparent the coherence of their shared intentions.

tional variety, i.e. a number of intentional states individual actors can possibly adopt in °system° implementation. The more intents and claims adopted by actors are compatible, i.e. shared, the smaller the number of possible states the °system° might evolve into. Shared purposes, goals and incentives diminish intentional variety between actors. Figure 14 illustrates this relation between actor intentionality and the intentional variety faced in °system° implementation.

3.1.1.3 Evolving °system° notions

An issue refers to what is the matter in °system° implementation, i.e. it points to those aspects of a situation (facts, attributes, and their relations) with respect to which actors do not yet share compatible distinctions. Thus, the appearance of an issue reflects a residual variety that actors are actually confronting in a certain situation throughout their engagement in °system° implementation. An issue may arise between them as a consequence of new developments or unclear, unshared actor backgrounds. Any perceived problems, needs, threats, and opportunities are °system° issues. Hence, issues are the momentary foci attended to for °system° implementation. In order to effectuate the appearance of their intended °system° states, actors need to continuously reconcile and attune each other into a concerted action. In any such situation, three types of issues have to be addressed and resolved continuously:

1.   environmental issues,

2.   operative or implementation issues, and

3.   governing and management issues.

Issues may be distinguished according to their complexity, diversity, and dynamics. The complexity of a °system° issue refers to the number of distinguishable states it may potentially develop into; the diversity of an issue refers to the underlying composition of °system° elements, facts or attributes. The dynamics of an issue refers to the cause of change of these °system° elements, facts and attributes over time.

Through continuous reconciliation of intents and claims actors mutually establish °system° notions. A social °system° is implemented by creating shared intentions and claims based upon a common notion of boundary judgements. As soon as actors adopt the view of a shared °system° notion, the entailed assumptions of purpose and boundary become part of their

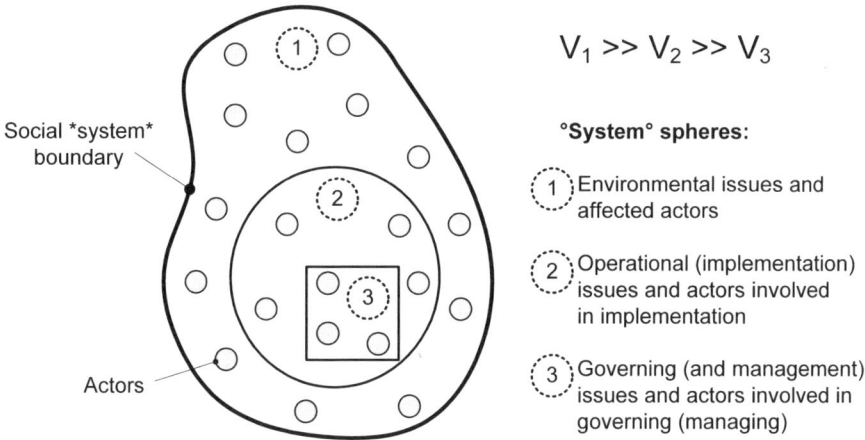

Figure 15. Three fundamental °system° spheres

lifeworld and subsequently predetermine their emerging images. Interaction takes place in reference to a °system° notion and to the claims attached to it. Actors refer to the common notions of purpose expressed in the definition of a °system° and join together to implement that purpose (e.g. a °company° or °community°). Hence, a social °system° is a shared boundary delimiting a set of intents and claims which leads actors to align in implementing the °system° notion.[155] In regard to a °system°, actors can refer to the intentional and contextual boundary judgements accompanying its specific notion, e.g. its purpose, clients, measures for improvement, etc. These claims may be more or less well defined, and, depending on the degree of intentionality and contextuality prevailing, actors may show different notions of the °system° and create different references to it. Nevertheless, when actors adopt the boundary of a °system°, they subsequently relate to it. Interactions create and recreate backgrounds in reference to that boundary. The higher the degree of contextuality and intentionality of a °system° notion, the less space remains for incoherent actor behaviour.

The following figure illustrates how a social °system° notion evolves through actors' mutual reconciliations. In that process, representations refer to and establish agreements on shared boundary judgements (SBJ), and claims and intents which point to shared governing elements (°images°, °instruments°, °actions°, and °actors°).

---

[155] Espejo, R. and Schwaninger, M.: (Organizational Fitness)

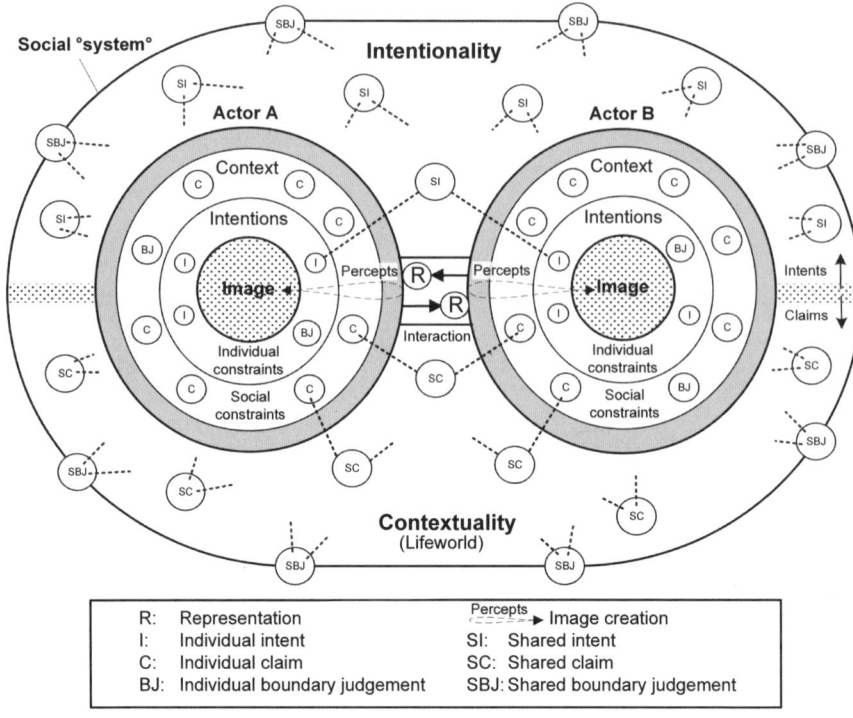

Figure 16. Interaction stretching up a social °system° notion[156]

3.1.1.4 Variety regulation

As soon as multiple actors commit to a °system° notion and engage in im-plementing it jointly, their individual varieties confront and lead to a °system° variety. That °system° variety refers to the predisposition of the involved actors to resolve a common °system° issue. Besides the individ-ual actors disposition, it relies on the structures established between actors regarding whether their potential individual answers (i.e. states) can be accommodated and integrated adequately to effect a requisite resolution of that °system° issue. Thus, a °system° notion provides requisite capacity to attend to a °system° issue if the interplay of the actors involved provides for requisite variety. In a football game, it is not only the individual play-ers' strength which is essential, but their ability to play together as a team

---

[156] This model reflects the interrelation between intentions and contexts as sug-gested by the model of interaction by Kooiman, J.: (Governing as Governance)

and jointly score as much as possible. And how they play together depends on the structures they have established.

Therefore, the structures established between actors have to be adequate to attune actors' individual contributions in a way that ensures °system° issues can be constantly attended to and resolved. Interactions are the means to conduct change. They provide the regulative[157] mechanisms which induce change in each other's backgrounds to mutually attune their individual actor varieties to a °system° variety that is requisite.[158] Through interaction, actors share distinctions about their °system° states and continuously dissolve the residual variety evolving through the decisions and agreements they reconcile.[159] According to the law of requisite variety, actor varieties must be attuned to cope with the varieties evolving from °system° notion, i.e. the issues that are constantly unfolding.

Depending on the type of facts, attributes, and their relations captured in the shared °system° notion, it may be possible or very difficult to determine the number of states actors actually confront in a °system° situation. Simply counting the number of states an actor can choose from in regard to a °system° issue is rarely useful because that number strongly depends on the individual actor and his ability to differentiate.[160] Only in the case that actors have reconciled a shared °system° boundary, may they agree on a specific number of states for a °system° issue (and thus share compatible opinions on relevant aspects and its solution). Sharing a °system° boundary is a necessary precondition for any meaningful application of the law of requisite variety.[161] However, even in the case where they share a highly compatible °system° notion, counting °system° states will usually result in numbers quickly becoming exorbitant.[162] It is therefore essential to empha-

---

[157] Beer, S.: (Heart); Every "transaction, everywhere in the system, can be considered in terms of the variety equations that bear upon it", in Beer, S.: (Heart), p. 390.

[158] Interactions are the control mechanisms implementing social °system° notions. "Only variety in the control mechanism can deal successfully with variety in the system controlled.", in Beer, S: Cybernetics and Management, New York, 1959, p. 50

[159] For the concept of residual or response variety see Espejo, R.: (VSM revisited)

[160] Ashby, W. R.: (Introduction)

[161] Espejo, R.: A cybernetic method to study organizations, in: Espejo, R. and Harden, R., The Viable Systems Model – Interpretations and Applications of Stafford Beer's VSM, Chichester, 1989

[162] Ashby, W. R.: (Introduction)

sise that the purpose of the variety measure does not rely on fixing a reasonable count for its measure.[163] Rather, it should be applied for illustrating vast divergences between sources of variety in a °system° notion, i.e. the variety generators or drivers, for instance, between environmental and implementation varieties, i.e. actors' potential to cope with it.[164] It is useful to give qualitative estimations of the variety deviations actors face when confronting their °systems° issues.[165] The variety measure should therefore not be applied simply to count the number of potential °system° states but to design the structural conditions of actors' interactions as required to influence actor backgrounds and to enable °system° implementation.[166]

The law of requisite variety states that °system° issues can only be resolved if actors can jointly provide requisite variety to attend to them.[167] For sustainable °system° implementation, the concert of interactions taking place must trigger the actors involved to perform adequate adaptations. It

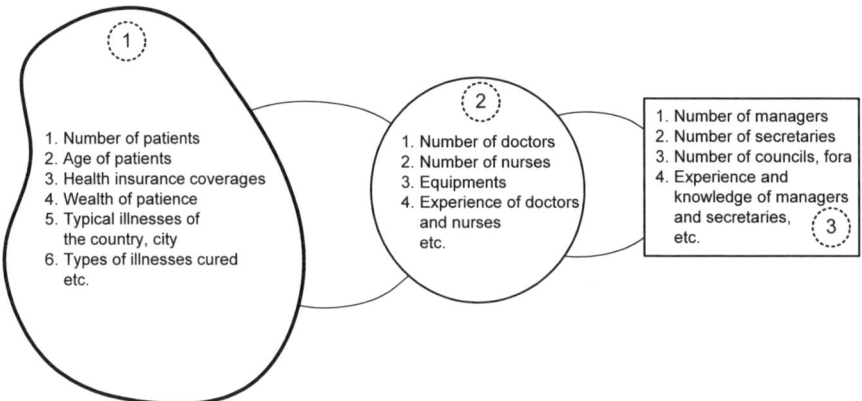

Figure 17. Exemplary variety drivers of a °health° notion, e.g. a hospital

---

[163] Ibid.

[164] Schwaninger, M.: What can Cybernetics contribute to the conscious evolution of Organisations and Society?, Systems Research and Behavioural Science, 21, 5, 2003; Beer, S.: (Diagnosing)

[165] Beer, S.: (Heart); Malik, F.: Understanding a Knowledge Organisation as a Viable System, in: Espejo, R. and Schwaninger, M., Organizational Fitness, Corporate Effectiveness through Management Cybernetics, Frankfurt a.M., 1993; Hayek, F. A. v.: Die Theorie komplexer Phänomene, Tübingen, 1972

[166] Beer, S.: (Heart)

[167] Beer, S.: (Heart); Ashby, W. R.: (Introduction)

must be ensured that their joint activities can match the variety of the
°system° issues continuously evolving. As soon as actors engage in issues
in regard to a specific °system° notion, the variety drivers involved can be
identified. Figure 17 shows the exemplary variety drivers faced when producing °health° in a °community°. These variety drivers, lead to the emergence of °health° issues. For instance, if the number of patients is increasing as a consequence of a wave of influenza, that will be an issue for the
doctors and hospitals of the °community° as they will have to initiate adequate measures. That will require the doctors, nurses, etc. involved to reconcile adequate agreements that enable them to cope with the increasing
demand, i.e. to increase opening hours and revise attendance schedules, to
maintain medical instruments, to provide extra rooms, to train assistants, etc.
If the variety provided by the actual °health° capacities of that °community°
is too small to cope with the surplus of influenza patients (i.e. with the additional states involved) it will need to be amplified.

In respect to the law of requisite variety, the structures of those involved
in implementing a °system° notion have to generate and absorb variety requisite to coping with the environment. Those involved in implementing a
°system° notion must be able to jointly generate requisite variety to counter
the possible environmental states and issues that evolve from the activities

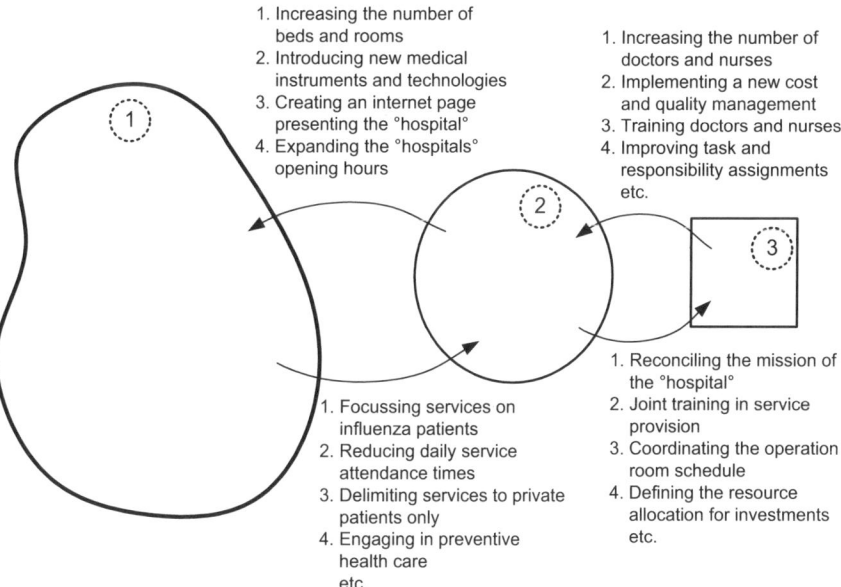

Figure 18. Exemplary amplifiers and attenuators of a °hospital°

of those affected by, or in this case, originating the °system° notion (through their need to be cured). Otherwise, the °system° notion will not be implemented as intended. In other words, the capacity of those involved to respond may not be less than the variety of the situation which the °system° proliferates.[168] Figure 18 illustrates possible amplifiers and attenuators actors may choose to provide requisite variety to cope with the influenza wave.

Thus, interaction is about attuning actor varieties in a way that allows actors to cope with the environmental issues that are being raised with a °system° notion. Designing structures between those actors involved allows to influence actors' joint capacity to provide requisite variety. The following figure illustrates how individual, unattuned actions are brought into concert to implement a joint °system° notion.

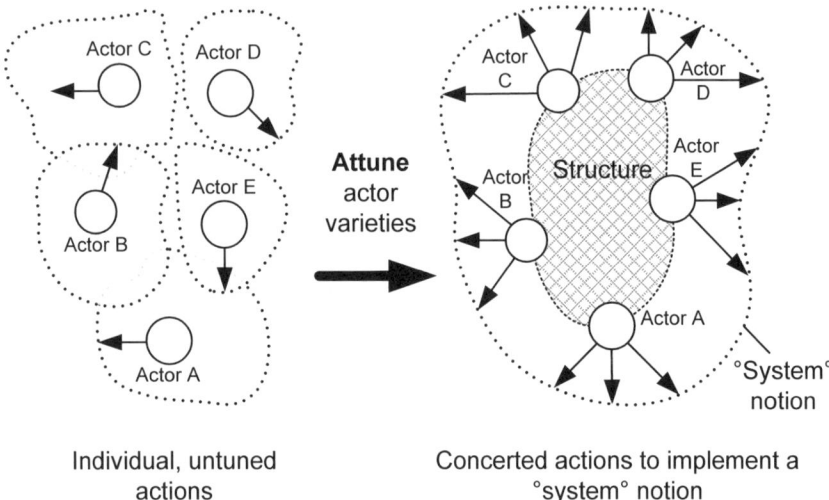

Individual, untuned actions

Concerted actions to implement a °system° notion

Figure 19. Individual untuned actions versus concerted °system° implementation

3.1.2 Aspects of structure

Structure is a fundamental property present in every °system° implementation. It refers to how the actors, involved in °system° implementation or affected by it, relate to each other. Structures are the relatively enduring patterns of behaviour and relationships that are established between actors to implement a social °system° notion. They shape the behaviour of the involved and affected actors. In cybernetic terms, structures provide the

---

[168] Derived from Beer, S.: (Heart), p. 89

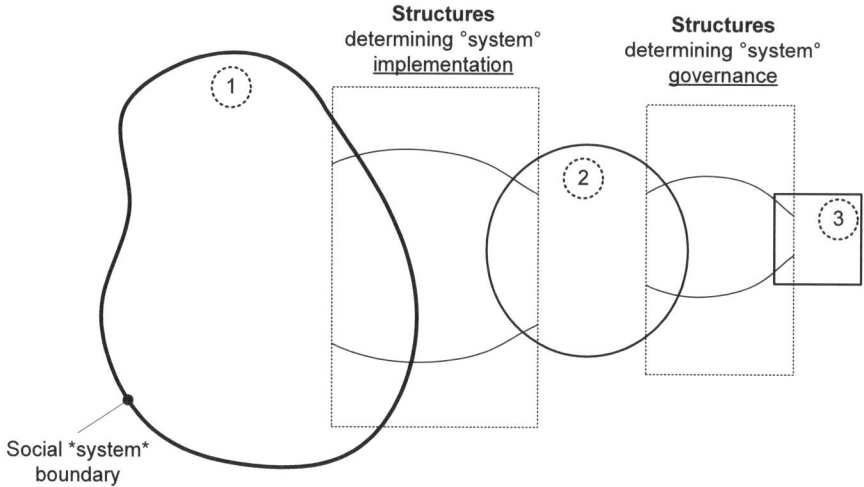

Figure 20. Structures of °system° governance and implementation

capacity to attend any °system° issues though continous amplification and attenuation of the varieties evolving in °system° implementation (Figure 20).

In the following, social structures shall be distinguished along the three fundamental capacities that bring about amplifications and attenuations in social systems:[169]

1. change or transformation capacity,

2. channel capacity and

3. transduction capacity.

Change or transformation capacity refers to the potential to address the relevant aspects of an issue when attuning actor backgrounds. Interactions create and continuously recreate messages and thus induce actors to add or subtract from the °system° states they can possibly adopt towards a °system° issue. Change or transformation of the number of potential states adopted takes place when boundaries are reconciled, agreements are settled on, priorities are set, relevant data is selected, etc. According to its change or transformation capacity, interaction exerts influence on actor variety, i.e. the states actors can possibly choose from when confronted with a °system° issue in a specific situation.

---

[169] Beer refers to these aspects in his organisational principles. Beer, S.: (Heart); Beer, S.: (Provenance)

Change or transformation capacity: the potential to recognize and address relevant states, i.e. the ability to transform given distinctions through adding or subtracting, amplifying or attenuating in order to identify relevant states of a specific situation. What aspects of an issue can be addressed? Do the methods applied in interaction express requisite variety? Change or transformation capacity refers to "How issues are brought to a solution and practical doing?", i.e. the practices, methods and instruments applied to execute changes.

Structures provide channels to expose messages. Channel capacity refers to the syntactical accuracy[170], the completeness and timeliness of the conveyed changes between relevant actors. It determines to what extent changes and transformations can be considered, actors can be involved, and to what extent they are enabled to contribute in due time.

Channel capacity: the ability to convey the change to be induced between actors, i.e. to express the proportion of relevant distinctions that can be made accessible to actors in due time to allow them to recognise the relevant states and changes to perform. Who is involved and what can each contribute? Thus, channel capacity refers to "Who relates to whom and when?", i.e. the relationships, tasks, responsibilities, and processes defined which determine actors' capacity to effectively conduct joint °system° implementation.

Transducers translate between different actor conditions and rationalities. They translate messages across actor, logical, and °system° boundaries.[171] Transduction capacity indicates to what extent a °system° structure is capable to translate messages across boundaries in order to make them compatible with the background of the actors involved, their languages, and rationalities.

Transduction capacity: the ability to translate changes according to the recipients' background and rationality, i.e. the proportion of relevant distinctions that can be put across between actors. What aspects of a statement can be made compatible, understandable? Thus, transduction capacity refers to "How mutual understanding is created?", i.e. the languages, conventions established.

---

[170] Whether it is "well-formed or not, in the sense of whether it can be 'read'", in Jackson, M. C.: (Managerial significance)

[171] Beer refers primarily to the necessity to cross over and translate between logical boundaries. As will be shown in chapter 3.4, there is a further valid requirement to cross over and translate between °system° and actor boundaries.

All three capacities are continuously and simultaneously in effect. The primary change or transformation capacity is constrained by the channel and transduction capacities. Together, they describe the potential of interactions to exert influence on actor varieties. As a consequence of all three capacities actors are challenged to adapt their individual varieties. Interactions can be characterised according to their capacity to cope with these three structural aspects, i.e. to what extent structures are capable to provide requisite variety in each aspect. Compliance with the law of requisite variety requires the sum of them to provide requisite capacity.[172] For interactions to be productive and sustainable in regard to a °system° notion, each of the three capacities must be requisite to allow actors to adequately address and solve the °system° issues.[173]

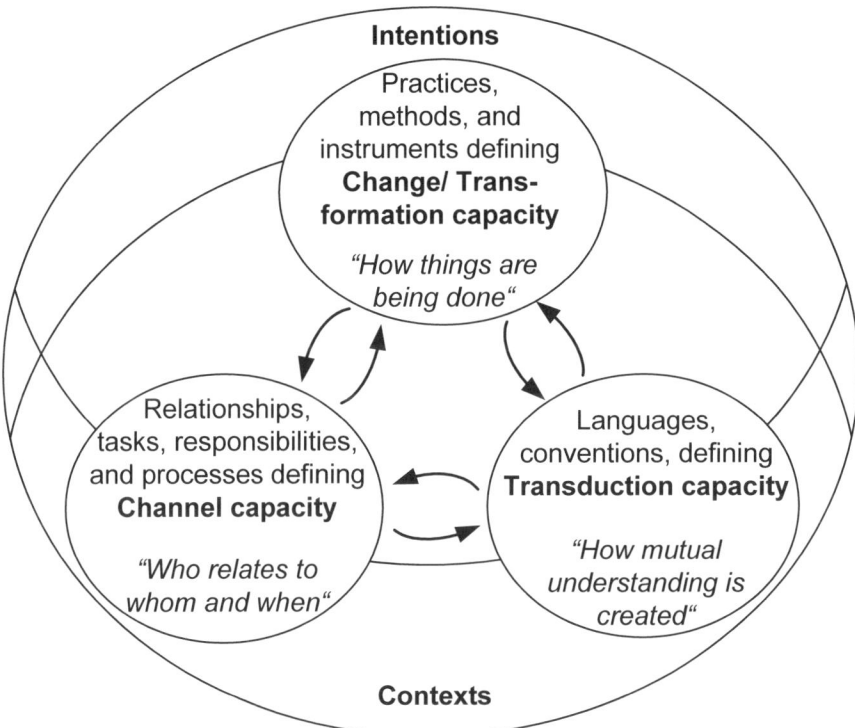

Figure 21. Change, channel, and transduction capacity

---

[172] Beer, S.: (Provenance)

[173] Beer, S.: (Diagnosing)

The three capacities (as summarised in Figure 21) can be referred to as aspects of structure. They are fundamental to interaction. In the following the requirements that apply to each of them will be deducted. Later on, characteristic interactions will be described with reference to the contribution of these aspects to the viability of a social °system° notion. Based upon the three aspects established, interactions can be categorised according to their function – as will be done later applying the criterion of viability.

3.2   Change or transformation capacity

Change takes place whenever actors attune their backgrounds and adapt their varieties in regard to a °system° notion. Actors' distinctions or potential choices emerge from their backgrounds.[174] To conduct change, interactions must trigger the residual variety of the issue to be resolved. Creating shared °system° boundaries and continuously reconciling the °system° issues evolving is required. As actors always act based upon their prevailing backgrounds, the issues they confront are in some way being settled in any case. At due time issues fall into their resolutions. Indeed, how they do and how actors behave and whether they act so in support of the aspired °system° notion is questionable. A normative judgement is required to guide the design of amplifiers and attenuators with respect to individual actors' means to influence others, their autonomy, and power. Any system boundary contains and implements such a normative judgement. The following normative, minimal requirements have to be met at all times:

> *Environmental, implementation, and governing issues[175] of a °system° notion are being solved continuously throughout time, manifesting themselves in certain occurrences. The underlying °system° varieties equate in the actual moment, the *now* when action takes place. Through interaction, actors reconcile agreements and create structures that allow them to influence and pre-condition the solution of their °system° issues and the realisation of their °system° notions. In the *now* then, their residual varieties confront and equate. Whether "how they equate" is favourable in the light of the °system° notion (and thus prevents damage to people and to cost) depends on the*

---

[174] Adapted from Gälweiler, Aloys: Strategische Unternehmensführung, Frankfurt/ Main, 2005

[175] Refers to the three °system° spheres established in Figure 15

practices, methods, and instruments performing adequate transformations. They should be designed to provide requisite change / transformation capacity with respect to a normatively legitimized °system° boundary.[176]

This refers to the possibility and the normative necessity to design the interactions taking place to constitute a social °system° in regard to their attenuative and amplificative potential. Through interaction, shared intents and claims are created by establishing, linking, reverberating or deleting from both. Actor varieties are attenuated or amplified. Any interaction taking place to attend to an issue and to provoke some attenuation or amplification with reference to some social °system° notion strives to induce some change.

Change or transformation capacity refers to whether the structures of interaction apply adequate methods to address °system° issues. Methods are adequate when the distinctions they reference and the way they are transformed leads to relevant results, i.e. provides requisite variety in regard to the issue addressed. For instance, a 'gun' is a useful representation to induce determent to criminals whereas a 'water pistol' is not. Obviously, the effect of the gun, to be frightening, requires both policemen and criminals to share the common knowledge and appreciation that guns are dangerous. They usually do so because they share a common lifeworld where 'guns' are known to be dangerous. If that were not the case, the method would not cause its effect. The policemen may then cause an effect by shouting a warning or giving a warning shot. In doing so, he emphasises his intention is serious. Policemen's guns only amplify their variety because criminals attribute dangerousness to them.

Messages are those specific sets of distinction actors intend to share for reconciling and resolving their issues. Their distinctions can be exposed and made accessible to other actors only by translating them into external

---

[176] Original text of the first organisational principle: "Managerial, operational, and environmental varieties, diffusing through an institutional system, tend to equate; they should be designed to do so with the minimal damage to people and cost.", in Beer, S.: (Heart), p. 97; Beer's metaphor of varieties "diffusing through an institutional system" might sound confusing, as variety itself cannot move or flow within a system but is a characteristic that can only appear or disappear. However, by emphasising that varieties "should be designed [..to equate..] with minimal damage to people and to cost", he clearly refers to how these °system° varieties are being attended to and brought to a solution by the actors involved rather than how the varieties "diffuse", i.e. are channelled between the actors involved. Further, see Espejo, R.: (VSM revisited)

phenomena through naming, qualifying, or attribution.[177] Representations are the conversational devices or objects expressing messages externally. They are recursive objects. For example, in script, a word is part of a sentence, which is entailed in a statement, which is part of a book, etc. (i.e. book(statement(sentence(word(sign)))))). Representations influence image creation and enable actors to mutually orient themselves and influence change.[178] As reflections of messages, they phenomenally explicate the distinctions expressed. Representations are individual or shared low variety derivates of messages.[179] Unlike images, they are manifested as linguistic, figurative, or auditory phenomena in language, writing, gesture, etc. In the same way as actors' images are subjective and incommensurate with external reality, representations are incommensurate to an even greater extent. Reality is not accessible to any form of classification, because of its variability, its changing and interlocking states as well as occurrences.[180] Any phenomena depicted in representation are secondary derivations of a reality exposed to trigger image creation. Representations are nothing but enablers of mutual change in regard to a certain message.[181]

3.2.1 Meaning

Representations depict sets of mostly linguistic phenomena such as letters, words, signs, movements, etc. Morphology refers to how such phenomena are formed in representation, whereas syntax refers to the way in which these signs are put together to form constituents such as sentences, phrases, clauses. Such linguistic, phenomenal agreements are fundamental rules, i.e. multiply confirmed claims entailed in actors' lifeworld. Assembling syntactic phenomena in representation enables actors to express the distinctions they wish to communicate.[182] This takes place under the premise

---

[177] Bateson, G.: (Mind and Nature)

[178] Espejo, R. and Schwaninger, M.: (Organizational Fitness)

[179] Beer, S.: (Diagnosing)

[180] Schaff, A.: Unscharfe Ausdrücke und die Grenzen ihrer Präzisierung, in: Grassi, E., Sprache und Erkenntnis und Essays über die Philosophie der Sprache, Reinbeck, Hamburg, 1974

[181] Adapted from Gälweiler, Aloys: (Corporate Strategy)

[182] Morpheme: "a speech element having a meaning or grammatical function that cannot be subdivided into further such elements.", in Collins author's: English Dictionary, 2005. For instance, in the English language, the letter 's' in the final position at the end of a word is a morpheme indicating plurality. A word may consist of one morpheme (e.g. need), two morphemes (e.g. need / less, need / ing) or three or more morphemes (e.g. un / happi / ness). Any suffixes and prefixes are morphemes.

that recipients share common linguistic phenomena and can actively draw upon distinctions entailed in representation. Though an actor may grasp the phenomena of representation, they do not necessarily have to be meaningful to him. Meaning is not an intrinsic property or quality of representation.[183] The formal syntax and morphology of representation does not itself contain and prescribe the individual actor's context and °system° boundary to identify distinctions. Different meanings can be imposed on a single representation, as actors have different contexts and therefore associate differently.[184] Meaning arises from active imposition by association upon the syntactic, phenomenal instructions formulated in representation.[185] Upon those instructions, it must be reflected with the discriminative capacity and rationality of the recipient.[186] Hence, the induced variety is not an attribute of representation transmitted in interaction, but of the individual actor's background.[187] Semantics arise from individuals projecting images upon representation.

Any change stimulated through the ascribed meaning of representation, its importance, validity, normative implications,[188] etc., always depends on how the °system° of reference is bound and which contexts the actors involved align with.[189] For instance, facts are those shared, multiply confirmed, and hence unquestioned contextual claims actors perceive as their reality. Interpretation of representation depends on the facts and values ascribed to it. And this depends on the adopted reference °system°.

---

[183] "The information conveyed is not an intrinsic property of the individual message.", in Ashby, W. R.: (Introduction), p. 124; also: "Note also that data are transmitted, not variety itself.", in Beer, S.: (Diagnosing), p. 45

[184] The distinctions are "not an intrinsic property of the set [representation; author]: the observer and his power of discrimination may have to be specified if the variety is to be well defined.", in Ashby, W. R.: (Introduction). For instance, irony is a stylistic device that gives expression to this.

[185] "Meaning that's abstracted from the book is not in the book; it is in the mind. […] We construct meaning by the associations we make. […] Meaning therefore is imposed. It emerges by our imposing associations.", in Arthur, Brian: (Cognition)

[186] "Variety is amplified or attenuated by the instructions that the data formulate; but those instructions must be adequate to the relevant variety selection.", in Beer, S.: (Diagnosing), p. 45

[187] "Information implies purpose, and causes the system to change in ways that favour achievement of system goals, while entropy does not.", in Beer stresses the same point; it is "the observer, who defines the system […] its variety.", in Beer, S.: (Heart), p. 36

[188] Ulrich, W.: (Reflective Practice)

[189] Checkland, P.: (Information Systems)

As soon as its boundaries are modified, other facts and values derive. Changing boundaries means actors adjust their values which make the facts look different.[190]

For instance, the description of a perceived action as *freedom fighting* by one actor may be perceived as *terrorism* by another drawing from a different individual context.[191] It is the common interpretation, based upon shared intentions and contexts, bringing about shared images and procuring cohesion between actors.[192] Only collectively shared intents and claims evoke compatible interpretations. An actor is informed only through those

Table 4. Qualifications of representation

Attribute	Qualification of representation
Noise	Simply insignificant.[193] May even not contain any facts.
Data	Points to *"observations or facts out of contexts that are [...] not directly meaningful"*.[194] State, *"which is the case"*[195].
Capta	Results of selecting or creating some facts for attention, creating a new category.[196]
Information	Structured data which have contextual meaning. That *"which changes us"*[197], i.e. those representations which attributed a certain meaning in a context.[198].
Knowledge	*"Larger, longer-living structures of meaningful facts"*[199]

---

[190] Ulrich, W.: (Reflective Practice)

[191] Checkland, P.: (Information Systems)

[192] Beer, S.: (Dispute)

[193] Beer, S.: (Heart)

[194] Zack, M. H.: Managing codified knowledge, Sloan Management Review, 40, 4, 1999

[195] Beer, S.: (Heart)

[196] Checkland, P.: (Information Systems)

[197] Beer, S.: (Heart)

[198] "Data becomes information – when the fact in them is susceptible for action", in Beer, S.: (Heart), pp. 282, 375; Information is "a difference that makes a difference", in Bateson, G.: Steps to an ecology of mind, 2000, pp. 437-459; Also compare to Heinz von Foerster's definition of information as the process of recognition, see Förster, Heinz von: Zukunft der Wahrnehmung: Wahrnehmung der Zukunft, in: Schmidt, S. J., Wissen und Gewissen, Frankfurt am Main, 1974

[199] Checkland, P.: (Information Systems)

representations which cause him to purposefully actualise, adapt or change his intents and claims with respect to his adopted °system° notion.[200] Those representations induce meaning for the individual actor and can be qualified as information. They are not meaningful themselves but induce meaning in their recipient. Change of actor backgrounds is the consequence of meaning induced through representation. Representations are secondary, low-variety derivations of reality that may be misunderstood.[201] They qualify as capta, information or knowledge if relevant to the °system° issue in focus (Table 4). This is the case whenever its distinctions trigger or dissolve some aspects of the °system° issue and thus bring about some kind of change in the backgrounds of the actors involved. Table 4 sums up the qualifiers for representations to indicate what is relevant for resolving an issue within a shared °system° notion.

3.2.2 Referencing situations and issues

3.2.2.1 Models

With models, representations provide descriptions of situations. They make situations tangible and referencable when attending to issues. Models are an idealised logical framework about the relevant factors that determine the states of a °system° notion. Thus, a model may describe the variety drivers relevant to a °system° notion (compare Figure 17 and Figure 18) and depict how they interfere with each other. Models enable actors to reason about their °system° notion and to identify the necessary levers to be taken. Further, they facilitate the creation of shared perspectives on °system° issues and topics. To provide for the requisite change / transformation capacity, the models actors use have to be

> "capable of generating a variety equivalent to the variety that has to be regulated – or" it "will fail".[202]

That means that the models represented must adequately reflect the variety of the issues and topics they apply to.

---

[200] Waelchli, F.: (VSM and Ashby's Law)

[201] Beer, S.: (Heart); Arthur, Brian: (Cognition)

[202] Beer, S.: (Heart); "Every good regulator of a system must be a model of that system." (Conant and Ashby, 1970); Ashby, W. R. and Conant, R. C.: Every good regulator of a system must be a model of that system, International Journal of System Science, 1 / 2, 89, 1970

3.2.2.2 Governing elements

Implementing the notion of a social °system° requires actors to constantly attend to the issues continuously evolving from it. With reference to an established °system° notion, four groups of °system° elements have been distinguished above (chapter 2.3.2): images, instruments, actions and actors. To address their °system° issues, actors form characteristic representations that address these characteristic elements: 'images', 'instruments', 'actions', and 'actors' (abbreviated as IIAA) and reconcile through them.[203] They are sketched as follows. As introduced above, single quotation marks indicate a representation, i.e. reference an °image°, °instrument°, etc.

Figure 22. Characteristic representations addressing governing elements

'Images' refer to actors' adopted views on °system° states, how they perceive the °system° to be or ought to be and what issues are involved. With 'images', they express their intents and claims about that °system° state and the issues involved, i.e. indicate *"what it is all about"* [204], where and how possibilities, opportunities, and limitations of dealing with the °system° state can be found.[205] They point to the phenomena considered as relevant, i.e. relevant characteristics, attributes, variables, and relations. In this way, 'images' give expression and interpretation to °system° facts, visions, presuppositions, problems, opportunities, judgments, wishes, goals, etc. By orientation towards 'images', actors form, discuss, and test their individual °system° images and reconcile them: problems ('images') are confronted

---

[203] Governing elements are a useful way to distinguish aspects of interaction in respect to governing. This is analoguous to the distinction between content and relationship aspects invented to address the conditions of inter-personal interaction in respect to the intentional states involved. See Watzlawick, P., Beavin, J. H., and Jackson, D. D.: Pragmatics of Human Communication. A Study of Interactional Patterns, Pathologies, and Paradoxes <German>, New York, 1967; Schulz von Thun, F.: Miteinander Reden Band I, 1981

[204] Kooiman puts it "what governing is about", in Kooiman, J.: (Governing as Governance)

[205] Kooiman, J.: (Governing as Governance)

with potential solutions (i.e. combinations of 'instruments', 'actors', and 'actions'), opportunities are scrutinised, capacities assessed, normative judgements are raised, discussed and tested.[206]

'Instruments' involve what is needed to implement an °image° and to achieve a certain °system° state. That means that the term refers to the devices, utilities, means, resources, and *"crafts applied"* to *"reach what they want to accomplish"*.[207] Actors inform, organise, and define rules to reconcile °instruments°.[208] To inform, they create representations that articulate the financial, human, or knowledge resource (allocations) that are being required for implementing °images°. For instance, defining a convention 'drive on the right side of the street' can be an 'instrument' that enables actors to implement states of flawless traffic. To announce rules, 'instruments' may depict laws, decrees, and regulations to be followed. Thus, 'instruments' assemble references that reflect plans, processes, responsibilities, incentives, actor constellations, roles, interplay protocols, etc. They create links between 'images' and 'actions' and point towards what is needed for their implementation.

'Actions' make explicit the activities that actors undertake or intend to undertake to achieve a certain °image° and to apply °instruments°,[209] i.e. to do something. They refer to all types of individual and collective behaviour coordinating the application of instruments. For instance, they may indicate the detailed activities and procedures required to create a plan, to define responsibilities, etc. Further, they may explicate the way these activities are to be performed, e.g. quickly, slowly, thoroughly, attentively, etc.

Finally, **'Actors'** identify and characterise those individual actors or established organisational entities who aspire to °images°, apply °instruments° and undertake °actions° for implementing and constituting a °system° notion. They may refer to actor names, attributes, and characteristics as they have evolved formally or informally. Perceived characteristics of 'actors' may include formal roles, positions, functions, and responsibilities, and informal charisma, personality, qualities, reputation, temperament, integrity, etc.

Legal norms, reconciled to create agreements upon appropriate and fair social behaviour in a °community°, are an example of how the characteristic

---

[206] Winograd, Flores as cited in Checkland, P.: (Information Systems)

[207] Kooiman, J.: (Governing as Governance)

[208] Ibid.

[209] To bring the "instruments into place", in Kooiman, J.: (Governing as Governance)

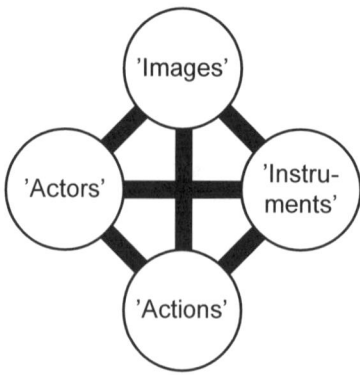

Figure 23. Four governing elements for addressing °system° issues

elements of representation apply. An 'article of law' is a conditional program for actor behaviour in a °community° which specifies some °system°
states to be achieved and some to be prevented. Therefore, it contains a
certain 'image' (corpus delicti) which refers to the 'instruments' used to
achieve those states and links to a certain 'action' (legal consequence).[210]
°Community° actors who have successfully reconciled and adopted an
'article of law' create an agreement (IIAA) as a shared background which
they follow consequently. Thus, they create pre-conditions that allow them
to permanently harmonise their behaviour throughout the implementation
of °community°.

To summarise, it can be said that governing elements are the invariant aspects referred to by actors when they reconcile their °system° notions and
issues. They enable actors to recognise their °system° issues and to create
compatible views on how to implement their °system° notion (and thus establish the pre-conditions for requisite variety). Any governing message,
statement, or concern links between an image, an instrument, an action, and
an actor. Each of the four elements has either to be articulated (as 'image',
'instrument', 'action', 'actor') or refer to a shared claim that has already
been established (an °image°, °instrument°, °action°, °actor°). Otherwise,
the oriented actors will not be able to align their activities to implement the
°system° notion aspired to.

---

[210] Of course, the conditional program itself can be an 'instrument' within a larger
context.

3.2.2.3 Logical levels of representation

Reference to °system° notions, states and issues can be made on different levels of abstraction and anticipation. This chapter develops a model of *Logical Levels of Representation (LLR)[211]*, which provides a basis for formulating the characteristics and benefits of abstraction and anticipation in representation.[212]

Essentially, logical levels provide a theory of abstraction and anticipation. They show what types of representations can be used in interaction to create coherent backgrounds on social °systems° notions. This means that a representation 'A' is considered superior or meta to 'B', if

'A' comments on 'B', or if, equivalently,

'A' contains 'B' as one of its parts (less than the entirety of 'A'), or, equivalently, if

'A' includes 'B' in its scope ('A' is about 'B').

Distinguishing logical types is required to dissolve the paradox of Russell's antinomy.[213] Following Russell's theory, representations (which are expressions of class / elements) of different logical type are to be kept separate. Mixing them would invite paradox. Adopting Russell's theory, it can be generalised that representations of normative, strategic, operative,

---

[211] Türke, R. E.: (Building blocks)

[212] It builds upon the Model of Systemic Control (MSC) as originated by Gälweiler and further developed by Schwaninger, in Gälweiler, Aloys: (Corporate Strategy); Schwaninger, M.: Integrale Unternehmensplanung, Frankfurt a.M., New York, 1989; Schwaninger, M.: Managing complexity: the path towards intelligent organizations., System Practise and Action Research, 13, 2, New York, 2000; Schwaninger, M.: Intelligent Organizations: An Integrative Framework, Systems Research and Behavioural Science, 18, 2, 2001

[213] Russell's antinomy is a paradox discovered by Bertrand Russell which shows that naive set theory is contradictory, see Russell, B: The Contradiction, Principles of Mathematics, Cambridge, 1903; Russell, B and Whitehead, A. N.: The Theory of Logical Types, in: Russell, B and Whitehead, A. N., Principia Mathematica, Cambridge, 1927. The barber paradox gives expression to Russell's antinomy: it considers a town with a male barber who shaves only any man who does not shave himself, and no one else. Such a barber cannot exist: if the barber does not shave himself, he must abide by the rule and shave himself. If he does shave himself, according to the rule, he cannot shave himself. Thus, the rule results in an impossible situation.

and tactical types are of different logical order and therefore must be kept separate. Each logical type of representation provides a different type of reference, reflection of a phenomenon (issues, facts, control variables[214]) and serves different anticipatory or regulatory purposes in regard to the social °system° notion aspired to.

For instance, 'solvency' and 'profitability' are indicators for describing the operative capacity of a °company°, its property of being able to pay all debts or its capacity to yield advantageous results out of its activity. Commonly, they are recognised as prerequisites for implementing a °company° notion, because in their absence most businesses activities cannot be conducted. Thus, 'solvency' and 'profitability' point to shared attributes of the °company° and serve to actively influence actors' activities.[215] Thus, each logically superior level of representation provides meta-expressions to its lower.[216] Agreements settled on at one level pre-condition and potentially pre-control those of the next level down. Logical levels are by no means independent; rather, each higher level envelops those below. If a normative agreement settles aspects of °system° identity, the range remaining for possible °system° strategies derives from these.[217] Obviously, the use of higher logical levels of abstraction in representation extends actors abilities to grasp complex issues and to reconcile them. At the same time, each higher level detaches the representation from the *isness* or *now* of the actual situation that is being perceived. The scope of phenomena expressed through the distinctions articulated increases from tactical to normative representations.[218] While higher degrees of representation broaden the scope of issues and facts that can be addressed, they clearly limit the extent to which the *now* can be be foreseen or influenced.[219] Abstraction and anticipation prepare and sensitise actors for addressing °system° states and for solving issues with requisite variety in their interactions. Adequate representations reflect both the degree of abstraction and the time frame of

---

[214] Variables are sets of phenomena which actors have reconciled to understand as meaningful descriptions of their °system° notion.

[215] Beer, S.: (Diagnosing)

[216] For other applications of the theory of logical types see Bateson, G.: (Ecology of mind); Bandler, R.: The structure of magic – Volume II, 1980

[217] Schwaninger, M.: (Framework Intelligent Organisations)

[218] Gälweiler, Aloys: (Corporate Strategy)

[219] Hayek, F. A. v.: Recht, Gesetzgebung und Freiheit: eine neue Darstellung der liberalen Prinzipien der Gerechtigkeit und politischen Ökonomie, 1986

the addressed issue. Long and short time horizons are inherent characteristics of representation.[220]

Certain principles expressed in normative representations (e.g. ethical and aesthetic ones) are largely timeless. Concerns of superior levels are not detached from those of the subordinate ones. A °system° notion does require value potentials to be implemented, i.e. converted into the benefit addressed with it.[221] Sharpening or broadening statements in representation between logical levels is not fruitful as such. For actors to inform each other, representations must be phrased according to the language of the adequate logical level relevant for the characteristics of the issue. Exaggerating the specification in a statement is as destructive as incautiously using vague expressions and ambiguous expressions.[222]

To sustain °system° notions, all logical levels of representation need to be used. Table 5 sums up the characteristics of the logical levels of representation. A primary level of tactical representations is added in regard to moment-to-moment representations.

Table 5. Logical levels of representation[223]

Logical level	Pre-conditioned phenomena	Anticipatory purpose	Logical Need
Tactical	Names, numbers, descriptions, signs, body language	(Inter-)Action	Efficacy
Operative	Productivity, quality, profitability, social benefit, ecological value, liquidity, solvency, etc.	Value, Benefit	Efficiency
Strategic	Core competences, problem solutions, technical substitutions, critical success factors, etc.	Value potentials	Effectiveness
Normative	Ethos, culture, social values, identity, vision, etc.	Viability and development	Legitimacy

---

[220] "The meaning created and the decisions taken based on them, are the more uncertain and dubious, the longer the temporal horizon being addressed. This is due not to the time span in focus, but to the operative type of representations which is generally incapable to anticipate longer periods of time.", as translated from Gälweiler, Aloys: (Corporate Strategy), pp. 55-57

[221] Schwaninger, M.: (Framework Intelligent Organisations)

[222] Schaff, A.: (Unscharfe Ausdrücke)

[223] With the tactical level added, slightly adapted from Schwaninger, M.: Intelligent Organizations – Powerful Models for Systemic Management, Heidelberg, 2006

Tactical

Tactical representations arise as an immediate, spontaneous reference on the *now* of the actual situation. They refer to the details individual actors face in their current situation. They are pointers, descriptions of phenomena perceived in actors images emerging.[224] Any successful °system° implementation depends on the naming, describing, articulating of °system° phenomena throughout the implementation. Tactical representations express 'what actors actually do' to implement their °system° notions. They concretise the four governing elements in respect to the characteristics of the situation. Whatever issue requires attendance is either resolved here or left to its own.[225] All tactical representations arise concurrently in the situation; they reflect the phenomena of the situation but there is no reflection upon themselves. Tactical representations do not have a time horizon. Sharing them ensures the efficacy of °system° implementation, i.e. enables its functioning.

Operative

Operative representations reference from actor backgrounds that express 'what can be done' and 'how it can be done' in order to implement a °system° notion. Operative representations address efficiency, i.e. the performance of actors when implementing a social °system° notion. It is a central characteristic of operative representations that they can capture, comment, and conclude on phenomena that have already occurred (in a former *now*). They do not provide evidence of the phenomena's causes and roots or the implied consequences for the future. With operative representations, actors align towards how to optimise the implementation of a °system° notion with its aspired °images° and °system° states. Therefore, operative 'images' specify the outputs to be achieved, the limitations and goals of resource consumption, etc. They emphasise how 'instruments' can be used to conduct 'actions' in the light of 'images' aspired to. A link is created between operative 'images', 'instruments', 'actions', and 'actors', describing who applies which means for aspiring which outputs.[226] Key °system° phenomena or variables pre-determined at this level are productivity, profitability, and quality. For instance, a known and precisely defined operative goal does define the adequate scope of action to take.[227]

---

[224] Gälweiler, Aloys: (Corporate Strategy)

[225] Schwaninger, M.: (Framework Intelligent Organisations), p. 140

[226] Ibid.

[227] Beer, S.: (Dispute)

Other examples are operative goals, guidelines, requirements, etc. The time horizon of operative representations is short-term.

Strategic

Whenever a situation requires the anticipation of future °system° states and issues, solutions based on today's circumstances, as expressed in operative representations, necessarily come too late.[228] Strategic representations enable actors to comment on operative issues and solutions with respect to how these are implemented. They point to 'what should be done' and 'what kind of phenomena °system° implementation should reveal'. They discuss the primary °system° states to be achieved, the °images° that the actors involved in °system° implementation actually head for. Therefore, they provide outcome descriptions, such as developmental goals, value, or quality potentials, critical success factors. Further, they reconcile means to aspire to those outcomes, e.g. capabilities, developmental plans.[229] With strategic representations, actors reconcile future states to be aspired (strategic 'images') and derive the strategic 'instruments' and 'actions' they intend to take for their implementation. What are the right steps and procedures taken for implementation? Strategic representations depict the long-term dependency of °system° factors relevant for the realisation of the aspired °system° states. They anticipate potential future states, such as what are our core competencies, how can existing problems be solved, etc.[230]

The reconciliation of strategic agreements enables actors to create and preserve the potential to successfully implement a °system° notion in future. They invent, develop, maintain, and preserve beneficial and reliable potentials to remain successful in consideration of the long-term limitations involved with respect to the social °system°, e.g. concerning its liquidity.[231] The potential to reveal and settle the intended °system° states, i.e. the primary °images° aspired to, is at the core of strategic interaction.[232]

Output descriptions for instance are reflections upon the ongoing production activities and therefore an operative representation. The appearance or absence of an output depends on the availability of production facilities, resource disposability, competencies, which are all required before an output can be produced. Therefore, it can be said that the appearance or absence of

---

[228] Gälweiler, Aloys: (Corporate Strategy)

[229] Schwaninger, M.: (Framework Intelligent Organisations)

[230] Gälweiler, Aloys: (Corporate Strategy)

[231] Ibid.

[232] Ibid.

an intended output depends on following strategic agreements taken before its appearance is prepared. With strategic representations, actors balance and align how they intend to deploy their strengths and outcome potentials. The crux of strategic representations is that they anticipate future trends and events by pointing to those phenomena or variables which, in turn, anticipate the °system's° outputs and their interrelationships.[233] Strategic representations express what future 'images' are aspired to by which 'actors' applying which 'instruments' and taking which 'actions'. Thus, they provide meta-statements for annotating, classifying, judging, criticising, or linking operative representations. The time horizon of strategic representations is medium- and long-term.[234] Any strategic agreement (defining 'images' and 'instruments', linking to 'actions' and 'actors') provides a basis for settling operative issues.

Normative

Normative representations enable actors to share understandings and evaluations of the overall situation of a °system° implementation.[235] They are used to reveal, discuss, and establish the underlying boundary judgements actors adopt[236] and make explicit 'what constitutes the social °system° notion', its epigenetic landscape. Further, through them actors initiate the creation and adaptation of °system° boundaries with respect to the purposes aspired to, the values to be followed, how the actors involved intend to arrange their relationships, which 'actors' are to be involved and what their tasks will be. Thus, they align actors' backgrounds in regard of shared

---

[233] Schwaninger, M.: (Framework Intelligent Organisations), p. 142

[234] Brühlmeier, D.: Politische Planung – Mittelfristige Steuerung in der wirkungsorientierten Verwaltungsführung, Bern, Stuttgart, Wien, 2001

[235] The "role of the 'higher' level is to express a perception of the scene observed by the 'lower' level. That is why the 'higher' level is able to formulate the epigenetic landscape. Moreover: the 'higher' level has a language to talk which is of a different logical order from the language of the 'lower' level. This is partly because it has a way of observing the impact of external disturbances on the 'lower' muddy box, and accounting for what is happening in his own language – whereas the only words for these shocks that are available in the 'lower' language are such as 'ouch' and 'help'. And it is party, because it is the recipient of a landscape from its 'higher' order, which (naturally) cannot be transmitted to its 'lower' order – because it would have no meaning there. [...] The 'higher' level is characterised not by its capacity to command, but by its order of perception and its order of language in logic.", in Beer, S.: (Heart)

[236] Ulrich, W.: (Critical heuristics social systems)

Table 6. Manifestations of governing elements on logical levels

	'Images'	'Instruments'	'Actions'	'Actors'
Tactical level Efficacy (what is)	actual state of affairs: positive or negative deviance to operative goals, task achievements, problem descriptions	actual use of resources: billboards, calendars, process descriptions, resource allocations, accounting, stock of inventory, status and quality of performance	moment-to-moment tacit activity descriptions, as entailed in advices, commands, directives, instructions, hints	name or denomination of an actor as entailed in commands, directives, instructions, indications, hints
Operative level Efficiency (what can be)	operative goals, output descriptions, capacity for change, operative know-how, experiences, social benefit, ecological value, profitability, quality achieved	optimisation of resource deployment: productivity, staff employment and responsibilities plan, defining process flows and procedures, resource allocation, performance and quality measurement, contracts, liquidity, solvency	aggregated, operative activity descriptions, short-term operating procedures and guidelines	task assignments, attendance and availability, training on the job
Strategic level Effectiveness (what should be)	developmental goals, outcome descriptions, critical success factors, environmental constraints, future prospects, threats and opportunities	developmental and strategic plans and programs, portfolio-, SWOT-[237], and value benefit analysis, resource disposability, system dynamics, sensitivity analysis	aggregated, strategic activity descriptions, long- and medium-term	core competencies, actor development and qualification, actor identity and profile, role descriptions, authorities
Normative level Legitimacy (what must be)	identity, ethos: culture, social values and norms, purpose descriptions, paradigms	normative laws, decrees and regulations, mission statements, how to aspire consensus among experts, involvement of stakeholders	customs, etiquette, formalities, manners, protocols, rules of conduct, social code	concept and dignity of man, understanding of equality, status, social class, recognition, fame, publicity, selection criteria

---

[237] A SWOT Analysis is a strategic planning tool used to evaluate the Strengths, Weaknesses, Opportunities, and Threats involved in a project or business venture or in any other situation of an organisation or individual requiring a decision in pursuit of an objective. See Wikipedia contributors: SWOT analysis, Wikipedia, The Free Encyclopedia, 2007

sources of motivation, power, and legitimacy. Only in reference to these agreements can actors prove the legitimacy of their ongoing behaviour in the light of the °system° notion. Hence, through normative representations, actors both create and comply with their °system° notions. They settle on agreements that apply in numerous, similar situations, regardless of the time intervals in which the addressed phenomena reoccur.[238] Ideally, normative representations provide permanent guidance. Their substantial contribution is to rationalise the constant reconciliation of issues on all lower levels in regard to time, expenditure, and quality.[239] They do so by linking, classifying, annotating, judging, or criticising strategic, operative, and tactical statements. They can be and often are reconciled without reference to a practical, present moment issue within which they are relevant. Their time horizon is indefinite or long-term, aiming at the sustainability and viability of the °system° notion.

With normative representations actors specify what abstract, idealised purposes, social values, norms, and identities ('images') will be aspired to through the application of what kind of 'instruments' and solution patterns ('actions') and under whose ultimate responsibility ('actors'). Table 6 briefly sketches some manifestations of governing elements for each logical level.

Thus, governing representations can be distinguished according to their logical level as well as the elements they express. They are used to induce intents and claims, which consequently can also be characterised through their logical level. Figure 24 shows how both logical levels and governing elements can be illustrated in a °system° notion.

As depicted an evolving shared °system° notion can be illustrated by generating a series of circles originating from the present moment, or simply the 'now'. The outer circle refers to the boundary that delimits the scope of intents and claims involved in the °system°. In between the present moment and the system boundary, shared °system° intents and claims appear as they have been reconciled. The distance from the present moment indicates their abstractness and timeliness. Outer intents and claims close to the boundary are far reaching or even completely timeless, and more generally valid. The closer the position is to the present moment, the more specific and immediately relevant it is to the ongoing implementation of the °system° notion.

---

[238] Gälweiler, Aloys: (Corporate Strategy); Brühlmeier, D., Haldemann, T., Mastronardi, P., and Schedler, K.: (Political planning)

[239] Gälweiler, Aloys: (Corporate Strategy)

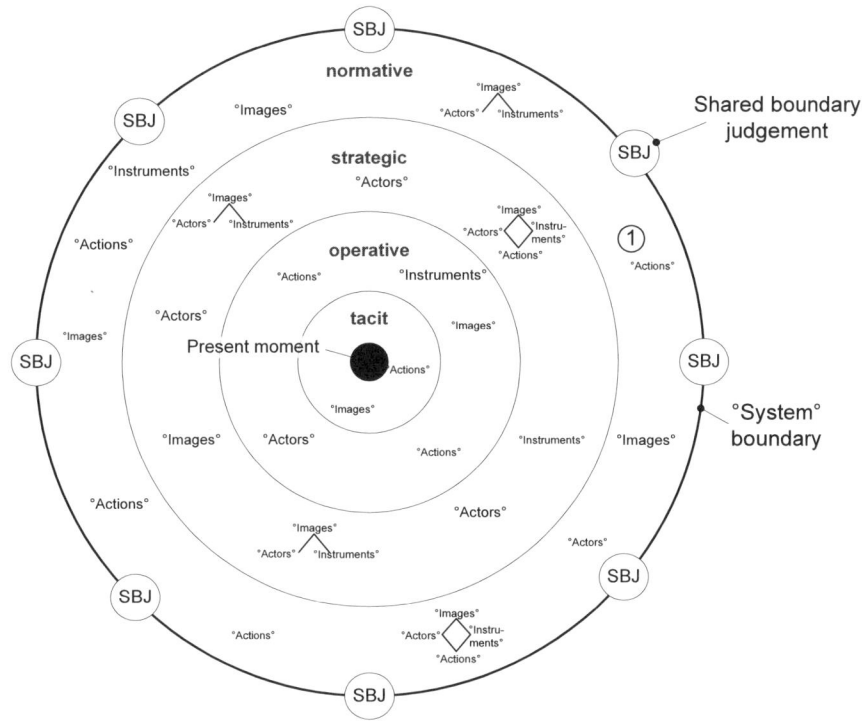

Figure 24. Logical spheres in a shared social °system° notion

3.2.3   Triggering change

Change of °system° notions means adaptations of both claims and intents. By referencing in representation, claims are addressed and modifications induced. By expressing concerns and solutions, intents are stimulated. Below is an elaboration of how references and concerns trigger change in °system° notions, thus affecting the contextuality and intentionality of the actors involved in the implementation of the °system° notion.

3.2.3.1 Contextuality

Interaction is always dealing with an issue addressed. To resolve their issues, actors must necessarily form and share representations that provide adequate reference to their relevant viewpoints, opinions, aspects. To do so, they cannot but apply logical levels of representation. Representations may reflect upon an issue on four logical levels, i.e. the (1) tactical, (2) operational, (3) strategic, and (4) normative level. On each level, actors create 'images' about what their governing is about, choose 'instruments' to achieve what they want to accomplish, and carry out 'actions' to implement the instruments chosen. Thus, on each logical level the four governing elements are addressed, which form a consistent °system° notion only when taken together. The potentially induced change primarily lies in the selectivity of distinctions referenced to depict an issue. Any reference of an issue provides account to the originator's underlying °system° notion and background and thus induces others to relate to it. Creating references of aspects, problems, issues of °system° implementation and making them accessible to others (e.g. by documenting it) can therefore be used to accommodate actor background and thus to induce amplification or attenuation of actor varieties. Similarly, eliminating or deleting references may induce amplification or attenuation. Furthermore, change or transformation can be induced by transforming the distinctions expressed in representation by

1. generalising distinctions to the next higher logical level,

2. specifying distinctions on the next lower logical level,

3. distorting distinctions on one and the same logical level.

This is illustrated in Figure 25.

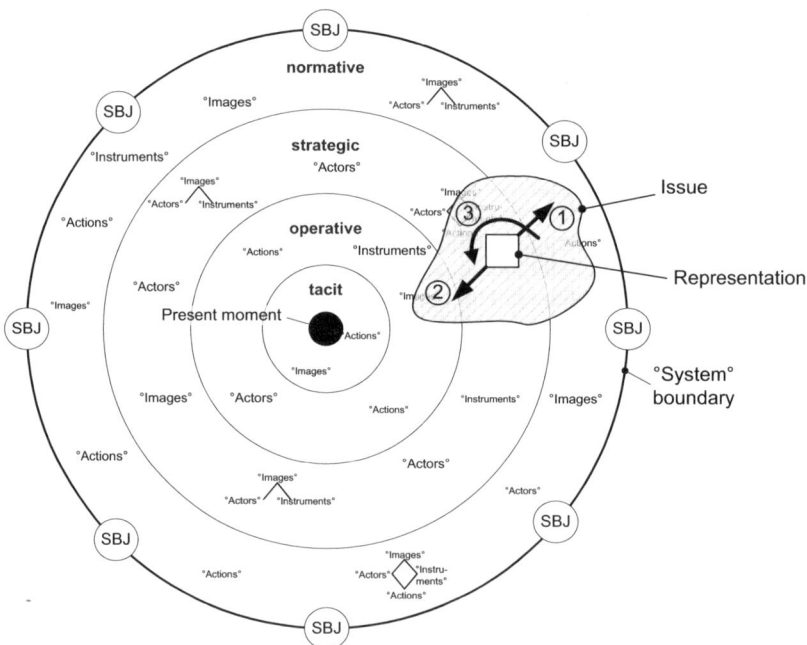

Figure 25. Three fundamental change triggers

The variety of an issue on a certain logical level cannot be eliminated or managed definitively by enumerating or dealing sequentially with its states.[240] Therefore, a meta-solution is required on a higher logical level, i.e. an operative issue requires knowledge of a strategic directions; a strategic direction in turn requires the normative grounding of a purpose definition of the °system° being implemented.

Let us imagine Paul wants to remove the tree in front of his house. He is not sure, how to do that, so he asks his friend Simon, who advises him that he should use a saw ('instrument'). This seems evident to Paul and attenuates his number of choices by order of magnitude, as he can now exclude many other possible 'instruments' such as dynamite, digging, etc. But as he goes to the do-it-yourself store to buy a saw, he recognises that there are different types to choose from … Nevertheless, Paul may still not know how to apply that special saw he has bought and how to cut the tree, i.e. how to set the cut, what sequence to follow, etc. References are his personal knowledge, others experts knowledge … Change or transformation capacity of interaction does not refer to the preconditions of the venture to 'cut the tree' but to Paul's ability to accommodate a solution to do it, i.e. his knowledge of an suitable method and practise for doing so. In respect to the actors, cutting a tree is a rather simple case, as actors are not disturbed. A forest ranger disturbing them and prohibiting their venture would indeed change the setting.

Change or transformation capacity depends on how far the distinctions actors make and expose in representation to reconcile their activities (i.e. the context) are capable to describe the issue and to derive a valid solution. The potential for change or transformation is inherent in any representation exposed, whatever form it may take. Change or transformation capacity lies in how relevant °system° distinctions can be depicted and transformed for referencing and resolving °system° issues. On the other hand, subsuming the aspects of an issue by wrongly using a statistical procedure (e.g. averages of averages of averages) will not lead to an adequate solution but rather create misunderstandings.

3.2.3.2 Intentionality

Interaction may occur either symmetrically, or hierarchically, depending on whether the shared intentions and claims applied in social °system° implementation express equality or difference.[241] With algedonic concerns[242],

---

[240] Waelchli, F.: (VSM and Ashby's Law)

[241] See Watzlawick's 5th axiom of communication: forms of interaction: "Inter-human communication procedures are either symmetric or complementary,

actors set out to actively influence each other's intents; they are means to express and enforce °system° intentions. With the formulation of positive activators such as wishes, desires, motivations, incentives, gratifications, or negative inhibitors such as moral pleas, fears, risks, restrictions, prohibitions, actors strive to induce their counterparts to perform a certain change.[243] Algedonic concerns delimit an actor's scope of behaviour by defining exceptions, or broaden it by opening up new alternatives. Role definitions subsume a set of both positive activators and negative inhibitors and thus describe a whole scope of determinants meant to guide the behaviour of an individual (see chapter 3.3.1). Algedonic concerns orient actors towards directives, conventions, agreements, contracts, roles, laws, etc. which express shared conditionings or create them. They challenge the receiving actors to perform changes through reward and punishment. Exerting influence is dependent on algedonic concerns, particularly in the reconciliation of 'images' such as goals and objectives and in continuously knowing what is going on with the 'actions' that have been expressed to attain those goals and objectives.[244] Algedonic concerns are means to execute power.

Autonomy is about how actors mutually influence each other's backgrounds. It refers to the degree to which influence is exerted through alge-

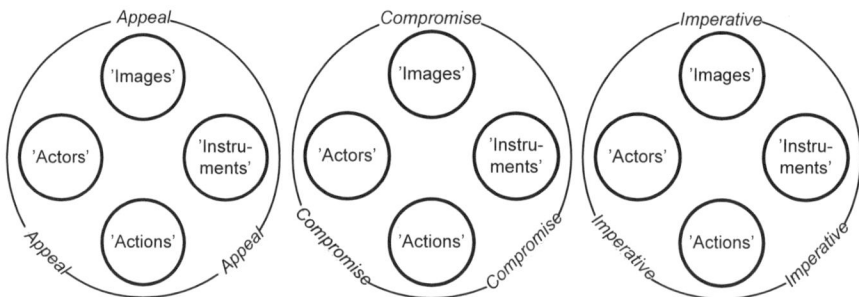

Figure 26. Algedonic concerns in representation

depending on whether the relationship of the partners is based on differences or parity.", in Watzlawick, P., Beavin, J. H., and Jackson, D. D.: (Pragmatics of Human Communication)

[242] Algedonic representations are manifested as signals and concerns. Algedonic signals are low-variety expressions that give expression to intentional states (chapter 3.3.3.1). Beer, S.: (Heart); Beer, S.: (Diagnosing)

[243] Willemsen, Maarten Helmut: Die Schweizerische Eidgenossenschaft als lebensfähiges System, 1992

[244] Beer, S.: (Dispute)

donic concerns in interaction. Three general types of algedonic concerns can be distinguished: appeal, compromise and imperative. Each has a specific capacity to challenge actors' prevailing backgrounds, their intents and claims. Whereas with appeals, the actors involved maintain their full autonomy, with compromises, each sacrifices a certain degree of his autonomy. And whenever imperatives are applied, the recipients completely lose the relative autonomy to perform the respective change (Table 7). Hence, the three kinds of algedonic concerns represent a scope of measures on the scale between freedom and determination. However, this does not contradict actors' autopoiesis. Algedonic concerns exclusively affect actors' relative autonomy. It is no contradiction that actors themselves, i.e. their image creation, remain autonomous as a matter of principle. Only with respect to the commonly adopted and shared °system° background can actors determine each other's image creation. Admittedly, this distinction between individual and relative autonomy may appear to be purely theoretical in all those °system° situations where actors face strong cultural imprint (such as machismo, feminism, rankism[245], etc.) or exceptional circumstances (such as war, violence, disaster, etc.). Nevertheless, the endless list of freedom fighters underpins the view that human actors remain ultimately autonomous, however conditional this may be. The following table depicts some manifestations of algedonic concerns:

Table 7. Manifestations of algedonic concerns

	Positive activators (Amplifiers)	**Negative inhibitors** (Attenuators)
Appeal	Wishes, desires, new ideas, ambitions, aspirations, expressions of curiosity, honest recognition, appreciation, tribute, acknowledgement.	Moral pleas, doubts, fears, nervousness, clarification of facts, subjective, inopportune praise.
Compromise	Offers, favourable arguments, motivations, opportunities, chances, positive rationales, justifications and reasons, constructive criticism.	Demands, unfavourable arguments, risks, constraints, negative rationales, justifications and reasons, unconstructive criticism, improper public plaudit.
Imperative	Incentives, stimuli, gratifications, positive rules, precepts, critical assessment.	Restrictions, prohibitions, negative rules, commands, sanctions, denunciation, condemnation, stigmatisation, blame.

---

[245] Fuller, R. W.: Somebodies and nobodies – overcoming the abuse of rank, Gabriola Island, 2003

Table 8. Amplifying and attenuating concerns (exemplary)

		Amplifying concerns Motivate other actors to expand their alternative options to solve the issue 'resource deployment'.	**Attenuating concerns** Induce other actors to reduce their alternative options to solve the issue 'resource deployment'.
Tactical How to use re- sources now?	Appeal	Wishes, desires, ambitions exposed to change the actual distribution and coordination of resources.	Doubts, fears, moral pleas that the actual resource distribution and coordination can be changed.
	Compro- mise	Offers, pros, and motivation to change the actual resource distribu- tion. Constructive criticism of the actual proceedings.	Needs, cons, and risks of changing the actual resource distribution.
	Imperative	Incentives, stimuli, gratifications to improve the actual process of re- source distribution.	Restrictions, prohibitions, and sanctions to change the actual proc- ess of resource distribution.
Opera- tive How to allocate resources between actors and gain synergy?	Appeal	Wishes, desires, and ambitions to optimise the overall allocation of resources.	Doubts, fears, moral pleas that the overall resource allocation can be optimised.
	Compro- mise	Opportunities, chances, and positive rationales in favour of an optimised allocation of resources.	Constraints, risks, and negative rationales coming along with a change of the allocation as it has been done hitherto.
	Imperative	Incentives, stimuli, gratifications to support optimised resource alloca- tion, e.g. de-formalising existing procedures, expanding individual responsibilities, financial incentives, broadening objectives followed.[246]	Restrictions, prohibitions, and sanctions restricting individual access to resources, e.g. highly formalised procedures, access limi- tations, non-compliance penalties.
Strategic How to deploy resources in the future?	Appeal	Wishes, desires, and ambitions to improve resource allocation in regard of future resource deploy- ment and outcomes.	Doubts, fears, moral pleas that resource allocation can be improved in regard of future threats and chal- lenges.
	Compro- mise	Opportunities, chances, and positive rationales of future resource deploy- ment, e.g. product innovations, value potentials.	Constraints, risks, and negative rationales of future threats and challenges.
	Imperative	Incentives, stimuli, gratifications to improve resource deployment and the outcomes achieved.	Ignore risks implied in future ac- tions, fix a planning horizon.
Norma- tive What must be done?	Appeal	Wishes, desires, and ambitions to broaden the purpose of resource deployment.	Doubts, fears, moral pleas that resource depletion is done precisely, consciously, and ethically.
	Compro- mise	Opportunities, chances, and positive rationales of broader system boundaries.	Constraints, risks, and negative rationales of existing system boundaries.
	Imperative	Incentives, stimuli, gratifications to motivate and liberate all aspects of resource deployment.	Restrictions, prohibitions, and sanc- tions limiting resource deployment.[247]

---

[246] Beer, S.: (Heart)

[247] "That is, preventive laws ('no access' curfews, identity papers) which restrict societary states imply less police amplification – because monitoring is a lower variety activity than coping with the unexpected.", in Beer, S.: (Diagnosing)

The effect of algedonic concerns is increased when they take care of and dwell on the recipients' intentions, e.g. by transforming relationships from 'win-lose' or 'zero-sum' modes to a 'win-win' situation.[248] The value of expressing algedonic concerns is not only to make explicit and decide upon an issue but to motivate actors to permanently adhere to the agreement that settles their solution. Ultimately, the value of any agreement manifests itself in actors' adherence to it in frequently recurring situations.[249]

Algedonic concerns are apt to exert a determining or guiding influence over an actor or a group of actors by inducing certain changes which are aspired to. They are used to provoke amplification or attenuation of the number of states, alternatives, solutions that are in question. The adequate level of autonomy can only be defined in relation to a social °system° notion that is aspired to. It is derived from the necessities the °system° faces in the light of its environmental challenges (see chapter 4).

3.2.4 Method

Change or transformation capacity of interaction is manifested in the method applied in interaction, whether these may be practices or instruments. Methods provide reference to issues and generate solutions. Any specific constellation of governing elements and algedonic concerns that is articulated on a logical level is a method (Figure 27). By composing representations, actors decide upon the methods applied: governing elements define which °system° issues are addressed and indicate how they are to be resolved. Algedonic concerns motivate change through appeal, compromise, and imperative, assigning responsibilities, defining incentives, and rules. Different degrees of abstraction and time horizons help to address the complexity, diversity, and dynamics of a perceived issue. High-variety representations reflect a plurality, low variety representations, a minority of distinctions. Any higher logical type of representation produces meta expressions upon the lower. The combination and configuration of governing elements, logical levels, and algedonic concerns in representation constitute the overall method applied and may give impulse to amplification or attenuation of actor variety. Methods induce mixed adjustments of amplification and attenuation. In fact, whether the specific contingency induced

---

[248] Espejo, R.: Giving Requisite Variety to Strategic and Implementation Processes: Theory and Practice, http://bprc.warwick.ac.uk/LSEraul.html

[249] Establishing an interaction channel could be the consequence of an algedonic concern. Compare similar Gälweiler, Aloys: (Corporate Strategy)

is viewed as one or the other depends on the °system° notion.[250] The
°system° notion provides the overall delimitation of the relevant choice for
selection.[251] Change / transformation capacity of interaction depends on
how well the method chosen addresses characteristics of the issue to be
resolved. Interaction can only provide requisite change / transformation
capacity if the method applied creates an adequate reference and turns it
into an adequate solution.

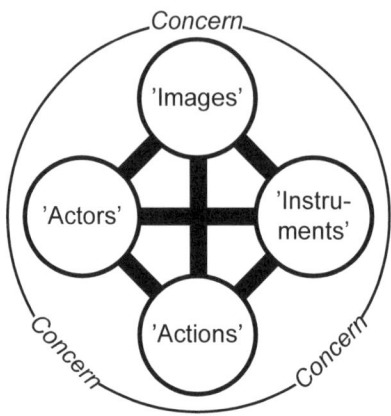

Figure 27. Method: a way to address an issue with a concern

A method is a certain way, approach, measure, or means for producing or
transforming distinctions in representation. A specific configuration of
representations is a result through which actor variety is attenuated or amplified in a particular situation. Actors use methods to reference their issues and to create the distinctions required to resolve them.[252] To induce
the desired effect, methods are always either positive activators or negative

---

[250] Beer, S.: (Diagnosing)

[251] "Variety is amplified or attenuated by the instructions that the data formulate;
but those instructions must be adequate to the relevant variety selection.", in
Beer, S.: (Diagnosing). See also Beer's 2nd organisational principle, in Beer,
S.: (Diagnosing), idem.

[252] A methodology describes the principles of method. It is independent from any
context. It provides a frame for how actors' different varieties with respect to
an issue can be meaningfully attenuated and amplified, i.e. captured, distorted,
generalised, and deleted. See for a similar definition Checkland, P.: Systems
Thinking, Systems Practice, Chichester, 1999

inhibitors enforced either in the form of appeal, compromise, or an imperative. Whether a method actually amplifies or attenuates actor variety also depends on the specific prevailing °system° situation prevailing. Describing the effect of a method always starts from the actual status.

This shows how essential it is to make clear, which are the desired boundaries of the °system° notion concerned. Any change of boundaries also changes the issues to be tackled and the varieties involved. Narrowing °system° boundaries by restraining purpose definitions, involving fewer clients, reducing the range of products, etc. severely attenuates the variety in focus. Similarly, widening °system° boundaries by extending purposes, involving more clients, etc. clearly leads to an amplification of variety.

To what extent interaction can reference and resolve the relevant aspects of a °system° issue and thus provide requisite change / transformation capacity depends on the characteristics of the method applied.[253] To conduct the change stimulus exposed in representation, the following aspects of representation essentially determine the change / transformation capacity of a °system° notion. Methods create references of issues and transform them into adequate solutions. The change / transformation capacity of a method expresses to what extent it enables actors to gain insight into the issue and to resolve or eliminate it. It depends on whether the applied method

1. creates adequate reference to °system° situations, i.e. meets its complexity, captures the diversity of its aspects, by applying an model;

2. addresses adequately the °system° issue at hand and references the governing elements, 'images', 'instruments', 'actions', and 'actors' required to express the intended impulse, qualifies as information or knowledge in the view of its recipients and exerts a determining or guiding influence over them;

3. transforms an adequate reference of the issue into adequate solutions;

4. motivates and effectuates others to perform changes through algedonic concerns, i.e. use appeals, compromises or imperatives to actually provoke recipients to amplify or adapt their individual backgrounds as required.

---

[253] "Still today most of the models in use rely on discrete, rather static pictures of organisational reality, inspite of the necessity to understand the patterns of behaviour generated.", in Schwaninger, M.: (Intelligent Organizations)

3.3 Channel capacity

Interaction is the mutual orientation of several actors towards representation. Actors instruct each other vis-à-vis representation[254] on how to amplify or attenuate their individual backgrounds, i.e. how to attend to, understand and resolve their issues. Whether their interaction succeeds depends not only on how the issues are attended to (change or transformation capacity), but also on the conditions and processes through which actors share these representations. The message and the instructions entailed must be exposed or channelled under conditions and at a rate that is *"adequate to the relevant variety selection"* [255] of the recipient, which means that they must be channelled at a rate that permits their recognition to deploy requisite variety.[256] This depends on the configuration of the channels for involving relevant actors and their capacity to distribute and preserve the content over space and time. Requisite channel capacity is a necessary, albeit not commensurate, condition for sustainable interactions between actors:

> *The channels established between the actors affected by or involved in implementing, governing or managing a °system° notion must provide a higher capacity to expose and transmit relevant distinctions per time unit than the originating actors have to generate per time unit. The interaction channels exposing and transmitting representations between actors' spheres must have a higher capacity to capture relevant distinctions per time unit than the originating actors have to generate per time unit.*[257]

---

[254] Beer referred to this process as "transmitting data"

[255] Beer, S.: (Diagnosing)

[256] "Suppose you are managing a production unit, and a critical situation develops in No 4 furnance. You have requisite variety to distinguish between furnances, and to distinguish between various degrees of crisis – of which 'critical' is the penultimately bad. Your boss, a mile away, also has requisite variety. Thus the first principle is satisfied (it is because you are both trained men). Now the crisis has put your telephone out of action, and you therefore send a message by word of mouth. The messenger is oafish sad to say. What he tells the boss is 'things are in a hell of state down there'. Well, he might have forgotten the real message. But I take the case where lack of knowledge means that he was incapable of registering it. 'No 4' and 'critical' were just not states of the system that he could recognize as distinguishable.", in Beer, S.: (Heart), pp. 99-100

[257] "The four directional channels carrying information between the management unit, the operation, and the environment must each have a higher capacity to

In other words, representations must be channelled between the relevant actors in due time and with the right frequency, enabling them to induce the required changes before the situation evolves. Only if the content expressed in representation can trigger the selection of intents and claims in image creation in due time, are actors able to adequately attend to their °system° issue and to deploy requisite variety. This points to the significance of time in interaction. Interactivity describes the degree of responsiveness of interaction, i.e. the capacity of the channels to capture and convey the distinctions that have to be induced between actors. It must be ensured that all distinctions exposed arrive properly at the recipient's side. The possibility of failure in transmission is always immanent in interaction, with the risk of failing to settle essential °system° agreements.[258] Channel capacity thus refers to the degree to which established channels enable actors to successfully perform their relevant changes.[259] A channel provides the space to conduct a specific interaction. It is the sum of the constraints effectuated. The capacity of the channels that perform interaction is manifested primarily as a consequence of

1. relationships, tasks and responsibilities;
2. sequences and time lags;
3. tacit and explicit shapes of representation;
4. physical settings.

These aspects essentially determine channel capacity and are therefore described below.

3.3.1 Relationships, tasks, and responsibilities

What actors perceive and what they can contribute to a shared °system° notion is largely determined by their individual contexts, which depend on their lifeworld. Channel capacity strongly depends on those parts of the in-

---

transmit a given amount of information relevant to variety selection in a given time than the originating subsystem has to generate it in that time", in Beer, S.: (Heart), p. 99

[258] Espejo, R.: (VSM revisited)

[259] It refers to the degree of interactivity established between actors. The "capacity of an actual channel depends absolutely on the rate of data transmission involved.", in Beer, S.: (Diagnosing), p. 44

dividual contexts which are already shared. Shared conditionings such as relationships, interrelations, roles, affiliations, memberships, formalisations, and other references pre-condition interaction and constitute lifeworlds and °system° notions. An algedonic concern stimulating a certain behaviour turns into a role, function, task, job, duty, or (or: and) formalised incentive when it is adopted implicitly or formalised explicitly as a shared intent or claim over a period of time.

Thus, channels strongly predefine an actor's ability to participate and to share. They provide a stable frame for interaction.[260] All interactions are bound to the established channels. At any moment, actors implementing the notion of a social °system° attune their backgrounds through the established channels. The tasks required to deploy the °system° notion are distributed between those actors involved and engaged in governing. They are assigned different roles, defining who provides which contributions based on which responsibilities. This may take place either in symmetrical constellations with actors assigning equal power to each other, or in asymmetric settings[261], where there are different levels of power being assigned.[262] A formalised rule can be used to create a channel, i.e. a fixed structure, that must be adhered to.

However, the channels evolving from actors' contexts, in the end, define their capacity to actually attune each other's background in the light of the °system° notion aspired to.[263] If the channels are inadequate, it cannot be ensured that every actor is contributing to the best of his abilities. Actors

---

[260] Espejo, R., Schuhmann, W., Schwaninger, M., and Bilello, U.: (Transformation and Learning)

[261] Fifth communicative axiom, in Watzlawick, P., Beavin, J. H., and Jackson, D. D.: (Pragmatics of Human Communication)

[262] Griffin, E.: A first look at Communication Theory, New York, 1997; Game theory addresses asymmetric settings between actors. It is a branch of applied mathematics that uses models to study symmetrical and complementary interactions with formalised incentive structures (i.e. games). It deals with issues between various actors aspiring to implement individual intentions. It studies the choice of optimal behaviour when costs and benefits of each option are not fixed, but depend upon the future choices of other individuals. Game theory originated with Morgenstern, O. and Neumann, J. v.: The Theory of Games and Economic Behavior, 1953

[263] "The stronger the culture, the larger the communication capacity of these channels and the leaner the structure can be.", in Espejo, R., Schuhmann, W., Schwaninger, M., and Bilello, U.: (Transformation and Learning)

then must necessarily fail to resolve the issues required to deploy the °system°.[264]

This can be illustrated by the contrast of team and group notions and their evolving characteristic relationships. The primary intention of constituting a °team° notion usually is to address and carry out specified tasks in a joint effort. Any valuable contribution of the actors involved to solve that issue will carry weight for the °team° as it promotes the implementation and resolution of that task. The quality of each contribution will therefore be assessed independent from any attributes of its originator. The authority of the °team° leader will derive from his capacity to moderate and manage those involved.

This is not the case with actors adopting the notion of a °group° to address the same issue. The specific hierarchy and order of precedence usually established with a °group° notion strongly defines the way the actors interact as group members. Here, it will be of primary interest to those responsible or in management functions to adhere to the established order and the rules that derive from it. Actor contributions will be evaluated based upon the originator's position within the °group° hierarchy. Actors who join such hierarchic °group° constellations will tend to be constrained in their individual autonomy and contribute less creativity and engagement. Obviously, the interactivity of a °group° in charge of a task such as to 'identify new innovative products' absorbs a clearly lower degree of the tasks' complexity. In the light of highly complex and dynamic issues its formal channels may break down and be substituted for by informal ad-hoc constellations. The formalisations established with the °group° setting provide only an average capacity for reconciliation. Actors will be forced to set up informal meetings if they intend to substitute what is missing to resolve their °group° issues.[265] To find new solutions for issues, °team° constellations are adequate; for implementing existing solutions, °group° constellations will serve better.[266]

With respect to the different degrees of autonomy as they can be established in channels, it is useful to distinguish three fundamental types of interaction: interference, interplay, and intervention. These will be introduced as follows.

---

[264] Espejo, R., Schuhmann, W., Schwaninger, M., and Bilello, U.: (Transformation and Learning)

[265] Beer, S.: (Heart)

[266] Example adapted from Löhner, M.: Führung neu denken – Das Drei-Stufen-Konzept für erfolgreiche Manager und Unternehmen, Frankfurt a.M., 2005

3.3.1.1 Interference

Interferences execute appeals, the most liberal form of algedonic concerns. They allow actors to openly interact flexibly and independently without constraint. Actors relate symmetrically to each other, autonomously following their individual intentions and contexts. Of course, behaviour still evolves within the context of actors' lifeworld, but there are no further restrictions on behalf of the °system° notion. Actors may initiate changes, but they do not give up their individual autonomy. There is no obligation at all for them to follow a specific protocol. Interferences are characterised through a low degree of formality or ceremony; they are generally informal. They are used to exchange opinions, positions, ideas, (hi)stories, etc. Actors will rarely resolve relevant °system° issues through interference. Rather, they use interferences to notice, realise, and discuss their °system° issues. Interferences are flows of moment-to-moment, extensively tacit representations. Examples for interferences are informal occasions where actors casually meet each other, simply enjoying being together to share current news, to get to know each other, to chat, or to celebrate.

3.3.1.2 Interplay

In distinction to interferences, interplays can be conceived as an interdependent process of interaction conducted until an agreement is settled on with respect to one specific °system° issue. In interplay, actors settle on a compromise for a °system° issue. They engage in reconciling purposeful agreements, striving to attune each other's views of the °system° issues by adopting shared °purposes°, °goals°, etc. Thus, actors reconcile a common solution for a specific issue. In the process, each actor involved agrees to sacrifice part of her or his autonomy in regard to that issue. Interplays engage actors mutually with either formal or informal protocols.

Interplays emerge in innumerable manifestations, representing rather independent or dependent forms. The way that interplays are conducted generally depends on the agendas, roles, courses of action, modes of governance, etc. that are followed. Interplays may be distinguished according to the number of actors that are involved, the topics that are being addressed, the process that is followed, the degree of autonomy applied, etc. The degree of autonomy reveals itself in the type of arrangement or ritual made for conducting the proceedings within a group of actors, determining the influence that actors have on each other.[267] Indeed, variants are not neces-

---

[267] Beer, S.: (Dispute)

sarily alternative, opposing options, but rather complementary types adequate to address different issues in different situations. Choosing between them is a question of the intentionality and contextuality prevailing with respect to the °system° notion (chapter 3.1.1).

3.3.1.3 Intervention

Interventions are ways to execute authority, rules, commands, etc. and are used to align an actor's background on a specific issue and thus to provide order and unity to action. It is a unilateral influence of the counterpart which draws on imperatives. By referring to legitimations such as prevailing roles, rules, power distributions, laws, or contracts, interventions induce dependence and actively compel the attenuation of variety to an intended state or number of states. It has lasting consequences for its recipients, forcing them to align themselves into a specified condition or state. Interventions enable their originators to induce high variety attenuations with low variety representations.

3.3.2 Sequences and time lags

No representation is capable of inducing change beyond the originating image it refers to.[268] Whenever actors confront each other – even with a history of knowing each other – the references and concerns articulated from their individual backgrounds presume a specific topic and assume certain roles, behaviours, knowledge, etc. Naturally, these assumptions will not always apply and recipients' behaviour may not be responsive. Disagreements about how to sequence interaction are at the root of all kinds of private, business, or political conflicts.[269]

---

[268] No representation is "competent to regulate anything beyond the real-world projection of the model it contains.", in Beer, S.: (Heart), p.72

[269] Watzlawick, P., Beavin, J. H., and Jackson, D. D.: (Pragmatics of Human Communication), p. 56: "Suppose a couple have a marital problem to which he contributes passive withdrawal, while her 50 per cent is nagging criticism. In explaining their frustrations, the husband will state that withdrawal is his only defense against her nagging, while she will label this explanation a gross and willful distortion of what 'really' happens in their marriage: namely, that she is critical of him because of his passivity. Stripped of all ephemeral and fortuitous elements, their fights consist in a monotonous exchange of the messages 'I withdraw because you nag' and 'I nag because you withdraw.'

Thus, channel capacity also relies on providing adequate ordering of the processes and sequences actors undertake with each other to resolve their °system° issues[270], i.e. to arrange, accentuate, emphasise, or lessen the messages conveyed in reconciliation. Sharing, talking, chatting allows actors to address different aspects of the issue at hand and to facilitate reconciliation.[271]

For instance, to address a complex issue, actors might first choose to conduct a broadening debate to assess the individual backgrounds of the chosen subject matter and to identify the issues' most important aspects or related topics. In a next step, they may carry on with sharpening their focus, i.e. extensively discussing specific, detailed aspects in small groups of interested actors and conducting an expert survey. In a last step, they may then reintegrate their previous results by creating summaries and related survey results. On the other hand, such a predefined sequence may constrain actors' ability to submit necessary contributions. If, for instance, a group meeting is set up with a detailed agenda that explicates the issues and sub-issues to be addressed, this pre-determines the outcome in advance. Such a setting promotes those who determined the agenda *"to ride their familiar horses"*.[272]

Generally, channel capacity is defined through the processes and sequences of the protocol applied in interaction. It varies with respect to the degree of formalisation applied by defining agenda, rubrics, roles, processes, etc. The protocol type "mediation", where an independent moderator facilitates the conflict resolution between parties, captures a broad scope of individual actor variety as actors can permanently exercise active influence according to their needs. In contrast, the protocol of a "survey" is much more formalised and provides only the limited, standardised capacity defined in its configuration.

In interplay sequences, the creation and reconciliation of issues considered relevant for the future always bears difficulties. Settling on resolutions for issues considered relevant at a future point in time by anticipation

---

[270] Fourth communicative axiom: "The nature of the relationship depends on how both parties punctuate the communication sequence", in Watzlawick, P., Beavin, J. H., and Jackson, D. D.: (Pragmatics of Human Communication)

[271] An example of this is provided by the demos project which was carried out by Luehrs, R., Malsch, Th., and Voss, K.: Internet, Discours and Democracy, in: Terano, T., New Frontiers in Artificial Intelligence. Joint JSAI 2001 Workshop Post-Proceedings., Heidelberg, 2002

[272] Beer, S.: (Dispute)

at an early stage of time, enables actors to turn to other issues, bearing in mind that the previous ones have been resolved already. But this process takes time. Unless the resolutions settled on are continuously kept up-to-date with respect to the newly developing aspects of the situation, they will lose ground and validity in the situation that unfolds (in the *now*), which will allow for all kinds of unforeseen factors to enter into the equation.[273]

Therefore, for any solution to sustain requisite variety with respect to its issue, the lag between the act of planning, decision taking and the accrual of results is essential, not the lag between planning and decision taking. That lag is determined by feasibility.[274] This leads to a mismatch between what has been made explicit in the resolution and the relevant aspects and phenomena of the issue. As a consequence, a seemingly definite resolution is in fact out of date, and individual actors need to change their minds before it turns into an unliked fact. Moreover, this may not be recognised and actors may cherish the illusion of knowing what is going on.

Obviously, it is not the fixation of a general plan that indicates the resolution of ongoing issues, but a continuous reconciliation between the actors involved as the issue unfolds and changes its characteristics and temporality.[275] Issues evolve instantaneously. To implement a timely resolution means not losing touch with the relevant underlying aspects of the issue through abstraction. In the ideal case, there is no need to abort plans because planning, decision making, and action taking are not distinguishable from each other; they are one. For instance, an actor who is showered with a plethora of advice provided by good friends to solve his marriage problems while he is solving a crossword will probably be unable to capture their inputs. Similarly, an actor who has just caused a car accident may say 'Sorry, it all happened too quickly'.

To prevent such conflicts, originating from time requires pre-conditioning or even pre-control.[276] The creation of agreements that anticipate issues, concerns, and solutions – i.e. planning – derives from the feasibility of intended action instead of a purported time-scale for achieving

---

[273] Beer, S.: (Dispute); Beer, S.: Brain of the firm, Chichester, 1981

[274] Beer, S.: (Dispute)

[275] The "process is what is important and not the plan; and what actually happens is the continuing spin-off of this process.", in Beer, S.: (Dispute), p. 151; "But planning ought to be a continuous process whereby things are done now – explicitly resources are committed – so that the future may be different", in Beer, S.: (Diagnosing), p. 40

[276] Beer, S.: (Heart)

results. Thus, planning is the creation of a shared °system° notion that pre-conditions actors adequately for future situations in °system° implementation.[277] Fruitful interaction depends on actors talking about the same issue. The processes and sequences conducted in interaction codetermine whether actors can adequately address an issue involving all relevant aspects to derive a sound solution in the light of the °system° notion. To design explicitly °system° processes and sequences in interaction is especially valuable when multiple actors are involved in treating a °system° issue. Admittedly, any reconciliation is always bound to the time frame, the feasibility, or the solvability of the issue.

3.3.3 Shapes of representation

Between the participants of interaction, further constraints apply which may hamper actors in finding solutions. This is due to analogue and digital appearances of representations provoking complications in interpretation.[278] In the following, tacit and explicit forms of representation will be characterised with reference to their channel capacity.

3.3.3.1 Tacit representations

The creation and exposition of representations occur either instantaneously, in moment-to-moment, unconscious formulation, or in a subsequent process of deliberative, conscious formation.[279] Instantaneous formulation creates tacit representations which mainly consist of analogue signs. Characteristically, analogue signs bear a likeness[280] to what they express, i.e. distinctions are represented through analogies with non-verbal signals such as scream, gesture, mimic, body- or eye-movements, and vocal signals such as accents, pauses and intonation.

---

[277] Beer, S.: (Dispute)

[278] Fourth communicative axiom: "Human beings communicate both digitally and analogically", in Watzlawick, P., Beavin, J. H., and Jackson, D. D.: (Pragmatics of Human Communication)

[279] Pragmatics is the linguistic discipline analysing the capacity of face-to-face settings in interaction. Watzlawick, Beavin, and Jackson claim general validity for the five communicative axioms which they derived from their observations of distorted communication. The communicative axioms were derived from their therapeutical practice. Watzlawick, P., Beavin, J. H., and Jackson, D. D.: (Pragmatics of Human Communication)

[280] Griffin, E.: (Communication Theory)

For a large proportion of intents and claims there are simply no representative correlates (signals) for articulation[281]; they are neither introspectable nor verbally articulable.[282] Tacit or implicit representations refer directly to actors' unconsciously emerging images and the actions they take. Tacit representations point to habits and cultures that the displaying actors themselves rarely recognise: *"We know more than we can tell."* [283] They reflect individual experiences, personal beliefs, practises, intentions, emotions, etc. Tacit representations evolve from actors' ongoing activities; they are inherently grounded in action. For instance, actors are usually unable to explain the grammatical or logical rules or social conventions they permanently apply.[284] An actor does not know how to ride a bike or swim because he reads a textbook, but only through personal experimentation, by observing others or being guided by an instructor. The whisper game provides a good example of how actors are limited to capturing, memorising, and conveying word-of-mouth messages.[285] Subject matter experts and key knowledge holders may not be aware of how – hence, unable – to articulate, communicate, and describe what they know. Therefore, tacit knowledge refers to those individual actor claims that are referred to as know-how. Hence, tacit representations can be broadly interpreted as they cannot specify, but only point to the underlying distinctions. They are generally difficult to identify,

---

[281] Leonard, D. and Sensiper, S.: The role of tacit knowledge in group innovation, California Management Review, Spring (electronic), Berkeley, 1998

[282] Wittgenstein's Tractatus says that one shall rather be silent on any general issues that one cannot express explicitly ("6.522 There are, indeed, things that cannot be put into words. They make themselves manifest. They are what is mystical. 7 What we cannot speak about we must pass over in silence."), in Wittgenstein, L.: Tractatus Logico-Philosophicus Philosophische Untersuchungen, Frankfurt / M., 1988

[283] Polanyi, M.: The tacit dimension, Garden City, N.Y., 1967

[284] Pylsyshyn, Z.: The imagery debate: Analogue media versus tacit knowledge, in: Collins, A. and Smith, E., Readings in Cognitive Science: A perspective from Psychology and Artificial Intelligence, San Mateo California, 1981

[285] Whisper game: as many actors as possible line up so that they can whisper into their immediate neighbour's ear but not be heard by any other actor. The player at the 'beginning' of the line thinks of a phrase and whispers it as quietly as possible to her/ his neighbour. The neighbour then passes on the message to the next player to the best of her/ his ability, and so on until it reaches the player at the 'end' of the line, who calls out the message she/ he has received. Usually, the final message bears little or no resemblance to the original, due to the cumulative effect of mistakes along the line.

locate, quantify, map, or evaluate. Indeed, some portion of the shared back-grounds evolves from an unconscious tacit origin and becomes codified or articulated over time[286] as actors consciously accept, agree, or submit to the conventions, rules, or laws implied. Nevertheless, only tacit representations can capture nameless aspects of a situation, e.g. "how something is said" [287] and express the implicit, underlying aspects that are required to address relationship issues.[288]

As a consequence of their broadness and lack of specificity, tacit rep-resentations cannot be easily grasped by other actors.[289] To enable actors to grasp tacit representations, channels have to be structured to allow actors to capture the understanding of the underlying contexts. This will require high channel capacity, e.g. through recapitulation, revision, coach-ing, etc.

---

[286] Busch, P. and Dampney, C.: Tacit Knowledge Acquisition and Processing within the Computing Domain: An Exploratory Study, 2000, Anchorage

[287] Third communicative axiom: "Communication has a content and a relation-ship aspect.", in Watzlawick, P., Beavin, J. H., and Jackson, D. D.: (Pragmatics of Human Communication); Griffin, E.: (Communication Theory); Watzla-wick refers to the relational aspect of interaction as "meta-communication". It is communication about communication. The relationship aspect refers to how actors see themselves, how they see others and how they see others see-ing themselves. Schulz von Thun further differentiates the relationship-aspect into appeal, self-revelation, and relationship. All aspects of a message may be part of both analogue and digital representations. Here, it is not fol-lowed the position of Watzlawick, who suggested with his distinction of con-tent and relationship aspects that the latter classifies the former and is there-fore a meta-communication. Rather, it is suggested, that there may be meta-representations on both sides, respectively that it does not make sense to dis-tinguish different aspect for prioritising one over the other. Watzlawick, P., Weakland, J. H., and Fisch, R.: Changing a system. Change, New York, 1974; For a more differentiated perspective on the relationship aspect see Schulz von Thun, F.: (Miteinander Reden I)

[288] Irony for instance is a form of expression that depends on the recipient recog-nising through tacit representations that things are not what they are said to be or what they seem. Tacit representations conceal or contradict the explicit rep-resentations exposed at the same time.

[289] Espejo refers to tacit representations as the operational domain and explicit representations as informational domain. Espejo, R.: Giving Requisite Variety to Strategic and Implementation Processes: Theory and Practice, http://bprc. warwick.ac.uk/LSEraul.html

3.3.3.2 Explicit representations

As soon as actors switch into a reflective mood, detaching themselves from the moment, they distance themselves from their moment-to-moment awareness, percepts, and feelings, and move into the domain of thought, consciously confronting, evaluating, and reflecting on their intentions and contexts. In such a reflective mood, actors think, contemplate, and deliberate about their own backgrounds. Explicit thought enables them to make sense of their ongoing issues by interlinking and prioritising aspects purposefully. Representations deriving from reflective thought are referred to here as explicit.[290] They are cognitive references not yet grounded in action. These are manifested in a descriptive form that primarily contains digital signs such as in script, diagram, graph, recording, etc. In contrast, digital representations expose conventionalised signs that follow a syntax that names them.[291] Digital signals are the primary source of explicit representation.

With explicit representations, actors can relate and reconcile their conscious models and explanations with their ongoing percepts of the world and use them in interaction and thus improve the coherence of their own °system° reconciliations, thoughts, explanations, and rationales.[292] Making representations explicit creates a shared reference between actors, which can continuously be synchronised until it approximates their images. Thus, actors are enabled to share anticipated abstractions of upcoming situations and issues. These can be used to assess actors' backgrounds and to increase

---

[290] Espejo distinguishes the 'operational and informational domains' of tacit, respectively explicit representations. Espejo, R.: Giving Requisite Variety to Strategic and Implementation Processes: Theory and Practice, http://bprc.warwick.ac.uk/LSEraul.html

[291] Griffin, E.: (Communication Theory)

[292] "By detaching ourselves temporarily from the action of the moment and becoming an observer, we abstract ourselves from the rest of the world of experience – the operational domain in which we constitute our realities – and move into the informational domain of ideas and mental constructs. The habit of observation is critical for developing not only self-awareness but also awareness of the actions of other people. Observation enables us to create in our minds mental models about situations. […] It is in conversational processes that people ground their ideas and relate their realities. Individual realities are bridged by constructs; i.e. shared mental models, created from grounding experiences on a shared model.", in Espejo, R., Schuhmann, W., Schwaninger, M., and Bilello, U.: (Transformation and Learning), p. 80

their action potential, i.e. their variety, by documenting relevant distinctions in support of their action. They even allow actors to depict complex interrelations of attributes and to explore different potential impacts of interaction by capturing, describing modelling and simulating complex situations.[293] Making explicit representation is a means to amplify the number of distinctions that can be referred to and reconciled. They can be stored, ordered, structured, scripted, etc. The main use of explicit representations is to share, record, broadcast, and duplicate them. Further, they are especially adequate for anticipating issues, concerns, and solutions by using logical levels of representation, thus helping actors to create shared backgrounds on future situations and issues.

For instance, writing down notes on paper makes the distinctions entailed available for later use. Examples are books, mathematical formulas, manuals, multimedia, etc. Even a work of art can be seen as form of explicit representation in which an actor's skills, motives, and knowledge are externalised.

Therefore, it is clear that the use of explicit representations is also static, since they must be assembled and therefore cannot capture the much more complex reality always immanent in moment-to-moment interpersonal interactions.[294] They can address specific topics and support the actors' intentionality and contextuality, e.g. to create a common language among participants by making apparent distinctions so far not recognised or shared by them. But explicit representations cannot depict the complete true aspects of any issue, simply because they are static, which means they inherently entail the problem of sequencing mentioned above.

Actors may use explicit representations to settle on their agreements and resolutions such as in contracts, etc. Whether representations are laid down in a written form is of secondary importance. The more actors are involved

---

[293] However, only if actors share a common background, explicit representations can be used as if they would point to an external reality; it is only then that the dictum "the map is not the territory" makes sense. For as long as the process is focused on creating a common background, such as by reconciling a °system° boundary the "map is the territory" of interaction. Harnden, R.: (Outside and then)

[294] Understanding the centrality of tacit representations and the largely supportive role of explicit representations is a crucial insight for designing and managing interactions for °systems°; Espejo, R.: Giving Requisite Variety to Strategic and Implementation Processes: Theory and Practice, http://bprc.warwick.ac.uk/LSEraul.html

and the more complex and abstract the issue, the larger the necessity is to make representation explicit and accessible to all actors involved. Representations should be made explicit whenever the issue and its related aspects, resolutions, concerns, etc. supersede the individual actor's capacity to capture the message. Making explicit representations supports actors in creating and sharing references of their common °system° issues. Indeed, it may mislead actors to believe that they have captured and resolved the issue, because what they have made explicit seems to be complete, elaborate, sophisticated, well thought-through, whereas the only thing they have reached is mutual agreement upon how they intend to view the issue. The potency of explicit representations does not lie in the formulation and fixation of a finalised, true resolution to an issue but in the creation of agreements that are considered permanently valid throughout the implementation of a °system° notion. Ultimately, the value of reconciling explicit representations manifests itself in actors being able to repeatedly reference and thus homogenise their understanding of the distinctions considered valid and relevant.[295] Nevertheless, by transforming their unfolding images into explicit derivates, they are captured, packaged and stored. This implies that actual thoughts, feelings and experiences can be revised – just as they once were – at another time. Thus, creating explicit representations stops time in its tracks and transforms life experience (the *now*) into patterns of data and symbols. However, while explicit representations can be captured, stored, accessed and processed, the actors tacit experiences underpinning it – and making sense of it – cannot.[296]

Making representations explicit proves adequate, the larger the number of actors, roles involved and the more complex the issues to be addressed in a social °system° notion. Without a sufficiently precise verbal or written representation, actors will often not be able to share their thoughts. Keeping records of the documents is an important and necessary aid in order to ensure that it is noticed by other actors and changes can be retraced later on.[297]

Depending on the setting of interaction, analogue or digital signals are important. Both modalities appear in face-to-face settings. Both are com-

---

[295] Gälweiler, Aloys: (Corporate Strategy)

[296] However, based on the *Weltanschauung* described, with its concept of autopoietic actors, explicit representations are also subject to re-interpretation, that is, there is no single way to construct meaning. The interpretation of a representation cannot be fixed or indicated as correct beyond the moment of mutual agreement between actors.

[297] Gälweiler, Aloys: (Corporate Strategy)

plementary; none can replace the other without a significant loss of content. Any translation from digital to analogue signals and vice versa bears the danger of a substantial loss of information. Any pure linguistic (and thus digital) debate by actors on relationship topics is extremely difficult because analogue phenomena (such as feelings, moods) have to be made explicit and expressed digitally.

Thus, it can be said that representations can never comprehensively reflect messages. While digital representation lacks the adequate semantics in the field of relationships, analogue interaction possesses semantics but misses an adequate syntax for the unambiguous expression of relationship issues. As referred to above (in footnote 287), Watzlawick distinguishes content and relationship aspects of representations. Content is "what" is actually said, while relationship refers to "how" it is said.[298] The following figure lists the attributes of tacit and explicit representations:

Table 9. Attributes of tacit and explicit representations

Tacit Representation	Explicit Representation
analogue modality	digital modality
highly dependent on individuals	low dependence on the individual, open to social reconciliation
have to be re-created	easy to document, duplicate
mainly face-to-face mainly	easy to broadcast
strong in expressing relationship aspects	strong in content transmission

Tacit and explicit representations serve different informative needs in interaction. The use of tacit or explicit modes of representation strongly determines the channel capacity provided in interaction. Tacit representations as dynamic, revolving expressions of analogue signals continuously being re-created enable actors to create trust, faith, certainty, confidence, hope,

---

[298] Third communicative axiom: "Communication has a content and a relationship aspect.", in Watzlawick, P., Beavin, J. H., and Jackson, D. D.: (Pragmatics of Human Communication); Griffin, E.: (Communication Theory); for a different view that does not interpret tacit representations as exlusively 'meta' in relation to explicit representations see chapter on logical levels in Bandler, R.: (Structure of magic II)

reliance, and to identify their opposites. To the contrary, explicit representations as static, socially agreed expressions of largely digital signals, are easy to duplicate and broadcast, are adequate for sharing and recording aspects, concerns, and resolutions of highly complex issues in a specific and precise way. Thus, they are predestined for establishing formalised structures.

3.3.4 Physical settings

Channel capacity also depends on actor settings, i.e. in which physical setting actors encounter each other. Multiple settings are possible such as face-to-face, teacher-pupil, round-table, etc. Face-to-face settings are different from indirect or distant multiple-actor settings, as all actors who attend to a situation face to face cannot but contribute in presence to others, enabling a more differentiated interpretation in interaction. Even if they are not actually speaking, or perhaps not doing anything, they still contribute their physical presence: some facial expressions, a way of sitting, being silent in general.[299] In face-to-face settings, any behaviour contributes to interaction in some way and influences the counterpart, who cannot but react in some manner. The addressed actor may misinterpret this non-intentional behaviour. Further, the characteristics of the physical location may influence channel capacity. Actors ought to choose a location that serves the purpose of reconciliation. Obviously, it should be quiet. If major differences are likely to erupt between actors, the location ought to be neutral territory. Uncomfortable seating or bad lighting interfere with people's ability to coordinate tasks at hand. Rows of seats set up in 'theatre style' do not allow for eye contact and therefore discourage collaborative interaction. A room filled with numerous small tables hampers group interaction and invites actors with similar viewpoints and interests to cluster.[300] Other external factors might be relevant. Thus, parameters such as the physical distance between actors, eye-to-eye contact, position of seating, lighting, meeting constellation, and grouping, etc. co-determine channel capacity of interaction. Thus, the physical setting provides an interactional structure, the frame within which the actors involved may move:

---

[299] First communicative axiom: "One cannot not communicate.", in Watzlawick, P., Beavin, J. H., and Jackson, D. D.: (Pragmatics of Human Communication)

[300] Susskind, L., McKearnan, S., and Thomas-Larmer, J.: The Consensus Building Handbook, 1999

*"The Rules of the Game do not inhibit players once they agree
to go on the field; the design of a cathedral, and decorous conduct inside it, do not set limits to praise and prayer."*[301]

3.3.5 Channel capacity

Channels set the stage for interaction by defining relationships, tasks and
responsibilities, actor constellations, sequences, and both, forms of representation and physical settings. They define what roles actors can take, set limits on their behaviour and on how they treat each other. Channels define the
space within which changes and transformations can be applied. Further,
attenuating and amplifying methods may be embedded in channels. With a
channel, the parameters indicating methods can be transmitted.[302] The establishment of a channel refers to the proceedings and sequences of interaction
determining who is involved, which topics are in focus, what is shared,
made accessible at what time, and in which form.[303] Any formal or informal
agreement actors draw on in a concerted process of interaction with respect
to the notion of a social °system° refers to a channel being established.
Channels are defined in conventions describing specific arrangements and
proceedings to be followed in interaction, e.g.

1. the actors to involve, their interdependency as manifested in roles,
   ranks, influence;

2. the constellation of actors among each other, their physical locations
   towards each other;

3. the topics to address, as settled in agendas, typical issues;

4. the methods, instruments and behaviours to apply, e.g. etiquettes,
   formalisations, principles, informal rules, or customs;

5. the sequences or processes defining which steps are to be taken at
   what time.

Generally, for the channels to be adequate to address a specific °system°
issue they must convey sufficient capacity for a little redundancy to ade-

---

[301] Beer, S.: (Dispute)

[302] Beer, S.: (Heart)

[303] Ibid.

quately communicate a certain message.[304] To attend to a °system° issue
with requisite variety, the relationships, settings, sequences, and modes of
representation must correspond to the coherence prevailing in actors background in regard to the °system° notion aspired to. In the case of low coherence (e.g. differences in the underlying *Weltanschauung*, attitudes, and
opinions), channels must allow actors to attend to a large number of issues
(and huge varieties) to enable participative reconciliation, or alternatively,
the structures must restrict actor's autonomy. For instance, high capacity
channels open up actors thinking about a °system° issue through brainstorm-
ing, free discussions, or mediations. Such channels are loosely formalised
and allow actors to contribute a diversity of individual perspectives towards
their issues. On the other hand, low capacity channels, such as agenda discussions or surveys, predefine certain topics or processes of reconciliation
and force actors to follow these conventions in interaction. Such channels
can provide requisite variety only in settings with higher levels of coherence in °system° notions (i.e. °system° intentionality and contextuality)
which do not face major challenges from their environment.[305] Applied in
settings with low intentionality or contextuality, these channels fail to provide for requisite variety.

Interaction as a means to balance actor variety inherently relies on
channels to allow actors to share adequate messages for the creation and
exchange of adequate representations. As a central point, the channels applied must provide the requisite capacity to capture and process the distinctions that enable actors to address their issues.[306] Ultimately, channel capacity depends on the extent to which relevant viewpoints are integrated in
the light of the °system° notion and competent actors can contribute adequately to attend to °system° issues. To do so, the channel capacity of interaction depends primarily to what extent

---

[304] The "channels must convey more than the variety of the schedules and reports
concerned, to allow for a little redundancy. Without a little redundancy (day
plus date, machine number plus name, figures plus words, and so on) ambigui-
ties will appear (due to omissions, bad writing, mistakes, and so on) that cannot be resolved.", Beer, S.: (Diagnosing)

[305] Structural restrictions, role-based instructions, and algedonic signals are examples of interactions which do provide leeway in variety generation for actors,
but constrain and steer in a certain direction at the same time. See Beer, S.:
Decision and Control – The Meaning of Operational Research and Management Cybernetics, London, 1966

[306] Beer, S.: (Heart)

1. the relationships established between actors, i.e. their roles, tasks, assignments, etc., allow them to adequately attend to current °system° issues and to support the changes required;

2. actor constellations involve the contributions and viewpoints relevant to attending to the topic in the light of the °system° notion;

3. the processes and sequences performed ensure that actors are involved according to different skills, knowledge, competencies, abilities, etc. and can make their contributions in due time;

4. explicit representations are used to create shared references that can be recorded and broadcasted to facilitate actors' mutual understanding of the issue and the reconciliation of its solution;

5. tacit representations are exposed to maintain trust, certainty, confidence, credence, faith, hope, reliance in their relationships, especially in regard to their °system° agreements.

3.4 Transduction capacity

Depending on their lifeworlds and contexts, actors use different languages and apply different rationalities when creating their images. Understanding is essential to know what the other is talking about. In interaction, actors cannot directly re-cognise the message sent to them and conclude according to the consequences that are induced (the states), because it is not tangible to them as due to their autopoiesis.[307] Human perception, as it has been introduced above, has to carry out transduction to make assessable the information exposed in representation.[308] When confronted with a message exposed in representation, the actor translates the phenomena entailed into the distinctions they point to with respect to the known linguistic conventions (characters, figures, signs, symbols, motions). This process of translation is referred to here as transduction. It is limited to the recognition of the distinctions that are expressed in representation. In contrast, active interpretation means applying changes, transforming the recognised distinctions through generalisation, deletion, and distortion. Interpretation takes place after that recognition of the distinctions. Interpretation and transduc-

---

[307] Ibid.

[308] Original definition: a „transducer [is] a machine, a device, protocol, or rule by which information is changed to an appropriate form and introduced into a system", in Beer, S.: (Brain)

tion can be distinguished as different logical processes though the difference between the two may not always be clear.[309] Regarding transduction, outward and inward transduction can be distinguished. Creating external representations is an outward transduction which translates a message into a representation displayed in a medium. On the other hand, perceiving representations refers to an opposite transduction, namely translating phenomena entailed in representation into distinctions that stimulate image creation. Transduction capacity of interaction manifests itself in the quality of the translation performed between actors' languages and rationalities.[310] In the process, the content of the original messages has to be maintained, so that the induced variety is neither amplified nor attenuated:[311]

The creation and reception of messages through representations underlies transduction, i.e. a process of making them compatible with the language and rationality of the recipient. Transduction must be capable of performing this translation without any loss or falsification of the content and the induced variety.[312]

The challenge of transduction may be illustrated with a senior managing actor providing report to the executive board of a large organisation.[313] He faces the challenge of translating his statements on the issues in his responsibility into a language which the board members can grasp. In doing so he should consider the underlying rationality of the board members with respect to the organisation. This will compel him to build a bridge between logical abstractions, e.g. by abstracting and specifying the technical terms and concepts that he uses from his detailed knowledge so as to be comprehensible to the board audience. Further, he will need to put special emphasis on those points which are of primary importance with respect to the role of the board members. Overall, he will have to pay the

---

[309] Prejudices for instance are a consequence of poor interpretation, but not usually of deficient recognition.

[310] Actors would "probably be more effective in establishing knowledge and changing behaviour in organisations, if the languages of the field were more precise, enabling ideas to be expressed with greater clarity and hence helping to stimulate better debate.", in Checkland, P.: (Information Systems)

[311] Beer, S.: (Heart)

[312] Derived from Beer's third organisational principle, original text: "Whenever the information carried on a channel capable of distinguishing a given variety crosses a boundary, it undergoes transduction; the variety of the transducer must be at least equivalent to the variety of the channel.", in Beer, S.: (Diagnosing); Beer, S.: (Heart)

[313] Compare with the example given by Beer, S.: (Heart)

utmost attention in order not to miss any relevant apects of the °system° issues he tackles.[314] To make sure that his messages are understood (i.e. transduced correctly), active rephrasing is required from the side of the board members.[315] As this example shows, three transduction boundaries can be distinguished as follows:

1. °System° boundaries – separated through different notions of °systems°;

2. Logical boundaries – separated through different logical types of representation;

3. Actors' boundaries, separated through different expertise, languages, knowledge, lifeworlds.

Each of the three transduction boundaries will be elaborated below.

3.4.1   °System° boundaries

Interpretation creates meaning only by reference to underlying intents and claims. As soon as refernence to them is made in the light of the notion of a °system°, implicit or explicit boundary judgements evolve. They constitute the rationales actors apply in the light of the °system°. Boundary judgements ground messages, statements, or propositions which would otherwise be arbitrary. Table 2 indicates the twelve major boundary judgements to be settled with any °system° notion.

Schedler, for instance, elaborates the different rationales adopted by actors in political-administrative °system° notions.[316] Table 10 states a set of typical boundary judgements °community° actors adopted to govern and manage their °community° issues: politicians, administrators, and citizens. The table shows that their dominating rationales are as different as can be: political actors are primarily engaged with winning and holding control over citizens. They usually adopt a °community° notion that focuses on the citizens with a right to vote, on the interests of individuals, and on the competition with others for power and leadership in political roles. Diametrically opposed, administrative actors lead and direct their °community° through

---

[314] This means that, in fact, one requires profound knowledge of the 'hobby horses' and 'hidden agendas' of the relevant actors involved in °system° implementation in order to understand them and support change.

[315] Beer, S.: (Diagnosing)

[316] Schedler, K. and Proeller, I.: (New Public Management); Brühlmeier, D., Haldemann, T., Mastronardi, P., and Schedler, K.: (Political planning)

the deployment and manipulation of financial, human, material, or intellectual resources. Their typical notion of °community° is a demand-and-supply-driven market of services with citizens as clients. They primarily engage in the implementation of specific services and activities in order to achieve the goals defined by politicians. Administrative actors do not depend directly on public opinion or vote. This could be further continued, but the differences in the underlying °system° notions should make obvious why actors interpret differently. The criteria inherent in boundary judgements trigger their interpretations concerning whatever °community° issues evolve. It is obvious that whatever role or expertise an actor adopts or is assigned to, and whatever he articulates, draws on a partial, selected, more or less well-considered and particular °system° boundary. Consequently, the actors cannot themselves justify their expressed statements. With respect to the boundaries of °systems° notions, there are between actors no natural, innate advantages of competence, knowledge, expertise, or power.[317]

To enable actors to find adequate resolutions to their °system° issues, actors must make explicit the underlying normative judgements.[318] To maintain the content exposed in representation and thus to induce requisite variety in interaction, structure must be capable of translating between different notions of °systems° and thus of providing requisite transduction capacity. Instead of disputing from different, unreflected, or unrecognised perspectives, different notions of °systems° should be uncovered and translated. Exposing statements of concern, resolutions, and declarations and stressing their rationality are tenable only if the underlying °system° notion with its boundary is made explicit.[319] The transduction of boundary judgements on °system° issues enables actors to join in a dialogue in which they recognise each others' rationality and reconcile the conditions for achieving a consensus in regard to the 'rightness' of the underlying normative content.[320] Therefore, outgoing transducers must articulate the originator's °system° notion with its underlying boundary judgements.[321] Only at that point are incoming transducers of the recipient capable of appreciating the originator's reference °system° and enabled to recognise the differences in

---

[317] Ulrich, W.: (Reflective Practice)

[318] Ulrich, W.: (Critical heuristics social systems)

[319] Ulrich, W.: (Quest for Competence)

[320] Ulrich, W.: (Critical heuristics social systems)

[321] Therefore the backgrounds constituting the boundary of a shared °system° notion must be defined precisely and clearly, thus enabling the derivation of valuable insights in other areas also. Beer, S.: (Provenance)

Table 10. Typical boundary judgements of key °community° actors

		Citizens (affected)	Politicians (involved)	Administrators (involved)
1	**Client** Who is the client?	human actors living in °community°	citizen with a right to vote, interest groups, individuals	market and clients demanding services, private sponsors
2	**Purpose** What is the purpose?	well-being in all aspects of life, viability, sustainability, solving problems	winning and holding control over citizens, and interest groups	organise and achieve legitimacy, implement goals
3	**Measure of improvement** What is the measure of improvement?	individual welfare, quality and standard of life, °community° services	gaining influence, election results	legitimacy, goal achievement, effectiveness, efficiency
4	**Decision-Maker** Who is the decision-maker?	mayor, community council, citizens deciding upon who represents them	mayor, parish, and community council	executive administrators executing policies delivered by mayor, parish, and community council
5	**Resources** What resources are controlled by the decision-maker?	material, human, financial resources, taxes	material, financial resources, taxes with respect to strategic allocation	material, human, financial resources, taxes with respect to operative optimisation
6	**Decision Environment** What conditions lie outside the decision-makers' control?	social situation of citizens, real income levels, overall standard of living, employment opportunities, social solidarity, crime, natural disasters, guidelines and directives from higher levels such as the state		
7	**Professional** Who is considered a professional?	actors with an appropriate reputation	experts belonging to or in line with the interests of the political party	experts belonging to or supporting the interests of the administration
8	**Expertise** What expertise is consulted?	internal knowledge, external consultants		
9	**Guarantor of Success** What or who is assumed to be a guarantor of success?	democratic interplay of politicians, administrators, media referring to independent consultants where adequate	publicity, public interest, all measures positively affecting the public spirit and affection	experience and intuition of those involved, political support, consensus among experts, involvement of citizens
10	**Witness** Who is witness to the interests of those affected but not involved?	political opposition, economic, local unions, interest groups, mass media, scientists		
11	**Emancipation** What secures the emancipation of those affected from the premises and promises of those involved?	re-election every turn, judiciary, possibilities for petitions, access to media, etc.		
12	**Worldview** What worldview is determining?	democracy is the best known form of ensuring that different ideas of improvement are considered.		

their opinions and standpoints to gain understanding and trust. For the transduction of the message it is secondary whether actors thereby agree on a common reference °system° as long as the established transducers enable them to appreciate one another's different rationalities.[322]

As a consequence, the separation of function – as useful it is for the division of labour – is replaced by critical interaction regarding boundary issues. It is only through critical interaction based on explicit boundary judgements that the relevant concerns become apparent and a rational discourse on °system° issues is enabled. In regard to their boundary aspects, all °system° issues are subject to an informed debate on the underlying presuppositions in which all of the actors involved and affected participate.[323]

Transduction between °system° boundaries is thus the fundamental prerequisite for productive interactions on all logical levels. Concerning boundary issues, relying on conventional monological justification, on deduction and empirical corroboration, or falsification is insufficient. This becomes clear when different opinions and behaviours arise in a situation. In such a case, messages must point to the underlying boundary judgements and make them explicit.

The Rationalities Model (RM) as depicted in Figure 28[324] illustrates the reconciliation required between politicians and managing administrators. Due to their different °system° roles, elected politicians and opposition members engage in wording policies, planning goals, measuring, describing, and evaluating effects for creating policies. In contrast, administrative managers engage in specifying goals, implementing and executing them as well as measuring and reporting goal-attainment and performance.

Obviously, politicians and administrative managers have to address and settle all °system° issues between specifying goals and reporting upon the effects that have been chosen. This is a consequence of the general rules and roles that have been assigned historically in representative democracy. It follows that they must be able to settle these intermediate issues and translate between the °system° notions. Transduction of °system° boundaries refers to the capacity of the established structures to clarify °system° boundaries. It identifies °system° issues and makes clear why the concerns, solutions and justifications articulated are seen as tenable in the light of the °system° notion. Only based on an adequate understanding of °system°

---

[322] Ulrich, W.: (Reflective Practice)

[323] Ulrich, W.: Critical Heuristics of Social Planning: A New Approach to Practical Philosophy, Bern, 1983; Jackson, M. C.: (Managerial significance)

[324] As depicted in: Schedler, K. and Proeller, I.: (New Public Management)

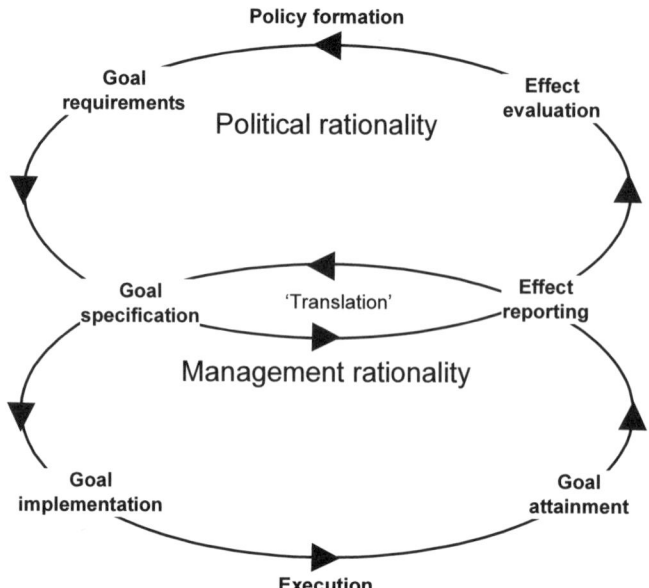

Figure 28. Rationalities model (RM)

boundaries can interaction be conducted as a rational discourse which guarantees that practical needs are translated adequately into technical questions and likewise technical answers into practical decisions.[325]

3.4.2   Logical boundaries

Along with the abstractness of the content exposed in representation, the variety addressed through it increases by orders of magnitude. The more abstract a message, the more interpretations will usually arise from different actor contexts. Figure 29 depicts the transductions required between logical levels of representation (LLR) in interaction. It shows four logical spheres, each of which produces expressions on a different logical type of abstraction. Logical types of representation express different abstractions of content, intents and claims, or a tactical, operative, strategic, and normative dimension. Each level employs a different logic, language, emphasis, and level of detail and serves to address specific issues (i.e. a characteristic variety) evolving in °system° implementation.[326] Each lower logical level is en-

---

[325]   Ulrich, W.: (Critcal systems heuristics)

[326]   Ben-Eli, M. U.: Strategic planning and management reorganization at an academic medical center: use of the VSM in guiding diagnosis and design, 1989

tailed in its superior. Representations of the different logical levels cannot be compared at all; ultimate consistency can be achieved only within, not between, these levels.[327] Circular processes broadly refer to the translation of expressions required between logical levels. By treating perceived phenomena of situations with respect to the adequate logical type, requisite variety can be articulated. The specific set and type of interactions required with respect to the viability of the °system° notion is depicted in chapter 4.

Representations must adequately reflect the variety of the °system° issue to be addressed. Besides a shared °system° notion, this requires actors to reference the adequate logical level the issue expresses. The degree to which °system° variety is expressed increases exponentially with each level. Logical types contain proliferating variety through cascading.[328] 'Images' expressed as goals, for instance, are pre-conditions for actors in social °systems° that can be defined on all levels in their normative, strategic, operative and tactical forms. When subsumed in a logical tree, the goals of the superordinate level pre-condition those on subordinate level issues, while at the same time these constrain subordinated goals. In this way, it is possible to configure representations expressing any amount of variety required (Figure 29).

Higher order °system° concerns such as calmness, peace, quality of life or justice have to be translated into lower order correlates which specify how these notions are to be understood and implemented, e.g. by defining what concrete set of phenomena counts as calmness, what measures should be taken to avoid noise, etc. The next lower level will further detail what measures can actually be taken due to existing resources, capabilities, etc. Finally, actors determine what is actually done based upon the claims that have been reconciled along this logical ladder. As can be seen, each level contributes further aspects and the complexity addressed, i.e. the number of states addressed, increases by orders of magnitude.

Let us imagine a °community° of actors, consisting of retirees and pensioners who have commonly agreed to maintain 'a quiet community'. This notion has been specified essentially with attenuating compromises such as 'to listen to music only at low volume after ten o'clock', 'no kids outside around midday' or 'not to mow the lawn on Sundays'. Actors are content, as they experience every day that their individual notions of peace and quiet are met, because they are shared and everyone complies with them. Obviously, these actors comply willingly in regard to keep 'peace and quiet'.

---

[327] Schwaninger, M.: (Framework Intelligent Organisations)

[328] Beer, S.: (Heart); Cascading refers to variety engineering through the creation of management levels and divisions, which contain proliferating variety.

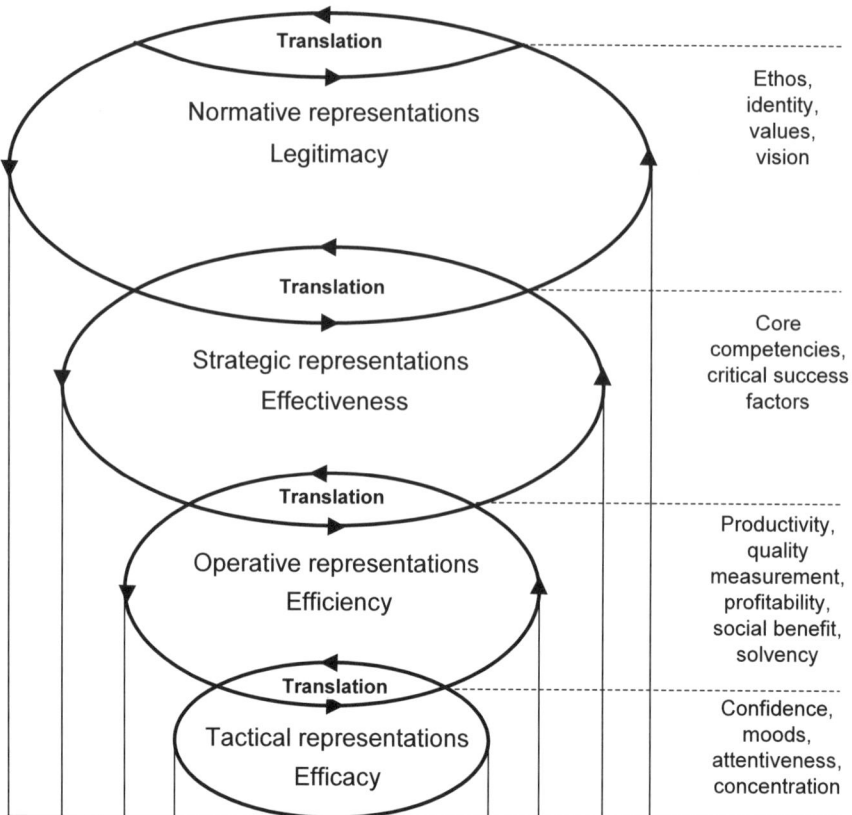

Figure 29. Logical levels of representation and their translation

Now, let us imagine some new inhabitants in the °community°, a family with three children. Obviously, telling these new people that 'this is a quiet community' will not be enough to induce the desired change. What those family members perceive as 'quiet' may well be different to the pensioners' notion. The new family will have to be informed by way of a higher-level transduction that explains what is considered as quiet in this °community°, e.g. through courteous requests, reminders, asking for cooperation. Thus, the message that this is 'a quiet and peaceful community' is made understandable to the new family. After a while, when the family has become accustomed to the pensioners, a much lower-level of transduction will suffice for them to get along with each other, as the family members have now grasped more of the °community° culture and learnt how to behave and assert their own interests. Another example is business developers announcing a strategic plan to the employees of a °company°. They will need to illustrate their °company° notion by providing operational examples. In doing so, they enable others to understand their underlying intents and claims. If instead the difference between strategic and operational levels is not recognised and the two levels are mingled, actors are most likely to end up in endless discussions and quarrels without any contribution to the desired improvement of their respective situations.

Thus, transduction of logical levels refers to the capacity of established structures to translate messages between different degrees of abstraction and anticipation. In ongoing interaction, such transduction between logical boundaries is essential, as actors will otherwise be caught in the trap of confusing logical levels with the consequence of not being able to gain the fruit of requisite variety.

3.4.3 Actor boundaries

A central characteristic of actors is that they build their backgrounds on individual histories, experiences, and lifeworlds, and autonomously create their individual intentions and contexts. Different languages, cultures, knowledge, competencies give manifold evidence of that. A primary function of transduction is the translation between actor boundaries. This means distinctions expressed in the phenomena of representation are translated into the language of the recipient. For instance, an actor trying to decrypt a morse code without intimate knowledge of the morse code alphabet will not be able to translate the perceived phenomena into relevant distinctions. By learning a new language, an actor builds up transduction capacity to interact with actors of another lifeworld. A primary school teacher who adapts his language with respect to the pupils' capacity to understand him uses his experience to make them understand what he is teaching. Similarly, a medical doctor chooses a different language when talking to his patients than with his colleagues. And so do any other experts, be they pilots, captains, priests, or managers. Transduction between actor boundaries is a necessary precondition of interaction. Without a minimum of shared commonality in language and concepts, any attempt to mutually influence each other must fail.[329] Thus, transduction of actor boundaries refers to the capacity of interaction to translate messages between individual languages, cultures, knowledge, competencies, etc.

---

[329] In linguistics this is the 'code' which is created (encoded) and deciphered (decoded). Bußmann, H.: Lexikon der Sprachwissenschaft, Stuttgart, 1990; A further example of this is group languages developing between social groups. See also Eco, U.: Semiotik und Philosophie der Sprache, München, 1985

3.4.4 Transduction

For individual actors, it is not always easy to identify whether a failure to grasp requisite variety facing a representation, i.e. a misunderstanding, is due to insufficient transduction or a lack of actor variety for its interpretation. The difference is that it may be either lacking claims (knowledge, experience, etc.) on the side of the recipient and, therefore, a problem of transduction, i.e. the message does not arrive at all. Or alternatively, there may be differing intentions (interests, preferences, wishes, fears, etc.) and consequently a problem of interpretation, i.e. the message arrives correctly at the recipient but is immediately re-interpreted in the light of his intentions and adopted °system° notion.

> *"Consciously to preserve requisite variety in our relationships with other people is helpful to those relationships; to attenuate variety in our perception of another is to degrade his or her humanity".*[330]

Thus, transduction refers to the capacity of interaction to get messages across in a form accessible to the recipient. It consists of activities such as defining, specifying, elucidating, explaining, translating, illustrating, elaborating, etc. Transduction capacity is contingent to what extent

1. different notions of °systems° can be made transparent and reconciled. Actors should adopt a critical tenor and make explicit the boundary judgements underlying their statements. Only in this way can the recipients be enabled to grasp the perspective on the °system° of concern which is aspired to.

2. statements, concerns and solutions can be translated between logical levels. With abstractness increasing, the meaning addressed in representations loses its grounding in the situation of concern. Higher order agreements must be specified and exemplified with respect to their subordinated underpinnings to clarify the exposed message.

---

[330] Beer, S.: (Heart); This is in line with the biblical commandment used by the Swiss writer Max Frisch in connection with his play Andorra: "Du sollst Dir kein Bildnis machen." ('Thou shalt not make unto thee any graven image'). This expresses that rather than making pretentious pronouncements, actors should try to bring critical understanding and open-mindedness to bear on the subjects of their concern. See Frisch, M.: Du sollst Dir kein Bildnis machen, in: Frisch, M., Tagebuch 1946-1949, Frankfurt a.M., 1949

3. disparities and incongruities of individual actor backgrounds, e.g. different knowledge, language, or skills, can be transcended. This is done by translation into the language and diction accessible to the recipient. This may be achieved either through reformulation by the exposing actor or with the help of a third actor's translation.

3.5 Sustainability of control

The success of interaction depends on the three structural capacities enabling the participating actors to perform the changes required:

> *The three capacities established with change / transformation, channel, and transduction capacities applied in interaction 1) to induce relevant changes, 2) to ensure adequate relationships, and 3) to achieve mutual understanding between actors must be provided continuously without hiatus or lags.*[331]

This means that whatever topics, issues or conflicts arise between actors, there ought not be any structural delays or breakdowns in interaction. °System° varieties have to be attuned constantly under requisite change, channel, and transduction capacity if they are to succeed in implementation. This principle thus invents a meta-criterion for structures to be sustainable. To ensure the sustainability of prevailing °system° notions the three structural capacities have to be provided continuously at all times. Incapacitated methods, inadequate role distributions, missing translations, or long response times hamper interaction and endanger the persistence of the °system° notion. Sustainable development relies on the quality of the interactions continuously performed; it depends on the three capacities. It is methodologies or didactics[332] that tell how methods, channels, and transducers can form 'symphony', i.e. how they can be concerted in a way that resolves the

---

[331] Adapted from Stafford Beer's fourth principle of organisation: "The operation of the first three principles must be cyclically maintained through time without hiatus or lags", in Beer, S.: (Heart)

[332] From Greek didaktikos, didaskein, which means to teach; something that is designed or intended to teach; something intended to convey instruction and information as well as pleasure and entertainment. See Merriam-Webster's authors: Online version of Merriam-Webster's Collegiate Dictionary, Encyclopædia Britannica 2005 Ultimate Reference Suite DVD, 2005

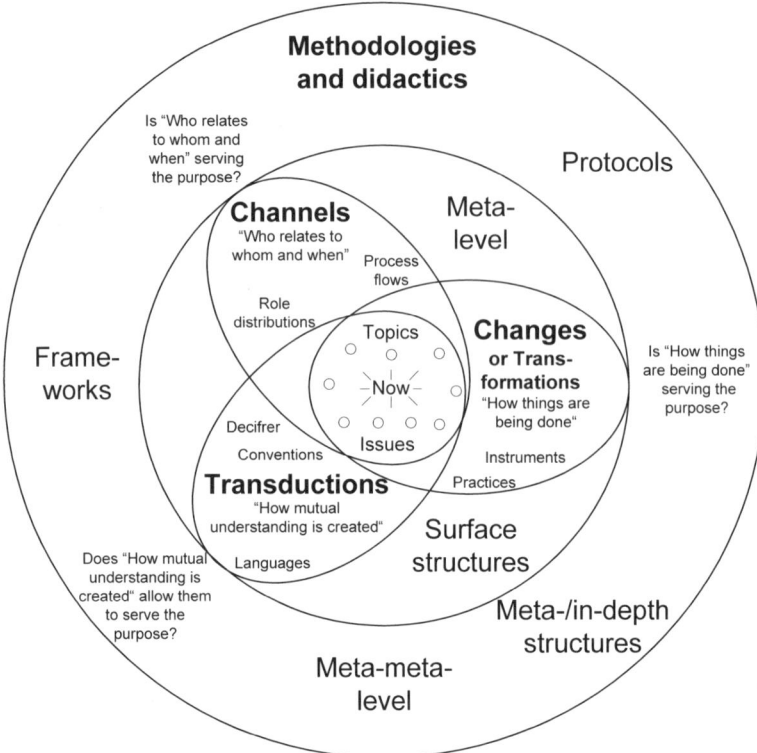

Figure 30. Sustainability as a meta-criterion of structure

ongoing issues on a °system° topic. A good methodology tells how requisite change, channel and transduction capacity can be provided for a certain °system° notion. Thus, methodologies guide interaction and how the pre-conditions for certain topics are to be set, which as a consequence, leads actors to reconcile more adequate, coherent and compatible actor images.

Figure 30 depicts how methodologies integrate the three aspects of structure (i.e. the three organisational principles). The current situation (the *now*) is depicted in the centre circle, the meta-level reflects upon the issues of the current situation ('How are issues being evaluated? How are they being addressed? What methods and instruments apply?'). Further, the meta-meta-level indicates how methods, channels, and transducers interrelate and how they can be captured and defined, who learns what, when, with whom, where, how, whereby, why, and what for.[333]

---

[333] Jank, W. and Meyer, H.: Didaktische Modelle, Berlin, 1991

Protocols[334] are commonly used to specify a methodological frame for interaction for a certain topic, event, organ, meeting, etc. For instance, the informal protocol of a festival theatre may require women and men to wear formal attire and prescribe a certain etiquette, defining the specific 'rules', 'habits', 'customs' actors are to follow throughout the evening. In scientific interactions, protocols are manifested in detailed plans of experiments, treatments, or procedures to be conducted.[335] Thus, protocols accord individual ways of conducting interactions; they are adopted agreements which describe the conventions governing interaction and the type and format of representations that are to be used. The protocol is crucial for productive outcomes of interaction.[336] This can be illustrated with the following example.

Teaching a °school class° depends on all the structures that determine the pre-conditions for the °school class° to be successful. Methodologies of learning aid in choosing methods, designing channels and transducers for facilitating, supporting and stimulating. For instance, when teaching a °school class°, some teachers follow the Montessori teaching methodology. This includes those pre-conditions which give expression to the relationship of the actors participating. How actors relate to each other in interaction does influence interaction quality. A methodology or didactic may therefore put particular emphasis on the organisation of relationships and the ongoing design of adequate protocols for teaching a °school class° (channel capacity). Table 11 summarises structural characteristics of methodologies applied for teaching a °school° class, dispensing justice at °court° and planning in a °company°.

Further, the established structures are strongly conditioned by actors' adopted cultures. Cultures are patterns, i.e. sets of intentions and contexts, shared between a group of actors involved in a °system° notion. They precondition actors just as structures do. A strong culture relieves actors from reconciling every detail by predefining what issues can be solved with

---

[334] Definition "A protocol is a rule which guides how an activity should be performed. Formerly used mainly in the diplomatic and government fields of endeavour to denote unwritten guidelines, by the turn of the twenty first century it had come into wide use in the computer and communications fields.", see Wikipedia contributors: Definition of 'protocol', Wikipedia, The Free Encyclopedia, 2004

[335] For definitions of synonyms see Merriam-Webster's authors: (Britannica)

[336] "Thereafter, the design of the meeting – agenda, protocol, rubrics – all variety reducers – is crucial to a productive outcome.", in Beer, S.: (Diagnosing), p. 31

Table 11. Structural aspects of exemplary °system° notions

	Teaching a °school° class	Dispensing justice at °court°	Planning in a °company°
Involved actors (elements)	School children, teacher, fathers, mothers, etc.	Judge, lawyers, prosecutor, accused, witnesses, public attendance, security, etc.	Chief executive office, head of strategic controlling, profit centre persons responsible, head of accounting, etc.
Change / transformation capacity	To teach, to present, to tell, to convince, to repeat, to coach, to discipline, to educate, exercise, to guide, to instruct, to practice, etc.	To argue, to explicate, to agitate, to clash, to contradict, to debate, to deny, to discuss, to doubt, to negate, to question, to refute, to toss around, to violate, etc.	To arrange, to bargain for, to brainstorm, to calculate, to contemplate, to devise, to draft, to engineer, to formulate, to frame, to invent, to organise, to prepare, etc.
Channel capacity	School building, class room, sequence of lessons in the class schedule, school subjects, teacher pupil roles, regular exams, frequency of school report, pupil representation, etc.	Court room, accused, solicitor, state attorney roles, court hearing, hearing, attendance of witnesses, proclamation of sentence, etc.	Actor roles defining contributions and authorities, budget cycle, capital spending plan, budget control, budget periods, etc.
Transduction capacity	School regulations, codes of behaviour, pictograms (of elephants, birds, etc. to substitute for letters), etc.	Prevailing case law, jurisdiction, paragraph conventions, etc.	Naming and labelling conventions, explicit descriptive or graphical illustrations, issue delineation, etc.
Methodologies (exemplary)	Montessori teaching, Waldorf education, etc.	American, German, Swiss, etc. country law of court proceedings, litigation, mediation, etc.	Strategic planning methodologies, delphi survey proceedings, etc.

whom in what way. To the contrary, a weak culture requires actors to provide a much larger channel capacity. Of course also the opposite is possible: a strong culture may avoid necessary reconciliations with its preconceived traditions. Thus characterising a culture to be strong or weak refers to its capacity to facilitate and support its followers' ongoing reconciliations.[337]

---

[337] It is not meant to imply any notion of dominance or submission between different cultures, which is another interesting question.

Thus, it can be summarised as follows. The concept of interaction as mutual orientation towards representation will be of particular importance, because it clarifies what structural aspects determine actor reconciliation of °system° issues. It thus makes accessible how actors can be facilitated in making compatible their underlying intents and claims in regard of their °system° aspirations. The capacity of interaction to accommodate actors depends on the methods, channels, and transducers that are in place. Adequate structures provide the capacity to induce requisite variety in actors' relationships. Interactions evolve and regulate social °system° notions and determine how varieties collapse into the *now*. To be productive and sustainable, structures must provide sufficient capacity for actors to share relevant distinctions in regard to their °system° notion.

Social °system° notions are created through interaction. Actors' capacity to attune mutually depends on how the capacity of methods, protocols and transductions to recognise, address and adequately resolve their °system° issues. The success of °system° implementations depends less on the coherence of the actors' individual appreciation of °system° states than on the interactive capacity positioned between them to accommodate °system° issues.[338] Without methods and instruments that create adequate references of °system° issues and transform them into solutions, they cannot be addressed. And even if the method applied is capable of performing the required change, it may be insufficient channels that do not transmit adequately the message between the actors involved. Actors constantly fail to reconcile °system° issues because there are no adequate channels established to recognise and address them. However valuable the solutions created might have been for implementing the °system° notion, they are ignored or not generated at all. Different channels produce different responses to the same issue.[339] Finally, without adequate transducers, actors will not be able to talk about the same issues and understand each other. The following figure offers a depiction of the three structural aspects as they have been detailed.

The specific set and interrelation of interactions required to evolve a social °system° notion will be derived from the metasystemic set of interactions described in the Viable Systems Model. This will be done in the following chapter.

---

[338] Espejo, R.: Giving Requisite Variety to Strategic and Implementation Processes: Theory and Practice, http://bprc.warwick.ac.uk/LSEraul.html

[339] Espejo, R. and Schwaninger, M.: (Organizational Fitness)

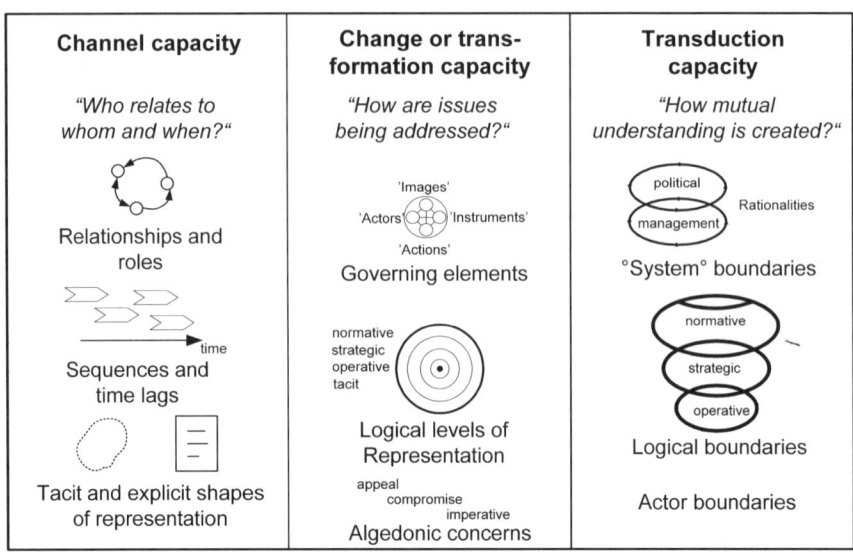

Figure 31. Aspects of structure (Organisational principles)

4 Viability

Actors wish that their common endeavours and ventures will succeed in the long run.[340] Stafford Beer's Viable System Model (VSM)[341] is a formal model identifying the necessary and sufficient structural conditions required for actors to evolve and maintain a social °system° notion.[342] These structures explicate the dynamic, adaptive and self-referential connectivity, i.e. the specific interactional features required for anchoring change and adaptability within °system° notions, thus creating the preconditions for lasting persistence.[343]

Actors implement a °system° notion by referring to their shared backgrounds, which are non-tangible.[344] To create shared actor backgrounds, interactions are required, as has been described above. The way interactional structures are manifested in channels, methods, and transducers is crucial for evolving viability. The notion of a social °system° can only be viable if the interactions taking place for its implementation equip actors to jointly provide requisite variety to attend to and resolve °system° issues.[345] As captured in the principle of sustainability of control, that requires the three aspects of structure to permanently supply sufficient capacities for maintaining a °system° notion. Structures – and that includes the cultures established – have to enable actors to jointly create requisite variety. The interactions performed, which predefine the distinctions actors make and

---

[340] Beer, S.: (Diagnosing)

[341] Beer, S.: (Heart); Beer, S.: (Brain); Beer, S.: (Diagnosing)

[342] Adam shows how the Viable System Model provides relevant contributions to the understanding of social systems. See Adam, M.: Lebensfähigkeit sozialer Systeme. Stafford Beer's Viable System Model im Vergleich, Bamberg, 2001

[343] "The laws of viability in complex organisms are not merely, or even primarily, concerned with the energy (like the metabolism of money) that propels them, but with the dynamic structure that determines the adaptive connectivity of their parts.", in Beer, S.: (Diagnosing), p. xi; Beer, S.: (Heart)

[344] The control of a system is an "integral, albeit non-tangible part of its architecture", in: Malik, F.: (Knowledge Organisation)

[345] Beer, S.: (Heart); Ashby, W. R.: (Introduction)

thus the °system° states that they jointly generate, have to match those states arising from the environment.

The viability of a °system° notion emerges as a consequence of adequate structures, rather than of the nature and talent of the actors involved. The VSM makes explicit the specific canon of structural conditions and features which leads actors to constitute a °system° notion and to sustain it for the long term. The theory of viability is a methodology (as characteristed in chapter 3.5, Figure 30) specifying what has to be reconciled for evolving a viable °system° notion.

The original convention of the Viable Systems Model defines a set of interrelated functions referred to as "*Systems One, Two, Three, Three*, Four and Five*". In the convention of Stafford Beer, both these systems and their interconnecting channels, refer to characteristic domains or "blocks of variety" which actors do address to predetermine °system° variety. Based on the interactional perspective introduced in chapter 3, a more differentiated convention can now be formulated. It is clearly distinguished between systems and systemic functions. Whereas "system" refers to a shared boundary established between actors to implement a °system° notion, systemic functions are applied to settle °system° issues. Both "Systems" and "Channels" as used by Beer can be understood and described as the characteristic topics actors have to address in order to continuously implement their °system° notion. The characteristic "blocks of variety" refer to the characteristic variety effects that these "Systems" and "Channels" induce. That means that actors always address characteristic, invariant °system° topics in their interactions. Each issue falls into one specific variety block or topic and have to be attended to and brought to resolution there. That meta-structure is configured in an invariant, recursive arrangement which sharpens the understanding of what is required for evolving a social °system° notion and how that relates to the actors involved and the relationships established between them (distribution of functions, autonomy). The aspects of structure (as they have been derived from Beers' organisational principles) apply to all the characteristic interactions involved. It is the specific concert of interactions satisfying the three aspects of structure that evolves the long-term viability and sustainability of a °system° notion.[346] Against this set of

---

[346] Malik, F.: (Knowledge Organisation); Schwaninger, M.: Das Modell Lebensfähiger Systeme – Ein Strukturmodell für organisationale Intelligenz, Lebensfähigkeit und Entwicklung, Diskussionsbeitrag des Instituts für Betriebswirtschaftslehre, 20, 2000

structural conditions and features, the way actors actually pursue the implementation of their °system° notion can be diagnosed, evaluated, analysed, and characterised according to its viability. Through this °system°-oriented approach, the concept of organisation is equipped with a framework that allows the comprehension of its functioning in a much deeper and integrated way, as in common organisational theories. Thus, the framework allows identifying when

1. established relationships between actors are inadequate or incomplete to implement the °system° notion aspired to;

2. processes do not involve the right actors or cannot be conducted in due time;

3. particular methods fail to produce valid solutions to ongoing issues;

4. transducers fail to mediate between logical levels of representation, °system° notions or actor boundaries.

A °system° notion can only be maintained as viable if the actors involved are enabled to adapt and to continuously reproduce it.[347] Successful adaptation of viable structures depends on actors' ability to self-organise[348] their mutual adaptation with regard to the °system° notion.[349]

4.1 Structural characteristics of °systems°

The following five principles describe the specific conditions of the characteristic interactions required for °system° implementation.[350] They are invariance, recursion, actor involvement, autonomy, and viability;[351] and are explained in detail below.

---

[347] Beer, S.: (Diagnosing)

[348] It is his capacity for self-organisation, the system 'adjusts itself', in Beer, S.: (Decision), pp. 359, 361

[349] Adaptation is actor's ability to perform "structural adjustments to a set of disturbances within the context of a set of overriding goals.", in Beer, S.: (Decision), p. 355

[350] Beer, S.: (Diagnosing); Beer, S.: (Brain); Beer, S.: (Heart)

[351] Schwaninger, M.: (Viable Systems Model)

4.1.1 Invariance

At an early stage in his professional career, Beer hypothesised the existence of invariances in the way actors govern the reconciliation and implementation of their purposes, i.e. in how they implement their °system° notions. He conducted research in neurocybernetics, social science, mathematics, and performed empirical fieldwork, recurrently strengthening this hypothesis. To identify invariances[352] between different °system° notions, Beer invented a method he called "topological mapping": the percepts of two situations in different °systems° are compared and found to be analogous. Each is transformed rigorously into a homomorphic mapping. The two rigorous formulations are then generalised into a final single model. This is done repeatedly in a yo-yo process of similes, analogies, homomorphs, and generalisations.[353]

In the wording of the interactional framework established here, there exist invariant, characteristic topic domains or *"blocks of variety"* [354] to which actors refer in interaction. These invariant blocks or °systemic° topics[355] can be addressed only through representations that specify distinctions dealing with a specific variety block.[356] In their interactions, actors concurrently address the invariant °system° topics. A °system° notion (as depicted in Figure 24) delimits and determines the invariant spheres actors create when implementing common °system° ventures. As a consequence, °systems° can be understood as emerging from the characteristic interactions actors use to adapt their variety in these invariant domains. Or to put

---

[352] Invariance draws on the cybernetic theorem of organisational isomorphism. See Bertanalaffy, L. v.: General Systems Theory – A New Approach to the Unity of Science, Human Biology, 23 / 1951, 1951

[353] Beer, S.: (Provenance)

[354] Ibid.

[355] It is essential to note the difference between °system° and °system*ic*° topics. °System° issues might be categorised into °system° topics, as for example marketing, controlling, finance, etc. However, these topics are not rooted in logical invariances of systems and therefore not anchored in the °system° notion that is being looked at. In contrast, the invariant variety blocks of a °system° notion are referred to as °systemic° topics.

[356] It is important to emphasise that only the characteristics of the variety blocks are invariant. What structures are established and what kind of social °system° notion manifests itself based on them may vary widely. Beer, S.: (Brain); Malik, F.: Strategie des Managements komplexer Systeme – Ein Beitrag zur Management-Kybernetik evolutionärer Systeme, Bern, Stuttgart, Wien, 2002

it the other way around, it is highly useful to distinguish interactions as addressing invariant blocks of °system° notions because that shows the roots that determine the implementation of the respective °system° notion. As invariances can be found in any °system° notion, they reflect a kind of in-depth structure or "skeleton" of any °system° organisation. Actors' activities to implement a °system° notion can always be characterised from the perspective of how they attend to the invariant blocks, i.e. what structures they establish to resolve the continuously evolving °system° issues. The invariances in °system° notions legitimise the formulation of a general theory that is concerned with how to create optimum structures to attend to those invariances.[357] With the Viable System Model, Beer has shown how the meta-structures of a °system° notion can be defined and what the characteristic invariant topics are that must be settled for its implementation.[358] It can be applied to any social °system° notion.

Table 12. Invariances and variables within a °system° notion

Invariant	Variable
Characteristic boundary judgements	Boundary agreements
°System° topics	°System° issues
Variety blocks	Information flows between actors
Meta-structures	Manifestations of system structures: actor relations, processes, etc.

4.1.2 Recursion

The recursion principle claims that the principle of invariance, i.e. the set of invariant blocks and topics, can be applied equally on different layers of °system° notions. Any °system° layer contains and is in turn contained in another °system° layer[359]. Lower layers are recursions of their meta-layers and vice versa.[360] Any layer defines a °system° notion that is logically embedded in a lower one and is as well part of superior notions. All notions have the potential to maintain an independent, separate existence. The

---

[357] Beer, S.: (How to run a country); Beer, S.: (Provenance)

[358] Beer, S.: (Provenance)

[359] Beer, S.: (Heart); Beer, S.: (Brain)

[360] Beer, S.: (Heart)

characteristic interactions relate to the specific layer that is chosen for investigation. For instance, a social °system° notion of a °community$^{o(layer\ n)}$ may be defined to consist of a set of invariant layers as its superior °region$^{o(layer\ n+1)}$, °state$^{o(layer\ n+2)}$, °continent$^{o(layer\ n+3)}$, etc. Each layer is equipped with the same invariant meta-structure.

And in the recursive logic, different layers do not depict a hierarchy. The major impact of recursive layers is that they allow the capturing of different sizes of °system° notions in the same way without simplification. Recursion takes care of the limitations of human actors to capture, process, and respond to relevant °system° issues. It enables actors to focus on the issues of one specific layer that is at the focus of interest and look at the others as black boxes. This is made possible through autonomy. Distinguishing recursive layers is thus a variety attenuating approach for analysing °system° structures.[361] Only those actors who actively engage in implementing a specific °system° notion and layer possess sufficient expertise and commitment to cope with its environment. Issues should be attended to locally, on the lowest layer possible, in close proximity to the situation, except for those residual aspects which are of superior interest and cannot therefore be handled directly in the situation.[362] On each °system° layer, structures must provide requisite capacities for actors to implement their °system° notions. Recursive interlocking °system° notions enable actors to resolve issues *"along the fronts on which variety unfolds"*.[363]

The principle of recursion thus provides a major conceptual aid for pre-conditioning the fulfilment of Ashby's law of requisite variety in °system° implementation.[364] It is a criterion to determine suitable °system° boundaries against which the systemic topics can be oriented. Focus can be put on a specific layer, and that °system° notion can be diagnosed and designed reasonably.[365] To unfold and delimit °system° notions in this way allows attending and resolving critical °system° issues at their logical origin or at their inception. It helps to develop effective structures for coping with topics and solving problems in the light of the °system° notions agreed upon.[366]

---

[361] Ibid.

[362] Espejo, R.: Giving Requisite Variety to Strategic and Implementation Processes: Theory and Practice, http://bprc.warwick.ac.uk/LSEraul.html

[363] Schwaninger, M.: (Conscious evolution)

[364] "Only variety can absorb variety", See chapter 2.2.4

[365] Espejo, R.: (VSM revisited)

[366] Espejo, R.: Giving Requisite Variety to Strategic and Implementation Processes: Theory and Practice, http://bprc.warwick.ac.uk/LSEraul.html

For instance, the sub-systems of a °company° may be defined as its independent °projects°, °profit centres°, °ventures°, °product lines°, °sales representations°, etc. In contrast, accounting will usually not be considered a °sub-system° of a °company°. Accounting is an activity by which financial aspects relevant to implementing the °company° are recorded, classified, summarised, interpreted, and communicated to enable actors to agree upon them.[367] It is therefore not an independent °system° notion that would make sense outside the °company° notion. Rather, accounting provides a support to the implementation of the °company° notion in various ways.

Assessing the viability of a °system° notion always concentrates on a single °system° layer and the implementation of that layer. By putting one specific notion into focus, a useful and, at the same time, comprehensive and sufficient set of aspects is chosen for examination. The °sub-system° boundary delimits one particular layer from the subsequent layer, and thus each of them can be assessed by diagnosis and design.[368]

4.1.3   Organisational entities and actor involvement

This principle emphasises that the characteristic interactions conducted to implement a social °system° may not necessarily relate to specific, clearly assigned actors.[369] It neither is necessary nor always possible that the invariant systemic topics are attended to by different organs, departments, workshops, human actors. In principle, organisational entities and actors may engage in multiple different °system° topics – and systemic topics have to be attended to by different actors. Characteristic interactions settle issues within systemic topics and thus regulate °system° varieties, but that does not indicate that a specific instance – organisational entity or actor – has to engage in implementation. The involvement of organisational entities and actors may be found to execute tasks and responsibilities on several °system° topics, and working fields of actors may flow one into another, thereby overlapping and requiring parallel or sequential processes to ensure that the °systemic° topics are attended to adequately.[370] To sustain the viability of a °system° notion, there are no prescribed, explicit °systemic°

---

[367] Espejo, R.: (Cybernetic method)

[368] Beer, S.: (Heart)

[369] Characteristically, Four arena interactions are not organized or formalised but disseminated over multiple actors who are unaware of each other's activity. Beer, S.: (Heart)

[370] Malik, F.: (Complex Systems)

roles for organisational entities or actors to adopt. This does not mean that
it is useless to suggest who should participate and play certain roles in the
implementation of a social °system°. It only means that the invariant systemic topics do not per se require a specific distribution of roles to organisational entities or actors. There are no rules on how to assign roles entailed in viability. Ideally, the assignment of roles is to be defined according to what organisational entities and actors can contribute to a °system°
topic as a consequence of their engagement, knowledge, experience, com-
petency, physical condition, age, etc.[371] Selection criteria for defining
°system° involvement can relate to individual actor characteristics and the
outcomes that are being sought. There are no general structural requirements for defining °systemic° actor roles. However, the necessity to ensure
that the systemic topics are attended to effectively should be reflected in
the role distributions, job descriptions, and actor assignments as well as in
process descriptions, methods and instruments, etc. Of course, in practice,
executing power is a major criteria for assigning actor roles.[372]

4.1.4 Autonomy

Any method chosen by actors to successfully implement their °system° notion asserts a certain degree of autonomy using appeals, compromises, or
imperatives to assert certain solutions and decisions upon other actors. For a
°system° notion to remain viable there is no specific degree of autonomy to
be set. Rather, the autonomy principle supports the maximisation of freedom
and minimisation of hierarchy as long as the social °system° notion in focus
is not affected negatively.[373] Strict intervention is legitimate only to avoid
behaviour that is at the expense of the overall °system° notion.[374]

---

[371] They may not be defined by assigned three actors exclusively, but may well
evolve from full-time working groups of actors involved in System One.
Within these groups consensus upon the regulations to be set up, changed or
adapted is reached. Beer, S.: (Heart)

[372] For example see Beer: To create the "algorithms to implement tactics should
be the role of those responsible for the activities defined by the tactical plan
and not those who defined it. This does not exclude anyone from involvement
in both activities. What it says is that the person or group that is held accountable for the outcome should be given responsibility for determining the action.", in Beer, S.: (Heart)

[373] Beer, S.: (Heart)

[374] Malik, F.: (Complex Systems)

Depending on the dynamics and complexity of the environmental issues being faced, hierarchy is to be exerted to a degree that secures the implementation of the °system° notion. Unrestricted appeals are suitable to stimulate actors to self-organise independently the implementation of their °sub-system° notions. In contrast, hierarchical imperatives, defining tasks, measures, and criteria are needed to cope with fundamental 'threats' to the °system°. Appeals and imperatives, autonomy and hierarchy are not opposites. Rather, autonomy induces self-organisation; actors amplify their capability to cope with the majority of issues on their own, leaving only a residual, minimal set of issues, conflicts, problems to be treated through imperative restriction.[375]

Thus, autonomy is a relative factor determined according to the actual disturbances actors face in their °system° environment and the cohesion of actors[376], i.e. the prevailing degrees of intentionality and contextuality of the °system° notion. The degree of autonomy is a characteristic topic to be reconciled as part of the implementation of a °system° notion.[377] Theoretically, the optimal degree of autonomy depends on the relation between a °system's° structural capacities and the respective °environmental° issues, problems or obstacles it is facing or expecting to face. The more problems and obstacles a °system° notion faces, the lower the degree of autonomy that can be tolerated will be. However, the less autonomy, the less actors will be able to self-organise their °system° notion. Essentially, the optimal degree of autonomy considered legitimate depends on the purposes, norms, and values defined with the °system° boundary in relation to the °system° environment.[378] Today, a tendency from hierarchical to more participative structures can be observed as a consequence of the broad proliferation of complexity (see chapter 1). Any loss of hierarchy in °system° structures requires the actors involved to compensate that loss in their reconciliations, which is possible only through more capacitative, participative structures.[379] Aspects of °system° issues usually cannot be meaningfully captured by one

---

[375] Espejo, R.: (VSM revisited)

[376] Malik, F.: (Complex Systems)

[377] Refers to the resource bargain of Three-One interaction. See chapter 4.5.3, in Beer, S.: (Diagnosing)

[378] Beer, S.: (Provenance)

[379] As "organisations try to move away from a structure of hierarchical bureaucracy, which remains the dominant organisational form today, they will continue to move towards more participative structures. To do so, they will have to solve the problem of 'proliferating complexity resulting from reduced centralisation.'", in Beer, S.: (Dispute), p. 344

viewpoint alone. Since multiple actors create multiple views, those actors who are actually confronted with the task of addressing the issues (and eliminating the respective complexity) should also be expected to resolve the issue.[380] Any set of methods applied to address a °system° issue should involve those actors who have the most intimate knowledge of and experience with it.[381] And those actors are commonly found on the lowest recursive layer where the issue has originated. Whenever actors are unable to dissolve variety participatively, e.g. in situations where the persistence of the °system° notion is under threat, requisite variety can only be achieved by reducing the autonomy of the °sub-systems°. This means that imperatives are required to ensure the implementation of the °system° notion.

4.1.5 Viability

The viability of a °system° notion manifests itself in the actors' capability to maintain it as a separate existence independent of other °systems° notions.[382] It relies on permanent compliance with the canon of principles mentioned in this chapter. But what state or condition does viability refer to? Actors may find social °system° notions to adopt a multiplicity of states and conditions[383], which they may describe as success, advancement, build-up, crop, growth, descent, collapse, survival, etc. Viability is a criterion for assessing the structures applied to implement °system° notions. It is not concerned with the characteristics of a perceived state of the °system° notion, but refers to the conditions under which actors can sustain the °system° notion for an indefinite time. A viable °system° may therefore not necessarily persist at all times but it will have the pre-requisites to maintain its existence and to conduct the necessary changes as required to implement its purpose.[384] Consequently, there is no viable state or condition into which a

---

[380] Espejo, R.: (VSM revisited); Beer, S.: (Heart); A protocol that empowers those directly involved in the day-to-day operations to develop procedures to deliver specific actions to achieve the set goals and objectives. Beer, S.: (Dispute)

[381] Espejo, R.: (VSM revisited)

[382] Beer, S.: (Provenance)

[383] A social system may adopt many different states of configurations, of which "the mere survival" is only one possibility. See Schwaninger, M.: Structures for Intelligent Organizations, Diskussionsbeitrag des Instituts für Betriebswirtschaftslehre, No. 20, 1996

[384] "The fact that the societary system is there does not guarantee that it will always be there: its days may well be numbered [...] The fact that a 'system' does exist does not prove that it is effectively there. Monoliths and monopolis-

°system° notion should evolve but only a viable structure, which enables actors to sustain and develop a °system° notion throughout its implementation.[385] As will be explained in detail below, viability emerges from the continuous provision of sufficient structural capacity to reconcile adequate solutions (i.e. to provide for requisite variety in attending the characteristic invariant interactions). The actors involved who adhere to a °system° notion face non-involved actors following other °system° notions. Threats and problems arise and initiate change in the further development of the °system° notion. Development and elaboration of °system° structures is an ongoing process in viable °system° notions. In that process, actors may well face the need to fundamentally change their °system° notions and structures as they face changing constraints from the environment and the °system° layers. Thus, the implementation of a °community° is constrained both by those involved in its °sub-systems°, producing °health°, °education°, °traffic°, °security°, etc., and those authorised by the °state° to accommodate neighbouring °communities°. Actors themselves can be understood as viable °systems° that can act freely based on their will. But they have social (superior °system° layer) and individual (lower °system° layer) constraints that limit their scope of thoughts, actions, and behaviour.[386]

Therefore the concept of viability does not simply address a single °system° notion and arrange for its survival. Rather, it calls for integrating and sustaining the °system° notions within the chain of their lower and superior layers. Weaving them into this chain enables survival beyond the margin of subsistence[387], in a specific, higher state or condition despite inimical or hostile disturbances from the environment. Hence, maintaining a viable °system° notion is a continuous, revolving process. It implies the possibility that °system° identity, boundary and all that may derive from them may change fundamentally in order to accommo-

---

tic systems often operate at the margins of viability, creaking and choking like the valetudinarian organisations that they are.", in Beer, S.: (Provenance); Malik, F.: (Complex Systems)

[385] Beer, S.: (Brain)

[386] Beer, S.: (Provenance)

[387] Glasersfeld argues from a constructivist perspective that 'survival' in the sense of adaptation is to darwinistic and therefore teleologically connotated. Rather, one should speak of "organisms, which remained viable", in Glasersfeld, E. v.: Wissen, Sprache und Wirklichkeit – Arbeiten zum radikalen Konstruktivismus., Wiesbaden, 1987

date new conditions.[388] Only the °system° structure itself and the source of identity remain unchanged.[389]

4.2 Invariant °system° topics

To evolve a social °system° notion, it is necessary to have a group of actors that actually produces whatever it is that has been defined to be the purpose of that °system°. This will require actors to actually engage in its °sub-systems°, e.g. °alpha°, °beta°, °gamma°, etc. The notion of °community° for instance may involve producing the notions of °health°, °education°, °security°, etc. Actors will be needed to engage in the implementation of each of these °sub-systems° of °community°. If °community° is the layer in focus which shall be looked at, then the pure °sub-system° issues are out of focus, as they belong to the next lower recursive layer of the °system°. Upholding °health° and °education° is different from governing the °community° notion.[390] Those remaining °sub-system° issues relevant to the overall °system° will be referred to as *One* issues here. °Health° and °education° may both depend on °infrastructure° so that such *One* issues can be expected to arise from the confrontation of °health°, °education° and °infrastructure° engagements.

But still these are °sub-system° issues. To realise a °community° notion, the actors involved will be required to share and resolve their °community° issues. Therefore, those actors involved have to continuously interact to align their °community° notions. To prepare for sound resolutions of *One* issues, the actors will have to engage with four invariant topic domains. With the distinctions of four logical levels, four topic domains have already been identified above (chapter 3.2.2.3). Issues of each topic domain can only be attended to and resolved with the respective characteristic, the logical type of representation, by applying its own language, criteria, figures of speech, etc.[391] As a convention, each of these topic domains can now be labelled by counting upwards: tactical *"Two"*, operational *"Three"*, strategic *"Four"* and normative *"Five"*.

---

[388] Espejo, R. and Schwaninger, M.: (Organizational Fitness)

[389] Jackson, M. C.: (Managerial significance)

[390] They themselves constitute orientations towards a viable °system° and are therefore conducted autonomously to cope with their respective environments. Beer, S.: (Heart)

[391] Beer, S.: (Diagnosing)

A social °system° notion can only remain viable if the interactions conducted for its implementation address these four invariant topic domains.
Each of these topic domains requires characteristic interactions to resolve
its issues.[392] Such interactions that exclusively attend to a single topic domain shall be referred to as arena interactions. Furthermore, interactions
that are required to reconcile and translate between these topic domains will
be denoted *DomainA-DomainB* interactions. For each interaction, characteristic channels, methods and transducers will be required to create adequate
representations. It must be ensured that all interactions cope with the topic's
peculiarities and resolve the attendant issues. Any implementation of a
°system° such as °community° manifests itself in resolutions to the four
topic domains. Indeed, whether the way how this is done sustains the viability of the °system° notion depends on the quality of the characteristic interactions (and their structures) to continuously resolve the issues arising
in all topic domains. A brief overview of *One* issues and the *Two, Three,
Four, Five* topic domains is given in the Table 13.[393]

In the following, the characteristic interactions required to create each of
the four topic domains are described and illustrated. This is done based
upon the theory of viability and using the concepts that have been developed so far. For each of the preceding topic domains characteristic, invariant representations will be identified and specified with respect to their
contribution. Therefore, the convention of the inverted comma ('') will be
used, and further, the logical level of representation (LLR) will be indicated with TR (tacit), OR (operative), SR (strategic) and NR (normative)
respectively. The environmental interactions taking place between actors
not involved in the implementation of the °system° notion are not included.[394] The entire statement reveals which kind of characteristic interactions are required to evolve °systems° and to maintain their viability. The
course of descriptions follows the convention of topics in ascending order,
however, this is arbitrary since there is no top-down or bottom-up hierarchy inherent in the invariant issues and interactions.[395]

---

[392] Harnden, R.: (Outside and then)
[393] Beer, S.: (Brain); for a more detailed description see: Schwaninger, M.: (Viable Systems Model); Malik, F.: (Complex Systems)
[394] Beer, S.: (Diagnosing)
[395] Beer, S.: (Dispute)

Table 13. Four invariant topic domains to solve *One* issues in °system° implementation

***One* issues** *One* issues articulate °sub-system° quarrels, conflicts, synergies, etc. They are expressed by groups of actors who actively engage in implementing the different °sub-system° notions and thus produce the purpose of the overall °system° in focus. *One* issues do not concern °sub-system° implementation, as these are being settled on the lower recursive layer. *One* issues are the remaining, unresolved issues of °sub-system° implementation.
***Two* topics – Coordination** *Two* topics concern the interdependency of °sub-system° interests and how they can be coordinated. What are actually the interdependent activities of the °sub-systems°? Where do activities of °sub-systems° clash and how can they be harmonised? What is the status of the ongoing attenuation of °sub-system° interdependency?
***Three* topics – Operative governing** *Three* topics focus on the 'inside and now' of the °systems° in-focus, the definition of °sub-system° notions, the synergy between them, the resources to be allocated, the actual capacity and efficiency of the overall °system°. What are necessary and reasonable requirements and constraints for °sub-systems°? How should *Two* issues be resolved? What is currently being done for °sub-system° implementation and how?
***Four* topics – Strategic governing** *Four* topics pertain to anticipations of future developments of the °system°. What external factors are to be considered relevant for sustaining the °system° notion? How do they affect the outcome? How can the actual situation be understood, interpreted, modelled? What could and should be done to prepare for future threats and problems?
***Five* topics – Normative governing** *Five* topics address the boundary judgements adopted by the actors involved and the norms deriving from them. What is and what should be the purpose of the °system°? Who is and who should be the client? What is and what should be the measure of improvement? How shall present and future as well as internal and external perspectives be accommodated? What criteria shall be applied for interpreting the environment? What supreme values, norms, and rules do actors have to comply with to legitimise their engagement in implementing the °system° notion?

4.3 *One* issues – °sub-system° implementation

°*Sub-systems*° produce the individual purposes which together create the purpose, the raison *d'etre*, of the overall °system°.[396] Following the principle of recursion, all interactions reconciling pure °sub-system° issues are out of focus here. °Sub-systems° are regarded as black boxes, with the only

---

[396] Espejo, R.: (VSM revisited)

exception being the unresolved issues, conflicts and problems evolving as a consequence of their parallel activities, which do affect and are relevant for the overall °system° notion in focus. Mutually dependent °sub-systems° are labelled One^{alpha}, One^{beta}, One^{gamma}, *etc* respectively. *One* issues express the problems, conflicts and potential synergies emerging from °sub-system° implementation. From the perspective of the actual °system° notion, the °sub-system° boundaries are the primary determinant pre-conditioning overall °system° purpose implementation. It will make a difference whether the °sub-systems° of a °community° are delimited by regions (in several °villages°) or living spheres (e.g. in °health°, °education°, °infrastructure°, etc.). Similarily, for a °company°, it will make a difference, whethere its °sub-systems° are delimited by products, technologies, locations or markets. More precisely, different °sub-system° boundaries will provoke different *One* issues to be governed.[397]

As follows, only the *One-One* interactions conducted for implementing the different °sub-systems° are described. *One-Three* and *One-Five* interactions will be explained within the corresponding chapters of *Two*, *Three* and *Five* interactions. Further, as an exception of the °sub-system° domain, a

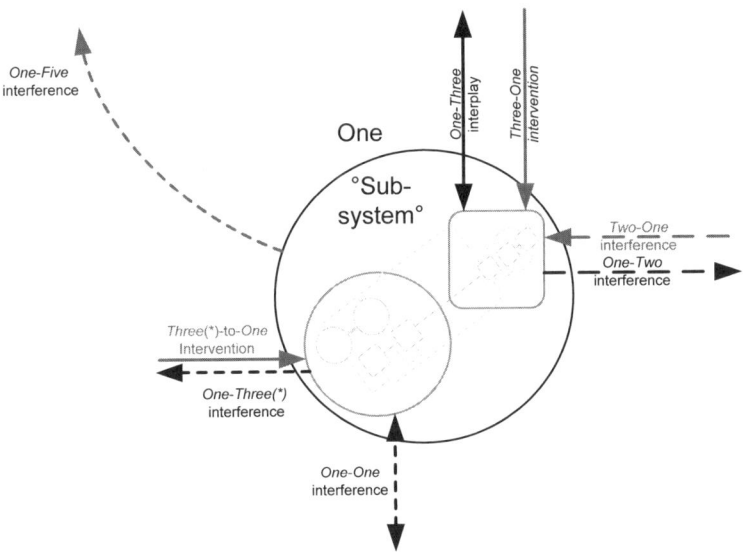

Figure 32. *One* interactions

---

[397] The determination and fixing of optimal °system° boundaries is therefore a primary question when a social °system° is being designed.

characteristic *One* arena interaction concerned purely with *One* issues does not exist. As a whole ° system° is implemented inside the *One* arena; actors engaged on the lower layer of the °sub-system° perform the whole set of characteristic interactions between *One*, *Two*, *Three* and *Five* issues, which will subsequently be described. The *One* arena is only the outer shell of the lower °system° layer and entails an independent and autonomous °system° notion. Wherever there is reference to the characteristic interactions and reconciliations taking place inside a *One* arena, this is indicated with the prefix *"Sub-"*. Figure 32 depicts this convention.

4.3.1 *One-One*

Actors implementing *One* issues may face interdependencies as a consequence of their behaviours being in conflict with each other or with the environment.[398] Actors engaged in the provision of °alpha° cannot do as they would like, because other actors implementing °beta° attempt to do what they like, and both confront each other. Enhancing the autonomy of °alpha° at the same time erodes the autonomy of °beta°.[399] For example, it is inevitable that the real estate used for building a new hospital to improve °health° will not be accessible for building a motorway which would be required to sustain °traffic°. Further, the implementation of °health° will require rescue services to be continuously supplied with fuel to use in their emergency ambulances, which does require °infrastructure° to provide sufficient fuel reserves. Such conflicting One^{alpha}, One^{beta}, One^{gamma} issues are recognised in *One-One* interferences ('squiggly lines'[400]), where actors use 'Demarcation^{TR}' to specify and coordinate their °sub-system° interdependencies. 'Demarcations^{TR}' reflect practical necessities or facts which cannot be abolished or neutralised by means of managerial 'Requirements^{OR}' but simply execute a severe restriction on the °sub-systems° °alpha°, °beta°, °gamma°, etc.[401] These interferences can solve only those issues purely concerned with the highly individual One^{alpha}, One^{beta}, One^{gamma} interests and do not address overall °system° needs.

This may require actors to interact either strongly or weakly. Strong *One-One* interferences reflect highly interdependent relations between °alpha°, °beta°, °gamma°, etc. If °beta° relies on some obligatory input from °alpha°

---

[398] Espejo, R.: (VSM revisited)

[399] Beer, S.: (Heart)

[400] Squiggly lines as used by Beer, in Beer, S.: (Diagnosing)

[401] Beer, S.: (Heart)

– such as receiving resources from it – and is required at the same time to pass on its output to °gamma°, then it is heavily constrained. Usually, even autonomous actors would not even think too much about how to solve these 'Demarcation^{TR}' issues, but just take them as given. Often the immense restrictions arising as a consequence of practical necessity are not even noticed. If actors are upset because of the loss of autonomy that goes along with 'Demarcations^{TR}', they may tend to blame managers for being autocratic.[402] However, usually the loss of autonomy, the erosion of freedom, is already implicit in the chosen boundary of the °system°.[403] In contrast, highly independent relations between °alpha°, °beta°, °gamma°, etc. require only weak *One-One* interferences. As each °sub-systems° can act largely independently here, there is not much need for mutual reconciliation.

Often, 'Demarcation^{TR}' issues, such as complaints of °alpha° with respect to why °beta° or °gamma° are much better in implementing their notion, cannot be solved in *One-One interference*. Some superior, pervasive solutions and conventions are required to dissolve 'Demarcations^{TR}' issues. Meta-interactions engage on systemic *Two, Three, Four* and *Five* topics. They will be described below.

4.4 *Two* topics – coordination

The confrontation of the interdependent, conflicting One^{alpha}, One^{beta}, etc. issues inevitably leads to instabilities and incompatibilities that are destructive and endanger the implementation of the overall °system° purpose and notion. Any kind of common, revolving °sub-system° interdependencies create *Two* issues, e.g. shared inputs (e.g. resource consumption, supplies), throughputs (e.g. knowledge, experiences), outputs (e.g. products, shared markets, or publics) or feedback (e.g. common evaluative concerns).[404] *Two* interactions address these instabilities and incompatibilities, continuously compile interdependencies ('what the system does') and avoid the reappearance of common interdependencies and conflicts by proposing

---

[402] Ibid.

[403] Ibid.

[404] Espejo, R., Schuhmann, W., Schwaninger, M., and Bilello, U.: (Transformation and Learning)

compatible solutions for solving *One* issues.[405] A typical example of *Two* activity is resource scheduling such as assigning the distribution of rooms in a school, reserving hotel rooms for clients, or creating a production schedule.[406]

The better *Two* interactions perform, the less residual variety remains that has to be attended to by *Three,* and the more leverage remains for those implementing the °sub-systems°.[407] As will be seen below, sound structures for *Two* interactions relieve *Three* from the need to manage these issues actively (via 'Requirements^{OR}').[408] Thus, *Two* activities harmonise *One* activities and facilitate *Three* activities. In doing so, the *Two interactions* secure a seamless transition of *Three* solutions (plans, programmes, and procedures) into *One* solutions.[409]

Successful *Two* interactions improve actor cohesion in °system° implementation with fewer comments and more standards.[410] The following characteristic interactions are required for attending to *Two* topics:

a) *Two* arena, which keeps track of °sub-system° interdependencies;

b) *Two-One,* which creates individual suggestions to eliminate interdependencies between °sub-systems°;

c) *Two-Three,* which reports to *Three* actors unresolved interdependencies and provides feedback for guidelines delivered by *Three* actors.

Figure 33 illustrates *Two* interactions.

---

[405] In the original model, each System One has its own System Two assigned to it. 'Lower' Systems Two spread their filtered information into a 'superior' one which is situated within the meta-system.

[406] A "Resource Bargain that 'knows' we can make 1000 units this month has to be amplified into a production schedule providing requisite variety: i.e. exactly what each machine has to do shift by shift.", in Beer, S.: Diagnosing the System for Organizations – Companion Volume to Brain of the Firm and The Heart of Enterprise- Brain of the Firm, Chichester, New York, Brisbane, Toronto, Singapore, 1985b

[407] Espejo, R.: (VSM revisited)

[408] Beer, S.: (Diagnosing)

[409] Two interactions are "the focus of homeostasis between management and operations.", in Beer, S.: (Diagnosing)

[410] Espejo, R.: (VSM revisited)

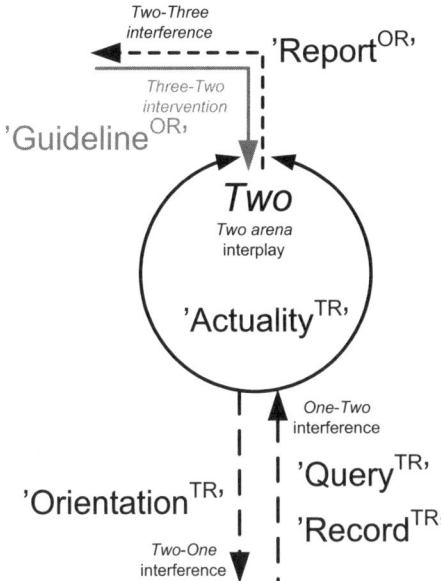

Figure 33. *Two* interactions

4.4.1 *Two* arena

The *Two* arena is a continuous interplay in which actors create 'Actuality^{TR}' to provide reference to the actual status, change, and deviation of °sub-system° interdependencies. 'Actuality^{TR}' reveals any incompatibilities of the °sub-system's° adopted concerns. It is a high-variety representation capturing the details of moment-to-moment 'Queries^{TR}' received on °sub-system° activity.[411] To be able to answer these, it is continuously being fed and actualised with 'Records^{TR}' about the ongoing °sub-system° activity. All *Two* interplays follow the 'Guidelines^{OR}' provided by *Three* that define their protocol and point to restrictions of the °system° 'Capacity^{OR}'. Thus, individual *One^{alpha}*, *One^{beta}*, etc. concerns are confronted with collective restrictions, making transparent the conflicting aspects of *One* activities and preparing the derivation of individual suggestions for *One* actors according to the procedures ('Guidelines^{OR}') provided by *Three*.[412]

---

[411] Ibid.

[412] Beer, S.: (Dispute)

4.4.2 *Two-One*

The *Two-One* relation consists of two separate, antipodal interferences. To enable the *Two* arena to capture individual and common concerns, *One-to-Two* interference continually provides 'Records[TR]' of the °sub-systems'° ongoing activities, describing their status as well as their efforts in terms of performance, quality, resource consumption, causes, and consequences of fluctuations, etc.[413] Further, °sub-system° actors pose 'Queries[TR]' whenever they address common °sub-system° concerns such as being willing to take interdependent actions or to utilise shared resources. *Two-to-One interference* provides 'Orientation[TR]' by articulating specific and tailored advice on how to resolve the interdependent issues. It derives from the actual situation as described in 'Actuality[TR]'. It is articulated as an appeal, as *Two-to-One* interferences do not restrict the autonomy of *One* actors. Rather, they are mere facilitators or services helping *One* actors to solve their interdependencies and to implement their °sub-system° notions.[414] 'Orientation[TR]' simply articulates anti-oscillatory suggestions to them.[415] The resolutions proposed foster self-organisation of °sub-system° implementation; they do not themselves constrain the autonomy of the °sub-systems° but may nevertheless be consequences of 'Requirements[OR]' formulated by *Three* and translated into 'Guidelines[OR]' relevant for *Two*. 'Orientation[TR]' does not call to account *One* actors who neglect to follow its coordinative suggestions. The concerns are always the *Two* issues of the recursive layer in focus[416], i.e. *Two* actors give 'Orientation[TR]' only to their assigned *One* actors in their coordinative issues.

4.5 *Three* topics – operative governing

Three topics address the 'inside and now' of a °system° notion, i.e. the assignment of °sub-system° notions and the optimisation of their resource allocation, performance, efficiency, exploitation of synergies, etc. *Three* interactions create and manage the operative issues actors face while implementing a °system° notion.[417] They are at all times concerned with the

---

[413] Every "kind of happenstance, from broken bolts to streaming colds, from lightning strikes to power failures, has to be monitored under variety attenuation in a reporting system.", in Beer, S.: (Diagnosing), p. 43

[414] Beer, S.: (Heart)

[415] Ibid.

[416] Beer, S.: (Brain)

[417] Beer, S.: (Heart)

activities of the °sub-systems° in the light of the whole. They concentrate on identifying and implementing optimum 'images', 'instruments', and 'actions' to achieve optimum resource allocation and to exploit synergies between °sub-systems°.[418] Their engagement in resource allocation and synergy distinguishes *Three* from *Two* interactions, which concentrate solely on balancing interdependencies. *Three* interactions execute the 'Strategy[SOR]' that they have agreed upon with *Four*. The following *Three* interactions can be distinguished:[419]

a) *Three-Two*, which configures the protocol of the *Two* arena and receives reports;

b) *Three-One*, which reconciles a 'Contract[OR]' on how to implement the °system° and defines the constraints of °sub-system° activity;

c) *Three(*)-One*, which conducts 'Audits[OR]' on °sub-system° activity and supplements 'Findings[OR]' with direct observations.[420]

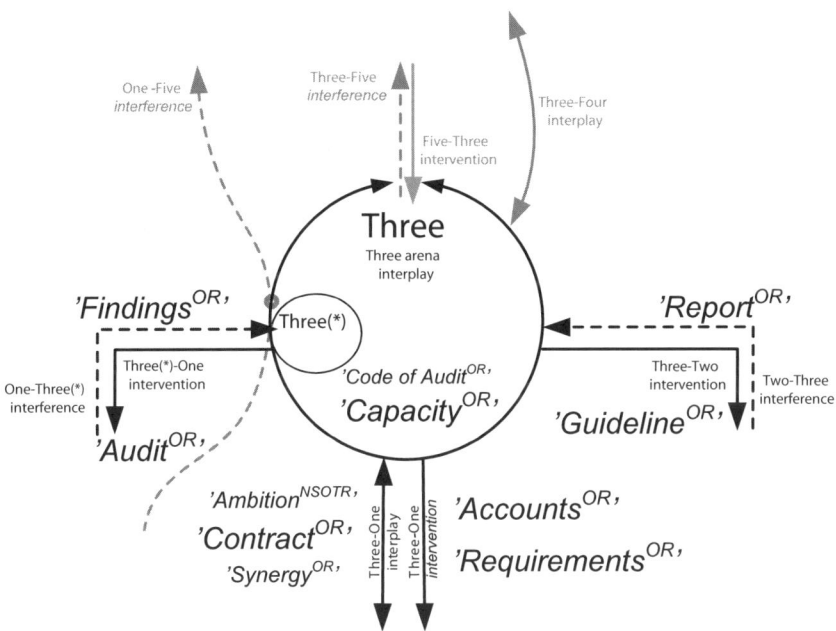

Figure 34. *Three* interactions

---

[418]   Malik, F.: (Complex Systems)

[419]   Ibid.

[420]   Beer, S.: (Heart)

Furthermore, *Three* evaluates the initiatives for change and innovation that are being issued by *Four*. These will be described with *Four* topics (chapter 4.6.3). Figure 34 illustrates *Three* interactions (which will be described in detail as follows.)

4.5.1 *Three-Two*

Two-One can provide practical advice for °sub-system° issues only in relation to known and precisely defined goals and procedures.[421] 'Guidelines^OR' define the protocol of the *Two* arena interplay. They entail the regulations, policies, and procedures on how to resolve *One* issues[422], e.g. consequences of °sub-systems'° fluctuations, criteria for judging these consequences, and measures for dissolving them. 'Guidelines^OR' are used to execute and implement *Three* solutions via *Two* interactions. For regularly monitoring *Two* performance (*Two-to-Three*) interferences suffice; for prescribing new 'Guidelines^OR' into the *Two* arena (*Three-to-Two*) interventions are needed.

One activities may turn out to be incongruent or incompatible in a way that is detrimental to the overall °system°, e.g. when they exceed the resources at *One's* disposal or harm each other in the implementation of their purposes. Further, the 'Guidelines^OR' for *Two* arena interplay may reveal inconsistencies – e.g. when different *Three* actors have not synchronised their contributions. A 'Report^OR' is created in *Two-to-Three* interference to bring those cases to a resolution.[423] Further, 'Reports^OR' express the status of the °sub-system° interdependencies and refer to the difficulties *Two* faces with ensuing 'Guidelines^OR'. They may also refer to the necessary steps to harmonise *Three* arena interplay. Thus, besides damping *One* interdependencies, *Two* actors also engage in synchronising *Three* 'Guidelines^OR'.[424] Generally, *Two-to-Three* interferences are calm, taking place on occasional demand and upon request. 'Reports^OR' are filtered and carefully selected operative interpretations of the actual *Two* perspective. They rely on interferences and are conducted at minimum intensity.

---

[421] Beer, S.: (Dispute)

[422] Beer, S.: (Heart)

[423] Ibid.

[424] Ibid.

4.5.2 *Three* arena

Primarily, the task of the *Three* arena is to create cohesion[425] and synergy of °sub-system° activity. As a consequence of its optimisation, °sub-system° activity will exceed the result that would have been acquired by the sum of individual efforts.[426] With the reconciliation of 'Capacity^{OR}', actors recognise and interpret the actual situation of the °sub-system° interdependencies and develop optimum procedures, processes, etc. To do so, the *Three* arena interplay constantly creates, discusses, evaluates, optimises, reconciles, and decides upon the overall 'Capacity^{OR}' based on a synoptic perspective of the °sub-systems°. In the *Three* arena, all operative information is brought together[427]: 'Norms^{NR}' and the adopted 'Strategy^{SOR}' constitute and specify the frame for the reconciliation of the 'Capacity^{OR}' of the °system°.[428] 'Proposals^{SR}' assess 'Capacity^{OR}' in the light of new prospects and challenges. 'Reports^{OR}', 'Accounts^{OR}', and 'Findings^{OR}' inform bottom-up about all aspects of the ongoing implementation of °sub-system° purposes.

'Capacity^{OR}' captures all aspects relevant for understanding and interpreting the actual situation and for acquiring the optimum synergy of the °sub-system° notions. Through it, actors continuously identify the optimum set of 'images', 'instruments', 'actions', and 'actors' for implementation of the °system° purpose. Operative 'images' describe the perceived °sub-system° performance, the modi operandi, and their potential for change, etc. Operative 'actions' specify the potential steps to be taken in order to implement 'instruments' and to aspire to 'images' of °sub-systems°. Thus, 'Capacity^{OR}' constitutes the fundamental reference for all other operative reconciliations, e.g. on target agreements, job descriptions, resource allocations, process descriptions, cost and activity accounts, cost and benefit analyses, etc. The operational character of 'Capacity^{OR}' facilitates an indication of the consequences of what has already occurred in the °sub-systems°. Solutions derived from 'Capacity^{OR}' always trace back to such descriptions of the actual situation and rely on methods restricted to taking such a perspective.[429]

---

[425] Ibid.

[426] Beer, S.: (Brain)

[427] All "direct links with all managerial units, which exist simultaneously and in real time", in Beer, S.: (Brain), p. 202

[428] On Feedback Adjuster and Adjuster Organizer, see Beer, S.: (Heart)

[429] Gälweiler, Aloys: (Corporate Strategy)

In 'Capacity^{OR}', the *Three* arena interplay considers resource allocations and tasks to implement operative goals and to optimise the output of the °sub-systems°.[430] Actors recognise characteristics and peculiarities of *One* issues as they manifest themselves. They engage in describing and assessing the constitution of the social °system° inside, i.e. its operational needs and constraints. This enables actors to understand and to gain experience regarding how the implementation of the °system° notion can be optimised and what its constraints are. This discussion enriches their conception of 'what can be done' and restrains the pursuit of useless options. A thorough, shared perception of what is feasible is a precondition to reconciling a common 'Contract^{OR}' and to evaluating developmental 'Proposals^{SR}' delivered by *Four*.[431] *Three* arena interaction relates to the adopted 'Strategy^{SOR}' temporarily fixed in *Three-Four* interaction. Whenever *Four-Three* interplay changes the 'Strategy^{SOR}', that has to be reflected in 'Capacity^{OR}'.

A further task of *Three* arena interplay is to ensure the sufficiency and integrity of 'Capacity^{OR}'. Therefore, an independent arena engaging in separate *Three*-One* interactions is created. *Three* arena interplay defines, develops and inspects the 'Code of Conduct^{OR}', i.e. the monitoring and control practices to be followed in that *Three(*)-One* relation.

4.5.3 Three-One

Three-One relationships reconcile and define the optimum conditions for implementing the °sub-systems°.[432] They consist of a resource bargain conducted as interplay and a constraint executed as intervention.

4.5.3.1 Interplay – resource bargain

Three-One interplay reconciles, *between One* and *Three* actors, a synergic allocation of 'images', 'instruments', 'actions', and 'actors' to be aspired to.[433] Based upon 'Capacity^{OR}', *Three* actors propose a 'Synergy^{OR}' that describes how °social systems° can be synchronised thus specifying the optimum frame for °sub-system° implementation. *One* actors advance their 'Ambitions^{NSOR}', which derive from their individual °sub-system° logics, i.e. their 'Sub-Norms^{NR}', 'Sub-Strategy^{SOR}', and 'Sub-Capacity^{OR}'. These indi-

---

[430] Malik, F.: (Complex Systems)

[431] Beer, S.: (Diagnosing)

[432] Beer, S.: (Brain)

[433] According to Beer, "Program Planning and Budgeting (PPBS) Systems typify these bargains", see: Beer, S.: (Diagnosing)

vidual 'Ambitions[NSOR]' are declarations of intent enriched with information on their °sub-system° aspirations[434], e.g. individual goals, budgets targeted, etc. They then negotiate a 'Contract[OR]', which specifies the activities to be implemented and the resources to be disposed of.[435] Thus, the °system° mission and goals to be accomplished[436] ('images'), the resources and rules[437] to be applied ('instruments') and the activities to be performed ('actions') are determined for each °sub-system°.

Along with the 'Contract[OR]', a certain degree of autonomy[438] is agreed upon by the *One* arenas, which depends on how specified and formalised the 'Contract[OR]' is. Following the principle of autonomy, the °sub-systems° have to be equipped with the maximum degree of autonomy for allowing optimising and sustaining their individual performance and does not impair the overall viability of the °system° in focus. Therefore, 'Contracts[OR]' should define only what is absolutely necessary to accord °sub-systems° synergistically and to dissolve the residual variety entailed, i.e. the remaining *One* issues that need to be attended to.[439] Synergy arises from a low variety 'Contract[OR]' that specifies how the °sub-systems'° interdependency can be attended to, i.e. what the temporary operative solution is. These are clearly much fewer than the total number of the °sub-systems'° issues.[440] Settling the 'Contract[OR]' is a most potent method of variety attenuation[441], as it prevents *One* from undertaking competing activities or investments.

4.5.3.2 Intervention

Three-One intervention ensures that *One* actors adhere to the necessary, indispensable operative 'Requirements[OR]' for °system° implementation. 'Contracts[OR]' are being enforced via 'Requirements[OR]'. The identity of °sub-systems° and their 'Sub-Boundaries[NR]' is defined as far as is relevant to the °system° notion in focus. That may include any other strategic, operative,

---

[434] Beer, S.: (Heart)

[435] Beer, S.: (Diagnosing)

[436] Ibid.

[437] Ibid.

[438] Ibid.; as has been described in the principle of autonomy, the degree of autonomy depends on the purpose of the system as well as the complexity, diversity, and dynamics of the environment.

[439] Espejo, R.: (VSM revisited)

[440] Beer, S.: (Heart)

[441] Beer, S.: (Diagnosing)

or tactical constraints with respect to the modus operandi applied to implement °sub-systems°.[442] Intervening in the ongoing implementation of °sub-system° notions may imply all degrees of predetermination including step-by-step commands.[443] For a °system° notion to remain viable it is essential that only the minimum restrictions necessary to sustain the cohesion of the whole °system° are applied. *Three* actors may define 'Requirements^{OR}' and constraints, i.e. cut back investments assigned to a °sub-system° or re-invest in another, only as long as it is done in the interest of the overall °system°. *Three-One* intervention ensures that *One* actors cannot threaten the viability of the overall °system°. *One* actors are orientated towards the operative 'Requirements^{OR}' of the °system° notion being focussed on. The choice of minimal interventions depends on the purposes ('Norms^{NR}') to be implemented and the conditions being faced in the environment (see chapter 4.1.4).[444] The challenge is to allow for a maximum degree of autonomy whilst maintaining °sub-system° cohesion. Indeed, increasing autonomy in 'Contracts^{OR}' and 'Requirements^{OR}' may lead to ever more inconsistent 'Ambitions^{NSOR}' of *One* actors.[445] 'Requirements^{OR}' have to be such as to increase actors' freedom to implement their adopted °system° notions unhindered, i.e. as laws against assault and theft do.[446]

As a response to 'Requirements^{OR}', °sub-system° actors have to provide an 'Account^{OR}' of their ongoing activities and guarantee their compliance with the °sub-system° 'Contract^{OR}' agreed on. In doing so, actors show that everything is proceeding as agreed upon in the 'Contract^{OR}' and thus justify the further assignment of resources from *Three*. 'Accounts^{OR}' can only provide a strongly summarized reflection of °sub-system° activity.[447] Naturally, they reflect the biases and communication problems of *One* actors.[448] 'Requirements^{OR}' define what is to be accepted as 'Accounts^{OR}' of °sub-system° activity (One-to-*Three*), they set the parameters for the 'Accounts^{OR}' to be returned and further execute interventions when the cohesion of the whole °system° is at risk. This greatly reduces the leverage of the °sub-

---

[442] Ibid.

[443] Ibid.

[444] Beer, S.: (Brain)

[445] Espejo, R.: (VSM revisited)

[446] Jackson, M. C.: (Managerial significance)

[447] Beer, S.: (Diagnosing)

[448] Espejo, R.: (VSM revisited)

system° activity (i.e. strongly attenuates their variety) setting the standards, i.e. which specific behaviour is to be considered as damaging. The more °sub-system° autonomy is curtailed by instructions from above, the harder it will be for the °sub-systems° to enlarge their scope of activities.[449]

4.5.4   *Three(*)-One*

Somehow, it has to be ensured that the actual °sub-system° implementation taking place remains consistent with the global 'Contract^{OR}', i.e. that the relevant °sub-system° issues are being recognised and the completeness, rightness, and integrity of 'Capacity^{OR}' is ensured. 'Reports^{OR}' of *Two-Three* interference can only describe the ongoing coordination of °sub-system° fluctuations. 'Accounts^{OR}' only provide an interpreted summary of °sub-system° activity. Therefore, a task force is needed to perform an independent investigation or 'Audit^{OR}', referred to as *Three(*)*. *Three(*)-One* gets in touch[450] and observes the actual activities carried out for implementing the °sub-systems°. Obviously, such a task force will not be capable to attend and accompany all °sub-system° activity and will therefore limit its investigations to a small set of aspects to be looked at. *Three(*)-One* interactions provide detailed information on the small set of aspects being examined and interpret it in the light of the °system's° 'Norms^{NR}', 'Strategy^{SOR}', and 'Contract^{OR}'.[451] They directly assess °sub-system° activities and complement *Three* arena interplay in regard to how the °sub-system° notions are being implemented. Therefore, they may address any °sub-system° actor individually at any time. 'Audits^{OR}' investigate °sub-system° notions exclusively; lower recursive layers are not included as involving lower levels of recursion would breach the integrity of the recursion levels and countervail the recursive function of portioning varieties between layers.

Three(*) actors use interventions to initiate 'Audits^{OR}', and create the 'Findings^{OR}' in highly formalised interplays with the selected *One* actors. 'Audits^{OR}' can be initiated only by *Three(*)* actors, and this occurs singularly at a certain point of time and lasts for the time defined by that actor. Thus, 'Audits^{OR}' may perform a study on process flows, investigate the condition of buildings or machines used, revise the cash management, or look at other aspects of °sub-system° activity. 'Findings^{OR}' are the inter-

---

[449]   Beer, S.: (Heart)

[450]   Espejo, R.: (VSM revisited)

[451]   "Monitoring is a low-variety channel that carries high variety about a few, specific issues.", in Espejo, R.: (VSM revisited)

preted reports on the current °sub-system° activity prepared for confrontation and integration into 'Capacity^{OR}' through *Three* arena interplay. As far as necessary and useful, they adopt the structure of 'Capacity^{OR}'. Further, *Three(*)-One* creates 'Conduct of Audit^{OR}', which defines the *Three*-One* interaction, i.e. the channels, methods, and transducers to be applied in *Three(*)-One*.

4.6 *Four* topics – strategic governing

Three deals with the "inside and now" perspective on a °system° implementation by engaging in how to optimise ventures and how to acquire synergy between °sub-system° activities. That view does not suffice for sustaining the viability of the °system° notion over the long term. Therefore, actors require ideas of 'where they are going' and 'what they should do'. They need to recognise changing circumstances in the environment and to prepare for future opportunities and risks by considering alternative options.[452] This is what *Four* topics are about.

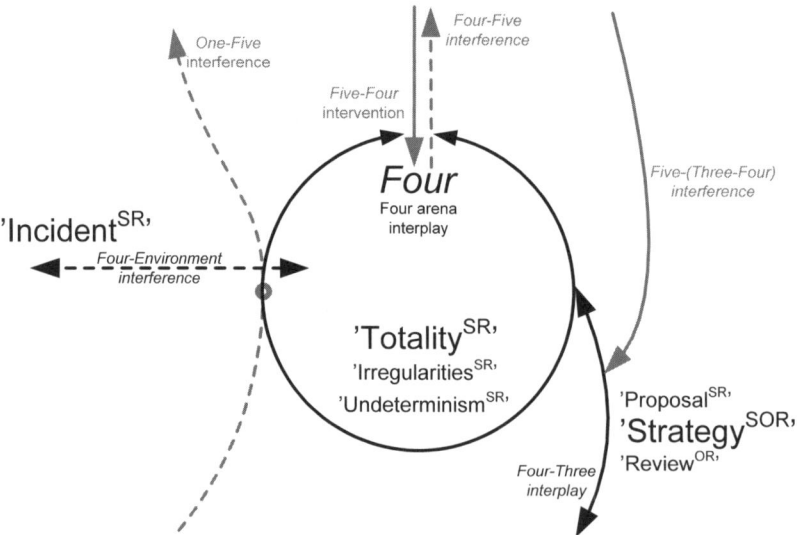

Figure 35. *Four* interactions

---

[452] Beer refers to these actors as the 'Development Directorate'. See Beer, S.: (Heart); Beer, S.: (Brain)

Four interactions identify important developments in the environment of the °system°, they simulate and forecast alternative options in different scenarios and initiate the adaptation of the °system° notion. Through them actors orient themselves towards the prevailing developmental possibilities of the °system° notion, i.e. the improvements latent in the current situation but not yet realised under present constraints.[453] The following characteristic interactions can be distinguished[454] for anticipating relevant °system° topics from an "outside and then" perspective. Again, each is described subsequently:

a) *Four* arena, which continuously creates an understanding of the 'Totality^{SR}' of aspects relevant for implementing the °system° notion;

b) *Four-Environment*, which constantly informs about 'Irregularities^{SR}' and 'Undeterminisms^{SR}' which the implementation of the °system° notion currently faces;

c) *Four-Three*, which creates 'Proposals^{SR}' of future activity, confronts them with 'Reviews^{OR}' of the current capability, and reconciles a temporary 'Strategy^{SOR}' with *Three* actors.

Figure 35 illustrates *Four* interactions.

4.6.1 *Four* arena

The *Four* arena interplays are used to anticipate the necessary developments in the environment and to prepare for the changes required in future °system° implementation. *Four* arena interplays create interpretations of how the °system° notion is to be implemented. Through them actors identify relevant opportunities and threats, find out how those developments can be approached or resolved, i.e. what 'images' should be implemented, which 'instruments' should be used and what 'actions' should be taken. They reflect on how the °system° actors are expected to react. Lower layer *Four* topics are involved in establishing the basis of *Four* arena interplay. Further, the following issues and solutions come together in the *Four* arena: 'Irregularities^{SR}' and 'Undeterminism^{SR}', which inform about significant trends and changes in the environment. 'Norms^{NR}' constitute and specify the frame for *Four* arena reconciliation and provide criteria for evaluating novel developments. Further, 'Reviews^{OR}' indicate the opera-

---

[453] Beer, S.: (Dispute)

[454] Beer, S.: (Heart)

tive restrictions and constraints that apply to future development from the perspective of the actual 'Capacity^{OR}'.

Four arena interplay is a sustained long-term effort[455] to reconcile and continuously re-create 'Totality^{SR}', i.e. an overview of all aspects relevant to the future and environment of the °system° notion including their interdependence (a *Wirkungsgefüge*).[456] It depicts a model of what is to be regulated,[457] a fundamental reference that enables actors to gain awareness of the relevancies in and the functioning of the °system° implementation.[458] 'Totality^{SR}' is self-referential and explains how the adopted °system° identity is currently being implemented and how it should be implemented in future. Therefore, the mutually influencing factors affecting °system° implementation from the environment producing the °system° notion and their interdependencies are revealed. The strategic, meta-operational type of representation of 'Totality^{SR}' permits actors to orient themselves to a larger time horizon.[459] This enables actors to share a holistic understanding of the °system's° future states and trends in its environment, including all relevant aspects and facts.[460] Sharing and continuously creating 'Totality^{SR}' enables actors to recognise incipient instabilities in °system° implementation and to stimulate alternative strategies for the future.[461] Both favourable and unfavourable developments can be anticipated, which enables actors to ground their decisions in a thorough understanding of the relevant developments in the environment as well as an in-depth understanding of the °system° organisation that has been assembled for implementation re-

---

[455] Schwaninger further emphasises that too many strategic efforts rest on established modes, while the precondition for genuine innovation to take place is re-framing the reference system (i.e. 'Totality^{SR}') completely, which then leads to the emergence of new modes of °system° implementation, e.g. of doing business, creating new opportunities, etc. See Schwaninger, M.: (Framework Intelligent Organisations)

[456] Beer, S.: (Heart)

[457] 'Totality^{SR}' is required because every "regulator must contain a model of that which is regulated", in Ashby, W. R. and Conant, R. C.: (Regulator); also see Beer, S.: (Heart)

[458] Beer, S.: (Diagnosing)

[459] Gälweiler, Aloys: (Corporate Strategy)

[460] Ibid.; Beer, S.: (Dispute); Malik, F.: (Complex Systems)

[461] Beer, S.: (Brain); Beer speaks of a 'stream of dialogue' that never stops flowing. Beer, S.: (Dispute); See also Schwaninger, M.: (Framework Intelligent Organisations)

flected in a section of 'Totality[SR]' referred to as the 'model of itself'[462]. That would not be possible based on a purely operational background.[463] Whenever the multiplicity of factors depicted in 'Totality[SR]' transcends actors' capacity to grasp them, the underlying model must be made explicit so that it can be questioned.[464]

4.6.2 *Four-Environment*

The environment includes those affected and not affected by °system° activities (or those inside and outside the °system° boundary). Environmental issues evolve from environmental actors, as for example clients in a market, citizens in a community, pupils in a school, car drivers on the road, etc.[465] Some of these issues may strongly affect the °system° notion; others may not affect it at all. Three types of actors have been distinguished above (chapter 2.3.2): firstly, those involved in the implementation of the °system°; secondly, those not involved but affected by the °system° notion; and thirdly, those neither involved nor affected by that °system° notion. *Four-environment* interaction engages in collective 'Incident[SR]' with those actors not involved and either affected or not affected. Therefore, this interaction brings some of these actors together in some kind of investigative interplay to uncover and detect the environmental issues relevant to it. In doing so, it fosters the recognition of the °system's° identity and its boundaries in the environment.

Primarily, *Four-Environment* interplay gathers, filters and interprets environmental issues and subsumes significant developments, trends and

---

[462] Figure 41 in Beer, S.: (Heart), p. 239 shows that the 'System Four Model of itself is embedded in the 'Model of total Viable System', see also Beer, S.: (Diagnosing)

[463] Gälweiler, Aloys: (Corporate Strategy)

[464] Beer, S.: (Heart)

[465] Besides Four actors, °sub-system° actors interact with the environment. Unlike *Four* actors, °sub-system° actors are confined to that part of the environment which is relevant on their level of recursion and makes up only a part of the whole environment-in-focus. In contrast, *Four* actors observe the whole environment of the °system° notion in focus. Both the well known and problematic part of the Four's environment transcend the sum of °sub-system° environments. The different markets a company serves do not in themselves constitute the complete environment relevant for the company. Malik, F.: (Complex Systems)

changes into 'Incident^{SR}', which it forwards to the *Four* arena.[466] It may be used to actively address individuals or group of actors, or simply to perceive the evolving environmental occurrences, such as signals of imminent unhappiness, the dissatisfaction of those affected, or danger and instability arising from other circumstances. Thus, *Four* actors can recognise the °system's° role in its environment. A well-known and a problematic part of the environment can be distinguished.[467] Observing the well-known part of the environment, its 'Irregularities^{SR}' is required for managing ongoing activities. For coping with newly evolving challenges in the environment the problematic part, or 'Undeterminism^{SR}', must be in focus. Well-known and problematic parts of the environment each require a different level of attention (or variety absorption) because they face different problems.[468] The 'well-known' part of the environment is to be observed regularly to detect 'Irregularities^{SR}'. Formalised protocols may apply here, which are to be adapted whenever this part of the environment undergoes major changes. Investigation into the 'problematic' part of the environment is conducted on the spur of the moment and uncovers any (even yet still unknown) 'Undeterminisms^{SR}' [469] the °system° is facing. Here, the applied procedure protocol tends to be tailored to the specific requirements each time in order to capture and trace problematic issues. Based upon this ongoing inquiry, the adequacy and validity of 'Totality^{SR}' to recognize prevailing 'Incidents^{SR}' is assessed.[470] To evaluate and interpret the relevance of the environmental issues for 'Totality^{SR}' and to identify novel developments, criteria are required. These criteria must allow actors to assess the perceived facts according to their relevance and importance with respect to the °system° notion.[471] These criteria are to be provided with 'Norms^{NR}' through *Five* interaction and to be referenced with 'Incident^{SR}' and 'Totality^{SR}' (chapter 4.7).[472] The proper recognition and interpretation of the significant developments and external factors[473] ensures that the implementation of the °system° notion

---

[466] Beer, S.: (Heart); Beer, S.: (Diagnosing)

[467] Beer, S.: (Heart)

[468] Malik, F.: (Complex Systems)

[469] 'Undeterminism^{SR}' has been chosen instead of 'Threats^{SR}' or 'Opportunities^{SR}' to avoid any emphasis on the °system° notion's pathologies or potentiality.

[470] Beer, S.: (Brain)

[471] Beer, S.: (Diagnosing); Beer, S.: (Heart)

[472] Beer, S.: (Heart)

[473] Willemsen, Maarten Helmut: (Is Switzerland viable?)

remains aligned with environmental developments. Simultaneously, *Four-Environment* transmits the overall °system's° identity and mission into the environment to exert influence.[474]

4.6.3 *Four-Three*

Four-Three interplay reconciles complementary *Three* and *Four* issues.[475] Building upon 'Totality^{SR}', *Four* actors develop, discuss, and reconcile 'Proposals^{SR}' illuminating future prospects, threats, and opportunities the °system° notion is expected to confront and how it is being planned to cope with these challenges.[476] 'Proposals^{SR}' give a developmental perspective and seek to implement the latent benefits, needs, and challenges in the situation. Typically, the propositions indicated cannot be realised under present constraints and require further investment of some sort, such as research, training, resources, etc. 'Proposals^{SR}' orient actors towards those factors in the °system's° *Wirkungsgefüge*[477], which develop the °system° notion into a desired state. Strategic solutions can never be better than their sources and the protocol that has led to them. Their quality depends completely on what is known about the environment and the °system's° organisation (as depicted in 'Totality^{SR}') and needs to be continuously updated.[478]

'Proposals^{SR}' have to be assessed in the light of the operative limitations of °system° implementation. The solutions they propose may at the same time be unrealistic as well as idealistic. Therefore, *Three* actors have to prepare 'Reviews^{OR}', which elucidate the actual needs, problems, and difficulties[479] faced when trying to assimilate those new developments described in 'Proposals^{SR}' which may not conform to the known procedures, cultures, and technologies.[480] 'Reviews^{OR}' orientate *Four* actors towards the operational constraints of °system° implementation, its needs and 'Capacity^{OR}' for change.[481] They devise an implementation that appraises 'what

---

[474] Beer, S.: (Heart)

[475] Espejo, R.: (VSM revisited)

[476] Beer, S.: (Heart)

[477] The German word *Wirkungsgefüge* refers to the network of relevant, interdependent factors that leverage °system° implementation.

[478] Gälweiler, Aloys: (Corporate Strategy)

[479] Ibid.

[480] Beer, S.: (Dispute)

[481] Ibid.

can, after all, be done'. 'Reviews^{OR}' are reflections of 'Proposals^{SR}' that address the gap between the desired and the current state of the °system° notion. They translate the opportunity and needs perspective of 'Proposals^{SR}' into a down-to-earth perspective detailed through particular goals and activities.[482] 'Reviews^{OR}' are primarily concerned with ensuring a tight fit between the operative 'images', 'instruments', 'actions', and 'actors' to be defined.[483] Thus, *Four-Three* interplay confronts 'Proposals^{SR}' with 'Reviews^{OR}', with *Four* promoting the °system's° opportunities and chances, pointing to the the 'Irregularities^{SR}' and 'Undeterminism^{SR}' – and with *Three* pointing to the operational constraints ('Reviews^{OR}')[484] the °system° faces when implementing the propositions.[485] Discussing the polarities of the 'Proposals^{SR}' and 'Reviews^{OR}' leads to the reconciliation of a 'Strategy^{SOR}' that offers a temporary resolution of strategic and operational issues. In 'Strategy^{SOR}', the aspects emerging from *Three* and *Four* are to be settled. For instance, a councillor suggesting a °community° to diversify its scope of services (thus making a 'Proposal^{SR}') may be vetoed by the chief financial officer, indicating that there are not enough human and financial resources left for some of the services aspired to (thus giving a 'Review^{OR}').[486]

As soon as a 'Strategy^{SOR}' has been reconciled, it provides the basis for all operative activity. It specifies the *strategic* and *operative 'images'*, *'instruments'*, and *'actions'* to be followed. Based upon 'Strategy^{SOR}', *Three* and *Four* now actualise and redirect their revolving versions of 'Capacity^{OR}' and 'Totality^{SR}'. 'Norms^{NR}' of fair play and a continuous 'Supervision^{NR}' ensure that the reconciliation between *Three* and *Four* succeeds. Both *Three* and *Four* actors should act in unison promoting the potential and capacity of the °system° notion.[487] Both the reconciliation of and the resolution established in 'Strategy^{SOR}' must align with the 'Norms^{NR}' defined by *Five* interactions. 'Strategy^{SOR}' reconciliation is continuously supervised in *Five*-to-(*Four*-to-*Three*).

[482] Schwaninger, M.: (Framework Intelligent Organisations)

[483] Hamel, G. and Prahalad, C. K.: Competing for the Future, Boston, 1994, p. 23 as found in Schwaninger, M.: (Framework Intelligent Organisations)

[484] Espejo, R.: (VSM revisited)

[485] Gomez, P. and Zimmermann, T.: Unternehmensorganisation – Profile, Dynamik, Methodik, Frankfurt a.M., 1997

[486] Espejo, R.: (VSM revisited)

[487] Espejo, R. and Gill, A.: The Viable System Model as a Framework for Understanding Organizations, Internetpage, 1997

4.7 *Five* topics – normative governing

Five issues are concerned with establishing and maintaining the fundamental °system° boundary to be adopted by the actors involved and the norms that derive from it.[488] *Five* interactions produce and guard the °system's° identity by continuously reconciling 'Boundary^{NR}'.[489] In so doing, they define the essential normative qualities of the reference °system°[490] and cultivate its culture and ethos, i.e. the ground rules, norms, values to be followed throughout implementation.[491] Thus, *Five* provides ultimate reference and logical closure[492] to all other interactions implementing the °system° notion. A context is defined only by the superordinated recursive layer, i.e. via the 'Super-Requirements^{OR}' provided by the °super-system° notion.

Its fundamental contribution is to frame the °system° notion, to provide criteria for taking decisions on the common grounds of the °system° notion.[493] *Five* interactions finally complete the set of characteristic reconciliations required for maintaining the viability of the °system° notion.[494] And this is the end, because any further challenging of the °system° notion turns the discussion to the next level of recursion. There, the whole set of characteristic topics and interactions applies again, from a different,

---

[488] Closure through self-referentiality is a fundamental and constituting characteristic of systems. Beer assigns this function to Five interactions. Further details can be found in: Malik, F.: (Complex Systems); Beer, S.: (Heart); Beer, S.: (Dispute)

[489] Beer, S.: (Diagnosing); this is not opposed to the fact that One interactions actually produce and implement viable °system° notions. See Beer, S.: (Diagnosing), pp. 124, 128: "'The purpose of a System is what it does'. And what the viable system does is done by System One. System Five, then, is 'only' thinking about it.".

[490] Herold, C.: Ein Vorgehenskonzept zur Unternehmensstrukturierung: eine heuristische Anwendung des Modells Lebensfähiger Systeme, 1991; Beer, S.: (Diagnosing): "I think that the rules come from System Five: not so much by stating them firmly, as by creating a corporate ethos – an atmosphere."; further: Herold's interview with Beer as cited in Malik, F.: (Complex Systems): Ethos is "the way we are".

[491] Beer, S.: (Heart)

[492] Beer, S.: (Diagnosing); Beer, S.: (Heart)

[493] Gälweiler, Aloys: (Corporate Strategy)

[494] Harnden, R.: (Outside and then)

broader perspective.[495] Ultimately, *Five* interactions guard the implementation of the °system° notion making sure that governing structures are adequate to perform and revise the aspired °system° notion (thus administrating requisite variety). The following characteristic *Five* interactions are to be distinguished:

a) *Five arena*, which continuously (re-)creates the °system° boundary;

b) *Five-(Three-Four)*, which observes the *Three-Four* interplay;

c) *Five-Four*, which secures the legitimacy of coping with the 'outside and then';

d) *Five-Three*, which secures the legitimacy of coping with the 'inside and now';

e) *Five-One*, which responds to and provides normative solutions to 'Urgencies^{OR}'.

Figure 36 illustrates *Five* interactions.

Due to the normative character of 'Boundary^{NR}', 'Norm^{NR}', 'Legitimacy$^{SR\&OR}$', and 'Supervision^{NR}', *Five* interactions reconcile abstract representations that indicate broad statements (high-variety resolutions). As

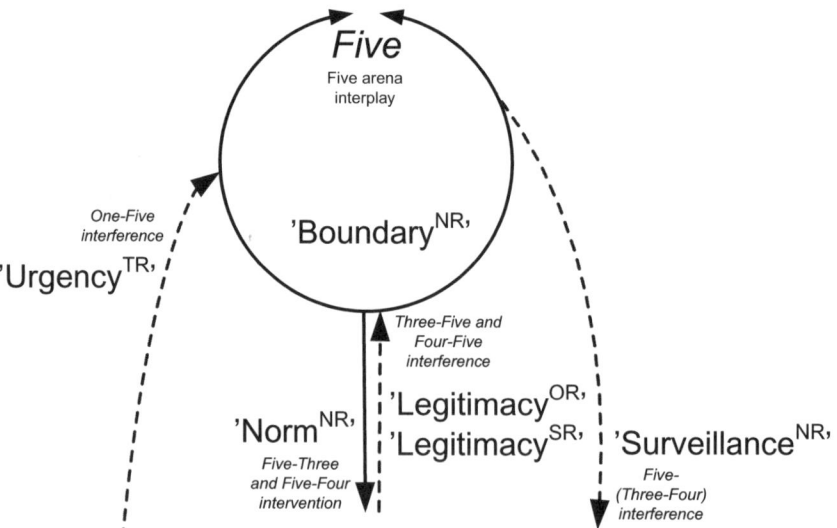

Figure 36. *Five* interactions

---

[495] Beer, S.: (Heart)

a consequence, they only have a limited structural capacity to absorb and process specific problems and issues. In principle, they cannot attend to and resolve issues that belong to the other systemic topics.[496] That is completely sufficient for fulfilling their task, i.e. to avoid uncontrolled conflicts in the other interactions.[497] *Five* simply engages in solving the remaining issues by providing the normative criteria upon which *Two*, *Three*, and *Four* interactions can dissolve the residual variety. Thus, *Five* concludes and closes logically the overall °system° notion.[498] It naturally follows that 'Boundary[NR]' and its derivations rely strongly on their sources.[499]

4.7.1   *Five* arena

°System° notions emerge and develop based on *Five* arena interplay. It subliminally influences the behaviour of all actors implementing the °system° notion[500] and executing their power to sustain it.[501] *Five* arena interplays give closure to all fundamental issues of the °system°.[502] The outcome of *Five* arena interplay is not a choice of 'instruments' or 'actions' to be implemented.[503] Rather, it addresses boundary issues and their normative

---

[496] Espejo, R. and Gill, A.: The Viable System Model as a Framework for Understanding Organizations, Internetpage

[497] Beer, S.: (Diagnosing)

[498] Beer, S.: (Heart)

[499] Ibid.; see Beer's third axiom of management, stating that the variety disposed by Five interactions equals the residual variety generated by the operation of the second axiom. First axiom: "The sum of horizontal variety disposed by all the operational elements EQUALS the sum of vertical variety disposed on the six vertical components of corporate cohesion.", in Beer, S.: (Diagnosing), p. 84; Second axiom: "The variety disposed by System Three resulting from the operation of the First Axiom EQUALS the variety disposed by System Four.", in Beer, S.: (Diagnosing), p. 121; Third axiom: "The variety disposed by System Five EQUALS the residual variety generated by the operation of the Second Axiom.", in Beer, S.: (Heart), p. 260; Beer, S.: (Brain)

[500] Malik, F.: (Complex Systems)

[501] Beer, S.: (Diagnosing)

[502] Espejo, R.: (VSM revisited)

[503] In distinction, Espejo claims that "Policy making is a process whose outcome is the choice of courses of action for the organisation.", in Espejo, R. and Harnden, R.: The VSM: an ongoing conversation, in: Espejo, R. and Harnden, R., The Viable System Model. Interpretations and Applications of Stafford Beer's VSM, Chichester, 1989

implications with respect to the °system° notion. In 'Boundaries[NR]' actors reconcile the normative judgements of what belongs to the °system° and what does not. They develop, discuss, and reconcile shared boundary judgements and derive ground rules (chapter 2.3.1). These boundary judgements are those intents and claims which delimit the background of a °system° notion in relation to its assigned °sub-systems°.[504] Some parts of boundary may be general values of the lifeworld which have evolved in the course of history and now constitute the °system°. Although parts of such °system° boundaries may correspond to formal, institutional boundaries, other parts usually do not. Most importantly, the frame delimited with the boundary judgements applies to *Two, Three,* and *Four* interactions as well as to *Five* interactions themselves.

Through orientation towards 'Boundaries[NR]', actors attune their individual boundaries and °system° backgrounds. As a consequence, they accumulate positive experiences and confidence in each other, which facilitates the stabilisation of their adopted °system° notions with respect to the integration of the individual. Shared boundary judgements are strong constraints on actor behaviour (variety attenuators)[505] because they expel the huge quantity of other possible selections from being implemented in the name of the °system° notion. For instance, they do so by legitimising resource demands, value potentials, operating procedures, compensation systems, etc. Different intentions advocate different values. In a cycle, values are adopted by those involved and affected by a social °system° and then implemented by the decision-makers: boundary judgements legitimise structures, structures evolve and shape governing issues – governing issues assess and re-shape °system° boundaries.

All *Five* arena interplays are paradoxical, since what they reconcile is inherently self-referential, creating and re-creating fundamental backgrounds based upon what has already been established in the lifeworld. The primary reconciliation of a °system° notion is a good example of this. It requires some fundamental agreement on how actors relate to one another. Some sort of such an agreement will generally be found in the prevailing cultural, political, social, economical conditions in an actor's lifeworld.[506] These pre-conditioned agreements have evolved in the personal

---

[504] Beer, S.: (Dispute)

[505] A "variety sponge of gigantic capacity", in Beer, S.: (Diagnosing), p. 125

[506] Beer refers to these conditions as "epigenetic landscape", in Beer, S.: (Heart), pp. 125, 259; Epigenesis stands for the accretion of design beyond the merely developmental process. See Beer, S.: (Diagnosing)

development of the actors' history and are determinative for their °system° notions now. Nevertheless, this evolutionary background of °system° notions does not guarantee that the notions are continuously actualised and kept viable. As has been seen above in the principle of autonomy (chapter 4.1.4), to maintain the viability of a °system° notion, interventions in other actors' backgrounds are legitimate only to the minimum degree required to sustain that shared °system° notion. Autonomy provides a useful criterion to distinguish between the implementation of the °system° notion and its °sub-system°. However, it does not tell whether that °system° notion does make sense and can be considered legitimate or which °system° layer should be considered normatively prime. These fundamental questions underpin any constitution of a °system° 'Boundary^{NR}'. They can be answered differently and have to be grounded in some way on some layer. The fundamental cybernetic law of requisite variety that has been the source of identifying invariant issues and interactions can only provide a hint, but no definite answer to these questions.

It can be argued that the only °system° notion that holds for grounding others is the actor himself, because only his boundary is experienced and delimited based on both percepts and contexts, as actors are both biological and social °systems°. This, as could be argued, legitimises them to be considered as the fundamental °system° in relation to which other purely contextual °system° notions are solely products of reflective thought and therefore have to be legitimised carefully. Such an argument gives primacy to human actors, adopts basic human rights, etc. Based upon such a fundamental 'Boundary^{NR}' agreement, limitations of autonomy can only be decided based upon the meaning and significance of a °system° notion for the affected actors.[507] It follows that, for the coherent reconciliation and implementation of a social °system° notion, all actors involved and affected by that notion have to own a legitimate claim to participate and contribute in its constitution, i.e. in the *Five* interactions taking place.[508] However, making the actors primary to legitimise °system° 'Boundaries^{NR}' does not imply that the wishes of all actors with legitimate claims on it can be met. *Five* arena interplay cannot achieve equality as that would require all actors to permanently reconcile and re-shape their °system° notion, with each single actor talking to every other at the same time.

---

[507] Ulrich, W.: (Reflective Practice)

[508] In regard to determining overall °system° purposes, "Beer has got to answer that they should be determined by all those with a legitimate claim on the relevant system.", in Ulrich, W.: A critique of pure cybernetic reason: The Chilean experience with cybernetics, Journal of Applied System Analysis, 8, 1981

Further, *Five* solutions are normative in character, which means they are abstract and do not necessarily entail their practical implications.[509] A 'Boundary[NR]' that has been decided upon and published in the name of a small legitimised group of actors (e.g. a company directorate) has not and will not be adopted in the same way by all actors involved. For instance, a 'mission statement' being published to describe a set of normative goals and values of a °company° does not in the least mean that all actors internalise it. Rather, it is most probable that actors will experience major differences in how it is being interpreted. Depending on the process that led to the mission statement, only a limited number of °system° actors might have been involved or the statement might have been announced by the company directorate. Based on such limited involvement, only little commitment can be expected from the side of the employees. The low-capacity *Five* channel is usually not capable to induce actor commitment.

Therefore, it is true that *Five* arena theoretically consists of everyone involved, be it e.g. politicians, public and private managers, the workforce, customers, or citizens (compare chapter 4.1.3).[510] It is generally not restricted to a selected group of actors. All actors, without exception, repeatedly undertake *Five* arena interplays, at least as part of their informal dialogues for opinion formation and decision-making. This may be sufficient in loose relationships to realise loose °systems° notions but not if actors are involved in the implementation of a challenging °system° notion which increases actors interdependency and urges them to surrender parts of their autonomy. Obviously, to equally involve a broad public in °system° constitution is purely idealistic. In such a situation, all actors would require common backgrounds, a common past, and synchronous time flow. Informal, interference- based dialogues are limited to accommodate and affirm an explicit 'Boundary[NR]'. Somehow, commitment has to be acquired. For °system° notions with many actors involved, *Five* arena interplay will therefore require some type of formalised protocol. Commonly, such a protocol nominates a smaller group of actors to be responsible for defining and reshaping 'Boundary[NR]'.[511] Some institutionalised body, such as a board, a constitutional court, or a constituent assembly, may be established. Involving the remaining actors may be formalised as with citizen initiatives, elections, and plebiscites.

---

[509] Espejo, R.: (VSM revisited)

[510] Beer, S.: (Heart)

[511] Espejo, R.: (VSM revisited)

Actors always create their individual °system° notions, purposes, clients, decision-makers, etc. as they evolve from their individual intentions and contexts. *Five* arena interplay cannot create equal °system° notions but only bring forth shared, accommodated individual °notions° that prove to be compatible and suitable in regard to certain issues in a certain period of time.[512] They are a compromise which reflects the prevailing culture and power relations between the actors involved.[513]

For this reason, nominating the 'Boundary[NR]' of a °system° is usually a profoundly controversial task. It requires actors to articulate their °system° notions, thereby realising and disclosing their individual boundary judgements. Making boundary judgements explicit and comparing them, provide evidence on how actors impute different boundaries to one and the same °system° label in regard to their interests. Usually, most boundary imputations will be found to be highly idiosyncratic.[514] Uncovering them will therefore not always be in the interest of all actors. Nevertheless, analysing articulated notions of a social °system° allows the determination of how authoritarian a °system° notion is by considering whether the 'Boundary[NR]' compromise being worked out is biased towards the overall °system° notion rather than towards its °sub-system° notions.[515]

Five arena interplays reconcile 'Boundary[NR]' judgements and enable the actors involved to observe and critically supervise all other interactions[516] and to make certain that the °system° notion is actually being implemented. Through them actors identify and correct communicative flaws and breakdowns occurring in °system° interactions.[517] Their normative perspective allows them to reconcile present and future, as well as internal and external °system° issues.[518] Ultimately, with 'Boundary[NR]' the identity[519] of the °system° notion and its environment is determined. In addition, they also encourage actors not participating in the constitution of the °system°

---

[512] Espejo, R.: Giving Requisite Variety to Strategic and Implementation Processes: Theory and Practice, http://bprc.warwick.ac.uk/LSEraul.html

[513] Beer, S.: (Diagnosing)

[514] Jackson, M. C.: (Managerial significance)

[515] Espejo, R.: (VSM revisited)

[516] Schwaninger, M.: (Viable Systems Model)

[517] Beer, S.: (Heart)

[518] Espejo, R. and Harden, R.: The Viable System Model. Interpretations and Applications of Stafford Beer's VSM, Chichester, 1989

[519] Beer, S.: (Diagnosing); "Closure is the talisman of identity.", in Beer, S.: (Heart), p. 260

'Boundary^{NR}' to consider critically whether those who actually set it up truly represent their intents and claims.

Any issue, concern, or solution claiming to be rational is not critically tenable unless it refers back to and makes explicit its underlying boundary judgements. Whenever an interaction oscillates or faces breakdown, *Five* interactions enable the participating actors to reveal their underlying 'Boundary^{NR}' and to examine its implications in the light of alternative °system° notions.[520] Before any topic issue, concern, or potential solution can be discussed meaningfully with respect to its validity, importance, or normative implication – the boundary of its reference °system° has to be made explicit with respect to its empirical and normative content.[521] Making 'Boundaries^{NR}' explicit creates legitimacy and practical rationality.

4.7.2   *Five-Four* and *Five-Three*

Adopted °system° boundaries substantiate interactions and frame recon-ciliations. 'Norms^{NR}' derive from the agreed 'Boundaries^{NR}'.[522] They are directives setting the standards against which ongoing interactions and actor behaviour is judged with respect to °system° implementation.[523] By adopt-ing and adhering to 'Norms^{NR}', their characteristic *One, Two, Three,* and *Four* interactions are orchestrated and monitored, thereby also impacting lower °system° layers. Thus, they can rationalise ongoing strategic, opera-tive, and tactical reconciliations with respect to the time and effort invested as well as the quality of the reconciliations taking place.[524] 'Norms^{NR}' pro-vide the criteria required to evaluate issues and situations.[525] They set the conditions for the concert of roles, competencies, and responsibilities.[526] They do not derogate autonomy or keep other interactions from carrying out their assigned tasks. They have leverage on *Four* and *Three* interactions, but exclusively with respect to setting up their normative underpinnings.[527]

---

[520] Ulrich, W.: (Quest for Competence)

[521] Ulrich, W.: (Reflective Practice)

[522] Beer, S.: (Dispute)

[523] Gälweiler, Aloys: (Corporate Strategy)

[524] Ibid.

[525] Beer, S.: (Provenance)

[526] Gälweiler, Aloys: (Corporate Strategy)

[527] "The boss is supplying closure – in a logical sense. He is not applying it by mas-sive variety inhibition: he is leaving variety absorption where it belongs, between Three and Four. His role is metasystemic.", in Beer, S.: (Heart)

'Norms[NR]' are conveyed as imperatives that ground actor behaviour without determining the execution of strategic, operational, and tactical functions.[528] The course of action of a °system° notion can only be determined through *Four* and *Three* interactions. *Five* interactions simply ensure that all other interactions execute the 'Norms[NR]' and thus promote the °system° ethos and values. They constitute the basis of these interactions, but never actually promote decisions.[529]

'Norms[NR]' specify and delimit the scope of issues and solutions to be reconciled. Those issues and solutions seen as irrelevant for the implementation of the °system° notion and its purposes are excluded. Therefore, they should be formulated as specifically and precisely as required to designate the scope of possible selections actors are expected to choose from. Strategic 'Norms[NR]' give direction to *Four* interactions.[530] They delimit the way *Four* actors perceive the environment by providing rules for the conduct and interpretation of inquiry.[531] This enables *Four* actors to evaluate and interpret the relevance of the inquiries that are gathered and to identify 'Irregularities[SR]' and 'Undeterminism[SR]' (see chapter 4.6.2). Whereas strategic 'Norms[NR]' address the conduct of *Four* interaction, operative 'Norms[NR]' specify the conduct of *Three* and indirectly also *Two* interactions.[532] Operative 'Norms[NR]' provide direction in *Five-Three* intervention by setting operational policies and proposing operational guidelines. Delimiting the impact of *Three* interaction in °system° implementation is necessary to avoid a unilateral focus on short-term 'Synergy[OR]' in °system° implementation. Even though this may seem worthwhile with respect to the short-term efficiency of the °system°, emphasis on 'Synergy[OR]' only curtails long-term success and ignores success potentials by fading out strategic issues. This would deteriorate the fundamental preconditions of success and viability.[533]

Through 'Legitimacy[SR]' and 'Legitimacy[OR]' operative and strategic activities are linked to the normative °system° boundary which they implement

---

[528]   Gälweiler, Aloys: (Corporate Strategy)

[529]   For a different notion of Five interactions see Espejo, R. and Harnden, R.: (Conversation)

[530]   Gälweiler, Aloys: (Corporate Strategy)

[531]   Beer, S.: (Diagnosing)

[532]   Gälweiler, Aloys: (Corporate Strategy)

[533]   Ibid.

and thus become meaningful activities perceived as making sense.[534] Via interferences, an account on the 'Legitimacy^{SR}' of *Four* interactions is provided. This regards the reconciliation of 'Totality^{SR}' and all its derivates, i.e. 'Irregularities^{SR}', 'Undeterminism^{SR}', and 'Proposals^{SR}'.[535] *Four-Five* interference does not provide detailed reference to *Five* but indicates that its activities comply with 'Norms^{NR}'.[536] It subsumes the current strategic activities and issues and provides evidence on how they are being adhered to, interpreted, and settled. Thus, it may be recognised that the established normative 'Boundary^{NR}' and its derived 'Norms^{NR}' needlessly restrict the implementation of 'Proposals^{SR}'. As soon as 'Proposals^{SR}' suggest new ways to relate to the environment, to develop or delimit the identity set up in the actual 'Boundary^{NR}',[537] it will require *Five* actors to rethink the established 'Boundary^{NR}' in the light of new developments. *Four-Five* interference orients *Five* towards this incongruence and enables it to induce the required adaptation of the °system's° identity.[538] *Five-Four* intervention provides 'Norms^{NR}' that legitimate the resolutions achieved in *Four* interactions.

Three's contribution to the implementation of the °system° is to provide an account of the 'Legitimacy^{OR}' of *Three* interactions. This regards the reconciliation of 'Capacity^{OR}' and all its derivates, i.e. 'Guideline^{OR}', 'Synergy^{OR}', 'Audit^{OR}', 'Requirement^{OR}' and 'Review^{OR}'. *Three-Five* interference does not give detailed reference to these statements but simply proves that they are implemented in regard to 'Norms^{NR}'[539]. It subsumes the ongoing reconciliation of operative issues in the light of their contribution to the im-

---

[534] Willemsen, Maarten Helmut: (Is Switzerland viable?)

[535] *Five* actors receive answers providing analysis and interpretation of the environment. These are contained in 'Totality^{SR}', which enables actors to reference all aspects of the °system° and constitutes the fundamental basis for self-awareness. Beer, S.: (Dispute)

[536] They do not themselves access the environment or reproduce aspects of other representations. Jackson, M. C.: (Managerial significance)

[537] Espejo, R.: (VSM revisited); Schwaninger further emphasises that too much of strategic efforts rests on established modes, while the essence of genuine innovation is reframing the reference system completely, which often leads to the emergence of new modes of doing business, creates new opportunities and may reshape entire industries, see Schwaninger, M.: (Framework Intelligent Organisations)

[538] Malik, F.: (Complex Systems)

[539] Beer, S.: (Heart); Beer, S.: (Dispute); Espejo, R.: (VSM revisited)

plementation of the overall °system°. Therefore, it may describe the efforts and performance of the ongoing optimisation of °sub-system° activities, the procedures and efforts achieved in resource allocation, or the success of auditing °sub-system° implementations, etc. Thus, *Five-Three* interference legitimates the solutions being reconciled in *Three* interactions.

4.7.3 *Five-(Four-Three)*

Any imbalance occurring in *Three-Four* interplay implies the danger of losing opportunities and increasing resource consumption in °system° implementation.[540] If *Four* produces 'Proposals^{SR}' at a higher rate than *Three* can provide 'Reviews^{OR}', *Five* will have to decide how to cope with the innovative, environmental surplus in the light of the purposes addressed by the °system° notion.[541]

As its major activity, *Five* creates the normative frame for *Three-Four* interplay and supports their reconciliation.[542] *Four-Three* interplay confronts long-term strategic 'Proposals^{SR}' with short-term, operative 'Reviews^{OR}' and negotiates a temporary 'Strategy^{SOR}'. Both are complementary statements for evolving, transforming, and implementing the overall °system° identity.[543] *Five* is designed to harmonise the influence of *Three* and *Four* to prevent overarching dominance and advantage of one side.[544] Therefore, *Five* actors supervise the *Four-Three* interplay and ensure that aspects of both topics are being considered adequately.[545] The more fruitful and productive *Four-Three* interplay is, the less influence has to be exerted.[546] Only when the reconciliation encounters unconstructive conflict, does *Five* add the criteria required for solving their controversy and thus dissolves the issue (i.e. the prevailing residual variety). Resolving the remaining issues (i.e. the residual variety) is done via *Five-Four* or *Five-Three*

---

[540] Espejo, R.: (VSM revisited)

[541] Ibid.

[542] Beer, S.: (Diagnosing); Absorbing the residual variety of Three-Four interplay is prime. Beer, S.: (Heart)

[543] Beer, S.: (Dispute)

[544] Espejo, R. and Gill, A.: The Viable System Model as a Framework for Understanding Organizations, Internetpage

[545] Beer, S.: (Dispute)

[546] Second managerial axiom: "The variety disposed by System Three resulting from the operation of the First Axiom EQUALS the variety disposed by System Four.", Espejo, R.: (VSM revisited), p. 87

intervention. It is *Five* actors' awareness of *Three-Four* interplay that is needed to adapt the °system° 'Boundaries^{NR}' and their derived 'Norms^{NR}', if necessary.[547] *Four-Three* interplay is a most vulnerable interaction for maintaining the viability of the °system° notion, as usually a °system° collapse is initiated here.[548] The quality of the solutions derived from *Three-Four* interplay depends on the quality of its 'Supervision^{NR}'.[549]

Three-Four interplay should make as much use of 'instruments', such as resources, as the circumstances of the situation permit. Continuous 'Supervision^{NR}' ascertains that all normative °system° concerns are being examined from both *Three* and *Four* perspectives. This is necessary to maintain the balance between investment into the future and maintaining the actual activities running. To do so, *Five* interactions critically challenge the underlying boundary assumptions of the actors involved with respect to the °system° boundary. *Five* interactions judge their activities with respect to the °system° identity. This enables them to observe, bring to the surface, critically discuss, and accommodate those underlying boundary judgements which differ or oppose the shared °system° 'Boundary^{NR,550}'.

4.7.4 *Five-One*

Five interactions further deal with 'Urgencies^{TR}' of the ongoing °subsystem° implementation. 'Urgencies^{TR}' are algedonic signals that characterise actual °sub-system° instability. They do not describe or explain analytically the why and how of the issue, but focus simply on labelling the 'Urgency^{TR}' as positive or negative, rewarding or punishing.[551] They arise directly from those involved in governing the °sub-system° notion.[552] On their way from *One* to *Five*, they must be labelled 'good' or 'bad' with respect to their impact on operative and strategic issues. Therefore, they pass the *Three* and *Four* arenas, which add their comments to the message.[553] *One-Five* channels ensure that 'Urgency^{TR}' cannot be manipulated or filtered by *Three* or *Four* actors. *Five-One* immediately enacts the 'Norms^{NR}' relevant to responding to these 'Urgencies^{TR}'.

---

[547] Beer, S.: (Heart)

[548] Beer, S.: (Dispute)

[549] Espejo, R.: (VSM revisited)

[550] Ibid.

[551] Beer, S.: (Heart)

[552] This channel is restricted to the cases of urgency. See Beer, S.: (Diagnosing)

[553] Beer, S.: (Heart); Beer, S.: (Provenance)

Algedonic signals are simple, non-analytical, spontaneous, and immediate. Actors use them to give expression to their °system° intentions, i.e. they articulate how a °system° issue is being evaluated.[554] A scream may be an algedonic signal, indicating that an actor finds himself in a dangerous situation. Algedonic signals do not describe characteristics or attributes of a certain issue or situation but point to its significance in the °system° context, e.g. with respect to the stability or instability of the °system° notion.[555] Resentment, initiatives, petitions, referenda and plebiscites give expression to algedonic signals. Essentially, algedonic signals point to problematic °sub-system° issues in the light of the °system° in-focus without commenting on their causes. They simply inform that there are critical, threatening issues evolving that endanger the implementation of the °system° notion. Further reconciliation will only be required to address the relevant aspects of the indicated issue. And that will be performed through the respective topic interactions.[556]

4.8 Integrated framework

It is only now that the necessary and sufficient conditions for the viability of a °system° notion have been set up. The integrated governance framework, which represents the outcome of this research, is now complete. Mainly, viability is a property of those °system° notions whose structures provide sufficient capacity (chapter 3) for the actors involved to reconcile adequate resolutions to issues on all system topics (chapter 4). Figure 37 provides a review of the invariant systemic topics that have been identified.

The governance framework is assembled as depicted in Figure 38. Therefore, the systemic topics (reflecting Beer's axioms of management) are plotted on the vertical axis whereas the aspects of structure (reflecting Beer's organisational principles) are indicated on the horizontal axis. In their architecture and design, structures have to promote the viability of social systems. Thus, it is demonstrated that structures are established to support °systemic° topic reconciliation. In the columns the structural aspects are indicated as they have been described above. The governance framework can be applied for any social °system° notion which has clari-

---

[554] Beer, S.: (Heart)

[555] Beer, S.: (Brain)

[556] Ibid.

fied its °system° and °sub-system° boundaries. Where it is applied, the prerequisites for productive interactions and sustainable development of the °system° notion can be identified. Social °system° notions that provide such adequate structures are viable only at a certain point in time. Those which maintain the balance continuously over time, i.e. through implanting or anchoring the described basic principles in their °system° structures, are sustainable over time. With the fourth's principle of organisation[557], permanence is an inherent property of viability. However, often the framework will be used in a diagnostic mode reflecting on a °system° notion at that specific point of time. To unleash the sustainability of a °system° notion, permanent supply of requisite capacity has to be ensured, as it has been demanded already.

Figure 38 can also be used to profile the viability and sustainability of a °system° notion. Therefore, the table has to be segmented into rows for each °system° topic and columns for each structural aspect, thus allowing the confrontation of systemic topics with structural aspects (compare Table 15).

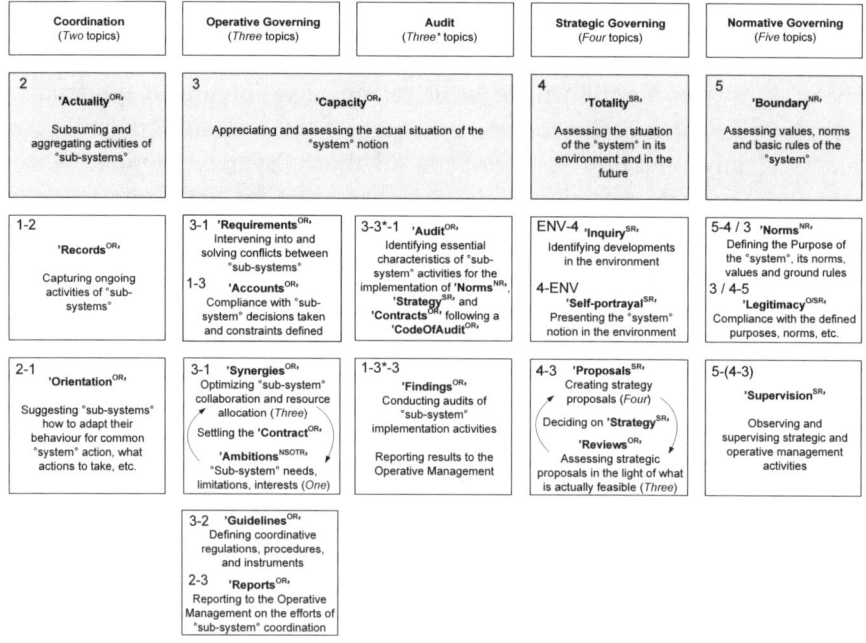

Figure 37. Invariant systemic topics

---

[557] See chapter 3.5

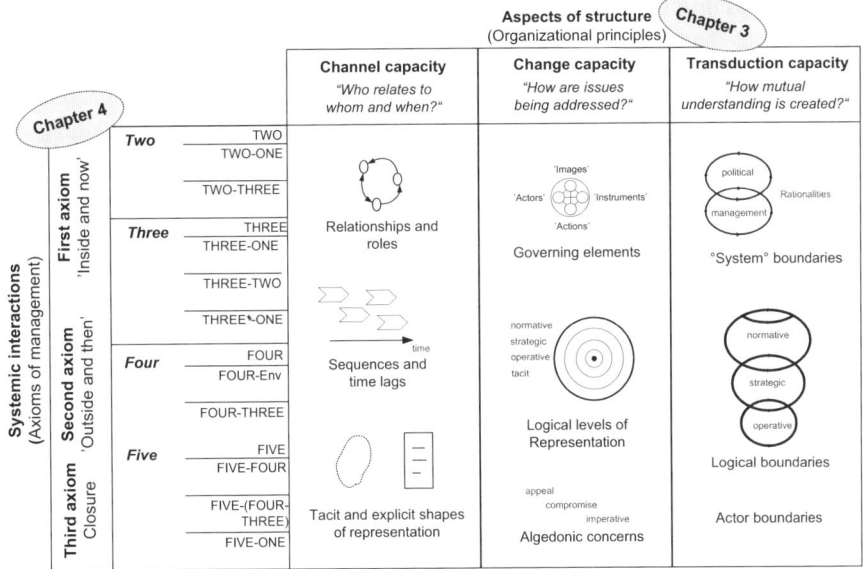

Figure 38. Governance framework for viability of °system° notions

In such a profile, each field can be used to indicate (e.g. with different colours) the actual status of the structural capacity that is provided. Thus, white fields would indicate "everything ok", yellow fields "improvement possible" and red ones "urgent action required". There can then be specific attention given to those structural properties which are of deficient and of primary interest for °system° implementation (compare case study, chapter 5).

The following typical questions indicate how the integrative framework can be applied in social °system° diagnosis and design. Similarily, it is verified here to what extent the established structures support the execution and solution of the systemic topics.

Channel capacity

A: Adequacy of actor roles, tasks, and responsibilities

1. Who is involved in °system° implementation?

2. What are the major formal actor settings, i.e. meetings, councils, departments?

3. What is the contribution of the major actor settings to comply with the systemic functions and to solve the °systemic° topics?

B: Processes and sequences of reconciliation

1. What are the processes and sequences followed in the major actor settings throughout the reconciliation?

2. Do these processes and sequences support actors in solving their °systemic° topics in due time? What are major obstacles, lags, and hurdles?

Change or transformation capacity

A: Aptitude of methods and instruments

1. What are the major methods and instruments applied for governance?

2. Are the transformations applied correct? Do the methods contribute to solving the °systemic° topics? What are their limitations and disorientations?

B: Interfaces between methods and instruments

1. How do the established methods applied interfere?

2. Does the interplay of the established methods and instruments promote compliance with the °systemic° topics?

Transduction capacity

A: Awareness of the °system° notion aspired to

1. Are the actors involved aware of the °system° notion being sought? Do they know about and agree with the major boundary judgements?

2. Do actors act conform to the °system° notion when they engage in the °systemic° topics?

B: Understanding and translation between logical boundaries

1. Do actors distinguish between logical levels of representation? E.g. are they aware that strategic issues are different from operative?

2. Do actors translate correctly between logical levels when engaged in °systemic° topics? For instance, do they recognise that operative results cannot be extrapolated into strategic goals?

C: Understanding and translation between actor boundaries

1. Do actors understand each other? Do they speak the same language? Do they understand each other's terminology?

2. Do actors understand each other when engaged in solving °systemic° topics?

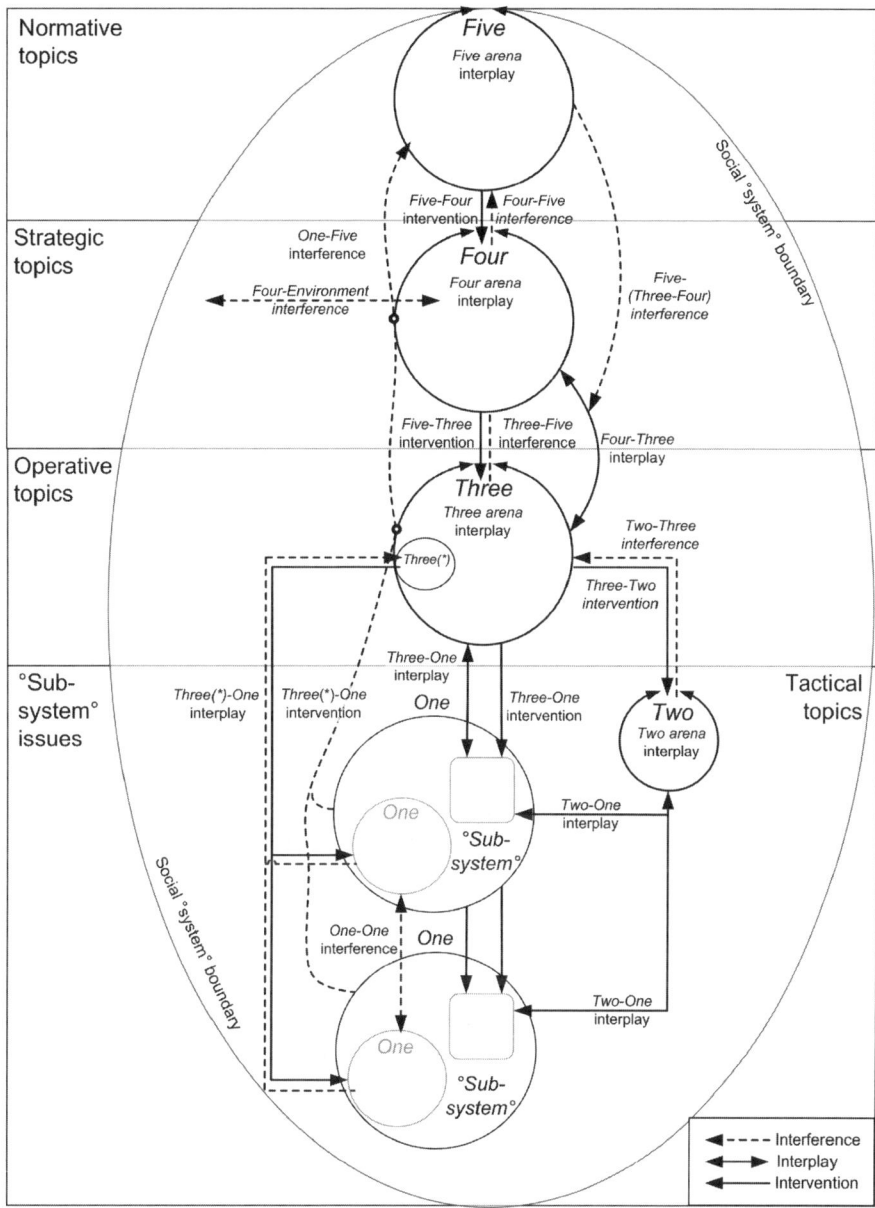

Figure 39. Invariant interactions required for °system° viability

The figures and tables on the following pages sum up the key features of the characteristic interactions. First of all, Figure 39 sketches the whole set of invariant °systemic° interactions as they were described. Then, the tables of Figure 40 to Figure 44 provide detailed descriptions of each invariant interaction that was identified. For each °systemic° topic, the following characteristics are indicated:

1. the name of the representation including as annotation the logical level that is being addressed (i.e. TR, OR, SR or NR);

2. the classification of contribution, to which this topic corresponds (e.g. Reference, Declaration, Concern, Solution or Justification)[558];

3. a description of the targeted topic or variety block including a typical question that points to the topic;

4. a description of the content structure of each topic based on the four governing elements that were introduced (e.g. "These 'images' are being aspired to", "These 'actors' are to be involved", etc.);

5. the sources that are logically required for reconciliation of each specific topic.

Furthermore, Figure 45 makes explicit the logical interdepencies and necessary interfaces between the invariant °systemic° topics. Therefore, it indicates how each °systemic° topic exerts influence on others, e.g. where

1.   topic 'A' makes a contribution, determines (a part of) topic 'B';

2.   topic 'B' is created as a reflection on topic 'A';

3.   topic 'B' describes an observation of topic 'A' or 'A' informs 'B'.

Based on the knowledge of these interdependencies between topics, the diagnosis and design of change or transformation capacity is facilitated. Methods and instruments can be analysed with reference to their interfaces.

---

[558] Compare chapter 3.1.1, Table 3

4.8.1   *One* issues

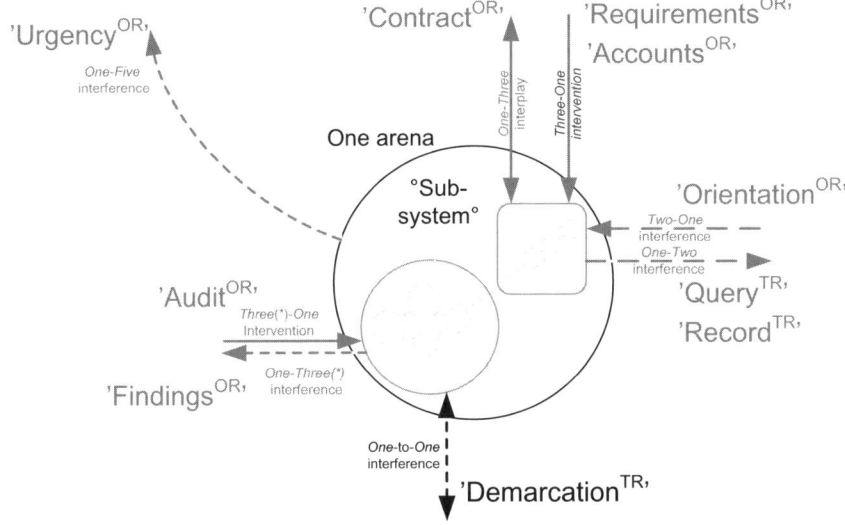

Figure 40. *One* issues

Interaction	\<Protocol\>		
	Representation	Targeted issues	Sources

One interactions			
***One* arena**	Implement the °sub-system°.		
(°Sub-system°)	**No single representation**	*Inside One arena, a complete °sub-system° is implemented. It entails all other characteristic interactions described.*	System-in-focus ('ANY')
One-One	Clarify operative issues without relation to interdependencies affecting the overall system.		
Interference (Squiggly lines)	'**Demarcation**TR'	*Where is the boundary separating a °sub-system° from others? How can it be resolved?*	
	Concern (instant)	a. What practical necessities or facts restrict °sub-system° implementation and need to be reconciled?	'Sub-ANY'
	Solution (temporarily fixed)	b. What compromise can be achieved between °alpha°, °beta°, °gamma° to solve 'Demarcation'TR' that does not affect the overall °system°?	
Overall context of *One interactions*: 'Boundary'NR', 'Norm'NR', 'Strategy'SOR', 'Contract'OR', 'Requirements'OR'.			

4.8.2 *Two* topics

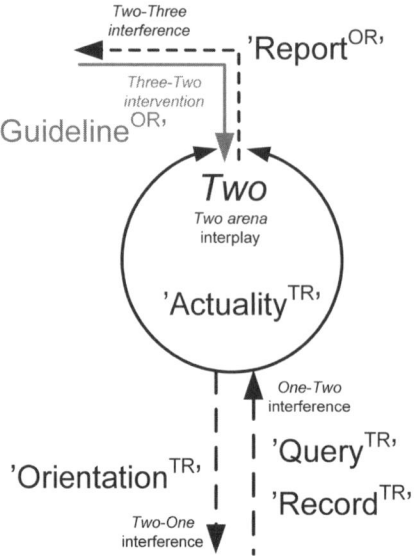

Interaction	<Protocol>			
	Represen- tation	Targeted topic (or variety block)	Content	Sources

Two interactions				
Two arena	Creates tactical plans of *what the system does.*			
Interplay	**'Actuality**[TR]**'** Reference (revolving)	*What constitutes the implementation of the °system° now? Where do °sub-systems° face interdependencies, fluctua-tions that need to be coordinated?* a. What 'instruments' are used where and for how long? Which are dispos-able? b. What is the current state of activities? Are they currently being executed, implemented, stopped, or prolonged?	Model	'Guideline[OR]', 'Record[TR]', 'Query[TR]'
Two-One	a) *Ones* continuously supply 'Records[TR]' describing their individual situation, b) *Ones* express 'Queries[TR]' to access 'instruments' or to undertake 'actions' which do affect the overall °system° notion, c) *Two* provides 'Orientation[TR]' to *One* arenas towards how they can eliminate interdependencies and conform to collective 'Guidelines[OR]'.			
One-to-*Two* *Interference*	**'Record**[TR]**'** Declaration (instant)	*What is the individual °sub-system° currently doing? What is its situation in relation to the others?* a. What individual activities are con-ducted now, what resources are used? b. What are causes and consequences of fluctuation?	These tactical 'images' are being aspired. These 'instruments' are being used. These 'actions' are being taken. These 'actors' are involved.	'Actuality[TR]' 'Sub-Actuality[TR]'

Figure 41. *Two* topics

Interaction	<Protocol>			
	Represen-tation	Targeted topic (or variety block)	Content	Sources
	'Query^{TR}' Concern (instant appeal)	*What concerns are being articulated for the implementation of individual °sub-systems°?* a. What 'images', e.g. facts, visions, problems, needs are relevant to °alpha°, °beta° etc.? b. What 'instruments', financial, human resources can °alpha°, °beta° access? c. What 'actions', e.g. appointments shall °alpha°, °beta° take?	What tactical 'images' should be aspired to? What 'instruments' should be used? What 'actions' should be taken? What 'actors' should be involved?	
Two-to-*One Interference*	**'Orienta-tion^{TR}'** Solution (instant appeal)	*What can and should °sub-system° actors do to resolve or dissolve their interde-pendent concerns with others?* 'images' facts, visions, presupposi-tions, problems, opportuni-ties, judgements, goals, causes, and consequences of fluctuations, etc. 'instruments' financial, human, and knowledge resources, ex-periences, structures, etc. 'actions' activity descriptions and characteristics, etc. 'actors' competencies, interests, etc.	These tactical 'images' are to be aspired. These 'instruments' are to be used. These 'actions' are to be taken. These 'actors' are to be involved.	
Two-Three		a) *Two* reports on the efforts of the activities to harmonise °sub-system° interde-pendencies, i.e. the conduct of the ongoing *Two-One interplay*, b) *Three* define and sets up 'Guidelines^{OR}' for the *Two* arena interplay.		
Two-to-*Three Interference*	**'Report^{OR}'** Declaration (instant appeal)	What are the efforts of harmonising fluctuations between the °sub-systems°? a. What is the actual status of °sub-system° implementation with respect to interdependent issues? d. What are unsolved, problematic issues of interdependency between °sub-systems°? e. What are causes of the fluctuations of °sub-systems°, f. What experiences are made with the 'Orientation^{TR}' of the °sub-systems°? g. What are incongruencies in *Three* 'Guidelines^{OR}'?	Efforts of harmonisation have (not) been successful, because a. these operative 'images' have (not) been achieved; b. these 'instruments' have (not) been used; c. these 'actions' have (not) been taken; d. these 'actors' have (not) been involved. These are relevant occur-rences, reasons, interpreta-tions.	'Actuality^{TR}'
Three-to-*Two Intervention*	**'Guideline^{OR}'** Concern (temporarily fixed impera-tive)	*How are °sub-system° interdependencies to be coordinated and what policies and decisions apply?* a. What 'images' are to be followed? Goals, resource allocations, activity plans; benchmarks for identifying and judging fluctuations between °sub-systems°; admitted performance loss due to fluctuation. b. How are 'images' to be implemented? Procedures for solving fluctuations; responsibilities; agendas.	Operative 'images' that shall be aspired. What and how 'instru-ments' are to be used. What and how 'actions' are to be taken. What and how 'actors' are to be involved. Criteria for interpretation.	'Capacity^{OR}'
Overall context of *Two* interactions: 'Boundary^{NR}', 'Norms^{NR}'.				

Figure 41 (continued)

4.8.3   *Three* topics

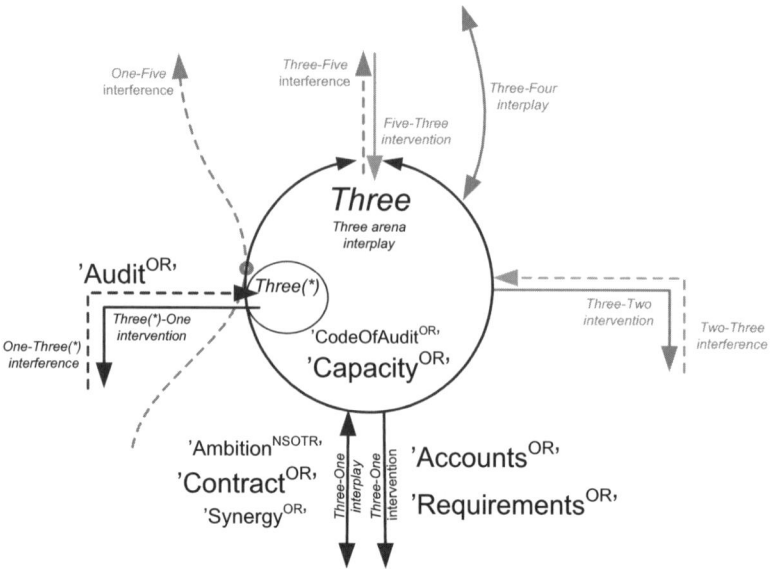

Interaction	<Protocol>			
	Representation	Targeted topic (or variety block)	Content	Sources

Three interactions supporting managerial interactions.				
Three arena	Create operational plans based on *what the social °system° can do.* a) Create and maintain 'Capacity^{OR}', relying on 'Reports^{OR}', 'Audits^{OR}', and 'Accounts^{OR}' to understand the operational needs and constraints of the system; b) Optimise 'Capacity^{OR}' to express how *the °sub-systems° can achieve synergy*; c) Develop and inspect the 'CodeOfAudit^{OR}' for *Three(*) interaction*.			
Interplay	'Capacity^{OR}' Reference (revolving)	*How is the current status of activities to be evaluated in the light of 'Norms^{NR}' and 'Strategy^{SOR}'?* a. What is the output, performance of °sub-systems° implementation? b. What are experiences with the modus operandi and the constraints of °sub-system° implementation? c. What is the capacity to conduct change? What is the gap between the required and actual capacity to change?	Model	'Norms^{NR}', 'Strategy^{SOR}', 'Account^{OR}', 'Report^{OR}', 'Audit^{OR}'.

Figure 42. *Three* topics

Interaction	<Protocol>			
	Representation	Targeted topic (or variety block)	Content	Sources
	'Code of Audit^{OR}' Reference (temporarily fixed)	*What should be monitored, when and in which time intervals?*	*Essentials of 'Boundary^{NR}', 'Strategy^{SOR}', 'Contract^{OR}' and 'Guidelines^{SR},*	'Capacity^{OR}'
Three-One (Resource Bargain)	a) *Ones advocate* their individual autonomy and 'Ambitions^{NSOR}' as expressed in their adopted 'Sub-Strategy^{SOR}' and 'Sub-Ethos^{NR}', b) *Three* puts forward a 'Synergy^{OR}', representing the interests of a synergic whole as recognized with its 'Capacity^{OR}' to implement the adopted 'Strategy^{SOR}', c) *Three* reconciles with each *One* upon a temporary 'Contract^{OR}', which defines *One's* degree of autonomy that incorporates the 'Requirements^{OR}'.			
Three-to-One inter-play	**'Synergy^{OR}'** Concern (instant)	*What can the overall social °system° do and what is it proposed to do to acquire optimal synergy of °sub-systems°?*	To acquire optimal allocation, a. these operative 'images' would have to be aspired to b. these 'instruments' would have to be used c. these 'actions' would have to be taken d. these 'actors' would have to be involved	'Strategy^{SOR}', 'Capacity^{OR}' 'Requirements^{OR}'
Accommo-dation	**'Contract^{OR}'** Solution (temporarily fixed, low-variety com-promise)	*What is the arrangement between the interests of the °sub-systems° and their synergy in regard to the overall °system° that is actually being implemented?* a. Goals for °sub-systems°, out-come expectations, resource allocations, degree of autonomy, specific tasks, etc.	Operative 'images' that shall be aspired. Which 'instruments' are to be used and how. What 'actions' are to be taken and how. What 'actors' are to be involved and how. Criteria of success.	
One-to-Three interplay	**'Ambition^{NSOR}'** Concern (instant)	*What is aspired to by the °sub-systems° to realise their intentions and °sub-system° notions?*	Any normative, strategic, operative 'images', 'instruments', 'actions' and 'actors' constella-tions aspired by °sub-systems°.	'Sub-Strategy^{SOR}', 'Sub-Ethos^{NR}',
Three-One (Account-ability and Constraint)	a) *Three* announces necessary constraints, i.e. the operative 'Requirements^{OR}' required for the synergy of the °sub-systems°, a) *Three* requests *One* actors to provide 'Account^{OR}' of their activities, b) *Ones* provide regular 'Account^{OR}' of their ongoing activities.			
Three-to-One Intervention	**'Requirements^{OR}'** (temporarily fixed)	*What rules must be kept? What must not be done by the °sub-systems° because it contradicts the notion of the social °system°?* a. Operative requirements, etc.	Adopt a tactical or operative 'image'! Use 'instruments' in a specific way! Use a specific 'instrument'! Take a specific 'action' or set of 'actions'! Involve a specific 'actor' or set of 'actors'!	'Contract^{OR}' 'Capacity^{OR}'

Figure 42 (continued)

Interaction	<Protocol>			
	Representation	Targeted topic (or variety block)	Content	Sources
One-to-Three Interference	**'Account**^{OR}**'** (instant)	*What provides account regarding the compliance of the °sub-systems° with the 'Contract*^{OR}*'?*	Throughout the implementation of 'Contract^{OR}', a. these 'images' have (not) been achieved; b. these 'instruments' have (not) been used; c. these 'actions' have (not) been taken; d. these 'actors' have (not) been involved.	'Sub-Capacity^{OR}'
Three(*)-One	a) *Three*(*) interactions directly and independently observe and interview °sub-systems° to ensure sound conduct and implementation of their 'Contracts^{OR}'. b) One arenas' answers produce 'Findings^{OR}' informing directly of ongoing primary activity.			
Three(*)-to-One Intervention	**'Audit**^{OR}**'** Concern (instant imperative)	*What are the efforts of One arenas to implement their °sub-systems°? What is actually being done?* a. Independent requests and investigation of °sub-system° effectiveness, efficiency, accountability, and legitimacy.	What 'images' are actually being aspired to? What 'instruments' are actually being used? What 'actions' are actually being taken? What 'actors' are actually being involved?	'Capacity^{OR}'
One-Three(*) Interplay	**'Findings**^{OR}**'** Justification (temporarily fixed compromise)	*How is °system° implementation actually being done?* a. What counts as an answer to 'Audits^{OR}'; b. Reflects on, or summarises a momentary observation of One activity, e.g. implementation of operating procedures, etc.	In the light of 'Norms^{NR}', 'Strategy^{SOR}' and 'Contract^{OR}', a. are the 'images' aspired supportive? b. are the 'instruments' applied productive? c. are the 'actions' taken efficacious? d. are the 'actors' involved reliable?	'Norms^{NR}' 'Strategy^{SOR}' 'Contract^{OR}' 'Sub-ANY'
Overall context of *Three interactions*: 'Boundary^{NR}', 'Norms^{NR}'.				

Figure 42 (continued)

4.8.4   *Four* topics

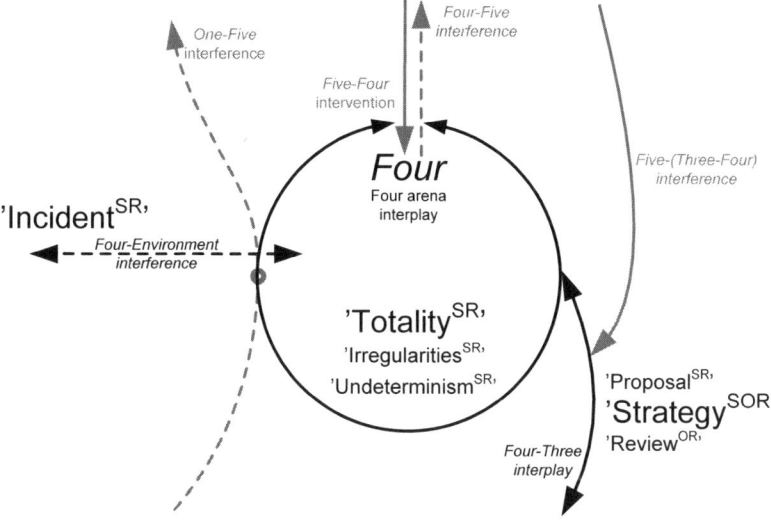

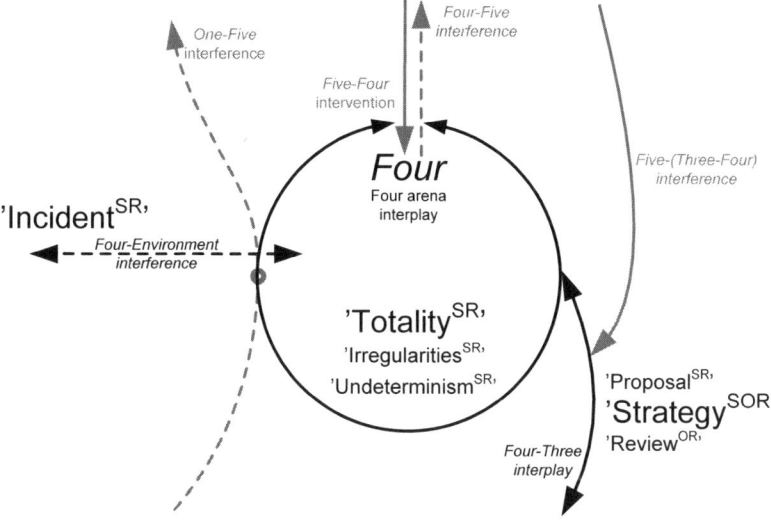

<table>
<tr><td>Interaction</td><td colspan="4"><Protocol></td></tr>
<tr><td></td><td>Representation</td><td>Targeted topic (or variety block)</td><td>Content</td><td>Sources</td></tr>
<tr><td colspan="5">Four interactions</td></tr>
<tr><td>Four-
Environ-
ment
Interplay</td><td colspan="4">Pose queries either to the 'well-known' or 'problematic' part of the social system's environment.
Capture environmental developments and constraints to recognise future prospects, threats and
opportunities.</td></tr>
<tr><td></td><td>'Incident[SR]'

Declaration
(instant)</td><td>What occurs in the 'well-known' and
'problematic' parts of the environ-
ment and is relevant in the light of
the °system° notion?</td><td>These facts, develop-
ments, occurrences are
relevant to
a. the 'images' that are
   being aspired to;
b. the 'instruments'
   that are being used;
c. the 'actions' that are
   being taken;
d. the 'actors' that are
   being involved.</td><td>Environment</td></tr>
</table>

Figure 43. *Four* topics

Interaction	<Protocol>			
	Representation	Targeted topic (or variety block)	Content	Sources
Four arena	Create and maintain a model of 'Totality^{SR}', describing the situation of the system and its determining parameters allowing to anticipate and conclude 'what constitutes the outside and then'. Continuously analyses 'Incident^{SR}' and 'Reviews^{OR}' to identify changes in the environment ('Irregularities^{SR}' and 'Undeterminism^{SR}') and to actualise 'Totality^{SR}' (*Wirkungsgefüge*) based upon their interpretation. Further creates an understanding about how the implementation of the °system° notion is achieved.			
Interplay	**'Totality^{SR}'** Reference (revolving)	*How is the situation of the °system° to be evaluated in regard of environment and future (outside and then)?* a. What determines °system° implementation? b. What are relevant 'Undeterminisms^{SR}' and 'Irregularities^{SR}'? c. What are the influencing parameters and the dynamics of the environment? What are key variables, value potentials relevant for maintaining the °system° notion? How are actors organised to implement the °system° notion?	Model	'Norms^{NR}', 'Incidents^{SR}', 'Undeterminisms^{SR}', 'Reviews^{OR}'
	'Irregularity^{SR}' (instant)	*What consequences arise from 'Incidents^{SR}' in the 'well-known' environment for the °system°?*	None	'Totality^{SR}'
	'Undeterminism^{SR}' (instant)	*What consequences arise from 'Incidents^{SR}' in the 'problematic' environment for the °system°?*	None	'Totality^{SR}'
Four-Three Interplay	a) *Four* derives 'Proposals^{SR}' from an assessment of 'Totality^{SR}' and illuminates *what should be done*, b) *Three* creates and advocates 'Reviews^{OR}' that assess 'Proposals^{SR}' in the light of 'Capacity^{OR}', c) *Three* and *Four* reconcile a finalised temporary 'Strategy^{SOR}' that makes explicit how 'Proposals^{SR}' and 'Norms^{NR}' should be implemented in the light of the system's 'Totality^{SR}' and 'Capacity^{OR}'.			
Four-to-*Three*	**'Proposals^{SR}'** Concern (instant)	*What should be done in future to sustain the social °system° in its environment?* a. What are future prospects and opportunities of the °system° under the constraints defined through 'Norms^{NR}'? b. What are the most promising ideas, goals, and plans, to cope with prospects, threats and opportunities?	Those 'images' should be aspired to address future prospects, threats, and opportunities. Those 'instruments' should be applied for implementation. Those 'Actions' should be taken for implementation. Those 'actors' should be involved.	'Norms^{NR}' 'Totality^{SR}' 'Capacity^{OR}'.

Figure 43 (continued)

Interaction	<Protocol>			
	Representation	Targeted topic (or variety block)	Content	Sources
Three-to-Four	**'Reviews^{OR}'** Concern (instant)	*Following 'Proposals^{SR}', what can be done to sustain the °system° notion in the light of its 'Capacity^{OR}'?* a. What operative needs and constraints of 'Capacity^{OR}' oppose the implementation of 'Proposals^{SR}'? b. What could be done to implement 'Proposals^{SR}'?	These strategic 'images' will be (un)feasible, (un)achievable. Instead those operative 'images' would be possible. These strategic 'instruments' will be (un)available, (deficient), (in)efficient. Instead... These strategic 'actions' will be (not) practical. Instead... These strategic 'actors' will be (in-)capable. Instead....	
Accommodation	**'Strategy^{SOR}'** Solution (temporarily fixed)	*What has been reconciled between future potentiality and actual capability, and is to be implemented?* a. What 'images' are to be followed? What are strategic and operative goals, outcome descriptions? b. What 'instruments' are to be applied? What are plans and rules for implementation?	These strategic and operative a. 'images' are to be aspired to; b. 'instruments' are to be applied; c. 'actions' are to be taken; d. 'actors' are to be involved.	
Overall context of *Four interactions*: 'Boundary^{NR}'.				

Figure 43 (continued)

4.8.5 *Five* topics

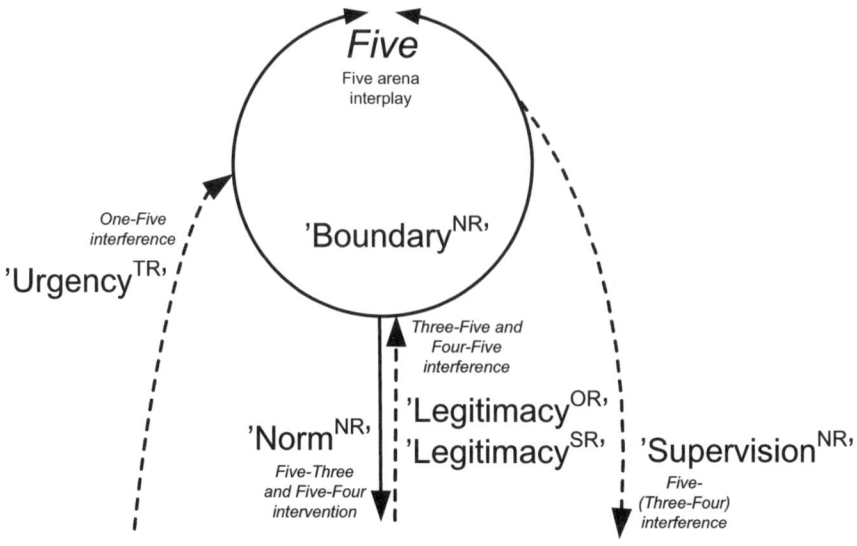

Interaction	<Protocol>			
	Representa-tion	Targeted topic (or variety block)	Content	Sources

Five interactions				
***Five* arena**	1) Continuously creates and maintains the 'Boundary^{NR}' of the social °system°, 2) creates a <protocol> for conducting *Five* arena *interplay*, 3) decides on regulatory 'Norms^{NR}' to respond to 'Legitimacy^{SR}', 'Legitimacy^{OR}' and 'Urgency^{OR}'.			
Interplay	**'Boundary^{NR}'** Reference (revolving)	*What constitutes the social °system°?* a. What boundary judgements apply? b. What are the basic rules of the °system°, i.e. its ethos, culture, norms, and values, purpose defini-tions, etc.? c. *What is the protocol of Five arena?*	Boundary judgements (compare Table 2)	'Super-Norms^{NR}', 'Legitimacy^{SR}', 'Legitimacy^{OR}', 'Supervision^{NR}', 'Urgency^{OR}'.
Five-Three	1) *Five* defines 'Norms^{NR}' for *Three* arena interplay, 2) *Three* reports to *Five* upon the 'Legitimacy^{OR}' of the inside and now.			
Five-to-Three Intervention	**'Norms^{NR}'** Concern (temporarily fixed)	*What has to be done to sustain the social °system° regarding operations?* a. What is the protocol for the *Three* arena interplay? What are opera-tional policies, purpose, guidelines, etc. of the overall °system°? b. *What are regulatory measures to counter the imbalance of Three-Four?*	When attending to solving *Three* topics, - aspire to these normative 'images'; - apply these 'instru-ments'; - take these 'actions'; - involve these 'actors'!	'Legitimacy^{SR}' 'Legitimacy^{OR}'

Figure 44. *Five* topics

Interaction	<Protocol>			
	Representation	Targeted topic (or variety block)	Content	Sources
Three-to-Five Interference	**'Legitimacy^{OR}'** Justification (instant)	*What accounts for the compliance of operative activities with 'Norms^{NR}'?* a. What operative activities and reconciliations have (not) been following 'Norms^{NR}'? b. Are 'Norms^{NR}' suitable to supporting operative activities in the current situation ('Capacity^{OR}', 'Reviews^{OR}', etc.) Are operative issues being resolved adequately?	Operative activities and reconciliations - followed these normative 'images'; - applied these 'instruments'; - took these 'actions'; - involved these 'actors' (not) in line with 'Norms^{NR}'.	'Capacity^{OR}'
Five-Four	1) *Five* defines 'Norms^{NR}' for *Four arena* interplay, 2) *Four* reports to *Five* upon the 'Legitimacy^{SR}' of the outside and then.			
Five-to-Four Intervention	**'Norms^{NR}'** Reference (temporarily fixed)	*What must be done to sustain the social °system° in regard to the development of strategies?* What is the protocol for the *Four* arena interplay, i.e. a. What are rules for creating 'Totality^{SR}' and the interpretation of 'Incident^{SR}' and 'Undeterminism^{SR}'? b. What is the boundary of the overall °system° notion, i.e. purposes, etc.? c. What are the regulatory measures to counter the imbalance of *Three-Four*?	When attending to solving *Four* topics, - aspire to these normative 'images', - apply these 'instruments', - take these 'actions', - involve these 'actors'!	'Legitimacy^{SR}', 'Legitimacy^{OR}'.
Four-to-Five Interference	**'Legitimacy^{SR}'** Reference (instant)	*What accounts for the compliance of strategic interactions with 'Norms^{NR}'?* a. Status and development of 'Totality^{SR}' in the light of 'Norms^{NR}' and 'Ethos^{NR}', b. Suitability of 'Norms^{NR}' produced by *Five* with respect to the adopted 'Strategy^{SOR}'. d. Report on the 'Strategy^{SOR}' of the overall °system°.	Strategic activities and reconciliations - followed these normative 'images'; - applied these 'instruments'; - took these 'actions'; - involved these 'actors' (not) in line with 'Norms^{NR}'.	'Norms^{NR}', 'Strategy^{SOR}', 'Reviews^{OR}'
Five-(Three-Four)	*Five* supervises *Three-Four interplay* to foster cohesion. Is *Three-Four* consistent with the 'Boundary^{NR}', e.g. the °systems° ethos, norms, values?			
Five-to-(Three-Four) interference	**'Supervision^{NR}'** Declaration (revolving)	*What are the efforts of reconciling 'Proposals^{SR}' with 'Reviews^{OR}'?* a. What quality have 'Proposals^{SR}' and 'Reviews^{OR}'? b. What disturbs *Three-Four* interplay, and what are the causes?	In the reconciliation between 'Proposals^{SR}' and 'Reviews^{OR}', - these normative 'images' have (not) been followed, - these 'instruments' have not been applied, - these 'actions' have not been taken, - these 'actors' have not been involved as defined in 'Norms^{NR}'.	'Proposals^{SR}', 'Reviews^{OR}', 'Strategy^{SOR}'
Five-One	1) *One* communicates urgent threats to the primary units; 2) *Five* takes quick consequences; 3) *Five* sublimely spreads the 'Boundary^{NR}', observes the primary units from a meta-perspective.			

Figure 44 (continued)

Interaction	<Protocol>			
	Representa-tion	Targeted topic (or variety block)	Content	Sources
One-Five interference via *Three* and *Four*	**'Urgency**[TR]**'** Concern (instant, algedonic)	*What actual occurrences endanger the viability of the social °system°?* a. What sudden threats, urgencies that affect the °system°? b. Which ongoing activities and consequences are critical? *Three* and *Four* label any 'Urgencies[TR]' as good or bad.	"Good!", "Bad!".	'Sub-Capability[OR]', 'Capacity[OR]', 'Totality[SR]'
Five- One interference, intervention via *Four* and *Three*	**'Norms**[NR]**'** Solution (instant)	*What normative judgements have to form the basis of current activities to sustain the social °system°?* a. Which normative rules and decisions are required for coping with 'Urgency[OR]'? b. Which *Four* and *Three* activities should be initiated?	To attend to 'Urgency[TR]' these normative, strategic, operative - 'images' are to be taken; - 'instruments' are to be applied; - 'actions' are to be taken; - 'actors' are to be involved.	'Urgency[OR]'

Figure 44 (continued)

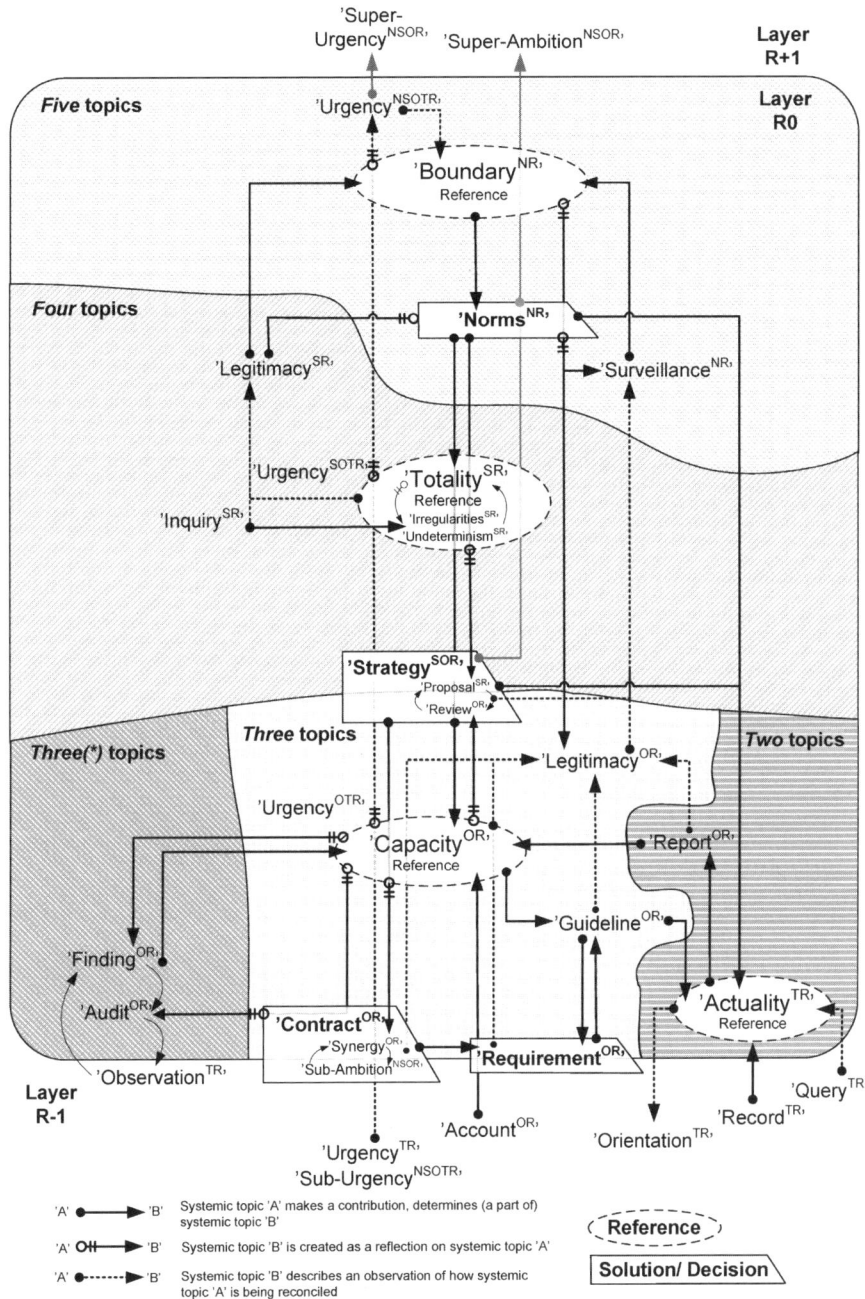

Figure 45. Interdependencies between invariant systemic topics

5   Case: Community

This chapter aims at explorative, empirical substantiation of the developed framework through application in the context of Hessian °communities°. Hesse is one of the 16 federal states embodied in the Federal Republic of Germany. Around 6.1m inhabitants live in 420 Hessian °communities°.

Therefore, with purpose and focus of the substantiation characterised, a 'case study' has been chosen as the appropriate method. Subsequently, the main characteristics of the selected case are described by defining the unit of analysis and the sources of percepts that have been involved.

5.1   Purpose

The essential focus of this research has been to find ways for the actors involved or affected in some social endeavor to appraise and improve the structures established between them in regard to the specific purpose they intend to implement. Hessian °communities° serve as an example to examine all of the interactions involved in settling the allocation of resources within themselves. The first and major part of the research is to identify how °community° life can be described and captured through the eyes of the governance framework. The research will reveal to what extent existing structures support the viability of communities and how it can be improved. Further, it will be deduced how viable structures can be supported by eMedia. Therefore, it focuses on identifying the obstacles and constraints immanent in the ongoing interaction of °community°. The focus is not to reflect in detail on the situation of a particular °community°, but to show what the quality of interactions looks like in the light of the governance framework.[559] To approach the exploratory research question formulated, a single, individual case has been conducted deriving the major relevant generalisations:

---

[559] Yin, R.: Case study research: Design and methods, Thousand Oaks, 1989, p. 6; Stake, R. E.: The Art of Case Study Research, Thousand Oaks, 1995, p. 16

1. Can the structures and characteristics of interactions provide adequate reference and solutions to the °system° topics evolving between actors?

2. What structures and characteristics do not yet meet the requirement of viability?

3. What can eMedia contribute to facilitating and improving the governance of Hessian °communities°? What is the potential of eMedia to promote the governance of a social system?

The conclusions derived shall be informative to all average °communities° sharing the same contextual conditions.[560] Furthermore, the hypotheses and propositions should motivate further inquiry into system-oriented logical frameworks.

5.2 Research methodology

A °community° notion is viable if the structures established between actors lead them to continuously resolve their °community° issues. It is only then that actors work well in concert supporting the purposes they aspire to. To examine the structures and characteristics of the interactions taking place, i.e. "to implement a °community° notion", means implementing a °research° notion. Doing so requires a clear and adequate °research° methodology[561] that allows

1. coping with settings of highly interdependent actors who cannot and will not be manipulated through the research activity;

2. handling different purposes and boundaries in °community° notions which are not clearly evident because they are continuously (re-)created by actors;

3. recognising °community° interactions and acquiring a thorough understanding of them.[562]

---

[560] Yin, R.: (Case study research)

[561] At this point, the research conduct draws from the theory it has created itself, i.e. the systemic Governance framework is applied to test itself. The interactions conducted throughout the activity "case study research" do follow some methodology. For sound research, the methodology applied has to have the capacity to provide for requisite variety (see "sustainability of control" chapter 3.5).

[562] Yin, R.: (Case study research); Stake, R. E.: (Art of Case Study)

The governance framework provides so to speak spectacles for classifying the percepts gathered throughout participation in the °community° notions and criteria for their interpretation. The logical model of interactions stipulates how the complexity of states and the diversity of actors and stakes in °community° governance can be captured.[563] Thus, it also provides a frame for categorising the dynamics taking place in interactions. As a major characteristic, the framework is not a linear sequence to be read from left to right or top to bottom. It is much more a structural frame of interaction that allows capturing all kinds of social contexts from the perspective of their prevailing intentionality and contextuality, i.e. the coherence of the backgrounds of the actors involved. The concepts established with "logical levels", "systemic topics", "governing elements", "system" and "boundary", "recursion", etc., can be filled with real-life experiences, which allows focusing on those aspects and phenomena of °community° governance which are of special interest. The continuous reconciliations of °community° actors can be traced, identified, and evaluated regarding their supportive or counterproductive contribution to the persistence of the °system° notion. A new quality of talking about and understanding °community° arises: typical topics and the channels, methods and transducers that are applied in different °communities° become identifiable, describable, and comparable – thus uncovering the underlying structure logically determining °community° life. Here, the governance framework is applied in a synthetic, diagnostic mode with a focus on some specific points of interest.[564] Essentially, diagnosing a social °system° notion is not only about analysing but essentially about synergising its elements and interrelations into a comprehensive holisistic perspective on it.

Thus, governing structures of a °community° notion cannot be captured by a narrowed perspective. Therefore, a theory has been provided allowing the examination of the nature of the interactions that are actually being applied to implement a °community° notion.[565] Now, the research methodology (the structure within which the research activity is taking place) has to

---

[563] For instance, 'Reports[OR]' depend on 'Actuality[TR]' but are independent of 'Capacity[OR]'; 'Capacity[OR]' relies on regular 'Reports[OR]'.

[564] "In a diagnostic mode, the method permits us to make visible mismatches between the complexity that particular managers appear 'to see' and the complexity that they should see for effective discharge of their duties.", in Espejo, R.: (Cybernetic method), p. 382

[565] Yin, R.: (Case study research)

be capable to holistically capture the interactions in the real-life °community° settings[566], to follow further the theoretical propositions developed, and to pursue the explorative and heuristic °research° notion (as defined in chapter 1.3). Therefore, it has to allow involving all relevant sources and to revise findings wherever required throughout the °research° process. What is required is a bird's eye view which evolves a rich picture of evidence, taking into account observations, documents, artefacts, actor

Table 14. Capacity of research methodologies

Capacities	Methodology		
	Case study	Survey	Experiment
Change	Summaries of observations, continuous refinement and reflection, application and continuous revision of the underlying theory.	Statistical analysis and evaluation. Logical conclusions.	Researcher formulates hypothesis and attempts to maintain control over factors that determine °community° interactions. Comparison of results in comparable °community° notions.
Channel	Researcher is observer of, and possibly active participant, in the °system° notion and may undertake any form of contact with involved actors. Actor involvement and research process are continuously being revised.	Limited contact with involved actors. Rigid focus on specific questions and answers throughout the whole research process. Fixed actor involvement.	Researcher is observer, creates stable conditions between actors of at least two °community° notions. Actor involvement is predefined. Process is predefined and repeated in different °community° notions.
Transduction	Researcher can assure his understanding of the involved actors through continuous questioning, repetition and confirmation.	Understanding is facilitated only in so far as explanations are provided in the survey documenttation and facilitate compatible interpretations.	Researcher limited in obtaining and communicating understanding through experimental protocol.

[566] Gassmann, O.: Praxisnähe mit Fallstudienforschung, Wissenschaftsmanagement, 6, 3, 1999

comments, and applied instruments to complete the puzzle.[567] Table 14 indicates the capacity of three typical research methodologies.

The case study methodology allows the research to grasp how the systemic topics are being addressed in °community°. Through them causal links between real-life percepts can be articulated which would be too complex for a survey or an experiment. In a case study, the researcher takes the role of an observer who continuously refines and reflects on his findings. The specific approach of the research (i.e. the channels, methods, and transducers to be applied) can be (re-)configured according to ongoing needs and requirements.

However, this is not to say that other research approaches could or should not be applied with the governance framework. Governance experiments or surveys can make highly fruitful contributions as soon as the °research° notion shifts from an explorative to an investigative focus. Such an endeavour will turn out to be much easier as soon as the basic underlying structures of the °community° notion in focus are known. The contribution of survey, experiment, and other methodologies would then be to concentrate on specific °community° or environmental phenomena. With their rigid focus on specific questions and answers, surveys are clearly limited in capturing interactional phenomena between °community° actors.[568] The methodology chosen here is particularly suited for primary applications of the governance framework in new °system° contexts. However, they could be highly useful in substantiating and generalising the specific topics found to be relevant in a case study.

Thus, the case study is the preferred research methodology, and only one single case will be looked at. The purpose is to create a representative case of °community°, not to lose itself in the details of local politics, specialities, cultures, etc. The emphasis is on describing the conditions of the usual implementation of °community° life as perceived through the eyes of the governance frame. Of course, °community° notions are quite different in the forms in which they are manifested. However, as the logic of the framework focuses on the established invariant structures, it allows us to look at the central characteristics of the structures established that determine °community° governance.

With the case study that follows, it will be shown that the governance framework can be applied, and how that can be done. The case depicts a subjective interpretation of the °community° implementations in Hesse; however, it does so within a strong frame that is independent from the set-

---

[567] Stake, R. E.: (Art of Case Study); Yin, R.: (Case study research)

[568] Yin, R.: (Case study research)

ting of application chosen here. It is primarily the framework and its descriptive, interpretative potential that is being developed, tested, and demonstrated here. However, it is evident – that this application could at anytime be transformed into an "objective" reflection of the situation in a specific °community°. Only for that reason would the criteria considered to be "objective" have to be defined within another research endeavor, e.g. with all executives, or 20% of the citizens involved in the inquiry, etc.

5.2.1 Unit and focus of analysis

The unit of interest is the interaction taking place between actors and the structures within which they take place. The focus will be placed on the common regulative constraints established for Hessian °communities° guiding and binding the actors involved in defining their °community° involvement, the methods and instruments they use, and the processes they perform to reconcile the evolving °community° issues. Interactions will be described as they are being performed between actors. In doing so, the conventions of the derived governance framework will be used.

As has been decided above, interactions will be examined with a focus on the settlement of the "resource distribution" issues between the primary activities performed in °community°. As the case study portrays the typical, representative case of Hessian °communities°, there is no necessity for disclosing true actor identities or for referring to specific circumstances in the individual political, civic, or geographic entities involved. This does not eliminate relevant background information, as the findings and conclusions seek to identify the general functioning of °community° governance in Hesse. Their formalised structures are to be contemplated. Variations do exist in some °communities°.

The case is centred on three of the six structural aspects identified (as indicated in grey in Table 15) and detailed below including the guiding questions for the case analysis. The guiding questions for the case analysis are as follows:

Channel capacity A: Adequacy of actor roles, tasks, and responsibilities

1. Who is involved in °community° implementation? What roles are defined?

2. What are the major formal actor settings, i.e. meetings, councils, departments?

3. What is the contribution of the major actor settings to complying with the systemic functions and to solving the systemic topics?

Change or transformation capacity A: Aptitude of methods and instruments

1. What are the major *Four-*, *Three-*, *Two-* methods applied leading to the settlement of 'Strategy^{SOR}' and 'Contract^{OR}'?

2. Do these methods contribute to compliance with the systemic functions? What are their limitations and disorientations?

Channel capacity B: Processes and sequences of reconciliation

1. What are the processes and sequences followed in the major actor settings throughout the reconciliation process?

2. Do these processes and sequences support actors in resolving their systemic topics and in due time? What are major obstacles, lags and hurdles?

Table 15. Selection of governance aspects and topics focused

		Aspects of structure (Organisational principles)					
		Channel capacity		Change capacity		Transduction capacity	
		Tasks and responsibilities	Processes and sequences	Methods & Instruments	Interfaces between methods	°System° and logical boundaries	Actor boundaries
Systemic interactions (Axioms of management)	*Two*						
	Two						
	Two-One						
	Three						
	Three						
	Three-One						
	Three-Two						
	Three-One*						
	Four						
	Four						
	Four-Env						
	Four-Three						
	Five						
	Five						
	Five-Four/ Three						
	Five-(Four-Three)						
	Five-One						

Thus, the work will identify to what extent the perceived conduct of interaction promotes or limits the viability of the °community° notion actors strive to implement. Subsequently, based upon the potential of eMedia to improve change, channel, and transduction capacity, the contribution of eMedia to the governance of Hessian °communities° will be derived. Further, it will describe to what extent and under what conditions eMedia application promotes actors in maintaining the viability of their °system° notion.

The focus of the case study is not on the specifics of the individual °community°, but on the commonalities of their structures. A large number of these structures have been defined on the higher °federal°, °state°, and °country° layers of recursion and are therefore valid for all °community° actions. Some of them are announced in the legal framework, Germany's federal law and Hesse's °state° law. These superordinate layer agreements clarify actor roles, interplay arenas, methods, and major issues of °community° and thus define the general conditions of how °community° notions are to be implemented.

5.2.2 Sources of percepts

The sources of data collection are the agreements settled on between actors defining how they implement their °community° notion, including:

1. Legal framework, Germany's federal and state law[569];

2. Community documents such as budgets, process descriptions, task and job descriptions, etc.;

3. Explanations and audit proceedings as used by the Hessian Audit Court[570];

4. Survey eGovernance – implications for governance[571]

5. New Public Management (NPM) literature as quoted.[572]

These activities have been complemented through the author's involvement in an audit program of the Hessian Audit court, which included 40 °communities° of which 20 have been visited personally by the author, each for a period of 3-4 days. Throughout the period from August 2004 to May

---

[569] Deutscher Bundestag: Grundgesetz für die Bundesrepublik Deutschland, 2006, BGBl.; Hessischer Landtag: Hessische Gemeindeordnung (HGO), 2005, Gesetz und Verordnungsblatt für das Land Hessen (GVBl. I); Hessischer Landtag: Gemeindehaushaltsverordnung (GemHVO), 1973, Gesetz und Verordnungsblatt für das Land Hessen (GVBl. I)

[570] German "Hessischer Rechnungshof"

[571] Türke, R. E.: Can eGovernance help to promote Good Governance?, hfp research publications, Kelkheim, 2001

[572] Selected previously existing literature, especially with respect to New Public Management and Governance, is a guide and referenced wherever used.

2005, comprehensive interviews with executive °community° actors were conducted as part of the °community° audit, including questionnaires on the topics of "Community profile", "Community future", "New Public Management", "Strategic planning", and "Community development". A broad involvement of political and administrative actors further allowed sketching different perspectives on actor roles, tasks and responsibilities, processes, autonomy issues, etc. Due to this research design, the reconciliations establishing °community° as they are reflected in the °community° documents have been a major source for this case. The interviews conducted and the observations made throughout the audit supplemented the understanding of how they were used, interpreted, etc.

5.2.3 Structure of chapters

The sequence of chapters reflects the logic of modules that correspond to the topics selected for examination. Within the module on processes and sequences, time is an important criterion. For this part of the case study the chronological order of budget reconciliation has been chosen for analysis.[573] Within each chapter, conclusions will be drawn based on the adequacy of the conducted interaction to support its systemic topic. Further, a suggestion will be formulated, subsuming the structural adaptations that are required. The following figure summarises the steps taken for conducting the case study:

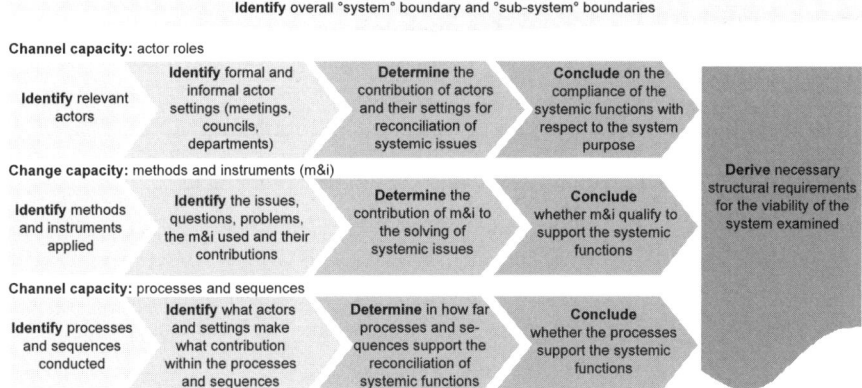

Figure 46. Steps of governance case study on Hessian °communities°

---

[573] Yin, R.: (Case study research)

As the research will require evaluating the structural facts, it will be useful to define some conventions characterising the compliance of the systemic functions in °community°. The following convention will be used to qualify the systemic contributions provided by the actors involved, the settings, councils, and fora engaged:

Table 16. Convention to qualify compliance of systemic tasks and responsibilities

Contributions (white background) are clearly defined or formalised. They can be identified clearly from the formalised structures (e.g. reglements). The actors involved have equivalent perceptions of their individual contribution to °community° implementation.	**White**
Contributions (light grey chequered background) are not clearly defined or informal. They may be created differently by different actors. Actors may follow different paths to reconcile these issues. E.g. individual interests and power relations may endanger compliance.	**Light grey**
Contributions (grey background) are not defined, unclear. Issues within these topics are not addressed and resolved. Inadequate to absorb the variety of a certain interaction as required for implementing the °community° notion.	**Dark grey**

The following convention applies for the methods and instruments applied:

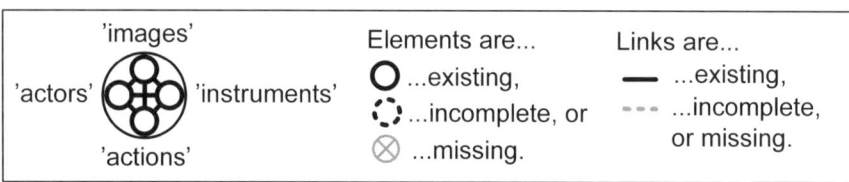

Figure 47. Convention to qualify systemic compliance of methods

6 Governance of Hessian °communities°

Community comes from Latin "communis", which means common, mutual exchange among each other. °Community° is an evolutionarily developed notion[574] like °family° that is a fundamental part of the lifeworld and forms the basis for implementing the German democratic °state°.[575] It refers to a group of actors who share a common place of living that is a geographically defined political entity. Actors who adopt a certain notion of °community° are called citizens. As a manifestation of the more comprehensive lifeworld, °community° actors who have adopted a shared °community° notion have a specific identity, language, (micro-) culture, and tradition. The most usual type of °community° notions are referred to by actors as municipality, city, town, suburb, etc. Its 'Boundaries[NR]' are geographically exactly defined, which enables citizens to identify with their notion and differentiate themselves from other neighbouring °communities°.[576] °Community° notions resolve local issues and problems and thus facilitate the creation and implementation of higher layers of recursion. In this case, the °community° notion refers to a German city or town with less than five thousand inhabitants somewhere in the state of Hesse.

The constitution or basic law ('Grundgesetz') of the Federal Republic of Germany[577] provides for a °federal° layer in which much power is reserved to the individual °states° ("Länder"). Within the °state° layer there are established °country° ("Kreis") and °community° layers ("Gemeinde"). The

---

[574] Klönne, A.: Zum Begriff und zur Realität von politischer Gemeinde, in: Ellwein, T. and Zoll, R., Gemeinde als Alibi: Materialien zur politischen Soziologie der Gemeinde, München, 1972; König argues that the distinction of artificial design and evolutionary, organic growth is void in the long term, since artificially created communities will over time form character traits of their own, and then appear to be organically grown. In König, R.: Grundformen der Gesellschaft: Die Gemeinde, Hamburg, 1958

[575] Sec. 1 HGO para 1 Nature and legal status of community

[576] König, R.: (Gemeinde)

[577] Deutscher Bundestag: (Grundgesetz)

notion of °community° and its fundamental purpose is described in the German constitution, which states that °community° actors have the right and duty to arrange for their self-governance, i.e. to resolve their local issues largely autonomously and responsibly through elected bodies and a separation of power.[578] Hence, it is true that the °community° layer is largely independent,[579] but unlike °federal° and °state° layers, it does not have an independent, constitutional status and does not have fully-fledged executive, legislative, and judicial bodies.[580] In consequence, this implies that °federal° and °state° layers can pass binding laws relevant for °community° implementation without the actors involved locally having a say in the matter.[581] The respective °state° layer defines the legal foundation for °community° following the °state's° constitution. Consequently, local °community° codes define structures that differ widely from one °state° to another. Today, prevailing political traditions and specific constellations have caused a diversification of °communities° into a wide range of different manifestations based on local traditions.

The actors involved are exclusively responsible for implementing a °community° notion within a region.[582] °State° law guarantees the autonomous conduct of °community° implementation. Supervision and interventions are limited to securing conformity with relevant laws adopted on the °state° layer.[583] Indeed, °federal° and °state° layer actors can assign tasks and duties to °community° actors by law or regulation to be implemented upon instruction.[584]

A °community° is considered here as an evolved °system° notion. The actors involved are those living within the established °community° boundary and actively engaged in its implementation; affected actors are those living within its boundary but not actively involved in implementation. Different °sub-system° notions of °community° provide the contribu-

---

[578] Art. 28 GG para 2; Sec. 2 HGO Community's sphere of influence

[579] Sec. 2 HGO Community's sphere of influence

[580] Although the respective functions are represented, i.e. the regulatory authority, e.g. the °community° police department ("Ordnungsamt"), has an executive function, the °community° arbitrator has a judicial function and the °community° council has a legislative function.

[581] Bundeszentrale für politische Bildung: Kommunalpolitik, 1998

[582] Sec. 137 Hessian Constitution para 1

[583] Sec. 4 HGO; Art. 137 Hessian Constitution para 3

[584] Sec. 4 HGO; Art. 137 Hessian Constitution para 4

tions which together implement the °community° notion. The adoption of °community° aims at influencing and shaping the interactions of all actors involved in a way that leads them to co-operate. If they succeed in doing so, the relevant °sub-systems° align and harmonise their activities, thus creating the overall purpose and task notions that together implement °community°.

Thus, the primary question for depicting °community° notion with the governance frame is: Which activities are conducted largely autonomously? Looking at °community° quickly leads to the recognition that some activities are distinct and depend on largely independent *Wirkungsgefüge* and can therefore be considered as the prevailing °sub-system° notions of °community°. Independent of whether the individual °community° notion has specified its overall mission and self-understanding, a set of typical purposes can be identified. Table 17 specifies the typical set purposes usually aspired to with German °community° notions.[585] Thus, independent social °sub-systems° of °community° are for instance °security°, °education°, °economy°, °health°. For the implementation of °education°, even lower °sub-sub-systems° could be defined such as °kindergartens°, °schools° or °gyms°.[586]

According to the different local conditions, °community° actors aim at implementing different purposes, dependending on their local priorities, cultures, social situations, etc. Activities can usefully be attributed to largely independent groups, compare Table 17. All °community° implementations visited throughout this research did pursue all of the indicated activities. It has been observed that there is always some tendency to give autonomy to the °living spheres°, because they require the actors involved to put strong focus on attendance to these issues – as a consequence of the independent *Wirkungsgefüge* that are effective. However, depending on local intentions, these activities have often not been organised in an independent way. Actors recognised °living spheres° as naturally separate in regard to their differences; however, they usually did not establish them as °subsystems° with formal boundaries. The degree of autonomy of their

---

[585] Bormann, M. and Stiezel, C.: Stadt und Gemeinde. Kommunalpolitik in den neuen Ländern, Bonn, 1993, p. 9

[586] The definition of °sub-sub-systems° depends on the focus of the diagnosis being aspired to. The body responsible for providing sponsorship of °kindergartens° (which in the case of Hesse is often the church) and °schools° (which in the case of Hesse is usually the county district) could, but does not necessarily require, these institutions to be rooted in °county° or °state° layers of recursion.

°living-spheres° reflected stark disparities from one °community° to the other. Nevertheless, the °sub-systems° of °community° are clearly delimitable along the fronts of their independent activities and *Wirkungsgefüge*. Therefore, the °living spheres° provide a sound boundary for this case. Together, they reflect the actors' needs, urging all actors involved to work toward sustaining °community°.

Besides the °living sphere° a more common and formalised boundary criterion found in °communities° is the region. All Hessian °communities° visited had established formal regional boundaries that existed concurrently with the °living spheres°. These are reflected in geographically defined °villages°[587] which have their own body engaged in the local governance issues of that area. In Hesse, °villages° are conceded an independent budget to organise and resolve their local issues.[588] Typical issues addressed in °villages° are land use and development planning, investment planning for public institutions such as kindergartens, youth clubs, play and sports sites, green and recreation sites, cemeteries, fire-brigades, and community centres, road designations, planning of gullies and sewers, roads, cycle tracks, traffic lights, and roundabouts, etc. Between the °sub-systems° of the two criteria in °community° there are usually no major conflicts in °community°. The issues to be addressed in °villages° are clearly defined in a °village° regulation[589] in regard to how °village° actors are to be involved in °community° (and potentially °living sphere°) reconciliations. Nevertheless, wherever the two boundary criteria are kept concurrently, °community° governance has to engage in optimising both. That means that resource consumption issues not resolved within °Housing° have to be looked at not only in regard to °health°, °welfare°, °education°, °security°, °culture° but also with respect to °village A° and °village B° (i.e. in 'Contract^{OR}' reconciliation).

°Sub-system° boundaries give expression to the means chosen for the implementation of the overall °community° boundary. Whereas regional boundaries are required to resolve the issues (absorb the complexity) that arise from the number of actors living together in geographic proximity to a village or suburb, °living sphere° boundaries stick to issues with-largely indepent *Wirkungsgefüge*. There is no contradiction in establishing two different criteria as long as the boundaries and the interdependencies are clearly defined.

---

[587] German "Ortsbezirk". See Sec. 81 para 1 HGO Constitution and Abolition

[588] Sec. 82 para 4 HGO Election and Tasks

[589] German "Geschäftsordnung des Ortsbezirks"

Table 17. Typical °living spheres° for creating °community°

°Sub-systems°	Purpose and exemplary institutions	Assigned Environ-ment
1 °Security°	Protect people against and help them to implement Police, fire brigade, emergency and rescue services, private security companies, trade supervisory board, building inspection, vehicle control.	All actors in °community° whenever exposed to some type of individual danger, etc.
2 °Education°	School administration Universities, schools, kindergartens, adult education centres, library, youth pro-grammes, after school care clubs, etc.	Students, any type of scholars, associations, lobbies, etc.
3 °Culture and leisure°	Cultural administration, associations Churches, theatres, tourist services, public swimming pools, wellness-center, clubs, cinemas, orchestras, playgrounds, sporting facilities, etc.	All humans within °community° whenever they spend cultural and leisure time.
4 °Health°	Public health department Hospitals and medical facilities, doctor's surgeries, cemetery.	All humans that suffer illness or are injured.
5 °Social wel-fare°	Legal authority administration, social ser-vices department, homeless service, unem-ployed support, etc. Court of justice, Nursing homes, youth centres, women's shelter, homeless asylum.	All citizens that require assistance with their basic needs for living.
6 °Infrastruc-ture / Mobility	Waterworks administration, Highway board department, road construction office, traffic provider administrations. Water, electricity, gas, bus-, taxi, and traffic.	All humans that need to cover a distance.
7 °Environment	Forest and park management, environmental services and protection Rangers, foresters, sanitation, gardeners, etc.	Forest, parkes, animals, etc.
8 °Economy	Department for business development, tour-ism, etc. Companies, industries, hotels, restaurants, supermarkets, business development.	Buisiness and industry. Any actors engaged in the exchange of goods.
9 °Supply and housing	Buildings and Construction departments, land-registry office, memorials preservation House construction, sewer system, city planning.	All inhabitants. Com-munity buildings, infra-structure, real estate.

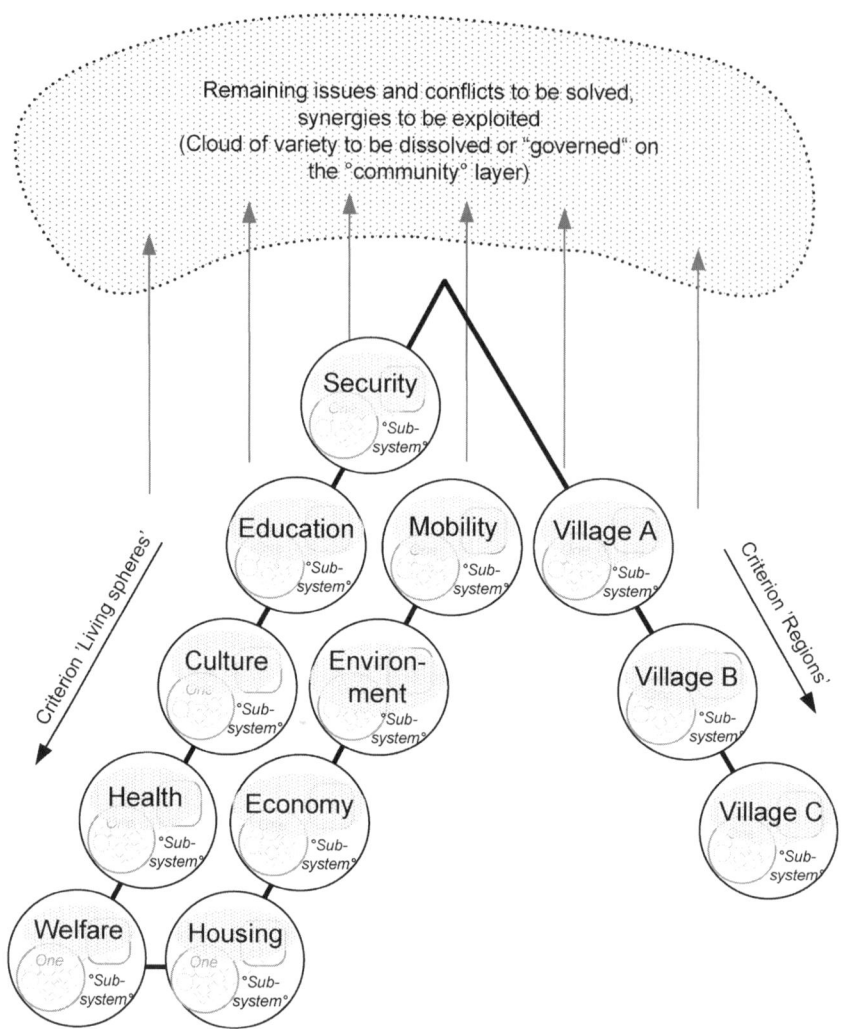

Figure 48. Common °sub-systems° of Hessian communities

Besides these two typical criteria, political, administrative, and public initiatives may engage in establishing new °sub-systems° based on different criteria. A public-private partnership may be established to run an independent °public company°. Alternatively, a citizen initiative may engage in building a new leisure park, therefore creating an independent °sub-system° (either of °culture and leisure° or °infrastructure and mobility°) to implement that purpose. Different °sub-systems° will be found in different °communities°, depending on the °community° 'Boundary[NR]', the 'Norms[NR]' and

'Strategy^{SOR}' that have been reconciled. However, the structure indicated in Figure 48 shows the usual °sub-system° boundaries found in Hessian communities. Specific local arrangements vary depending on the particular purposes that have been defined and the degree of autonomy that has been assigned to °living spheres° locally (with the respective overall °community° boundary). The question in focus for this case study is how the governance of the typical °sub-system° arrangement as indicated can be improved. Therefore, the assumed °community° notion focus defines the typical setting of °sub-systems° with °living spheres° and °villages°.

With the °community° notion in focus, both higher and lower layers are considered black boxes. °Community° is described based on the higher °state° layers frame taken as given. The fundamental structures of °community° are predefined on these higher layers. For instance, °federal° and °state° layer legislations are a major source for implementing °community°. They predefine the structure of the major reconciliations taking place between the actors involved.

6.1 Channel capacity: actor roles

6.1.1 Actors and settings

In Hessian °communities°, power is separated between community council (CC), as the representative body and the magistrate (M) as the executive body under the chairmanship of the mayor. Both councils are set up to be collegial partners. Furthermore, there are boards and factions which form sub-groups of the community council, and commissions which form sub-groups of the magistrate. The administration engages in preparing and implementing the resolutions and decisions of both the community council and magistrate. Private and public companies, all kinds of associations, churches and parties engage in implementing the activities and creating the benefits associated with °community°. Figure 49 gives an overview on the actors involved. Shaded areas indicate the typical involvement of the actors on super- and sub-ordinated layers of °community° recursion. The following synthetic viability mapping will particularly specify °super-system° layer contributions, as these set the frame for the actors engaged in °community°. °Sub-systems° are considered black boxes; their activities can therefore legitimally be omitted from exploration.

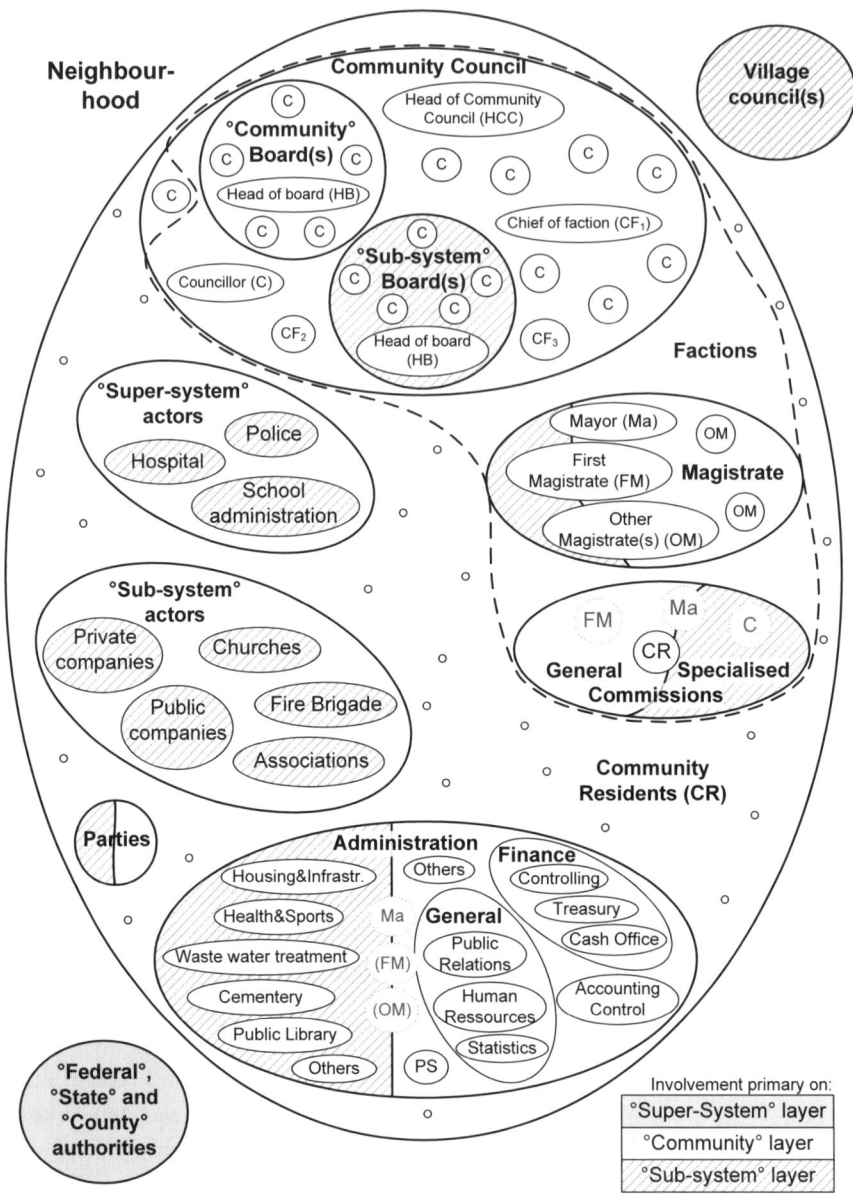

Figure 49. Major actors of Hessian °community°

6.1.2   Systemic contributions

In the following, the roles of the community council, its factions and boards, the magistrate and its commissions, the administration, the enterprises, the churches and associations, and the °community° residents are described as the major actors and settings involved in implementing °community° notions in Hesse.

6.1.2.1 Community council

The community council or German *Stadtverordnetenversammlung*[590] is the primary and most important setting of community. Depending on the number of residents, it consists of at least 15 elected councillors who choose a head among themselves (HCC).[591] Individual councillors may suggest topics for the agenda. All community council sessions ought to be open to the public unless there is a special reason for its exclusion.[592] Final resolutions and decisions are adopted through majority vote of the councillors.[593] In doing so, all councillors are in principle independent and act in regard of public interest based upon their personal convictions. However, in practice that independence is confined through their affiliation to factions and political parties. Councillors serve on an honorary and unpaid basis[594], which constitutes the necessity of other employment in addition to their °community° activity. As a consequence, they can often devote very little time and sparse background knowledge and have to strongly rely on the preparative work of the professionals in magistrate, boards, and administration. Although they are not formally bound in any way, the vast majority of councillors are members of factions, which promote them for election to the community council. Throughout their work as councillors, the factions facilitate their will formation and decision making. All factions of the community council are given space to create, elaborate, and reconcile their views and to

---

[590] The community council comprises all community representatives, German 'Gemeindevertreter'; in larger °communities° these representatives are referred to as town or city councillors, German 'Stadtverordnete', see Sec. 49 HGO Composition and denomination in the community council.

[591] Sec. 38 HGO Number of councillors

[592] Sec. 52 HGO Public

[593] Sec. 54, 55 HGO Reconciliation and elections

[594] Sec. 35 HGO para 1-2 Independence; Sec. 36 HGO Term; Bundeszentrale für politische Bildung: (Policy in community)

present them publicly.[595] Usually, but not necessarily, the factions correspond to the political parties which the councillors join to attain power and
to merge forces for promoting a common goal or a set of common goals.
Comparable to other parliaments, a certain hierarchy can usually be observed among the councillors, developing primarily in favour of the head
(HCC) and the chiefs of factions (CF). Shrewd councillors – as well as mayors and executive public servants – know to whom to introduce to their
ideas, plans, and interests in order to gain support for their implementation.[596] Councillors' relation to public servants is often tense as they tend to
doubt their competence and strive to restrict their spheres of influence.[597]

The community council is the legally assigned body to take °community°
decisions and to be accountable for them[598] ('Strategy[SOR]', 'Norms[NR]', 'Contract[OR]', 'Requirements[OR]', 'Guidelines[OR]'). It supervises the other actors and
councils involved, primarily the magistrate and the administration ('Supervision[NR]', 'Legitimacy[OR]' and 'Legitimacy[SR]'). Thereby, the emphasis is on the
management and allocation of the °community's° resources for which it
grants discharche to the magistrate ('Legitimacy[OR]', 'Accounts[OR]').[599] However, the community council does not have to fulfil all of these functions
itself. It may depute tasks and responsibilities for certain issues to a board or
to the magistrate and draw them back to itself at any time ('Norms[NR]').[600]
Some tasks and responsibilities are exclusively assigned to the community
council and cannot be delegated, such as the announcement of administrative rules, regulations, and statutes ('Norms[NR]', 'Guidelines[OR]')[601], the holding of elections ('Boundary[NR]') and the creation, adoption, and suspension
of statutes, decrees, establishing public companies, property rights, etc.
('Norms[NR]', 'Guidelines[OR]').[602] Also, the community council is responsible

---

[595] Sec. 36a HGO para 1, 3 Factions

[596] Informal 'tabacco' conferences are common phenomena in Hessian communities. See Bundeszentrale für politische Bildung: (Policy in community)

[597] Baier, H.: Operative Planung in Kommunen – Neukonzeption auf der Basis
einer Kosten- und Leistungsrechnung, Köln, 2002

[598] Sec. 9 HGO para 1 Organs.

[599] Sec. 50 HGO para 2 Duties of the community council

[600] The transmittal of certain issues to the magistrate is to be fixed in the primary
statute. Sec. 50 HGO para 1 Duties of the community council

[601] Sec. 51 HGO clause 6; Art. 28 para 2 GG; Legislative, Exekutive, Rechtspre-
chung, Bund – Länder – Kommunen

[602] Issues and affairs as specified in Sec. 51 HGO Exclusive responsibilities of the
community council

for deciding on unbudgeted and unscheduled expenditures, and the appointment of public taxes and private fees, which are relevant to the community residents.[603] Furthermore, due to its legal status, the community council can decide to intervene on all issues ('ANY') independent of any previous assignment or delegation to the magistrate or the administration.

6.1.2.2 Boards

As has been mentioned above already, the community council can decide to form sub-ordinated boards (B), which elaborate proposals and prepare resolutions. These are then in charge of supporting and preparing proposals for presentation and debate in the community council. Such boards may be convened and dissolved at any time. Only the financial board is obligatory; there may be other boards, but such were not found in the °communities° visited. Boards regularly report on their activities to the community council.[604] They may allow the participation of those community residents and experts whenever they are affected by their decisions or can provide valuable contributions.[605] Like the community council, all board meetings are

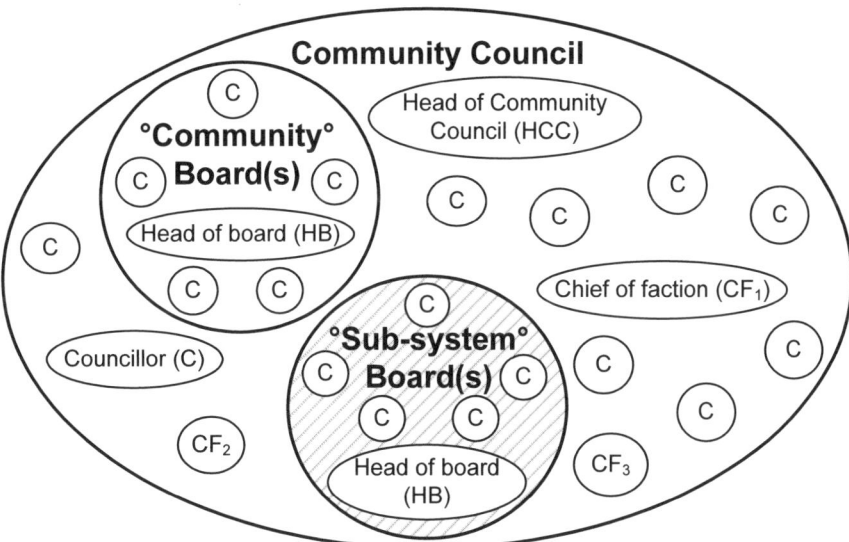

Figure 50. Community council

---

[603] Sec. 51 HGO para 6-15 Exclusive responsibilities of the community council
[604] Sec. 62 HGO para 1 Boards
[605] Sec. 62 HGO para 6 Boards

open to the public. A board is established whenever a quarter of the °community° mandates it or one faction decides in its favour.[606] The results of such board councils then form the basis for plenary meetings and debates. Legally, boards have no authority to take decisions, but concentrate on preparation, proposals, and advice ('Guideline^{OR}', 'Synergy^{OR}', 'Proposals^{SR}', 'Boundary^{NR}', 'Norms^{NR}') and recommendations ('Contract^{OR}', 'Requirements^{OR}', 'Strategy^{SOR}') for the community council. However, if the community council explicitly assigns responsibilities for certain topics to them, they may pass final resolutions themselves.[607] Not all boards are active on the layer of the °system° in focus. Rather, a distinction has to be made between °community° boards (e.g. financial board, administrative board, environmental board, main board) and specialised °sub-system°-layer boards (sport, culture, social welfare, education).

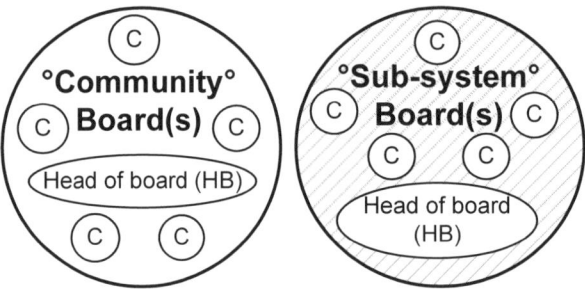

Figure 51. Boards (B)

6.1.2.3 Factions

As previously mentioned, councillors (C) can join factions. A faction can take on councillors who are not members of the faction's political party. The formation of a faction, its size, rights and obligations are to be regulated in the community council. Minimally, a faction consists of two councillors. Factions may invite magistrate members and others to their meetings.[608] Primarily, the factions facilitate public will formation and support decision making in the community council; they prepare proposals for presentation and discussion in the plenary sessions of the community council. Further, they may present their views publicly whenever they consider that to be

---

[606] Sec. 50 HGO para 2 Duties of the community council
[607] Sec. 62 HGO para 1 Boards
[608] Sec. 36a HGO para 1 Factions

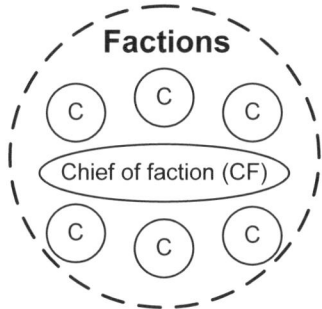

Figure 52. Factions (F)

relevant ('ANY', 'Sub-ANY').[609] They can be granted financial resources to cover their management expenditures by the community council.[610]

6.1.2.4 Magistrate

The 'Magistrate', or German 'Gemeindevorstand', actively leads the implementation of °community°[611], which is why it is commonly referred to as the executive authority. The magistrate consists of the mayor (Ma), first and possibly secondary magistrates (FM, OM). The mayor is elected in direct majority vote by community residents;[612] the first and secondary magistrates are elected by the community council. The mayor prepares the resolutions of the magistrate(s) and defines their tasks.[613] The mayor is the chairman of the magistrate; he is a *primus inter pares*, the chief of administration.[614] He distributes assignments to the magistrates[615], but he can be overruled and is obliged to implement all resolutions settled by the community council ('Norms^{NR}', 'Strategy^{SOR}', etc.). It is primarily the mayor who prepares magistrate decisions and implements them if that has not been delegated to the administration. All magistrate members may assign public servants of the administration to prepare, support, and execute tasks for them

---

[609] Sec. 36a HGO para 3 Factions

[610] Sec. 36a HGO para 4 Factions

[611] Sec. 9 HGO para 2 Organs

[612] Sec. 39 HGO para 1a Election and term of the major

[613] Sec. 70 HGO para 1 Tasks of the mayor; a single actor may not participate both in the community council and in the magistrate with the exception of the mayor.

[614] Sec. 73 HGO para 2 Human resources

[615] Sec. 70 HGO para 1 Role of the mayor

('ANY'). Legally, the mayor has no means to influence the agenda of the community council. *De jure* he cannot submit proposals in the community council himself, only the magistrate as a panel can do so. However, *de facto* it is usually he who prepares the proposals for the community council.[616] The magistrate participates in all meetings of the community council and is obliged to respond to councillors' requests on any issue that is being debated ('ANY').[617] Further, it is his duty to supervise the financial accounting of °community° ('Legitimacy^{OR}').[618] In the case of 'Urgencies^{TR}' being communicated to the mayor, when the magistrate cannot convene, he himself decides on the required resolutions and immediately reports to the magistrate.[619]

Magistrate members are the active representatives engaged in managing the attendance to °community° issues ('Contract^{OR}', 'Requirements^{OR}', 'Orientation^{OR}') following the decisions ('Norms^{NR}', 'Strategy^{SOR}', 'Contract^{OR}', 'Guidelines^{OR}') settled on by the community council.[620] In fact, they prepare and implement these decisions and settle °community° and °sub-system° issues that have been assigned to them by the community council ('Norms^{NR}', 'Requirements^{OR}', 'Sub-ANY').[621] Essentially, they create the resource allocation as it has been negotiated by the treasurer with the °sub-system° actors and is to be determined in the budget ('Contract^{OR}').[622] In doing so, they follow the laws of the °state°[623] and the instructions of the °states'° supervisory authority ('Super-Requirements^{OR}').[624] The magistrate continuously informs the community council on important tasks and regulations defined by superordinated authorities of the °state° ('Super-Requirements^{OR}').[625] Furthermore, it supervises the community council ('Supervision^{NR}'). Whenever a resolution of the community council

---

[616] The mayor may communicate his disagreement regarding magistrate decisions to the state's supervisory body but, nevertheless, has to implement it.

[617] Sec. 59 HGO Participation of the community council

[618] Sec. 66 HGO para 1 no. 6 Duties of the magistrate

[619] Sec. 70 HGO para 1,3 Role of the mayor

[620] Sec. 66 HGO para 1, Duties of the magistrate

[621] Sec. 66 HGO para 1-3, 5 Duties of the magistrate; all issues to be dealt with must be entailed in the duties of the magistrate, in Sec. 69 HGO Summoning of magistrate meetings.

[622] Sec. 66 HGO para 1 no. 6 Duties of the magistrate

[623] Sec. 66 HGO para 1-3, 5 Duties of the magistrate

[624] Sec. 66 HGO para 1-3, 5 Duties of the magistrate

[625] Sec. 50 HGO para 3 Tasks

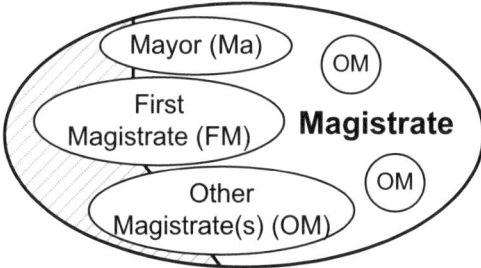

Figure 53. Magistrate (M)

violates the law or endangers the implementation of °community°, the mayor must formally state his protest ('Legitimacy^{OR}', 'Legitimacy^{SR}'). With his protest, the respective resolution is suspended and may not proceed until the community council has met a second time. If the revised resolution again violates the law, a lawsuit is to be initiated.[626]

6.1.2.5 Commissions

The magistrate can form subordinated commissions (Co) for permanent attendance to specific issues or for the completion of temporary assignments. Commissions may consist of the mayor (Ma), members of the magistrate, members of the community council (C) and, if appropriate, of competent community residents (CR). The mayor or one of his magistrates (FM, OM) presides over the commission.[627] However, commissions are not regularly established in all communities. Commissions are optional panels institutionalised to support the magistrate, there are no topics as

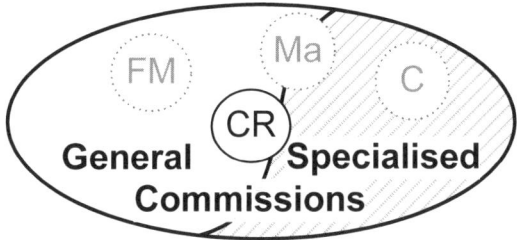

Figure 54. Commissions (Co)

---

[626] Sec. 63 HGO para 1 Protest and complaint
[627] Sec. 72 HGO para 1, 2, 3 Commissions

signed formally to be handled in commissions. Consequently, their specific contribution can be determined only with respect to the specific circumstances of a local context. This will not be done here, as none of the °communities° visited in the audit had established a commission.

6.1.2.6 Administration

Administration is the group of public servants (PS) responsible for supporting and executing the strategic and operative decisions that have been made. The mayor (Ma) is the chief of administration; next in the hierarchy is the first magistrate (FM, OM). Both mayor and magistrates have the right and responsibility to create and design the organisation of administration. Within the legal framework of Hesse, they themselves can decide how to subsume issues and tasks and which organisational units to create. However, since the 1950s a general model of organisation which proposes a typical division of departments has been established and adopted widely in °communities° all over Germany.[628] Generally, this model reflects a distinction between central and professional organisational entities. Central are entities such as controlling, treasury, human resources, and public relations, which engage in issues relevant to the whole °community° (°community° layer). Professional entities such as housing, infrastructure, and public libraries deal primarily with issues of the living spheres (°sub-system° layer). Consequently, not all public servants are involved in °community° topics such as the mayor, magistrate(s) and the treasury, human resources, and controlling departments. Others focus on °sub-system° issues, e.g. waste water treatment, cementery, public library, etc.

However, the consequences of having central and professional organisational entities which are, in fact, contributing to different recursive layers, i.e. °community° and °sub-system°, are still not recognised in Hessian communities. Departments are usually not treated as largely autonomous entities. Rather, they are managed through the community council and magistrate in all details of the issues (via 'Requirements[OR']'). Ongoing reform agendas have set the topics of decentralisation and budgeting. However, these developments have not yet been adopted and implemented in the majority of small Hessian communities. Rather, mayor and executive public servants tend to question the value added with largely independent entities and declare that there is a lack of competent actors capable of governing these entities.

---

[628] Kommunale Gemeinschaftsstelle für Verwaltungsvereinfachung (KGSt): Verwaltungsorganisation der Gemeinden, 1979

As the layer of °community° is in focus here, the central actors and departments engaged in °community° issues, usually referred to as cross-functional, will be discussed below. The most important central departments of Hessian °communities° are concerned with finance topics (such as the cash office, treasury, and controlling), and general topics (such as general administration, public relations, statistics, and human resources). These are predominantly engaged in *Two* and *Three* topics of °community°, as will be described subsequently.

6.1.2.7 Treasury

Treasury in German °communities° is the department of a public administration taking care of financial affairs and setting up the budget. Usually, both the department of real estate properties and the tax division are attached. In the °communities° visited, the main tasks of the treasury were:

1. Creating the overall and long-term financial plan and the investment plan ('Proposals^{SR}')

2. Preparing the draft of the budget statute ('Synergy^{OR}', 'Contract^{OR}')

3. Compiling the budget, accounts, and cash book ('Records^{OR}', 'Actuality^{TR}', 'Reports^{OR}')

4. Administrating reserves, shares, and debts ('Actuality^{TR}', Reports^{OR}')

5. Directives to the Cash Office, Supervision ('Guidelines^{OR}', 'Audit^{OR}', 'Findings^{OR}')

6. Cost and activity accounting ('Records^{OR}', 'Actuality^{TR}', 'Reports^{OR}')

7. Treatment of tax affairs of the city, recovery of taxes and fees ('Requirements^{OR}', 'Ambitions^{OR}')

8. Execution of the budget, managing and reporting unscheduled incomes and expenditures ('Synergy^{OR}', 'Contract^{OR}', 'Actuality^{TR}')

9. Cash flow management, including credits and debts ('Records^{OR}', 'Actuality^{TR}', 'Reports^{OR}')

Within the budget reconciliation, the treasurer is entitled to issue his personal statement if the magistrate does not agree with his suggestion in the budget draft. Further, he may present his view to the community council and its boards.[629]

---

[629] Sec. 97 para 1, 3 sentence 3 HGO Acceptance of the budget statute

6.1.2.8 Cash Office

The cash office settles all cash issues occurring throughout °community° implementation.[630] These comprise the following tasks:

1. Receiving income and making cash payments ('Records^{OR}', 'Orientation^{OR}')
2. Administrating funds and safe-keeping objects of value ('Actuality^{TR}')
3. Bookkeeping records and collection of vouchers ('Records^{TR}')

6.1.2.9 Human Resources

Human Resource departments usually cope with the following issues:

1. Bookeeping and statistics on human resources ('Actuality^{TR}')
2. Planning and staff appointment ('Proposals^{OR}', 'Synergy^{OR}', 'Actuality^{TR}', 'Orientation^{OR}')
3. Recruiting, deployment and development of staff ('Proposals^{OR}', 'Contract^{OR}')
4. Internal personnel matters such as vacations, illnesses, salary accounts, remunerations, wages, pension payments, benefits, travel accounts, etc. ('Actuality^{TR}', 'Orientation^{TR}')
5. Social support to the personnel ('Orientation^{OR}', 'Requirements^{OR}')
6. Safety and health in employee working environment ('Super-Requirements^{OR}', 'Requirements^{OR}')

6.1.2.10 Accounting Control Office

°Communities° with more than 50,000 inhabitants must establish an Accounting Control Office; others can voluntarily do so. In °communities° with no accounting control, these issues are executed by the °country° authority, which is to be remunerated. Primarily, accounting control has to examine and confirm the annual account (i.e. to take 'Account^{OR}').[631] Therefore, it examines the annual account (i.e. by looking at the actual 'Reports^{OR}') to see whether

---

[630]   Sec. 110 HGO Cash Office

[631]   Sec. 128 HGO Revising the annual account

1. the estimates are kept;

2. each single invoice amount is factually and calculatorily justified and documented;

3. incomes and expenditures accord with regulations;

4. the annex of the annual account is complete and correct.

Thus, accounting control performs an 'Audit^{OR}' and summarises its 'Findings^{OR}' in a final report.[632] To prepare for these tasks, accounting control concurrently examines cash procedures and vouchers ('Actuality^{OR}', 'Orientation^{OR}', 'Records^{OR}'), which are the basis of the annual account. Such monitoring is conducted continuously, both at regular and irregular intervals. Magistrate, mayor, the designated financial magistrate, and the community council can assign further tasks to accounting control, such as the examination of stocks and assets, awarding of contracts, efficiency and effectiveness of the administration, the management of the profit centres, cash management and book keeping, etc.[633] Accounting control acts independently from the other actors engaged in *Three* issues. It is generally free to choose its method of observation, investigation, and analysis

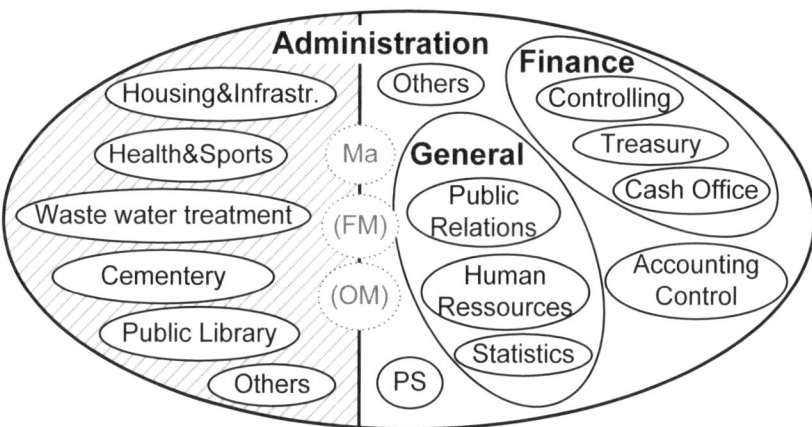

Figure 55. Administration (A)

---

[632] Sec. 128 HGO para 1-2 Revising the annual account

[633] Sec. 131 HGO para 2, Duties of the Accounting Control Department ("Rechnungsprüfungsamt")

('ConductOfAudit^{OR}', 'Audit^{OR}').[634] The magistrate is not allowed to instruct accounting control in regard to the scope, character, or the results it provides (i.e. in respect to 'Findings^{OR}'). However, the authorities and duties of the magistrate remain unaffected. Only the community council is allowed to mandate accounting control and to define specific queries to be investigated ('Audits^{OR}').[635]

6.1.2.11 °Super-° and °sub-system° actors

Police, hospitals, and school administration execute primary services relevant for the people living in the geographic boundaries of °community°. However, in Hesse these services are rooted in the °state° layer of recursion. As a consequence, the actors involved in °community° implementation do not exert direct influence on them, i.e. these activities are not part of the °community° notion. Any major issues or conflicts evolving in these spheres are addressed through the °state° layer of recursion. Other activities, such as fire brigade, public and private companies, or associations, are largely independent entities engaged in implementing the various °sub-systems° of °community°. Aside from making their intentions, needs, and interdependencies explicit with other °sub-systems° ('Records^{TR}', 'Queries^{TR}', 'Ambitions^{OR}'), they are not formally involved in topic reconciliations on the °community° layer. Nevertheless, they often engage in direct contact with councillors and magistrate members on an informal basis. The intensity and quality of relationships between magistrate, administration, and °sub-system° actors strongly determines the economic and cultural development of °community°. Cooperations and partnerships can facilitate °community° implementation. However, in some cases °community° councillors, magistrates, and executives have been seen to engage in responsible °sub-system° roles as well as in °community° activity. Thus, in the case of one °community°, the treasurer of the administration was also chairman of the board of directors of a local company. Although actors may very well be involved in several systemic topics and on different layers of recursion, such double assignments following different °system° notions bear the potential for conflicts (for instance, in the reconciliation of 'Contract^{OR}').

---

[634] Sec. 129 HGO para 1, Accounting Control Department ("Rechnungsprüfungsamt")

[635] Sec. 130 HGO para 1-2, Legal status of the Accounting Control Department ("Rechnungsprüfungsamt")

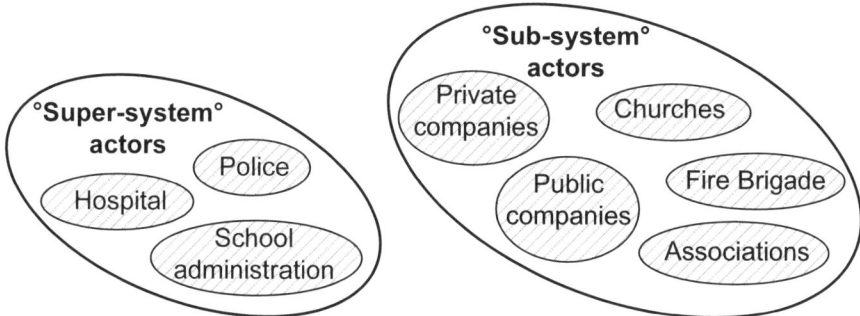

Figure 56. °Super-° and °sub-system° actors

6.1.2.12 Community residents

Community Residents (CR) are all those actors having their place of residence in the district of °community°. Citizens are those of them who are entitled to vote and thus to define who is in charge of representing the °community° in the community council and as mayor ('Boundary[NR']).[636] Citizens are both beneficiaries of °community° implementation and the subjects that constitute it.[637] Their involvement is obviously indispensable for implementing °community°, as their views primarily form the 'Boundary[NR']' of °community°.

Voting is their primary constitutive means of influencing °community° implementation ('Boundary[NR']). A citizen assembly is to be held at least once a year ('Boundary[NR']', 'Norms[NR']', 'Totality[SR']', 'Legitimacy[SR']').[638] Citizens have the right to conduct a referendum ('Proposal[SR']') and to take plebiscites on °community° issues ('Strategy[SOR']', 'Contact[OR']').[639] They can formulate petitions for the community council on important °community° issues ('Norms[NR']', 'Proposals[SR']', 'Reviews[OR']', 'Inquiry[SR']').[640] Further, com-

---

[636] Those who have German or European citizenship and have reached the age of 18, Sec. 8 HGO Residents and citizens; Sec. 30 HGO Active voting rights

[637] Although residents of neighbouring °communities° may, of course, participate in °community° implementation.

[638] Sec. 8a HGO Citizens reunion

[639] Any citizen motion must be signed by 10% of the citizens, Sec. 29 HGO para 1 Election principles

[640] However, such petitions and plebiscites ought not concern managerial competences of the magistrate, the internal organisation of the administration, legal issues of the councillors, magistrate members or public servants, the budget statute

Figure 57. Commity Residents (CR)

mon means of involving community residents are public opinion polls conducted by the administration, complaint, and suggestion management,
and internet fora ('Inquiry^{SR}'). In smaller communities, residents often
give active support to °community° implementation by engaging in building
houses, infrastructure, sport facilities, etc. (°sub-system° implementation).

6.1.2.13 °Federal°, °state° and °county° authorities

As mentioned above, °federal°, °state°, and °county° layers of recursion can
pass binding laws relevant for °community° implementation without community councils and actors having a say in the matter ('Super-Require-
ments^{OR}').[641] °Community° actors can be assigned tasks and duties by
°federal° or °state° layer law. Thus, these authorities define the legal frame
of °community° implementation following the °state's° constitution, including all the fundamental governing actors and institutions as they are
described here. This includes the frame within which the °community°
'Boundary^{NR}' is to be reconciled, how the rights of the actors involved and
the implementation of their duties are to be ensured.[642] Such superordinated directives are usually of general character (effecting 'Norms^{NR}',
'Strategy^{SOR}') although some do dictate detailed proceedings to be followed ('Contract^{OR}', Requirements^{OR}').[643]

---

and the municipal fees and tariffs charged by the communities' supplying and
transporting enterprises, the statement of the annual account, or any illegal suggestions or proposals. See Sec. 8b HGO Petitions and citizen decisions

[641] Bundeszentrale für politische Bildung: (Policy in community)

[642] The European regulation on self-monitoring sewage works (German "Verord-
nung über die Eigenkontrolle von Abwasseranlagen", EKVO) is an example of
detailed intervention in °community° from a super-ordinated layer; Sec. 11
HGO Supervision

[643] Sec. 4 HGO Authority to issue directives

Figure 58. °Federal°, °state° and °county° authorities

6.1.3 Compliance with systemic functions

The table on the following pages (Table 18) summarises the basic structure of °community° implementation applied in Germany's federal state of Hesse. The table reflects the typical political setting, depicting who usually provides what systemic contribution to °community° governance. How the key topics ('Norms^{OR}', 'Strategy^{SR}', 'Contract^{OR}') are resolved depends mainly on the most influential locals actors, be it the mayor, his magistrate, individual councillors or individual public servants who support or give their blessing to particular resolutions. With respect to the channel capacity provided by the legal framework of Hesse, the following findings have been observed.

6.1.3.1 °Sub-system° boundaries

Generally, there was no clear understanding of °community° versus °sub-system° layers of recursion. °Sub-systems° are not yet perceived as autonomous entities; many °sub-system° issues are being attended to on the °community° layer. Only a relatively small number of °communities° had created formal °sub-system° structures with all consequence of conceding autonomy to them. As long as °sub-system° actors are not formally assigned responsibility for their activities, not commited to achieving certain outputs or outcomes, not legitimised to dispose of their own independent budget, all these tasks must be executed and answered on the °community° layer by those who manage the entities (mayor, magistrate, administration, etc). This means that they have to understand and capture the details of all emerging °sub-system° issues (i.e. the whole complexity inherent in °sub-system° activities) in order to find the optimum solution. For instance, the planning of human resources allocation (i.e. 'Contract^{OR}' reconciliation) relies strongly on the existence of responsible °sub-system° actors who define the demand from the perspective of the individual °sub-system° ('Ambition^{OR}') as opposed to the treasurer's perspective on it ('Synergy^{OR}'). Without °sub-system° autonomy it cannot be ensured that the allocation of human resources will involve the requirements of the °sub-system° purposes. A purely central planning activity cannot replace such a function; it would require an disproportionate amount of time and effort to achieve the same results.

6.1.3.2 Two topics

The creation of 'Actuality^{TR}' is a major activity of the administration and thus of the public servants employed. On the °community° layer, primary *Two* topics in budget reconciliation are dealt with by the treasury department, which engages in setting up the budget, preparing the budget statute, compiling the budget, administrating reserves, etc. Therefore, treasury takes 'Records^{TR}', merges them in archives and electronic databases ('Actuality^{TR}') and reports on the current financial situation to magistrate and community council. Similarly, the cash office and human resources continuously engage in coordinating their resources. However, as a consequence of the vague °living sphere° boundaries and marginal autonomy assigned to parties responsible for °living sphere°, both °community° and °sub-system° issues are being coordinated on the °community° layer. Although the majority of *Two* activities were performed by administrative actors, there was usually confusion between them about who is expected to engage in coordinating °living spheres° and °villages°. It was recognised that the coordination of primary °community° issues such as financial and human resources was performed thoroughly and in-depth, however with strong and detailed participation of both mayor and magistrate members. Further, as a consequence of the distribution of tasks in professional functions within the administration, 'Orientation^{TR}' was usually not made accessible to other departments. Thus, the °housing° department would not engage in informing others about changes in the real-estate properties of °community°.

6.1.3.3 Three topics

To assess the 'Capacity^{OR}' of a °community° engaged in certain issues and undertaking specific actions requires not only the support of the mayor but also the financial, human resources and controlling departments. Councillors may submit requests regarding 'Capacity^{OR}' issues to the administration at any time. However, these issues are not usually addressed from an integrated perspective as administrative departments usually consider them from their own point of view only.

Further, there is obvious confusion about layers of recursion (i.e. about °community° versus °sub-system° layers), which is reflected in the resource bargain (*Three*-One on 'Contract[OR]'). The specialised administrative departments, profit centers, and special purpose associations[644] contribute exclusively to the °sub-systems° of °community°. However, these do not regularly participate in resource planning and budget negotiation ('Contract[OR]'). There is generally a low participation of °sub-system° responsible persons in budget negotiation. Typically, the plan for optimal resource allocation ('Synergy[OR]') is compiled solely by the treasurer. In consequence, a large proportion of °community° resources are assigned to °sub-systems° without the involvement of those actually engaged in their implementation. Sometimes those actors have not even been formally assigned responsibility. For instance, the costs of personnel are usullay planned by the human resources department on °community° layer without the required °sub-system° involvement. Similarily, the costs for building houses are often planned centrally without the participation of the respective department of °housing° and °infrastructure°.[645] As a consequence of this inherent confusion (which is expressed further in the methods and processes of the input-oriented cameralistic accountancy system applied), °sub-system° actors are usually not even interested in the accuracy of their expressed 'Ambitions[OR]' and 'Accounts[OR]' as they fear that this might lead treasurers to cut the budget positions assigned to them.

6.1.3.4 Three* topics

A *Three** function is legally assigned to the accounting control department. In smaller °communities°, these tasks are performed by the °county° authority. According to legal regulations, the magistrate and community council may mandate accounting control to audit the efficiency and effectiveness of the administration. However, in Hesse they usually did not make use of this option. The majority of accounting control departments did not have the general expertise to conduct °community° 'Audits[OR]' regarding °sub-system° implementation. Rather, they usually restricted their engagement to the examination of financial statements, books, ledgers, and reports only. A true audit function to examine administrative departments

---

[644] German word: "Zweckverband"

[645] They are captured in summary certificates ("Sammelnachweisen"), which are extrapolated sums of the overall °community's° personnel costs, material for maintenance, etc.

in all their systemic contributions was not established on the °community° layer. A comprehensive audit function to examine all °sub-system° activities regardless of their implementation through the administration or other °sub-system° actors has not yet been thought of.[646] However, because of the small size of the °community° administrations that were visited throughout this research, the major actors engaged in *Three* roles, i.e. mayor, councillors, treasurer, and public servants were the same people or closely in touch with those engaged in implementing the °sub-systems°, thus performing a kind of informal, independent 'Audit[OR]' without a shared, explicit 'Finding[OR]'.[647] However, these informal 'Audits[OR]' are not carried out systematically and the actors involved are usually not aware of their *Three** role. The extent of the individual actors' active engagement determines their perceptions ('Findings[OR]') of the *Three* interplay, where they are required to enhance the reconciliation of 'Capacity[OR]'.

6.1.3.5 Four topics

Discussing and deciding on °community° 'Strategy[SOR]' is the essential task of the political mandates, i.e. the mayor and the councillors. It is they who are held responsible by law for taking these decisions. The legal frame does not compel them to formally engage in four topics. However, there is nobody explicitly assigned to elaborate and reconcile a shared view of the total °community° and its *Wirkungsgefüge* ('Totality[SR]'). The creation of a common basis for understanding what relevant factors are, how they relate to each other, and how they shall be evaluated, has not been institutionalised. Councillors, magistrate members, and public servants do engage in continuous interplay, but there is no explicit, systematic reconciliation of a common understanding of °community° and the critical factors for exercis-

---

[646] This cannot only be compensated through the audit activities taking place on °county° and °state° layers. In the audit conducted throughout this research a comparison of 40 communities was performed. However, usually only °community° topics are being addressed; °sub-system° topics are the exception in °state° layer audits.

[647] A Three(*) interaction is formalised with the °county° layer's Accounting Control Department. However, this AC Department only examines the annual account of °community° and its substrats regarding whether: 1. the estimates are kept; 2. each single invoice amount is factually and calculatory justified and documented; 3. incomes and expenditures accord to regulations; 4. the annex of the Annual account is complete and correct. Accounting control (ACD) summarises its 'Findings[OR]' in a final report. Sec. 128 HGO para 1-2, Revision of the annual account

ing influence. In consequence, there is no explicit total view of understanding °community° ('Totality^{SR}') being shared. At times, this deficiency is compensated for one issue or the other through ambitious councillors, magistrate members, public servants, and skilful moderators succeeding in reconciling the dialogue in the different councils, enabling the actors involved to discuss their views extensively – thus ensuring that the relevant points are made, heard, and adequately introduced into the related topic discussion. However, this is more often not the case, since the discussion about 'Proposals^{SR}' and 'Reviews^{OR}' taking place tends to draw primarily on the personal and political views and interests in play. There has been no establishment of a common understanding of how to view the external determinants and the internal organisation of the °community° notion. For instance, 'Proposals^{SR}' are usually prepared by the magistrate and administration with very little involvement of the councillors. Due to the limited involvement of the honorary part-time councillors, they tend to strongly concentrate their engagement on simply confirming and finalising magistrate 'Proposals^{SR}', perhaps making some annotations and suggestions. Their part-time engagement strongly constrains their involvement and influence. Nevertheless, legally they are and usually they feel obliged to engage in the full range of operative, strategic, and normative °community° topics of 'Norms^{NR}', 'Strategy^{SOR}', 'Contract^{OR}', 'Requirements^{OR}', and 'Guidelines^{OR}' including both °sub-system° and °community° layers. Furthermore, the law reserves them the right to intervene on any ongoing issue being addressed.[648] Councillors' limited engagement does not enable them to attend adequately to how these issues are governed and managed. As will later be seen, the established methods and instruments further complicate their reflection on and resolution of *Four* issues.[649] Thus, councillors face enormous difficulties in reconciling a clear 'Strategy^{SOR}' that defines goals ('images') and assigns implementable and revisable tasks ('instruments' and 'actions') to the magistrate and administration, forcing both to either muddle through or to actively counteract the confusion through intense communication. Councillors often complain that the imbalance between them and the administration results for them in a loss of influence.[650]

---

[648] Sec. 50 HGO para 1-3 Tasks (of the community council)

[649] As will be seen in the next chapter, some of the methods and instruments themselves are inadequate for solving the issues (change or transformation capacity) and do not even depict them in a way that councillors can grasp (transduction capacity).

[650] Counter-proposals which would change this in principle have not yet been developed. For an improved approach compare the Hessian system to the con-

Furthermore, in the established °community° structures it remains unclear who is in charge of preparing 'Reviews^{OR}' of strategic 'Proposals^{SR}'. This is not reflected in the legally defined or locally observed actor roles. The mayor, councillors, treasurer, and executive public servants all engage in some manner in the creation of 'Reviews^{OR}' by commenting on them, but there is no particular person assigned to consider them in the light of the operative 'Capacity^{OR}' of °community°. The following example illustrates this: If there is a strong mayor supporting the 'Proposal^{SR}' "building of a new gym" in the °community° in order to please the voters of the °community's° sports associations (engaged in °culture° and °leisure°), he may arrange to assert that interest without facing anyone reviewing whether that effort lies within the °community's° 'Capacity^{OR}'. If the decision "to build the gym" then binds many resources and is enabled at the expense of e.g. the sub-system °infrastructure° – such as reducing the maintenance of the °community's° gutters and sewers – this imposes incalculable, even ir-revocable, consequences which will be felt at a later date.

Furthermore, a thorough 'Inquiry^{SR}' of the °community° environment is not established. Magistrate and councillors engage in contact with the community residents, however this is not done systematically in regard to the °community's° environment, future opportunities, and risks and is not presented in a form that could be used for reflecting *Four* issues ('Totali-ty^{SR}'). In consequence, the majority of °communities° face the danger that relevant changes in the environment are not employed to gain the best un-derstanding of the actual situation ('Totality^{SR}') and not translated into adequate measures ('Proposal^{SR}'). A common example of the lack of this function is the capacity planning of the local kindergartens. The majority of the °communities° visited did not recognise the demographic changes caused by the nationwide decline in birth rates, which in turn would affect the local demand for young children's care. Some of them nevertheless invested in building new children's facilities without a thorough recogni-tion of the underlying changing circumstances. In °communities° that lack a systematic 'Inquiry^{SR}' of the environment, any non-organised interests will scarcely be perceived.

---

stitution of Germany's northern states (the "Norddeutsche Ratsverwaltung"). See Bundeszentrale für politische Bildung: (Policy in community)

6.1.3.6 Five topics

°Communities° are usually aware of the importance of common normative foundations such as norms, purposes, understandings, etc. The laws of Hesse set the general normative frame for the °communities°, defining their general purpose, actors, and processes for addressing normative issues. Thus, community residents are given the right to vote and therefore to determine who will be participating in the community council and will be the head of the magistrate. Further, it gives community residents the right to take the initiative through referenda and plebiscites ('Boundary[NR], 'Norms[NR]'). However, further contributions of actors derive from their legally defined interrelations and roles. These role definitions focus strongly on defining the interrelations between the actors. On the whole, they do not substantiate how actors contribute to the systemic topics.

As in *Three* and *Four* topics, in *Five* topics it is also not clear which contributions the various actors are expected to make for settling normative issues. The missing or poorly established *Four* interaction is a consequence of this. There is no awareness that strategic topics have to be kept separate from operative topics, and that the attendance to *Three* and *Four* topics has to be legitimised and supervised independently from a normative perspective (*Five-Four, Five-Three and Five-(Four-Three)* are dark grey in Table 18). 'Norms[NR]' tend to focus on specifying the frame of operative reconciliations only. Yet they would need to attend also to strategic topics and to balancing the reconciliation of strategic and normative topics.

This seemed to be more apparent with operative issues. The community council and magistrate did actively engage in defining operative 'Norms[NR]' according to their roles (*Five-Three* is white in Table 18) but were less aware that defining 'Norms[NR]' also requires them to prove the 'Legitimacy[OR]' of how operative topics are being addressed. This needs to be specified as well as how strategic topics are to be addressed. Generally, the mayor is engaged in reporting to the community council, but usually he reports on single °sub-system° issues and how they have been managed (which corresponds to 'Reports[OR]', 'Accounts[OR]') and elaborates less on how the synergistic operative governing of the °sub-systems° is achieved ('Capacity[OR]', 'Synergy[OR]'). In doing so, he in fact legitimated past governing proceedings without actually elaborating on their 'Legitimacy[OR]' in the light of the established °community° 'Boundary[NR]' and 'Norms[NR]' (*Three-Five* is light grey in Table 18).

The following figure illustrates the current involvement of °community° actors in the systemic topics. All major conglomerates, i.e. community council, boards, commissions, and magistrate, did engage in the full

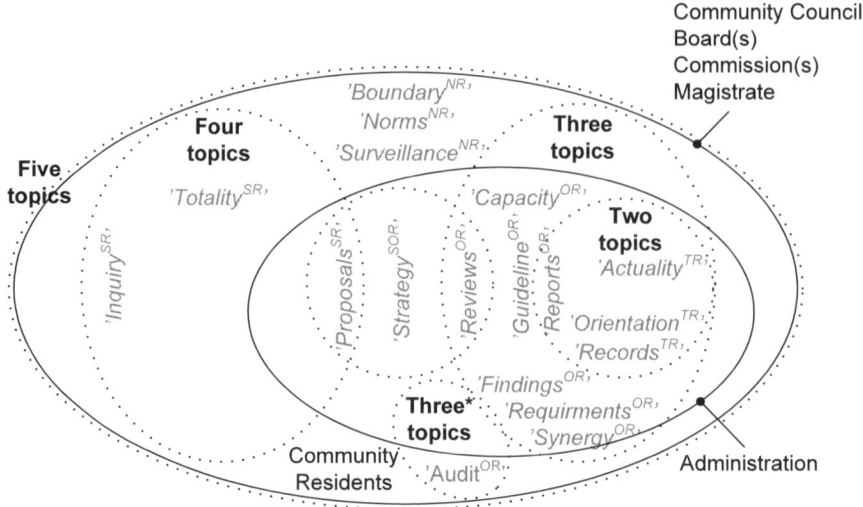

Figure 59. Current assignments of topic spheres to community councils

range of topics (and furthermore attended to °sub-system° issues and topics of all kinds, which is not depicted here). The administration has a slightly restricted focus on operative topics and 'Strategy^{OR}' reconciliation. In fact, all of the administrations visited showed professional instead of systemic functions and consequently also lacked focus on systemic topic reconciliation.

Councillors generally feel overwhelmed, which results from their board involvement in all °sub-system° and °community° issues on tactical, operative, strategic, and normative levels. Treasurers cannot competently assign resources if they are not in touch with the implementation of °sub-systems° themselves.

Generally, it can be observed that °community° actors, especially the most influential magistrate and administration, strongly orient their behaviour to conforming to norms, rules, and regulations, which is simply a logical consequence of their lack of links to the purposes that they are supposed to strive toward. The structures established do not ensure that actors comply with the logical systemic functions. In addition, there are no incentives concerning the fulfilment of their individual tasks. Instead, there is widespread confusion regarding what the different actors can and should contribute with respect to their individual involvement, time, expertise, etc. The structures defined in the legal framework tend to cause confusion, as they fail to clarify actors' contributions (i.e. tasks and responsibilities) in a way that ensures that all systemic functions are being addressed.

Table 18. Systemic contributions of °community° actors

Interaction / Systemic topic	Community Council (CC)			Magistrate (FM, OM) (honorary, part-time)	Mayor (Ma) (professional, full-time)	Central Administration (A) (professional, full-time)	°Sub-system° (SubS) Fire Brigade, Churches, Priv. & Publ. Comp	Community Residents (R)	°Super-system° (SuperS) State, county authority
	Councillors (honorary, part-time)	°Community° Boards (B) (topic focus)	Factions (F) (interest focus)						
°Community° topic									
Two topics									
Two-One									
°Query^TR° (←)					REQUESTS OF °SUB-SYSTEM° DEPARTMENTS		Requests of SubS responsibles		
°Record^TR° (←)						CONDUCTING ENQUIRY	Providing records		
°Orientation^TR° (→)						ADVICE TO °SUB-SYSTEMS° DEPARTMENTS	Receiving advice		
Two arena									
Actuality^TR° (↔)						COLLECTING AND ADMINISTRATING FACTS OF ACTUAL SITUATION			
Two-Three									
°Report^OR° (→)	Suggestions, Assig. B, Ma, A, FINAL DECISION SUSPENSION	Preparation Advice to CC Assign. Ma, A Recommendation CC	Preparing suggestions for B, CC	APPROVING REPORTS	CREATING REPORTS	CREATING REPORTS	CREATING REPORTS		
°Guideline^OR° (←) / Rules, statutes, and decrees on: °sub-system° implementation				Suggestion>CC Announcement Supervision	Preparation>Ma Issuing Continuous adaptation				BINDING STATE AND DISTRICT REGULATIONS

Table 18 (continued)

Interaction / Systemic topics — °Community° topic	Community Council (CC)			Magistrate (FM, OM) (professional, full-time)	Mayor (Ma) (professional, full-time)	Central Administration (A) (professional, full-time)	°Sub-system° (SubS) Fire Brigade, Churches, Priv & Publ. Comp	Community Residents (R)	°Super-system° (SuperS) State, district authority
	Councillors (honorary, part-time)	°Community° Boards (B) (topic focus)	Factions (F) (interest focus)						

Three topics

	Councillors	°Community° Boards (B)	Factions (F)	Magistrate	Mayor	Central Admin (A)	Sub-system (SubS)	Community Residents (R)	Super-system (SuperS)
***Three* arena**									
Capacity^{QR+} (↔)	*Informal dialogue*	*Informal dialogue*	*Informal dialogue*	*Interpretation of actual situation*		*Preparing interpretation of actual situation*			
CodeOfAudit^{QR+} (↔)								*Informal dialogue*	
***Three-One* interplay**									
Synergy^{QR+} (→) *How can the °sub-system° implementation be optimised from a °community° perspective?*	Suggestions Assig. B, Ma, A	PROPOSAL FOR CC Assig. Ma, A	Preparing agenda, suggestions and...	Suggestion=CC Prioritisation Deputation		Preparation of plan for optimal synergy of SubS	Requests of requirements of °community° synergy		
Ambitions^{NSOTR+} (←) *What are °sub-system° intentions, suggestions?*	Assessment Assig. B, Ma, A	Assessment Assig. Ma, A	assessments for: B, CC	Evaluation of SubS ambitions		Request of SubS ambitions	Formulation of SubS ambitions		
Contract^{QR+} (●) *Agreement on °sub-system° tasks, resources, goals, etc. (e.g. budget)*	APPROVAL	Recommendation to CC	(CALL TO VOTE CONSISTENT)	ONGOING DECISIONS ON RESOURCE ALLOCATION		MODERATION PREPARATION OF DRAFTS			
***Three-One* intervention**									
Requirements^{QR+} (→) *What must be done in order to implement °community° purpose? (e.g. defining public expenditures, establishing public institutions)*	GENERAL DECISIONS	PREPARATION ADVICE TO CC	PREPARING SUGGESTIONS FOR B, CC	DECISIONS ON ONGOING ISSUES		PREPARING DECISION REQUIREMENTS			
Accounts^{QR+} (→) *Proof of °sub-systems° complying with aspired achievements ('Contract^{QR}')*	APPROVAL	Recommendation to CC		Approval		Report of SubS persons responsible (PS) to Ma, Ma to CC	Report of SubS responsibles (PS) to M, CC		
Three(°)-One									
Audit^{QR+} (→)	Individual councillors observations			Observations through involvement in implementation		Exposition throughout implementation			STATE AND DISTRICT REGULATIONS DECISIONS
Findings^{QR+} (←)							Complaints Feedback		

Table 18 (continued)

Interaction / Systemic topics °Community° topic	Community Council (CC)			Magistrate (FM, OM) (honorary part-time)	Mayor (Ma) (professional, full-time)	Central Administration (A) (professional, full-time)	°Sub-system° (SubS) Fire Brigade, Churches, Priv & Publ. Comp	Community Residents (CR)	°Super-system° (SuperS) State, district authority
	Councillors (honorary, part-time)	°Community° Boards (B) (topic focus)	Factions (F) (interest focus)						
Four topics									
Four arena "Totality°^{SR}" (↔)	*Informal dialogue*						*Informal dialogue*	*Preparing statements, views*	
Four-Three "Proposals°^{SR}" (→) *What are relevant strategic plans to cope with future opportunities and risks in the light of °community° Totality°^{SR}?*	*Suggestions* Assig. B, Ma, A	PROPOSALS PREPARATION ADVICE TO CC Assig. Ma, A	Proposals/Agenda Preparing suggestions for B, CC	*Initiation Preparation Specification Suggestion*		Preparation Suggestion	Propositions Suggestions	*Initiative through petition*	
"Reviews°^{OR}" (←) *What constraints limit the implementation of 'Proposals°^{SR}' in regard of °community° Capacity°^{SR}?*	*Assessment* Assig. B, Ma, A	Assessment Assig. Ma, A	Preparing assessment for B, CC	*Assessment of CC sug. reg. feasibility*		Preparation Assessment	Concerns Objections	*Initiative through petition (rare)*	
"Strategy°^{SOR}" (●) *Agreement on a strategic plan (e.g. budget statute, investment program)*	FINAL DECISION THROUGH VOTE	Recommendation to CC	(CALL TO VOTE CONSISTENT)		Recommendation to CC			REFERENDA, PLEBISCITE	STATE AND DISTRICT REGULATIONS
Four-Environment "Incidents°^{SR}" (←) *What occurrences in the environment of °community° are relevant?*	*Individual councillors observations*			*Individual observations*		Public opinion polls	Complaints, Petitions		

Table 18 (continued)

interaction / Representation (°Community° issue)	Community Council (CC) Councillors (honorary, part-time)	Community Council (CC) °Community° Boards (B) (topic focus)	Community Council (CC) Factions (F) (interest focus)	Magistrate (FM, OM) (honorary, part-time)	Mayor (Ma) (professional, full-time)	Central Administration (A) (professional, full-time)	°Sub-system° (SubS) Police, Parties, Churches, Priv. & Publ. Comp.	Community Residents (R)	°Super-system° (SuperS) State, district authority
Five arena									
Boundary^SR (↔) E.g. public elections, mission statements; geograph. boundaries, etc.	Suggestions / Decision / CONDUCT ELECTIONS	Suggestions / PREPARATION ADVICE TO CC	Preparing suggestions for CC	Moderation / Representation of R	Support of dialogue / Suggestions			Dialogue / Decision by vote	Legal regulations, roles, duties
Five-Four									
Norms^NR (→) on. coping with strategic (Four) topics Rules, regulations, and statutes; Defining responsibilities of B, Ma	Suggestions / DECISIONS AND ANNOUNCEMENT, SUSPENSION	Suggestions / Recommendation to CC	Preparing suggestions for CC	Preparation / Suggestion	Preparation / Suggestion			Initiative through petition / Referenda, plebiscites	Legal regulations, roles, tasks, duties of actors
Legitimacy^SR (←) of operative activities Proof of compliance with strategic 'Norms'^NR (e.g. conduct of extraordinary legal disputes, approval of Ma)	APPROVAL	PREPARATION ADVICE TO CC	Preparing critical assessment for CC	Reporting to CC					
Five-Three									
Norms^NR (→) on. coping with operative (Three) topics Rules, regulations, and statutes; Defining responsibilities of B, Ma	Initiation / DECISIONS AND ANNOUNCEMENT, SUSPENSION	Initiation / Recommendation to CC	Preparing suggestions for CC	Suggestion				Initiative through petition / Referenda, plebiscites	Legal regulations, roles, tasks, duties of actors
Legitimacy^OR (←) of operative activities Proof of compliance with operative 'Norms'^NR (e.g. approving the annual financial budget, approval of the Ma)	APPROVAL	PREPARATION ADVICE TO CC	Preparing critical assessment for CC	*(Reports to CC)*	*Preparing Reports on operative activities*	*Preparing Reports on operative activities*			
Five-(Four-Three)									
Supervision^SR (←) Supervision of reconciliation between 'Proposals'^SR and 'Reviews'^OR	SUPERVISION OF	Ma, A	Preparing critical assessment for CC	Supervision of CC	Supervision of CC			Supervision of Ma; CC, A	Supervision of CC; Ma
Five-One									
Urgency^TR (←) Urgencies jeopardising °community° implementation				Judgement / Appraising / Proposing consequences	Signalling °sub-system° urgency	Signalling °sub-system° urgency	Signalling °sub-system° urgency		

6.1.4 Suggestions

The governance framework showed the viability of a social °system° notion requires that the structures established can attend to all °system° issues of the five systemic topics. The description of the typical actor involvement in Hessian °communities° has shown that there is a lack of focus in actors' roles, causing confusion between them. The tasks and responsibilities of all °community° actors need to be defined in their particular contributions to enable compliance of the systemic functions.

Related to the systemic topics, the confusion about actors' involvement on different layers of recursion should be eliminated. Therefore, the distinction made by actors between °sub-system° and °community° should be made visible, thus creating awareness of its significance. In doing so, it will become apparent that both °living sphere° and °village° layers are to be seen as autonomous, viable °system° notions with all consequences for the actors involved, i.e. being largely independent and self-organised. °Sub-system° actors should be assigned responsibility for addressing their issues and provided with maximum autonomy to implement their aspired goals. °Community° actors should be allowed to take °sub-system° decisions only when that is necessary for the °community° to remain viable, e.g. because the actors responsible are suspected of fraud or cannot cope with their duty for other reasons. Such expanded autonomy would enable self-organisation and thus improve efficiency and effectiveness on both °sub-system° and °community° layers.

Secondly, the contributions of the established councils and fora should be clarified. As has been recognised, there is a lack of focus on 'Proposals^{SR}', 'Strategy^{SOR}', 'Synergy^{OR}', and 'Contract^{OR}' in reconciliations. Thus, the recommendation is to put these topics on the agenda and to clarify systemic contributions of the community council, magistrate, and administration as well as boards and commissions. Thus, it would be ensured that all systemic topics are being addressed and brought to resolution. A potential way of eliminating the confusion of contributions would be to assign topics and decision competences to the different councils, i.e. to formulate customised systemic assignments that describe their contributions. One possible way of doing that is indicated in the following topic map (Figure 60).

Tasks and responsibilities are not to be defined by specifying outcomes or outputs to be achieved by the community council, magistrate, etc. but by specifying the actors' contributions to solving the systemic topics. Outcome and output responsibilities in 'Contract^{OR}' and systemic responsibilities

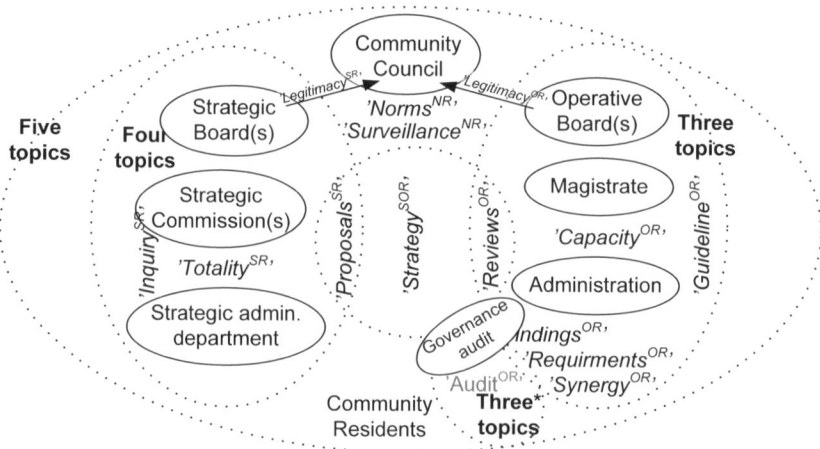

Figure 60. Proposed assignments of topic spheres to community councils

should be assigned for councillors, magistrate members, public servants engaged on °community° layer.

Such topic assignments defining the scope of issues and decision competences of the actors involved in °community° could even be formalised legally in order to ensure that all °communities° adhere to the assignments. However, as the mayor is free to design °community° organisation independently, a legal formalisation is not a must.[651] Council assignments could very well be reconciled as a part of °community° implemention. Local actors would, consequently, simply need to reconcile and fix a systemic distribution of topics and responsibilities within their °community° and °subsystem° boundaries. These general topic assignments would then be specified and continuously adapted according to the specific competencies and interests of the actors engaged to contribute to the systemic funtions.

In the proposed topic assignments, councillors and the majority of boards engage primarily in strategic topics. The main assignment of both operative and strategic boards is to suggest initiatives in *Four* and *Three* reconciliations, to approve the decisions taken by those in charge in *Three* and *Four* topics and to affirm the 'Legitimacy[O&SR]' of their activities. Thus, the boards would act as initiators, supervisors, and final decision takers of operative and strategic topics respectively.[652] Compared to today,

---

[651] Sec. 70 HGO Tasks of the mayor

[652] According to Sec. 62 HGO Boards, the community council can delegate issues and topics to boards for final decision making. Sec. 51 HGO Exclusive assignments

the boards would be strengthened in their ability to take decisions; general overlaps of agendas in various boards would be either eliminated or clarified in their mutual contributions to the resolution of their respective systemic topic. Both strategic board(s) and especially strategic commissions would involve °sub-system° actors to ground *Four* topic reconciliations in the realities of the °sub-systems°. The primary assignment of the community council would then be to set the normative frame of °community° implementation, i.e. to decide on topic and actor assignments, thus defining the 'Norms^{NR}' actually relevant for °community° implementation. Further, it would engage in the supervision of the interplay between *Three* and *Four* councils and actors ('Supervision^{NR}') and approve finally all strategic decisions taken by the *Three* and *Four* actors responsible ('Strategy^{SOR}'). Finally, the community council would be responsible for ensuring the involvement of the community residents, i.e. taking care of involving them where necessary and informing them about the purpose of the resolutions and decisions defined.

Based upon such a general frame of topic assignments, suggestions on the details of *Three* and *Four* topic assignments can now be derived. For addressing *Four* topics, strategic administrative tasks and responsibilities would have to be defined, perhaps even a department to be set up for clarifying and moderating a common understanding of the future situation of °community° in its environment, including an understanding of the °community's° *Wirkungsgefüge* and the crucial leverage to influence it ('Totality^{SR}'). A common or at least compatible understanding of the °community's° 'Totality^{SR}' is the basis for strategic governance and the crucial leverage of politics. It should be continuously re-created and therefore be assigned to a council or actor that can permanently attend to it. To keep in touch with environmental developments, it will be necessary that some actors are assigned the responsibility of observing the environment and identifying the relevant developments and changing needs of the community residents. Based on the initiatives of the strategic board and continuously advised by a strategic commission, the strategic responsible persons or departments would elaborate the 'Proposals^{SR}' of °community°. The councillors of the community council and the strategic board(s) now concentrate merely on initiating these activities. This would allow them to focus their engagement on setting the political dialogue, setting emphases and priorities. For addressing *Three* topics, the magistrate would be in charge of moderating a common understanding and interpretation of the actual situation of °community° ('Capacity^{OR}') and assign responsibility for sound 'Reviews^{OR}'. For 'Strategy^{SOR}' reconciliation a special meeting would be defined, moderated by the mayor, with strategic and operative actors participating. That meeting would be assigned pre-decision capability, which means that all decisions would be taken there with only those of outstanding importance for °community° to be authorised by the community council. All operative issues would be actively dealt with by the administration. The magistrate would actively lead through that process. It would be empowered to take final decisions on all operative issues ('Capacity^{OR}', 'Reviews^{OR}', 'Requirements^{OR}') as long as there were no veto from the councillors on the boards or the community council. General administrative departments such as treasury, controlling, human ressources, etc. would engage in addressing the remaining *Three* issues, i.e. 'Synergy^{OR}', 'Requirements^{OR}' and 'Guidelines^{OR}'.

6.2 Change or transformation capacity: methods

°Community° actors apply specific methods and instruments to adequately address and reconcile their ongoing issues. In view of the large number of actors participating in °community°, some central methods and instruments applied in °community° actor reconciliations have been made explicit and formalised legally or established through practice. These formalised methods and instruments are at the heart of systemic topic reconciliation – they are therefore presented here. In Germany, each of the °states° constructs its own legal frame, defining generally the type of methods and instruments to be used in °community°. Although these °state° layer regulations are roughly congruent, there are many variations in the details. Generally, Hessian laws prescribe the following instruments as obligatory for community:

1. Budget

2. Budget statute

3. Annual account[653]

Furthermore, some °communities° also use the following instruments:

4. Cost and activity accounting (optional)

5. Product catalogue (optional)

---

[653] Sec.112 HGO Annual account

This list of instruments was in effect during the author's participation in the general audit. As demonstrated by the following synthesis, these established instruments show major weaknesses. At the beginning of the 1990s, a fundamental reform of German community administrations was initiated, and controversial discussions continue to be carried on.[654] The discussion centered on the question of the design of the methods and instruments to be applied. It is not a Hessian speciality, but does occur in all other °states° in Germany, and similarly in other countries as well. Since the beginning of the 1990s, under the guidance of New Public Management (NPM), there has been a shift from traditional authority to a modern service enterprise demanding the transfer of economic management methods as applied in private companies to public administrations. Originally, New Public Management stipulated a change from the input to output orientation, initiating a transformation of traditional bureaucratic enterprises into modern service centers. Today, the focus of NPM is more to provide an approach for the reorganisation of the control and governing procedures in public administrations.[655] However, the emphasis of this case study is not to summarise or reflect on the ongoing wide-ranging discussion, which evolved from scientific discussions and historic developments. That has been elaborated elsewhere.[656] Instead, the case study intends to highlight how the systemic contribution of the specific methods and instruments applied can be identified and evaluated, and furthermore, how that consolidates (i.e. synergises) into a global picture of °community° governance and viability. The following synthesis

---

[654] Fundamental discussions concerning the theoretical foundation of governance research are ongoing. For instance, see proceedings of the European Group of Public Administration (EGPA) conference in Milan, 6th-9th September 2006. A workshop topic has been: "After public policy and management frameworks. What's the next step?", http://soc.kuleuven. be/io/egpa2006/, retrieved on 7th of February 2007.

[655] Thus, the self-conception of the Swiss pendant of NPM, commonly referred to as Results-oriented Public Management (RoPM). For a definition see glossary on http://www.idt.unisg.ch/org/idt/pmce.nsf/, retrieved on 7th of February 2007.

[656] See for instance: Schedler, K. and Proeller, I.: (New Public Management); Grüning, G.: Origin and theoretical basis of New Public Management, International Public Management Journal, 4, 2001; Barzelay, M.: (How to argue NPM); Steiner, Reto: New Public Management in Swiss Municipalities, International Public Management Journal, 3, 2000; Kiesel, B.: Wirkungsorientierte Steuerung einer Landesverwaltung, Wiesbaden, 2005

will show how the governance framework applies to depicting the methods and instruments a °community° uses for the reconciliation of its unfolding issues. As an example, those methods and instruments shall be looked at which are used for conducting resource allocation (*Two*, *Three*, and *Four* interactions). Their systemic contributions will be identified, synergised, and assessed with respect to their capability to promote the solution of the systemic topics required for the viability of the °community° notion.

6.2.1 Systemic contributions

6.2.1.1 Budget

The budget authorises the magistrate to incur expenditures and to commit to obligations.[657] It is said to be the community council's political program "expressed in figures". Throughout the year, it provides the binding instructions depicting the expected incomes and expenditures, assigning tasks and allocating resources to those involved in °sub-system° implementation. Whenever substantial deviations to incomes and expenditures arise, a hearing in or permission from the community council is mandatory. In the °state° of Hesse, the budget consists of the following main components[658]:

1. Budget statute ("Haushaltssatzung")
2. General plan ("Gesamtplan")
3. Activity field plans ("Einzelpläne") of the Administrative and Capital budget ("Verwaltungs- und Vermögenshaushalt")
4. Summary certificates ("Sammelnachweise")
5. Staff appointment plan ("Stellenplan")

Further, the budget annex consists of:

1. Preliminary report ("Vorbericht")[659]

---

[657] The budget neither justifies nor compensates any claims, titles, or liabilities. Sec. 96 HGO para 1-2 Budget

[658] Sec. 3 GemHVO para 1, 2 Pre-report

[659] Review, overview, and preview of budget keeping in previous, current and upcoming financial years. Sec. 3 GemHVO Pre-report

2. Financial plan and investment program ("Finanzplan und Investitionsprogramm")

3. Overview of commitment authorisations ("Übersicht der Verpflichtungsermächtigungen")[660]

4. Overview of debts and financial reserves ("Übersicht über den Stand der Schulden und Rücklagen")

5. Overview on the budgeted range of activities ("Übersicht über budgetierte Tätigkeitsbereiche")

In addition to this list, the annex entails the capital report and asset records, economic plans, financial statements of special estates and public companies, and an overview of the financial resources provided to the factions of the community council. However, these do not provide supplementary data to aspects of °community° implementation and are therefore not considered here. These budget components are described briefly below with respect to their systemic contribution and commented on wherever relevant.

General plan

The general plan ("Gesamtplan") comprises of the following parts[661]:

1. A summary of incomes, expenditures, and commitment authorisations of the activity field plans in the administrative and capital budget that provides an overall sketch of the activities of the °community° and depicts a 'Report^{OR}' of the type (These 'instruments' have (not) been used) and provides 'Orientation^{OR}' (These 'instruments' are to be used).

2. A budget profile ("Haushaltsquerschnitt") summarises the incomes, expenditures, and commitment authorisations for each activity field, e.g. security, schools, etc. Budget positions are aggregated to show how the figures relate to the income and expenditure groups (taxes, general administration, personnel expenditures, subsidiaries, etc.). Further, adequate multiples, e.g. per inhabitant, are indicated to facilitate the interpretation. The budget profile is a 'Report^{OR}' (These 'instruments' have (not) been used), standardised to facilitate comparison with other municipalities ('Super-Report^{OR}').

---

[660] Shows the impact of existing contracts on expenditures for the next three years.

[661] Sec. 5 GemHVO Activity field plans

3. A grouping survey ("Gruppierungsübersicht") that summarises the incomes and expenditures for each kind of income or expenditure, e.g. personnel. It reveals the proportions between different types of incomes and expenditures. The grouping survey shows to what extent the current income allows the financing of primary substance forming expenditures as well as the proportional relationship of equity capital to external funds. It may thus be used to identify the total expenditures in the maintenance of the °community's° properties. The survey depicts the transactions that have taken place and allows a general judgement of the financial aspects of the °community° implementation. It thus gives expression to 'Report^{OR}' (These 'instruments' have (not) been used).

4. A summary of financing ("Finanzierungsübersicht") depicts all transactions financing the °community's° activities, e.g. how it covers its deficits, what has been added to and withdrawn from the financial reserves, what admissions and repayments of debts are, etc. It thus also reflects a 'Report^{OR}' of the type (These 'instruments' have (not) been used).

The general plan is a written statement of the expected cash-flow of the year it is enacted for. It is a summary 'Report^{OR}' of the type (These 'instruments' have (not) been used) that is defined legally and contributes to actors' understanding of 'Capacity^{OR}'. It is the result of the democratic process of resource bargaining (*Three*-One interplay) for elaborating and arguing between 'Ambitions^{NSOR}' and 'Synergy^{OR}'. Furthermore, it is the reference point for 'Reviews^{OR}' (These 'instruments' will (not) suffice and / or (not) be efficacious) when responding to strategic 'Proposals^{SR}'.

Activity field plans

The activity field plans ("Einzelpläne") of both the administrative and capital budget depict the incomes and expenditures as they are planned for the upcoming year and as they have been realised in the two preceeding years. The following activity fields are distinguished:[662] 0. general administration; 1. public security; 2. schools; 3. social security and welfare; 4. culture, research and science; 5. health, sports and recreation; 6. construction, housing and transport; 7. public institutions, business development;

---

[662] State of Hesse: Sample specifying Sec. 4 para 3 GemHVO General plan, 1973, Gesetz- und Verordnungsblatt für das Land Hessen (GVBl I)

8. private companies; 9. public finance. Thus, the activity fields reflect both the °community° and °sub-system° activities. Each activity field plan is structured according to standardised groups and sub-groups.[663] Incomes are linked to their origin (e.g. fees, charges, taxes); expenditures refer to their specific purpose expressed with the cost centre structure. Planned positions of the actual financial year are stated along with the income and expenditure extrapolations for the previous year and the final results of the year preceding the last year. Further, for each investment, the total expenditures needed and expended up to that point are indicated.[664] Generally, two sets of activity field plans are to be distinguished, capital and administrative budgets. All incomes and expenditures affecting the the °community's° capital or debts are depicted in the capital budget ("Vermögenshaushalt"). The administrative budget ("Verwaltungshaushalt") contains all the current incomes and expenditures required for task fulfilment, e.g. personnel, maintenance and operating expenditure, fees, rents, current assignments, etc. From each entry it can be derived whether the respective activity increases or decreases the °community's° capital. Arrangement and grouping of both the administrative and capital budgets are defined in the Hessian °state° law.[665] Thus, activity field plans give expression to 'Reports[OR]' and 'Legitimacy[OR]' by subsuming previous year figures.[666] Further, they give expression to 'Contract[OR]' by stating the expected figures ("Soll") of the current year. Therewith, they are part of 'Actuality[TR]', and help to provide 'Orientation[OR]' to °sub-system° actors.

Summary certificates

Summary certificates ("Sammelnachweise") are summaries of incomes and expenditures that belong to the same subject category. They provide an overview of how the °community° rations its subject spheres such as "personnel", thus providing a 'Report[OR]' of the type (These 'instruments'

---

[663] Activity fields are defined in State of Hesse: (Sample GemHVO) as: 0. taxes, 3rd party funds, 1. administration and operation, 2. other, 3. income capital, 4. personnel expenditures, 5.&6. expenditures for administrative maintenance, 7. grants & funds for third parties, 8. other, 9. expenditure capital.

[664] Sec. 5 GemHVO Activity field plans

[665] State of Hesse: GemHVO on the Administrative and Capital Budget, 1973, Gesetz- und Verordnungsblatt für das Land Hessen (GVBl I)

[666] This means the budget for the year 2007, which was elaborated in 2006 subsumes values from 2005.

have (not) been used by the °sub-systems°). However, there is no general and official guideline in existence defining a useful set of subject categories and enabling the reader to identify the origin of the incomes and expenditures summarised. Summary certificates do not indicate what financial resources have been invoiced on what categories. For instance, the certificates list expenditures such as "building materials" without indicating the specific buildings the materials have been used for. As a consequence, it is not possible to interpret these figures in the light of an aspired optimum allocation to °sub-system° activity ('Synergy^{OR}'). Therefore, it would be necessary to know what amounts refer to which buildings to enable optimisation of the allocation. Thus, the summary certificates obfuscate the allotted budget. At best they provide only a limited description of 'Capacity^{OR}'.

Staff appointment plan

The *staff appointment* plan indicates the full-time equivalents of those currently employed in each department of the administration, according to the terms of their contract (public servant, office staff, and workers). It indicates the total number of positions required on different levels of remuneration in the current and previous year. The plan shows expected and potential changes from the previous year's numbers and comments on them.[667] Employees of the °community° are assigned generally to no specific administrative entity (e.g. administration, building yard). The plan entails no indication regarding the actual tasks of the actors.[668] It is thus a 'Report^{OR}' depicting the current status of personnel employment of the community, focusing on (These 'instruments' have (not) been used). It is based on the previous year's plan as it affirms the personnel and employees deployed for °sub-system° implementation. However, it depicts the quantities of the actual distribution in general terms but does not indicate the link between the actual activities ('actions') being performed and the costs that are involved with them ('instruments'). For the reader, it remains unclear to what extent the chosen distribution of resources has been adequate or optimal to implement °community°.

---

[667] Sec. 6 GemHVO Staff employment plan

[668] For instance, a worker from the building yard may work as a pool attendant in the °community's° public outdoor swimming pool during summer time and in snow clearing during winter.

Preliminary report

The preliminary report is the only formal, written assessment of the °community's° actual situation. It sketches the current state of affairs and the development of the financial resources of the °community°. Major points are

1. the development of the most important types of income, expenditures, capital, debts in the two previous years and the expectations for the coming year;

2. how financial stability can be evaluated, expressed through the alternating allocation between the administrative and capital budget and their relation to the break-even requirements as indicated in the financial plan; and

3. which investments are planned for the upcoming year and what their financial consequences for the subsequent years are.[669]

The preliminary report thus contributes to the collection of 'Reports[OR]' as a summary and evaluative assessment of the current situation specifying (These 'images' have (not) been aspired to; these 'instruments' have (not) been used; these 'actions' have (not) been taken; These 'actors' have (not) been involved). Its significance varies largely in the different communities depending on whether alternative investments are explained, the development of expenditures is addressed and illustrated visually, imputed costs are indicated, etc. Usually, no or spartan illustrations, explanations, and interpretations are provided to comment on the budget. However, one of the °communities° visited did release a further document during the year where it commented on actual incomes and expenditures.[670]

Financial plan

The budget of °community° implementation is based on a five-year financial plan. The first year of the financial plan is the current fiscal year. It defines the total volume and structure of expenditures and indicates how they are to be met.[671] It entails all planned expenditures for investments

---

[669] Sec. 3 GemHVO Pre-report

[670] With the introduction of double-entry accounting in Hessian °communities° in 2009 regular underyear reports will become mandatory.

[671] Sec. 101 HGO Financial planning

and incentives and links to the expected incomes and expenditures of the administrative and capital budget.[672] It is meant to estimate the development of the °community's° financial situation as accurately as possible to enable the magistrate and councillors to actively influence incomes and expenditures. It elaborates on the development of incomes as a function of taxes, personnel expenses, etc.

Thus, the financial plan reflects the adopted 'Strategy^{OR}' of the °community°. However, usually only foreseeable and preferred developments of the near future are considered in its reconciliation. It concentrates on planning the use of 'instruments' by specifying financial inputs and outputs and thus follows the type (These 'instruments' have (not) been used). It does not clarify how these financial resources ('instruments') relate to the desired outcomes and future states of the system (strategic 'images'), i.e. what is being aspired to with the allocation of resources. Further, the financial plan does not link monetary figures ('instruments') with the intented outputs ('images'), such as specifying the child care capacity of the local kindergartens maintained or the extent of streets maintainenance that must be carried out in the upcoming years. Thus, it does not indicate the 'actions' to be taken and the 'actors' to be assigned. Furthermore, it lacks reference to a thorough analysis of the expected consequential costs of potential investments.

Investment program

The investment program[673] explains the envisaged investments of the planning period for each administrative department of the year. It shows both ongoing and new investments, with the amount valid for the respective year and the overall sum per investment project.[674] Thus, it gives expression to the 'Strategy^{SOR}' that has been accepted by the majority of councillors. It explicates in which fields and with which resources actors will create facilities to support life in the °community° in the coming years. However, in most cases it did not adequately depict the consequential costs of the planned investments, i.e. the respective depreciation and calculative costs of the investments or the values resulting from personal contributions

---

[672] Sec. 24 GemHVO para 1 clause 1 Financial planning and investment program

[673] The investment program is grouped according to the °communities'° fields of activity. Sec. 24 GemHVO para 1 clause 1

[674] Insignificant investments and incentives may be summarised according to the fields of activity. Sec. 24 GemHVO para 2

on own account ('Reviews^{OR}'). Often the investment program accommodates a distorted view of the interests of the political faction in majority.

Overview of commitment authorisations

The overview of commitment authorisations depicts which expenditures are foreseeable for the years to come. Whenever the coverage of these expenditures is not indicated in the financial plan, it is specified here. Thus, this document reflects 'Report^{OR}' of the type (These 'instruments' have (not) been used).

Overview of debts and reserves

The overview of debts and reserves provides information on the execution of the budget changing the financial resources of the community. For this purpose, the ongoing financing transactions (in particular the admission and repayment of credits, the increase or decrease of reserves) are illustrated in incomes and expenditures. Thus, the overview of debts and reserves explicates a 'Report^{OR}' of the type (These 'instruments' have (not) been used). However it usually does not indicate the conditions and terms of the debts and reserves. But the total amount in interest paid on debts clearly delimits the financial options of the °community°. The overview of debts and reserves often lacks the essential information required for adequate appreciation of the °community° 'Capacity^{OR}'.

Overview of budgeted activity fields

The overview of budgeted activity fields is meant to provide information on which tasks and issues budgets have been assigned and can be managed by the respective °sub-systems°. However, the vast majority of Hessian °communities° did not furnish genuine budgets with all consequence of explicitly assigning autonomous responsibilities. Rather, groups and sub-groups of the activity field plans are being defined as mutually coverable, such as for instance the income from speeding offenses or the expenditures for youth clubs.[675] Similarly, personnel expenditures are usually not budgeted. The overview of budget figures is an expression of 'Contract^{OR}'.

---

[675] See Overview on budget of the city of Bad Hersfeld, in Kreisstadt Bad Hersfeld: Haushaltsplan 2003, 2002, p. 488

6.2.1.2 Budget statute

The essence of 'Requirements[OR]' is expressed in the budget statute ("Haushaltssatzung"); it forms the legal basis for the execution of the budget.[676] The statute is a necessary supplement to the budget. It defines up to which amount loans may be raised and cash credits may be taken. The budget statute must be approved by the °county° layer ('Super-Requirements[OR]'). It is officially announced in a public meeting of the community council. It is thus an expression of 'Requirements[OR]' of the type (Use these specific 'instruments'). As practice shows, the majority of °communities° tend to use large parts of their cash credit potential without adequate revenue expectations as a justification. In consequence, this ties up their budget in deficits. In a situation of generally increasing interest rates, they quickly run out of funds. Without the friendly environment of a generally booming economy, they find themselves trapped by the need to administer scarcity. It is the purpose of the budget statute to avoid such a situation through approval by the °county° layer. However, a majority of °communities° nevertheless faced major cash-credit deficits.

6.2.1.3 Annual account

In the Annual account[677] ("Jahresrechnung") the result of the °community's° financial transactions including capital and debts is documented at the beginning and end of the financial year. The results are commented in the notes to the annual account statement ("Erläuterungsbericht"); both are 'Reports[OR]' of the type (these 'instruments' have (not) been used).[678] In the annual account, estimated incomes and expenditures of the current and subsequent years are confronted with the actual incomes and expenditures of the finalised account of the previous year. Surpluses are forwarded to reserves; deficits are forwarded to the next financial year. In the notes to the annual account, the most important results and substantial deviations from the previous year's results are described.[679] It is the result of the political decisions (investment decisions, budget estimates) and the administrative actions (resource management and accounting) that have been taken. And it is to be approved by the accounting control department of the °county°

---

[676] Sec. 94 HGO para 1 Budget statute

[677] Sec. 112 HGO Annual account

[678] Sec. 112 HGO Annual account; Sec. 38-42 GemHVO Annual account

[679] Sec. 42 GemHVO para 4 Appendix of the annual account

layer ('Super-Requirement^{OR}'). The annual account justifies all °community° actions by specifying the exact amounts of income and expenditures, thus providing 'Account^{OR}' of the type (these 'instruments' have (not) been used) of the °community's° activities on a yearly basis. Internally, the annual account is the basis for the approval of the magistrate through the community council.

However, it is a weakness of the annual account that it can be 'distorted' through the transfer of expected incomes ("Kasseneinnahmereste") on the credit side or through the estimation of expected liabilities ("Haushaltsausgabereste") on the debit side. Such manipulations narrow the adequacy and significance of the information expressed in the annual account.

6.2.2   Compliance with systemic functions

The following chapter synergises the described formal methods and instruments concerning their systemic contributions typically used in the administrations visited in Hesse. Further methods and instruments are described wherever relevant. The conclusions reflect the situation found in the °communities°, even though the structural deficiencies identified here were partly compensated through the informal governing activities of competent mayors, public servants, etc.

6.2.2.1 Two topics

The following 'instruments' contribute to solving *Two* topics:

Table 19. Methods and instruments for addressing *Two* topics

Systemic topic	Formal methods and instruments applied
'Records^{TR}'	receipts, letters of referral, vouchers, sales slips, etc.
'Query^{TR}' 'Orientation^{TR}'	single budget positions, staff assignments relevant to individual department actors
'Actuality^{TR}'	files and records, databases; all adopted and announced documentations of previous decisions, e.g. budget (all components), staff appointment plans, statutes, regulations, norms, adopted financial plan, adopted investment program.
'Reports^{OR}'	aggregated budget (with all components)

'Records^{TR}'

To capture their ongoing interdependencies, °sub-system° actors continuously create documentation to provide evidence of their ongoing activities, resource utilisation, and consumption. 'Records^{TR}' are required to provide evidence of the actual transactions taking place between the °sub-systems°, e.g. by documenting them with receipts, letters of referral, vouchers, sales slips, etc. The data documented and filed in Hessian °communities° focus primarily on capturing the ongoing monetary flows,[680] the consumption of oil, gas, water, electricity, as well as the usage of community-owned cars, etc.[681] Thus, they merely capture 'instruments'; they do not link 'instruments' to the 'images' aspired to. However, to reflect comprehensively the 'instruments' used persistently, 'Records^{TR}' would have to identify also the planned depreciations, amortisations, and changes in capital such as omitted maintenance investments, internal labour, etc. Further, they currently do not capture the status of the °community's° real estate properties, i.e. information on whether they are sellable, valued, on offer, etc. However, this information would provide useful insight into the property's resource consumption and may be relevant for their optimum use in the °sub-systems° of °community°. Typically, these facts are known only by the responsible paraties in administration who are engaged in specialised °housing° activity. Thus, huge shares of capital may be bound up in property; high administrative and maintenance costs may be involved, or there may be a huge demand for housing and trade properties in the community. However, all these circumstances are not recognised due to the lack of creating comprehensive ongoing 'Records^{TR}' of the type (These 'instruments' are being used).

'Actuality^{TR}'

All the details entailed in the 'Records^{TR}' need to be organised, arranged, tabulated, and filed to be made accessible and analysed when necessary. 'Actuality^{TR}' captures the facts of °sub-system° interdependencies and depicts what is considered relevant to understanding the actual situation.

---

[680] Sec. 13 GemHVO para 1 Cash in transit

[681] Further documents kept are: civil status records of community residents (birth, marriage, and death), reference documentation for building construction, architectural plans, bidding documents. For a typical list of the documents held in °community° see: City of Staufenberg: Overview on community documents, 2007

Furthermore 'Actuality^{TR}' is a repository that entails all adopted 'Guide-lines^{OR}', 'Contracts^{OR}', 'Strategies^{SOR}' and 'Norms^{NR}' needing to be made accessible to °sub-system° actors for mutual reconciliation. Any relevant facts (e.g. the outputs and outcomes to be achieved ('images') and the steps ('actions') that have been taken to obtain them) not captured through 'Records^{TR}' do not enter 'Actuality^{TR}' and are consequently not accessible for examination, interpretation, or advice by *Three* actors. 'Actuality^{TR}' is an incomplete and disintegrated, fragmented puzzle that has not yet established its own logic but still follows the logic of the individual °sub-systems° activities. An optimum integration would require 'Records^{TR}' to derive 'Reports^{OR}' and 'Orientations^{TR}' in all aspects regarding coordinative issues on the °community° layer.

'Queries^{TR}' and 'Orientation^{TR}'

'Queries^{TR}' are used by actors to initiate mutual coordination, e.g. for ascertaining the availability of certain resources, applying to access them, etc. Any use of the shared resources of the °community° such as technical infrastructure, vehicles, public buildings, and rooms is applied for through 'Queries^{TR}' (These 'images' are (not) aspired; these 'instruments' can (not) be used; these 'actions' cannot be taken). Because of the incomplete and fragmented 'Actuality^{TR}', the possible 'Queries^{TR}' are limited to what can be derived from these methods and instruments. For instance, the assignment of resources in °sub-systems° activities (i.e. to answer 'Queries^{TR}' with 'Orien-tation^{OR}') requires taking 'Records^{TR}' and subsuming ongoing resource consumption to describe the current state of the °community° ('Actuality^{TR}'). Distributing financial resources requires °sub-system° actors to reconcile and specify how many resources they are authorised to use, and who is permitted access to them, at what time, and for what purpose ('Contract^{OR}'). Only based on such regulations can coordinative *Two* methods and instruments be established.

'Reports^{OR}'

As a consequence of the restricted base of 'Actuality^{TR}', the 'Reports^{OR}' derived are limited to depicting the efforts at resolving the financial aspects of *Two* topics. 'Reports^{OR}' of the administration inform magistrate and councillors about the efforts of financial resource distribution. Their quality depends on the information gained on how resources are being used, in regard to which activities, etc. The 'Reports^{OR}' created, based on traditional input- oriented methods, are limited to describing cash flow. They do not explain outputs, quantities, and qualities achieved and lack the actors' assigned responsibilities and processes.

The main *Two* methods applied to address and resolve *Two* topics are established in Hessian communities. However, as the majority of °communities° still rely on bureaucratic accounting methods, major relevant facts required for harmonising °sub-system° interdendency are not yet included. The adequacy of the applied methods and instruments to reference ongoing resource consumption, disposal, availability, etc. (i.e. the use of 'instruments') predetermines the extent to which *Three* actors are able to optimise and accomodate their use and to resolve *Three*, *Four*, and *Five* issues.

In the transformation from 'Actuality^{TR}' to 'Report^{OR}', the 'images' are lost because 'Actuality^{TR}' misses the link between 'images' and 'instruments'. However, for interpreting 'Actuality^{TR}' and creating operative 'Reports^{OR}', these links are needed to derive meaningful statements and to make sound decisions.

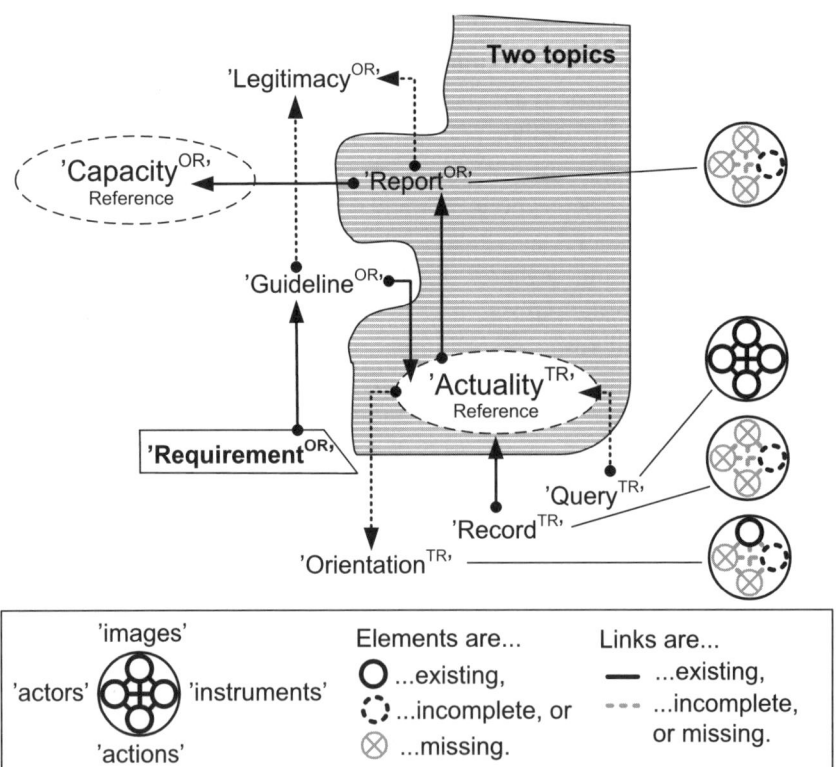

Figure 61. Compliance of methods with *Two* topics

Currently applied methods and instruments	Problems	Possible changes, alternative, additional methods (exemplary)
'Query^{TR}' and Orientation^{TR}'		
Single budget positions, staff assignments relevant to individual department actors	Requires actors' in-depth knowledge. Inaccessible to honorary councillors and citizens.	Detailed interpretations and application advices of service and target agreements.
'Record^{TR}'		
Single receipts, vouchers indicating costs per cost center	Incomplete. Lacking service costs, cost types not comparable.	Cost and activity accounting, Quality management.
'Actuality^{TR}'		
Adopted budget, adopted staff appointment plan	Fragmented, desintegrated.	Cost and activity accounting, Quality management.
'Guideline^{OR}' (1) and 'Report^{OR}' (2)		
1) Aggregated budget (all components), annual account	Rigid, does not address specific information needs.	Real-time reports capturing all aspects of °sub-system° interdepency.
2) Aggregated budget (all components)	Rigid, political. Lacking links to 'images' and 'actions', incomplete (e.g. cash flow, financial and human resources), difficult to comprehend.	Defining °community° goals and purposes to be aspired to. Changable in periods less than a year (cash credit).

Figure 61 (continued)

6.2.2.2   Three topics

The following 'instruments' contribute to solving *Three* topics:

Table 20. Methods and instruments for addressing *Three* topics

Systemic topics	Formal methods and instruments applied
'Capacity^{OR}'	None
'Guideline^{OR}'	Community council resolutions, magistrate decisions, administrative regulations
'Account^{OR}'	None
'Requirements^{OR}'	Budget statute, community council resolutions, all community council and magistrate decisions into °sub-system° issues
'Ambition^{NSOR}'	Individual °sub-system° applications for budgets, reasons
'Synergy^{OR}'	Extrapolation of previous year figures
'Audit^{OR}'	Informal. Councillors', mayor's, magistrates' informal talks with public servants and community residents; casual inspection of building sites

'Capacity^{OR}'

'Capacity^{OR}' is used to reflect on, assess, and evaluate the actual situation of °community°. It attends to all evaluations and analyses conducted on the basis of existing 'Reports^{OR}', 'Findings^{OR}', and 'Accounts^{OR}' in the light of the actual 'Strategy^{SOR}' to judge the current situation. It provides a critical assessment of the planned activities, resource consumption, and administrative activity of the °community°. It fundamentally enables the magistrate and councillors to appraise the current situation. Thus, 'Capacity^{OR}' is the precondition for actively influencing and controlling activities.

Logically, 'Capacity^{OR}' relies on the completeness, accuracy, actuality, timeliness, and quality of its sources, primarily on 'Reports^{OR}'. The existing limitations of °community° 'Reports^{OR}' causally restrict the evaluation of 'Capacity^{OR}'. A one-sided emphasis put on 'Reports^{OR}' on incoming and outgoing cash flows complicates the recognition of the efficacy, efficiency, and synergy of ongoing °community° activities. Further, the assessment of the °community's° 'Capacity^{OR}' is restricted through the lack of focus on 'Strategy^{SOR}' (see below). There are no verbalised operative 'images' which would be applicable for comparing desired targets with actual outputs and performance. Without knowing what is being planned, i.e. with respect to quantities and qualities, *Three* actors have no criteria to evaluate their activities and resource allocations. Still, the vast majority of small Hessian °communities° with less than 5,000 inhabitants still apply traditional budgeting methods focusing on depicting cash flows instead of resource consumption. Further, as a consequence of the cash-flow-oriented budget and annual account ('Reports^{OR}'), the outputs implemented and the performance achieved in the current situation remain unspecified. Consequently, it is difficult for the actors involved to evaluate the current status of activities. Councillors face major difficulties in reconciling their individual appraisals of the modus operandi of the °community° and its capability for change. Enabling actors to confront the related activity-oriented costs, qualities, performances, etc. of the °community° issues is a precondition to permitting them to attend to *Three* topics and optimising their resource allocation. Based on this information, instruments such as benchmarking and statistics would then allow them to create thorough comparisons with other °communities° facilitating the interpretation of 'Capacity^{OR}'.

'Ambition^{NSOR}', 'Synergy^{OR}' and 'Contract^{OR}'

The unclear 'Capacity^{OR}' of °community° affects the resource bargain (*Three*-One) taking place between treasurer, magistrate, and councillors on the one side (°community° actors°) and fire brigade, hospitals, public library, housing, and infrastructure departments, etc. on the other side (°sub-system° actors). If different actors engage in creating and announcing a 'Strategy^{SOR}' and determining optimal resource allocation ('Synergy^{OR}'), those engaged in the latter must be aware of the agreements settled on by the former. Therefore, 'Synergy^{OR}' has to be derived based on a solid understanding of °community° 'Capacity^{OR}', which then has to be linked to the relevant 'Strategy^{SOR}'. For instance, a desired strategic outcome (strategic 'image') to reduce by half housebreaking incidents cannot be specified as an output (operational 'image') without reference to actual 'Reports^{OR}' telling what the actual figures are and 'Ambitions^{NSOTR}' specifying °sub-system° actors interests. *Three* actors must engage in assessing the natural consequences of strengthening °Security° – by employing new police-men, investing in new equipment, starting citizens' initiatives – to other °sub-systems°. 'Reports^{OR}' inform on past experiences, 'Ambitions^{NSOR}' inform about °subsystems° actors' potential to implement these conditions.

Thus, whatever goals aspired to in 'Strategy^{SOR}' – such as to 'reduce housebreaking incidents' without any additional personnel, yet with an extra budget of 20,000 Euro – the chances for its implementation will necessarily depend not only on the methods and instruments applied for optimizing ('Synergy^{OR}') but on the whole chain of methods that predetermine 'Capacity^{OR}' and its predecessors (i.e. 'Reports^{OR}', 'Findings^{OR}', 'Ambitions^{OR}'). In Hesse, 'Synergy^{OR}' is in fact being assembled by the administrative treasurer in consultation with the magistrate. A sound optimisation of the resource allocation would require comparison between different alternative operative measures in the light of a clarified (and at best explicitly formulated) 'Strategy^{SR}' and 'Norms^{NR}'. In turn, this would require cost accounting ('Reports^{OR}') to provide a definition of the costs per 'action' (i.e. the 'instruments' required to conduct 'action'). As a consequence of the cash-flow-oriented accounting, resource allocations ('instruments') are being estimated as straight forward extrapolations, usually estimating the plausibility of the indicated sums based on previous' year's figures. 'Synergy^{OR}' is not at all grounded in the explicit outputs ('images') being aspired to. Traditionally applied methods and instruments for bookkeeping ('Report^{OR}'ing and understanding 'Capacity^{OR}') do not support the optimisation of the resource allocation. Usually, not even the most obvious background information ('images' and 'instruments') relevant to substantiate the interpretation and analysis required for optimisation is used here (thus specifying 'Capacity^{OR}'). For instance, if the specific demand of °educational° child care services has not been reflected in 'Reports^{OR}' and therefore not been considered in the °communities'° 'Capacity^{OR}', magistrate and treasury will not be able to gain an understanding of the optimum 'Synergy^{OR}'.[682] Further, as an explicit 'Strategy^{SOR}' does not exist, there is a lack of clear direction and goals to focus the optimisation. As a consequence, there is no comprehensible and traceable basis to determine optimum resource allocation. 'Contracts^{OR}' cannot be optimised regarding the intended purposes and are specified into rather artificial budget positions. The concerns of the °subsystems° with their individual needs cannot be met. Therefore, treasurers are constantly blamed for proposing resource distributions which cope with the overall °community's° necessities insufficiently. Ultimately, the majority of the involved actors are discontented with the results of the estimations settled on. The established structures require councillors of the financial and special boards and the treasurer to compensate these insufficiencies through intense interactions: recurrent requests, replications, etc (e.g. an increased channel capacity). As a consequence of councillors limited time to engage with the °community° the methods and instruments applied for 'Contract^{OR}' reconciliation are clearly deteriorating their chances to create sound solutions. The conditions are further complicated as a consequence of the vagueness and missing autonomy of the recursive layers, as mentioned above. Comparing alternative activities for helping disabled children would be a °social welfare° issue and not a °community° issue. °Community° optimisation is about how resources should be used for the new sports gym (°culture and leisure°) and / or the renovation of the old kindergarten (°education°), and / or for the local theatre (°culture°) based on the priorities given in the actual 'Strategy^{SOR}'. As there are no responsibilities assigned to the °sub-systems° (see chapter 6.1.2) for the different activity fields, they are usually not even interested in applying adequate methods to provide accurate estimates ('Ambitions^{NSOR}'). To what degree the resulting 'Synergy^{OR}' reflects an optimum resource allocation required for implementing the 'Strategy^{SOR}' and the °system° purpose expressed in 'Norms^{NR}'[683], or rather the priorities set by the treasurer, depends largely on the personal influence of the actors involved.

The indicated weaknesses originate in the °community° budget ('Contract^{OR}'). It settles the modalities of °sub-system° activity and the allocation of resources. However, the budget as applied in Hesse only specifies

---

[682] And neither will they be able to formulate 'Reviews^{OR}' that reflect competently on strategic 'Proposals^{SR}'.

[683] Which both did not exist in an explicit documented form in Hessian °communities°.

the financial resources ('instruments') to be used but does not provide links to outputs (operative 'images') and activities ('instruments'). Thus, it does not give a clear direction to the °sub-system° actors enabling them to organise their activities in the light of the °community° 'Strategy^{SOR}'. Outputs intended and measures to be taken are expressed only in the session reports of the community council or magistrate. The budget does not specify the output expected for a short- and midterm period. The outputs ('images') intended are not made explicit. Further, the resources assigned in the budget (i.e. the 'instruments' of the 'Contract^{OR}') are not linked to actors responsible for their implementation (i.e. the 'actors' of the 'Contract^{OR}'). The budget is arranged by artificial group categories without specifying °sub-system° responsibilities. It does not clearly identify the aspired states of the °community° ('images'), as operative 'images' are not explicitly discussed and prioritised on the level of the °community°. Such a general subsumation of primarily financial values ('instruments') cannot be sufficient for clarifying the binding 'Contract^{OR}' of the °community° with its °sub-systems° notions.

'Requirements^{OR}', 'Accounts^{OR}'

With 'Requirements^{OR}' the necessary decisions are being taken to accommodate conflicting °sub-system° issues. In Hesse, this is done both by the community council and the magistrate. The definition of the budget statute and the release of community council resolutions are formal expressions of 'Requirements^{OR}'. Further, all ongoing decisions taken by the mayor to control public servants engaged in °sub-system° issues can be seen as 'Requirements^{OR}'. As has been seen above, it is a consequence of a lack of °sub-system° autonomy when the mayor is too closely involved in the details of °sub-system° issues. From the perspective of change or transformation capacity and with a focus on the budget reconciliation process, the budget statute is the relevant reflection of 'Requirements^{OR}' for this case. A major weakness of formulating 'Requirements^{OR}' with the budget statute has been seen in its unilateral focus on prescribing the 'instrumental' conditions relevant for °sub-system° actors. The overall cash credit rates to be used were fixed to avoid excessive exploitation of the °community's° financial° resources. The necessity of such a constraint is a consequence of the unilateral focus of the budget ('Contract^{OR}') on financial aspects. If the °community° 'Contract^{OR}' entailed clear descriptions of the 'images' to be aspired to and the 'instruments' to be used by every °sub-system°, then the use of financial resources would be pre-controlled and the utilisation of the cash credit could be avoided.

By 'Accounts[OR]', the actors' engaged in and responsible for °sub-system° implementation justify their activities in the light of the 'Contract[OR]' settled on. As °sub-system° boundaries have not been clearly defined in the °communities°, this task corresponds most likely to those public servants engaged in housing and infrastructure, health and sports, waste water treatment, etc. providing account to the magistrate and the community council on their ongoing activities. However, this was done only in regard to financial aspects and without any formal reference to achieved outputs ('images'). As none of the °communities° visited explicitly assigned °sub-system° responsibilities, it was only the magistrate and, primarily, the mayor who took the °sub-system° role to provide 'Account[OR]' to the community council. Wherever there was some established form of delegation to executive servants, i.e. through flexibility and coverability between the cost of the kindergarten or the fire brigade, 'Accounts[OR]' were still provided only informally. Usually a trustful mutual relationship between the mayor and the public servants took the place of a formal 'Account[OR]'.

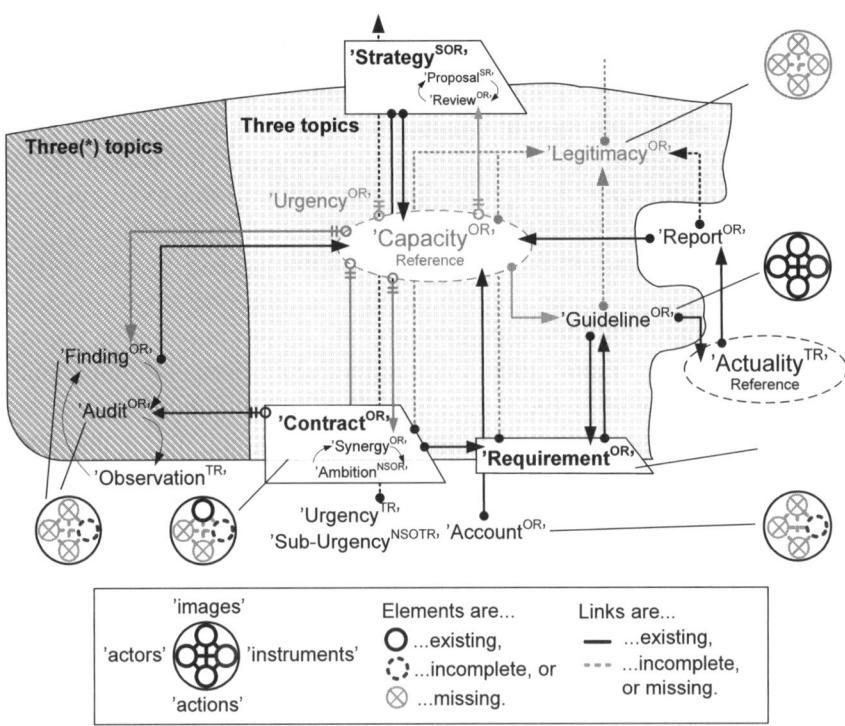

Figure 62. Compliance of methods with *Three* topics

Currently applied methods	Problems	Alternative, additional methods (exemplary)
'Capacity^{OR}'		
None, purely informal.	Relies on insufficient sources ('Reports^{OR}', 'Findings^{OR}') Reconciliation depends on engagement and competence of engaged actors.	Benchmarking, statistics, qualitative indicators, goal-achievement indicators, etc.
'Ambitions^{NSORT}' (1) versus 'Synergy^{OR}' (2) resulting in 'Contract^{OR}' (3)		
1) Individual departments' applications for budget.	Focus on financial resources ('instruments'). Tendency to apply for more than needed.	Individual department outputs and outcomes intended and restrictions effective. Contracts defining budget responsibility and competences.
2) Extrapolation of previous year financial figures	Focus on financial resources ('instruments'). Tendency to maintain last year's amount regardless of changed situation.	Target descriptions making explicit which °sub-system° states are considered optimum under currently defined 'Norms^{NR}' and 'Strategy^{SOR}'.
3) Preliminary budget draft, adopted budget making explicit budget positions and estimates.	Lacks intended outputs ('images') to be aspired to. Does not specify what resources ('instruments') to apply and which activities ('actions') to be taken by whom ('actors').	Service and target agreements making goals, product quantities and qualities, costs, budgets explicit.
'Requirements^{OR}' and 'Accounts^{OR}'		
Budget statute, community council resolutions. All ongoing informal decisions, primarily of the magistrate.	'Requirements^{OR}' do attend to both °community° and °sub-system° issues. Budget statute focuses on 'instrumental' aspects. 'Accounts^{OR}' of °sub-systems° unclear as consequence of ill-defined °sub-system° boundaries and unspecified 'images' in 'Contract^{OR}' and 'Requirements^{OR}'.	General 'Guidelines^{OR}' to be enforced via *Two* interactions. Detailed instructions are the exception. Detailed instructions on all kinds of aspects that have not been settled with the budget, e.g. how to decide, prioritise, manage °sub-system° issues.
'Audits^{OR}', 'Findings^{OR}'		
Councillors', mayor's, magistrates' informal talks with public servants and °Community° residents; irregular inspection of construction sites	Unilateral focus on financial resources ('instruments'). Lacks output ('images') and activity ('actions') analyses.	'Audit^{OR}' methods such as observation, questionnaires, etc. instead of merely finance-based accounting control. Linking to previously conducted 'Audit^{OR}' activities.

Figure 62 (continued)

6.2.2.3 Four topics

The following 'instruments' contribute to resolving *Four* topics:

Table 21. Methods and instruments for addressing *Four* topics

Systemic topics	Formal methods and instruments applied
'Inquiry^{SR}'	Citizen surveys, suggestion boxes, internet pages, external evaluations, etc. Direct informal exchange between political actors, administration and community residents
'Totality^{SR}'	Political dialogue in community council, boards, magistrate, administration
'Proposal^{SR}'	Councillor's applications, draft five year financial plan and investment program
'Review^{OR}'	None
'Strategy^{SR}'	Strategic political resolutions, i.e. adopted investment program, adopted financial plan

Recognition and illustration of the environmental conditions and developments taking place are reflected in 'Inquiry^{SR}'. For the community council to ensure the effectiveness of its decisions, it has to be able to observe and appraise these external conditions and developments. Possible methods and instruments for conducting 'Inquiry^{SR}' are interpersonal contacts with citizens, surveys, suggestion boxes, internet pages, external evaluations, predictions of tax incomes[684], etc. However, the majority of the Hessian °communities° visited relied on informal 'Inquiry^{SR}' as personal contacts with the community residents. Rarely are there systematic activities to support the understanding of the environment ('Inquiry^{SR}'). This may seem to be sufficient in some small, untroubled °communities° where political and administrative actors can manage to keep up with developments and satisfy citizen needs. However, this changes with a growing number of

---

[684] It is difficult to predict the income of a community. The German tax system is so complex that even new methods (e.g. statistic prognosis, plan cost calculation) do not supply reliable results. Changes in the calculation basis of °state° allowances and long time lags until they are received may change numbers quickly. The majority of the communities relies on the tax estimates of the Hessian Federation of Cities and Communities. See Hessischer Sädte- und Gemeindebund: Internetpräsenz, Internetpage, 2007

citizens, involving more actors and issues to be addressed and even more different roles to be taken. For instance, the development of the birthrate and the demographic change as relevant for planning child care capacities of kindergartens has not been part of 'Inquiry^{SR}' in the °communities° visited. The issue, therefore, did not enter the political dialogue (engaged with understanding 'Totality^{SR}' and deriving 'Proposals^{SR}'). Further, the need for improved child care services as a consequence of young mothers' working activity has hardly been recognised yet.

'Totality^{SR}'

Similarily, actors create their common understanding of the essential aspects and factors determining °community° life (i.e. the 'Totality^{SR}') solely on an informal face-to-face basis. With 'Totality^{SR}', actors create a common understanding of how issues and their determining factors interrelate, thus facilitating their reconciliation. 'Totality^{SR}' has not been made explicit. Just as °community° actors do not engage in making explicit a shared understanding of 'Capacity^{OR}', they do not create shared views on the essential influencing factors and their interrelations affecting °community° implementation ('Totality^{SR}'). There is no systematic debate on strengths and weaknesses. In some of the °communities° this appeared to be working well; there seemed to be a broad consensus among all governing actors and the affected community residents about determining factors and the possible alternative steps that could be taken. Thus, there was no necessity for a formalised examination of the future and the °community's° *Wirkungsgefüge*. Clearly, this depended primarily on the individual actors' intentionality to really resolve °community° issues. The overall size of the °community° and the intensity and quality of public dialogue are factors that promote the creation of coherent perceptions of the °community°. In larger, more culturally diverse municipalities an intense public dialogue that settles both normative and strategic issues cannot usually be maintained on a face-to-face basis anymore. The mayor, magistrate and councillors are simply unable to consider both individual needs and overall interests. Indeed, as more actors become involved, more and more of their issues will interrelate. The same happens when resources are in short supply. Cultural, economic and environmental interests coincide, clash, and have to be reconciled.

Hessian communities as visited in this audit have not yet engaged in continuously actualising and sharing an explicit, common 'Totality^{SR}' view of their °community°. The debates of both the community council and the magistrate are typically operative, with a high degree of detail and a lack of a complete overview. The same is valid for citizen meetings and assemblies. The conditions and necessities required for intending and implementing certain purposes, ideas, and goals are not yet expressed in an explicit and shared *Wirkungsgefüge* of the °community°. Thus, the lack of a shared foundation in the °community° notion and a low level of contextuality create a tendency to rely on promoting individual interests and intentions. As a consequence, strategic reconciliations are becoming increasingly difficult. Reconciliations then focus on politics, i.e. the creation and marketing of opposing views, aggravating public dialogue, instead of a gaining a sound understanding of the issues and finding productive resolutions.

'Proposal^{SR}'

'Totality^{SR}' provides the reference on how strategic ideas, goals, plans (i.e. 'images') link to 'instruments' and 'actions'. It is the basis for deriving sound 'Proposals^{SR}' on alternative solutions to future issues. The absence of a shared 'Totality^{SR}' leads political and administrative actors to remain vague in specifying their primary strategic aspirations ('images'). Instead of specifying their intentions, councillors tend to hold on to vague goals, propositions and ideas. 'Proposals^{SR}' are derived based on individual actor backgrounds and strongly determined by individual and political convictions and affiliation to a political faction. Further, councillors tend to concentrate on tacit and operative issues of the topics actually considered relevant. This has an immediate effect on the 'Proposals^{SR}' they formulate. To a large degree, the suggestions made in 'Proposals^{SR}' and commited to in 'Strategy^{SOR}' remain arbitrary and volatile under such circumstances. Emphasis is put on the details of particular issues, missing the strategic and normative aspects of the °community° layer. Non-organised public interests are not heard at all. As a consequence of the low level of °sub-system° autonomy, the actors involved in °community° implementation (usually the administration and / or the mayor) tend to elaborate fragmented 'Proposals^{SR}' with detailed °sub-system° suggestions such as urban planning, village renewal programs, welfare planning, etc. Thus, their primary task is to engage in these issues only from the perspective of the °community°. As they are clearly too overextended to attend to these issues in the community council or boards, what in fact happens is that the issues are being "artificially dissected" and then introduced into the budget process only to promote lobbying or to generate immediate budget effects. As a consequence, important 'Undeterminisms^{SR}' or 'Urgencies^{TR}' cannot be recognized, and they remain unnoticed because of the fragmented and short term focus of topics in political debates.

'Reviews^{OR}'

Strategic 'Proposals^{SR}' require operational assessment and substantiation through 'Reviews^{OR}'. Preparing a 'Review^{OR}' means reflecting on a 'Proposal^{SR}' in the light of 'Capacity^{OR}'. In a broad, general form this is part of the political dialogue in the community council and the magistrate. However, these are primarily reasonings set up to convince and gain advantage in the public political discussion. As just mentioned, these debates are fraught with °sub-system° issues. Not only are they based on 'Proposals^{SR}' which remain vague, they are also based on an understanding of operational issues which itself is founded on a partial or rudimentary view on 'Capacity^{OR}'.

Thus, for instance, the established budget procedure in Hessian °communities° does not regularly assess proposed new investments ('Proposals^{SR}') with cost accounting and rigorous cost-benefit analyses that reflect on the issue based on 'Capacity^{OR}'. Hence, it is not at all transparent to councillors, magistrate, and community residents which costs are expected to follow in the wake of specific investments, which values are involved in the assets, and which political goals are being pursued. Further, the general dependence of strategic decisions and the expenditures involved on legal guidelines (laws, regulations, contracts, allowance answer) ('Super-Strategy^{SOR}') is not made explicit. To receive such essential information, political actors must actively pose requests to the administration.

'Strategy^{SOR}'

A sound 'Strategy^{SOR}' entails all agreements needed to determine the future activities and resource allocation of the °community°. It is agreed to be valid and binding for some period of time. In Hesse the formal instruments used to express the °community° 'Strategy^{SOR}' are the investment plan and the financial plan. Furthermore, capital and administrative budget entail the extrapolated costs and thus also enter 'Strategy^{SOR}', although they are in fact extrapolated operational data (derived from 'Reports^{OR}'). Thus, the °community° 'Strategy^{SOR}' is a subsumation, an operational reflection based on the past. There are no specific strategic outcomes or goals (strategic 'images') being defined. Typically, the outcomes and goals formulated by the community council or the magistrate have a general character, such as "promotion of the economy" or "improvement of security and order". Thus, the 'Strategy^{SOR}' loses its orientating, direction-giving character. It does not indicate the linkage between outputs (operative 'images'), resources ('instruments'), and activities ('actions') and thus makes it arbitrary as to how different actors involved interpret the direction in which it is headed. The adopted 'Strategy^{SOR}' is a logical precursor to the interpretation of the actual situation ('Capacity^{OR}') necessary for the optimisation of the resource allocation in 'Synergy^{OR}'. Without a clear understanding of what is being intended, i.e. both with respect to quantities and qualities, actors cannot meaningfully optimise their resource allocation. Additionally, 'Strategy^{SOR}' has to be binding. Yet the investment plan is not given any formal statutory force.[685] As it is not binding, it is, as a result, hardly noticed by either political or administrative actors.

As seen above, °community° actors in Hesse do not seem to be aware of the necessity and particularities of attending to strategic topics. There are no councils, departments, or responsibilities assigned to attend to strategic

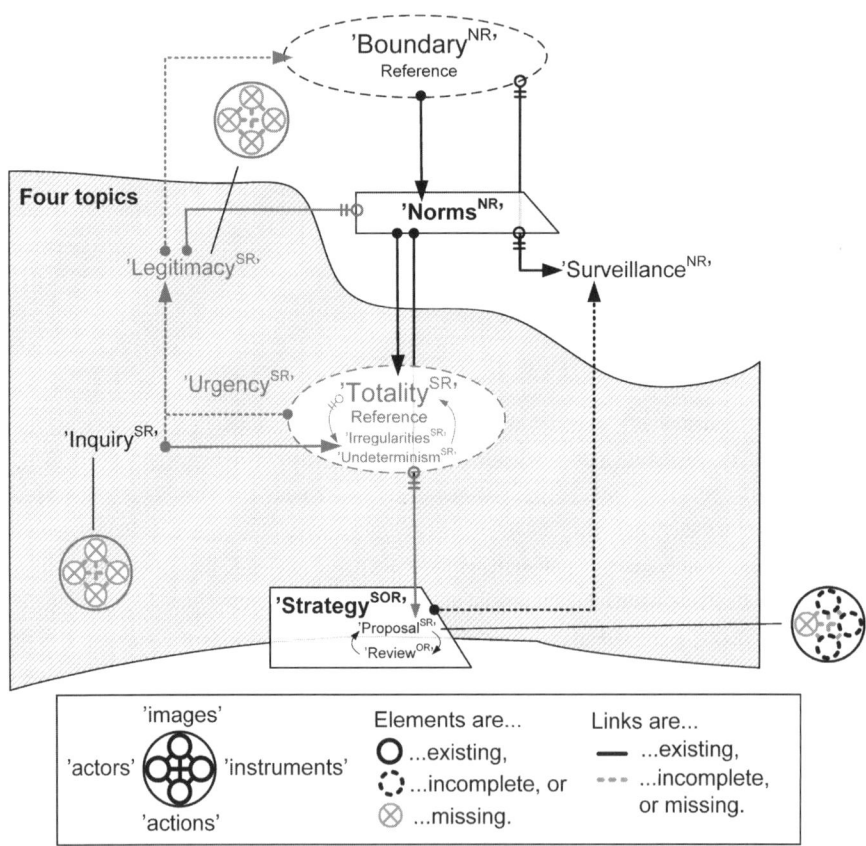

Figure 63. Compliance of methods with *Four* topics

---

[685] Sec. 24 GemHVO Financial plan and investment program

Currently applied methods	Problems	Alternative, additional methods (exemplary)
'Totality^{SR}'		
Political dialogue in community council, boards, magistrate, administration (created informally)	Lack of awareness of strategic issues. Strong tendency to rely on operative methods and instruments.	SWOT-analysis, stakeholder analysis, scenario-techniques, portfolio-analysis, sensitivity analysis, system dynamics.
'Inquiry^{SR}'		
Direct exchange between political actors, administration, and citizens	Rarely addressed systematically.	Complaint and suggestion boxes, opinion polls and surveys, public hearings.
'Proposals^{SR}' (1) versus 'Reviews^{OR}' (2) resulting in 'Strategy^{SOR}' (3)		
1) Councillor's applications, draft of five year financial plan and investment program	Not rooted in 'Totality^{SR}'. Tendency to remain vague and formulate broader goals. Focus on single cases.	Cost-benefit analysis from a 'Totality^{SR}' perspective, involving future developments and trends.
2) Political dialogue, manifesto	Informal, lack of resolution, orientation.	Cost-benefit analysis from a 'Capacity^{OR}' perspective, in regard to actual capabilities.
3) Adopted investment program, financial plan for upcoming legislature, planned positions in budget.	Vague and non binding. Extra-polation of financial estimates.	Integrated task and finance plan, legislative plan, product group budget, balance scorecard.

Figure 63 (continued)

topics. Consequently, strategic topics are not attended to at all and the central strategic decision of the °community° ('Strategy^{SOR}') is solved based on operative estimations of past facts. This shows the strong concentration on actual, operative issues in political debates. Lacking the focus and priorities of a 'Strategy^{SOR}', the political actors tend to change their issues quickly. The selection of issues discussed evolves largely arbitrarily based on actors' political interests. Systemic topics are not addressed methodically. The lack of autonomy of °sub-systems° leads to an excess of tacit and operational facts depicted in the budget and its components. All that leads to a fragmented approach on singular issues instead of an integrated, systemic focus on solving governing topics. Thus, the quality of the strategic solutions that is acquired actually depends on the primary political actors', usually on the mayor's and executive public servants' ability, will, and ability to compensate these structural deficiencies.

How *Five* topics are typically resolved in Hessian °communities° has not been examined. However, these do play a major role, as they set the frame ('Boundary^{NR}', 'Norms^{NR}') within which all the other topics can be addressed. However, in Hessian °communities° there is usually no clear understanding of the °community° 'Boundary^{NR}' because it is often not addressed in the °community° reconciliations (e.g. the citizen assembly). When lacking a shared understanding of the 'Boundary^{NR}' in their °community° notion, actors are not at all able to agree on the central °community° decisions, i.e. 'Norms^{NR}', 'Strategy^{SOR}', and 'Contract^{OR}'. Thus, for a °community°, declaring for instance *"The town of Ehrenberg (Rhön) – a natural beauty"* is much easier because it follows for

1. 'Norms^{NR}' that industrial parks will rarely be allowed because they would disturb the nature and landscape of the °community°;

2. 'Proposals^{SR}' that the setting up of a traditional weekly market which sells local products may be suggested, or alternatively that the establishment of a tourist information office might be suggested;

3. 'Contract^{OR}', 'Requirements^{OR}' and 'Guidelines^{OR}' that °sub-systems° will face restrictions to preserve their environment.

6.2.2.4 Excursus on products

Products refer to desired outputs ('images') and usually correspond to applying certain 'instruments' and taking specific 'actions'. °Community° products draw actors' attention to the external beneficiaries, i.e. the community residents. They point to services implemented by the °sub-systems°, i.e. they specify a certain benefit to be produced for the community residents. Products are used to describe what contributions the administration provides to implement some purpose. Products can thus be used as a currency across °system° boundaries to reconcile interdependencies. For community residents (the environment), they reflect the services on offer. Introducing products as 'image' references creates a binding element between the systemic topics and the different methods and instruments used (cost accounting, reporting, budgeting, etc). Products provide a consistent reference relevant to all systemic topics. None of the Hessian °communities° visited used products as an 'instrument' in its governing system. If so, these were still used in probationary, testing mode and not actively used by the

°community° actors. In none of the °communities° were products used for daily decision making.[686]

First of all, products enable °sub-system° actors of the °community° to identify their interdependencies and to negotiate their mutual support. In the °community°, those actors engaged in °living spheres° can use products to specify, reconcile, and coordinate the 'instruments' they share with each other. Hospitals and medical services (°health°) may require provision of water and electricity (°housing°) for maintaining their services, schools (°education°) may gain support through associations (°culture°) in teaching pupils social responsibilities, etc. With products the 'images' aspired to can be made explicit, quantified, and qualified. The results can be documented ('Records^{TR}'), stored and aggregated ('Actuality^{OR}') to facilitate coordination of and between °sub-systems° activities ('Orientation^{TR}', 'Demarcation^{TR}'). Further, products may be used to subsume quantities and qualities in the light of °community° purposes ('Reports^{OR}') and thus be exploited for interpretation and evaluation ('Capacity^{OR}'). They may be utilised for calculating and optimising outputs ('Synergy^{OR}') concerning aspired outcomes that have been fixed ('Strategy^{SOR}'). They can also be used to fix agreements and restrictions of °sub-system° activity and to define responsibilities ('Contract^{OR}', 'Requirements^{OR}') as well as to provide an account of what has been achieved ('Account^{OR}'). They can be used for the assignment of budgets[687] and facilitate the supervision and control of °sub-system° activities ('Audits^{OR}', 'Findings^{OR}'). They provide references for future planning ('Proposals^{SR}') and citizen benefit analyses ('Inquiry^{SR}'). Further, they are the primary reference of communication with the community residents. They facilitate the expression of political programs through the councillors ('Proposals^{SR}', 'Strategy^{SOR}'). They allow the formulation of needs and necessities of the community residents ('Inquiry^{SR}'). They enable citizens to gain insight into the work of the community council and the organisation of administration. Thus, they allow them to take democratic control ('Supervision^{NR}').

Products enable councillors to pre-control public servants' activities by deciding in the budgetary reconciliation which quantities and qualities will

---

[686] Kommunale Gemeinschaftsstelle für Verwaltungsvereinfachung (KGSt): Das Neue Steuerungsmodell. Definition und Beschreibung von Produkten, Köln, 1994, p. 11; Kommunale Gemeinschaftsstelle für Verwaltungsvereinfachung (KGSt): Verwaltungscontrolling im Neuen Steuerungsmodell, Köln, 1994

[687] NPM suggests that product groups should be the focus of reporting and budgeting. Siehe Ösze, Daniel: Managementinformationen im New Public Management: am Beispiel der Steuerverwaltung des Kantons Bern, Bern, 2000

be aspired to. Thus, the products themselves are the object to which a certain budget is assigned, i.e. the community council formulates its budgets ('Strategy^{SR}') based on products. Corresponding to the level of activity: subsumations of products into product groups can be used for reconciling medium- and long-term plans ('Strategy^{SOR}'). The use of products as cost units enables the translation of outcomes (strategic 'images') into specific outputs and activities (operative 'images', 'instruments', and 'activities' as in 'Contract^{OR}') to be offered to community residents. Products are therefore fundamental entities relevant to all actors involved and for all systemic topics.[688] Products can thus be used to focus activities on the actual beneficiaries by drawing attention to what is produced as well as to what is needed. They facilitate the execution of the *Three** function as well as the formulation of 'Legitimacy^{OR}' and 'Legitimacy^{SR}' by clarifying what has been achieved in the operative and strategic interactions and how.

6.2.3 Suggestions

It has been shown that actors' ability to implement °community° strongly depends on them applying adequate methods to cope with the information they have to share in order to reconcile their ongoing °community° issues. Any method or instrument applied has a certain potential to support the compliance of systemic topics. It has been explained that the methods and instruments currently applied complicate the attendance to systemic topics.

In regard to coordinative *Two* topics, there has been continuous improvement and implementation of methods and instruments that can more adequately take 'Records^{OR}' of °sub-system° activity and integrate them into a comprehensive, current perspective on °sub-system° interdependencies ('Actuality^{TR}'). The bureaucratic, cameralistic accounting has proved to be inadequate as it does not include the outputs achieved through the performed activities. The 'Report^{OR}' derived from it does not allow actors to gain a comprehensive understanding of the °communities° 'Capacity^{OR}' and constrains the ability to determine the 'Synergy^{OR}' of optimum resource allocation. Cost and activity accounting instruments enable the assignment of financial resources ('instruments') to the activities ('actions') under-

---

[688] They are, for instance, used in the Integrated Task and Finance plan for midterm planning. See Haldemann, T.: New Public Budgeting, in: Schmid, H. and Slembeck, T., Finanz- und Wirtschaftspolitik in Theorie und Praxis, Berne, 1997 as cited in Schedler, K.: Performance Budgeting in Switzerland – Implications for political control, Internetpage, 2007

taken within the °community°. They are therefore much more adequate for reconciling financial resource distributions.[689]

Attendance to operative issues in the °community° is a highly responsible task. To determine optimum 'Synergy^{OR}', actors have to clarify the 'Strategy^{SOR}' of what they consider needs to be done, and they have to be able to assess the 'Capacity^{OR}' of what the °community° can actually do. Therefore, they require 'Reports^{OR}' on what °sub-system° actors actually do and both 'Accounts^{OR}' and 'Findings^{OR}' to ensure the accuracy of the 'Reports^{OR}' and the reliability of °sub-system° implementation. Currently applied methods do not enable actors to address and reconcile these issues. They primarily lack references to outcomes and outputs ('images'). It should be integrated in a way that aids actors in gaining an understanding of and in resolving the °community's° central systemic topics. Therefore, the product concept provides a valid basis as it invents the output as a category which can be used as a central element for addressing all systemic topics. Wherever the central resolutions to °community° issues ('Norms^{NR}', 'Strategy^{SOR}', 'Contract^{OR}') give expression to more than one element (e.g. 'images' and 'instruments'), there should be a link established between them to enable the actors involved to comprehend the context entailed.

Alongside the clarification of °sub-system° and °community° layers, 'Contracts^{OR}' should depict low-variety statements. Rather than defining detailed resource allocations ('instruments'), activities to be taken ('actions') and 'actors' to be involved, only the minimal specifications should be made to bind °living spheres° and °village° implementations. This would enable the autonomy of the °sub-systems° to unfold. The 'Contract^{OR}' to be reconciled focuses on fixing independent °sub-system° outcomes and outputs ('images') by specifying goals, tasks, budgets, quantities, qualities, etc. Specifying the outcomes aspired to ('images') in 'Contracts^{OR}' massively reduces the complexity of operative planning as both councillors and public servants will require less involvement in °sub-system° issues. Specific output descriptions possibly spelled out in goals, quality, and quantity descriptions (operative 'images') should refer to those assigned responsibility for their implementation (operative 'actors'). Thus, the autonomy of °sub-systems° implementation would be raised by limiting intrusion into their activities and formulating 'Contracts^{OR}' as low-variety statements that define service and target agreements with op-

---

[689] The introduction of cost- and activity accounting instruments is already scheduled to be implemented in Hessian °communities° by 2009.

erative 'images', i.e. goals and outputs in quantities and qualities as they are to be achieved.[690] The service and target agreements are used to supplement 'Contract^{OR}' for specifying 'images, 'instruments', 'actions', and 'actors' as far as minimally necessary to ensure the purpose implementation of the respective °sub-systems°. In order to emphasise the °community° layer of recursion, the budget should be structured into categories and depict all information relevant to the independent °sub-system° layers. As soon as autonomous °sub-systems° are identified, the criteria for their delimitation should be reflected in the budget.

Strategic topics are logically distinct from operative issues. That has not yet been recognised in Hessian °communities°. To solve strategic topics, a common understanding of 'Totality^{SR}' has to be reconciled continuously; 'Inquiries^{SR}' are needed to keep it up-to-date. But still today 'Totality^{SR}' is not a consciously addressed topic in the °community°. Actors do not engage in reconciling their individual ideas and experiences of the °community's'° *Wirkungsgefüge*. Systematic and continuous approaches to sharing 'Totality^{SR}' can create a much better understanding of the situation and enable the actors involved to share a differentiated view on the most important factors relevant to the °community°, identifying strengths and weaknesses, future opportunities and risks, thus assessing alternative scenarios of the future. A SWOT analysis can provide the impulse to identify it. Other methods such as Sensitivity Analysis or System Dynamics enable its depiction. However, providing for adequate channel capacity will be more important than the application of sophisticated instruments. This means that, at a minimum, 'Totality^{SR}' should be put on the agenda for reconciliation involving all actors engaged and interested in *Four* topics. They should be aware of it in pre-conceiving the creation of 'Proposals^{SR}'. The distinctness of operative und strategic topics should be clarified and the methods and instruments appropriate for their resolution should be defined.

The elaboration of 'Reviews^{OR}' to counter 'Proposals^{SR}' should be made obligatory, e.g. with cost-benefit analyses of all major initiatives planned. 'Reviews^{OR}' must enable councillors to recognise and assess the

---

[690] This position very much corresponds to the service and target agreements that are known from contemporary NPM approaches, within which the 'Con-tract^{OR}' focuses on making explicit outcomes, goals, tasks, budgets, quantities, and qualities, etc., thus specifying the 'images' to be aspired to by the °sub-systems°. Kommunale Gemeinschaftsstelle für Verwaltungsvereinfachung (KGSt): Kontraktmanagement: Steuerung über Zielvereinbarungen, Köln, 1998; Winter, C.: Das Kontraktmanagement, Baden-Baden, 1998

consequences of any 'Proposals^{SR}' in the light of 'Capacity^{OR}' of the overall °community°. 'Strategy^{SOR}' should clarify both outcomes and outputs expected ('images') by specifying goals, qualities, and quantities. It may further detail the resources to be used ('instruments') and the activities or projects to be taken ('actions'). As NPM suggests, the operative part of 'Strategy^{SOR}' defines the product group budget or performance budget. It is the political actors' 'instrument' for answering the political question of whether the relationship of spending ('instruments') and activities ('actions') to expected outcomes (strategic 'images') is satisfactory. Therefore, the product group budgets have to specify to strategically relevant priorities and detail them operationally.[691] A link between outcomes (strategic 'images'), outputs (operative 'images'), the resources involved ('instruments') and activities ('actions') should be established in all 'Strategy^{SOR}' agreements. This should be documented in the budget. Intended outcomes (strategic 'images') and outputs (operative 'images), required resources (strategic 'instruments'), existing resources (operative 'instruments') and activities (operative 'actions') of the investment and financial plans should be brought together. The essence is to define strategic and operative 'images', 'instruments', and 'actions' as loosely as possible to describe the state of °community° aspired to. Therefore, the central 'Strategy^{SOR}' agreement must be binding.

6.3   Channel capacity: Sequences and time lags

Of course, all the governing interactions described take place or are conducted in a certain process or sequence of time and with a certain actor involvement. Processes and sequences may, more or less, support resolving the °community° issues. To provide an example, the sequence of the primary process of budget reconciliation will be described. Other primary processes would be mission statement reconciliation, an Agenda 21 process[692] or a village renewal program.

---

[691] Brühlmeier, D., Haldemann, T., Mastronardi, P., and Schedler, K.: (Political planning)

[692] For further information see UN Department of Economic and Social Affairs: Agenda21 process, 2007; Hessisches Ministerium für Umwelt, ländlichen Raum und Verbraucherschutz: Implementation of Local Agenda21 in Hesse, 2007

6.3.1 Systemicity of budget reconciliation

Budget reconciliation is the major act of planning in °community°. The budget is the central representation of political will, i.e. the °community's° 'Strategy^{SOR}' and 'Contract^{OR}' that have been reconciled. It runs through the following process:

1. Creating the budget draft

    1.1 Call for °sub-system° claims ("Haushaltsverfügung", 'Ambitions^{NSOR}')

    1.2 Identification of °community° claims, negotiation ('Synergy^{OR}')

    1.3 Optimising and balancing of claims ('Synergy^{OR}')

    1.4 Budget draft and investment program (pre-'Contract^{OR}', 'Strategy^{SOR}')

2. Counsels and meetings

    2.1 1st Reading in the community council

    2.2 Board meetings

    2.3 2nd Reading in the community council

    2.4 Finalising the budget as a statute ('StrategyS^{OR}', 'Contract^{OR}'), resolution

3. Execution of the budget (forthcoming year)

    3.1 Accounting and reporting ('Records^{TR}', 'Reports^{OR}')

4. Proof of legitimacy of budget execution ('Accounts^{OR}')

The creation of the budget draft starts with a written call for planning ("Haushaltsverfügung", 'Ambitions^{NSOR}') issued by the treasurer and sent to his colleagues in the °sub-system° departments in the August previous to the year planned. Department actors are requested to elucidate their financial needs, wants, and necessities ('Ambitions^{NSOR}') for the upcoming year. Usually, they then submit completed forms that indicate their planned income and expenditures for their departments' budget. In doing so, they rely on the previous year's figures and estimates for the developments in the forthcoming year. Thus, they are expressing their 'Ambitions^{NSORT}' and defend their 'Sub-Strategy^{SOR}' solely by declaring their financial resource demands, i.e. their specific incomes and expenditures on the basis of their current financial budget. Usually, this process runs bilaterally in the administration between treasury and department actors. Sometimes, they do not even share much actual information but simply rely on what is filled in

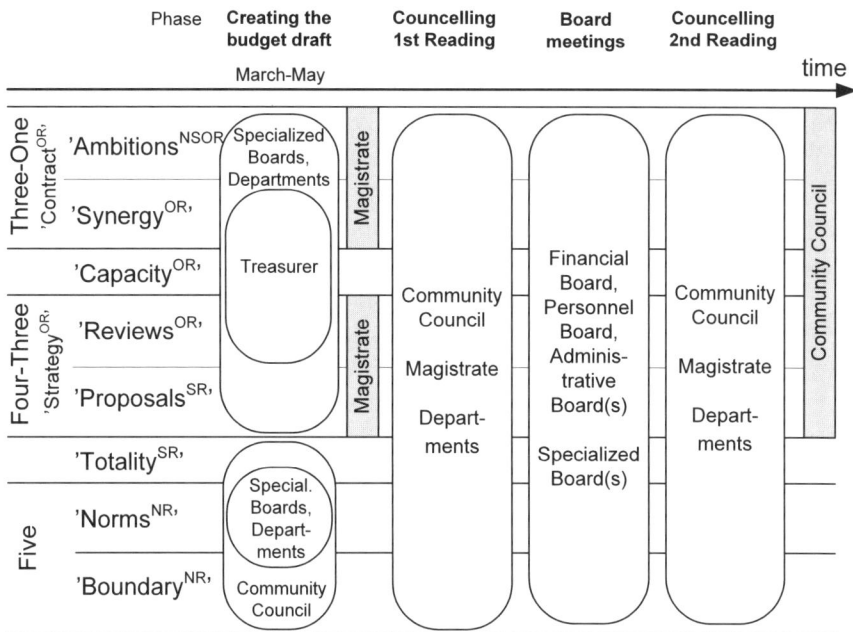

Figure 64. Systemicity of the traditional process of budget reconciliation

on the planning forms on their specific financial needs ('Ambitions[NSOR]').
Further, they articulate their individual investment plans.

All these planning forms are then collected and summarised by the
treasurer. The subsumation of the individual drafts represents the total
'Ambitions[NSOR]' of the departments (°sub-systems°). The treasurer com-
pares them against the presumably existing financial resources available
('Capacity[OR]'). Usually, the total sum of expected expenditures exceeds
the expected income. The treasurer now engages in bargaining with the
heads of department, adapting the plan until the overall sums are balanced
with respect to the total financial budget available ('Capacity[OR]') and reflect the overall °community° interests as perceived by the treasurer
('Strategy[SOR]', 'Synergy[OR]'). Typically, the treasurer is primarily concerned with reducing the individual departments' resource claims in this
process. Some treasurers do not even engage in bargaining and simply
define numbers themselves. The persons responsible in the various departments, usually in expectation of cutbacks, tend to apply for much
higher resources than actually required in order to improve their bargaining position and to prevent negative consequences from cutbacks to their
own department. In case of conflict between the treasurer and the depart-

ment representatives, the magistrate clarifies the issue and takes the final decision. As soon as reconciliations have been successful, the primary budget draft (i.e. the budget statute including all annexes) is announced by the magistrate, forwarded to the community council for final adoption and then laid open for public access for seven days ('Contract^{OR}').[693] Community residents and other actors with special interests (such as property owners or businessmen) may then submit their objections. These must subsequently be attended to in the further discussions of the community council.

In a similar procedure, the magistrate creates the investment program and the financial plan.[694] Usually, the treasurer, the mayor, or the first magistrate are in charge of compiling the drafts. The treasurer may comment on the draft of the magistrate and submit the commented version to the community council.[695] The financial plan must be submitted to the community council with the draft of the budget statute.[696] Both financial plan and the investment program are adapted annually to match with recent developments ('Inquiry^{SR}').[697]

Phase 2: Counselling and re-counselling

In the first reading of the community council, the mayor and councillors share their thoughts, concerns, and intentions (by formulating 'applications') of what is necessary ('Proposals^{SR}' versus 'Reviews^{OR}', 'Synergy^{OR}' versus 'Ambitions^{NSOR}') based upon the proposed resource allocation of the primary budget draft. This takes place independent of the issues' financial relevance. For councillors, budget debates in boards and the community council are the platform for illustrating and conveying their individual and faction interests. Throughout the first reading, heads of departments have the opportunity to present their wants, needs, and necessities as well as to indicate changes that have occurred in the meantime ('Ambitions^{NSOR}'). Subsequently, these concerns for modification are debated by the °subsystem° boards (for social boards, fire-brigade, building board, etc.) and in the financial boards with respect to °community° interests ('Proposals^{SR}', 'Reviews^{OR}', 'Synergy^{OR}', 'Ambitions^{NSOR}'). As the boards usually do not

---

[693] Sec. 97 HGO Adoption of the budget statute

[694] Sec. 101 HGO Financial planning; Sec. 24 GemHVO Financial planning and investment program

[695] Sec. 101 HGO para 3 Financial planning

[696] Sec. 101 HGO para 4 Financial planning

[697] Sec. 101 HGO para 5 Financial planning

have authority to take decisions, issues are usually discussed several times in different boards.[698] After consultation in the °sub-system° boards, all important issues are again addressed by the financial board and then final-ised for the community council by the administration. The results of the board meetings are then part of the second reading of the community council. Usually debates are closed until the second reading. The budget is then finally and formally adopted with the budget statute in the community council.[699] Therefore, a majority vote of the legally required number of councillors is needed. In the last year of the legislative period there may be no substantial changes of the budget statutes anymore.[700] The budget stat-ute may be published as soon as its legitimacy ('Super-Accounts[OR]') has been confirmed and permission has been granted by the supervisory au-thority. Therefore, budget statute and plans, as decided by the community council, are to be submitted to the legal supervision authority at the latest on the first of December before the planned year.[701] If a °community° does not submit the budget before the beginning of the new year, a provisional budget has to be enacted.[702]

The described procedure begins its cycle with the call for planning in summer (August) and is supposed to end just before the beginning of the new financial year at the end of the current year. However, only a small number (usually a tenth) of the °communities° finishes this process by the end of November. All others are much later. The usual explanation for that is that it takes until November for the °state° layer to deliver sound esti-

---

[698] Sec. 62 HGO Boards

[699] The statute may fix the required appointments for a two-year period but is usually restricted to one year, since the two-year perspective has generally not proved to be reliable (Sec. 94 HGO para 3, 2 clause 1-3). At the core of the budget statute are the essential fiscal regulations, e.g. the total sums of incomes and expenditures; the total sum of the debts; the total sum of commitment au-thorisations; the maximum of cash debit; property and business tax rates, which impact the total tax income of the °community° and others.

[700] Sec. 6 HGO para 2 Main statute

[701] Sec. 97 HGO para 4 Release of the budget statute

[702] If parts of the budget are subject to authorisation (e.g. loans, commitment au-thorisations, and changes of the cash volume), it comes into effect as soon as the °state° layer's supervisory department has approved it. That should occur within six weeks. However, it is usually the case that this takes from two to four months. Throughout this period, the °community° is operating based on a provisional budget. See Sec. 99 HGO Provisional budget conduct.

mates on the expected °community° income (taxes, subventions, allocations). If the budget is issued too early, the estimates are still inexact and it
is then most probably necessary to elaborate one or more supplementary
budgets, which requires considerable effort. Thus, the internal planning
period with the departments requires approximately one to two months.[703]
The first and second reading of the community council and the board
counsellings in between until the final adoption of the budget usually cover
another four to five months depending on the specific circumstances of the
community. Altogether, the entire planning process covers a period of five
months. At the same time as the budget reconciliation is taking place, the
°community° fees are re-examined and re-calculated if necessary.

Phase 3: Execution

The third phase is the execution of the budget. With the budget execution,
the financial claims of °community° are constituted and enforced (e.g. the
assessment of taxes and concessions) and obligations for °community° are
incurred and fulfilled (for instance the implementation of a construction project). Further, cash management and accounting are part of the budget execution process. The documentation of the cash management ('Records[TR]')
starts with collecting entries throughout the financial year. At the end of
the financial year, the final accounts are created ('Reports[OR]'). The annual
account must be set up by the finance department by the end of April of
the following year. Subsequently, the annual account is examined by the
°community's° accounting control department. At the latest, four month
after the end of the budgeted year, the magistrate has to confirm the annual
account.[704] After this, a superordinated examination of the annual account
is conducted by the °counties° accounting control department ('Super-
Audit[OR]').[705] The magistrate is to be informed about the substantial con-
tents of this examination ('Findings[OR]').[706] Hence, the budget cycles for
the different financial years inevitably overlap. While the budget of the
current year is being executed, the budget for the subsequent year is already being set-up. At the same time accounting is still engaged in finalising the preceding financial year's annual account statement. The resulting
consequences are to be considered in the new budget.

---

[703] In larger communities this period easily takes up to four month.

[704] Sec. 112 para 2 HGO Annual account

[705] Sec. 128 HGO Examination of the annual account

[706] Reif, K.: Der Haushaltsplan – kein Buch mit sieben Siegeln. Die kommunalen
Haushaltsgrundsätze, Die Gemeinde (BWGZ), 16 / 2004, 2004, pp. 604-605

Supplementary budget

Within the one-year validity of the budget, there may well be extraordinary or unscheduled expenditures such as changes in legislation, unexpected economic developments ('Undeterminisms^{SR}') or 'Urgencies^{TR}' which suddenly arise. A supplementary budget is obligatory in case of serious changes of the adopted budget. It is not sufficient simply to issue a new budget statute. The complete budget with all its components must always be re-issued. That means if the °community° recognises it needs to revise its cash credit or requires a new loan, the whole procedure starts over again. Then the community council decides on the supernumerary and unscheduled expenditures.[707] The magistrate authorises extraordinary expenditures as long as the community council does not define any different assignment. The community council must be informed and accept substantial changes to the planned expenditures.[708] When setting up the supplementary budget, the same processes and rules apply as for the ordinary budget. However, the reconciliation of a supplementary budget is an extensive and time consuming task, as this process again requires both adoption through the community council and the permission of the supervisory authority.

6.3.2 Compliance with systemic functions

All essential decision-making processes of °community° stem from the community council, board meetings, and the preparatory work of the mayor, magistrate, and administration ('Norms^{NR}', 'Strategy^{SOR}', 'Contracts^{OR}', 'Requirements^{OR}'). Councillors make individual applications, receive 'Proposals^{SR}', which are sometimes prepared by the administration, discuss and modify them and jointly pass resolutions by vote. The five-month period of counsellings between the community council and its boards forces the administration to start the internal planning process very early. However, since in the summer of the current year reliable assessments of the past year (the annual account, 'Reports^{OR}') are not available, planning for the subsequent year ('Proposals^{SR}', 'Reviews^{OR}', 'Synergy^{OR}', 'Ambitions^{OR}') cannot be expected to be optimal. This time lag is usually worsened by the time required for the realisation of the accounting control. It often takes up to three years before the accounting report ('Super-Findings^{OR}') is formu-

---

[707] Sec. 51 HGO para 6-15 Exclusive responsibilities of the community council

[708] Sec. 100 HGO Supernumerary and unscheduled expenditures

lated and the annual account is finally confimed.[709] In the summer months before the upcoming period, many developments in the °community's° environment such as changes in legal constraints ('Super-Requirements[OR]') and income estimations ('Capacity[OR]') can only be broadly guessed at as financial consequences which usually result in broad, flat estimations. This is worsened because the treasurer and other public servants engaged in planning do not actualise, retrieve, and revise the raw data of the plans with the person responsible for the °sub-systems° ('Records[OR]', 'Actuality[TR]'). As a consequence, the plans as they are announced in autumn only involve the most obvious and serious adaptations in relation to the original plans that have been created in August. Most probably, major adaptations will be necessary at the end of the year. Thus, although the prognosis for the subsequent year is highly complicated, the planning results derived from 'Strategy[SOR]' and 'Contract[OR]' are yet lacking.

In the whole process of budget reconciliation, there are principally no established rules, directives, or guidelines for shaping the agenda and debates in the panels. Usually, no general strategic direction is defined ('Norm[OR]', 'Strategy[SR]') before the optimisation of the resource allocation. Further, the separation of the budget reconciliation between political councils and administration is problematic. Until the presentation of the primary budget draft through administration, there is no opportunity for the councillors to influence the priorities. Thus, the budget draft represents a finished 'Proposal[SR]' of the administration on which the political councils can only exert minor influence in the process which follows due to the tight time schedule.[710] As has been mentioned already, councillors tend not to engage actively in identifying and reconciling their understanding of the °community's° *Wirkungsgefüge* ('Totality[SR]'). In the preparation and discussion of the budget draft, they tend to restrict their perspective on the issues relevant to themselves due to their personal intentions and involvement in political factions. The budget draft (a 'Proposal[SR]' derived from 'Report[OR]') delivered by the administration primarily addresses the financial aspects of °community° issues and does not reflect on 'Totality[SR]'.

---

[709] If the supervisory authority of the °county° demands a precautionary budget concept for the approval of the budget, it is discussed again in the financial board.

[710] Similar see Schwarting, G.: Effizienz in der Kommunalverwaltung, Teil I: Dezentrale Verantwortung und Finanzsteuerung durch Budgetierung, Berlin, 2004

In the absence of such a common understanding of the relevant °community° factors, councillors usually concentrate on a limited number of budget positions in their sphere of interest. Sometimes their discussions solely address at length the meaning and importance of individual budget positions. In fact, budget estimates are extrapolated based on previous year's budget figures without any systematic recognition of the changes that have taken place in the meantime. Neither the defined actor roles (as described above) nor the processes and sequences between the °community° actors support the budget reconciliation. Which topics are being reconciled is not defined, and the process of budget reconciliation does not lead the actors involved to settle the relevant 'Inquiry^{SR}' and 'Totality^{SR}' issues of their °community° for preparing final decisions ('Norms^{NR}', 'Strategy^{SR}', 'Contract^{OR}'). Rather, the opposite is the case. All actors and councils are engaged in more or less all topics (see Figure 59), and those boards who are engaged in special °community° topics have no decision authority. Generally, the distribution of topics between them does not reflect the necessity to settle the systemic issues. As a consequence, councillors usually feel too overwhelmed to cope with the complexity of °community° issues. Often, informal agreements are settled on with the majority faction to minimise effort and conflicts in the council. Thus, an open-minded and factual process is complicated and hampered substantially. Missing and incomplete strategic agreements (e.g. 'Proposals^{SR}') cannot be substituted through close and frequent interactions between the members of the financial and special boards and administration. Commonly, all major decision processes ('Norms^{NR}', 'Strategy^{SOR}', 'Contracts^{OR}') are characterised by extensive discussion and a long accommodation period. The legal primacy of the community council and the overload of issues in budget reconciliation bring about long time lags. These time lags become greater with the number of boards, committees, and local advisors[711] under the same circumstances.

The recognition of the real strategic priorities suffers from the lack of timeliness in the attendance to strategic issues. Characteristically, failures and lapses in attending to strategic issues can rarely be corrected at a later point in time. The current budget reconciliation process focussing on a short-term perspective is liable to miss important developments in the environment and thus not to implement these in due time.

---

[711] German "Ortsbeirat"

6.3.3 Suggestions

For viability and sustainability, all interactions between °community° actors have to have a continuous focus in order to prepare for sound decisions on 'Norms^{NR}', 'Strategy^{SOR}', 'Contract^{OR}', and 'Requirements^{OR}'.[712] Therefore, a systemic conduct of budget reconciliation replaces commonly sequential, consecutive processes with an integrated, organic flow of reconciliation in which taking decisions takes place permanently according to the requirements and timeliness of the °community° issues that are unfolding. However, the establishment of such a process strongly depends on systemic channels being clarified and established in the social °system°, i.e. the tasks and responsibilities assigned to actors and councils. Thus, it is insufficient to attend to these processes only once a year at a formally defined date.

Figure 60 describes a possible distribution of strategic tasks and responsibilities for °community°. °Sub-system° actors and boards are not expected to engage in budget reconciliation on the °community° layer, but contribute to it by clarifying °sub-system° 'Ambitions^{SOR}'. However, that does not imply that °sub-system° actors cannot or should not participate in the reconciliation of °community° issues (compare chapter 4.1.3). Their contributions will be highly useful, for instance, for attending to strategic topics (*Four*). Therefore, to place their contributions, they should be invited by those committees (e.g. strategic boards, strategic commissions) who engage in resolving these issues.

In the proposed systemic distribution of topics on the °community° layer, strategic boards, commissions, and departments primarily engage in strategic issues, whereas operative boards, magistrate, and general administration attend to operative issues. 'Proposals^{SR}' are prepared in the strategic committees and the administrative department (if existent), moderated and finalised by the magistrate. 'Strategy^{SOR}' decisions are then taken by the strategic board. The community council only engages in determining the general direction by giving normative direction to the strategic and operative processes; it does not itself engage in strategic and operative decision making.

'Synergy^{OR}' (budgeting of the °sub-systems°) is prepared primarily through the administration (and an operational committee if existent). The reconciliation with 'Ambition^{NSOR}' and the decision of the 'Contract^{OR}' based on the current 'Strategy^{SOR}' is moderated by the magistrate

---

[712] Compare Beers second organisational principal, chapter 3.3.

who takes the final decision. Thus, based on a systemic distribution of roles[713], the following characteristics of a systemic process of budget reconciliation can be derived:

Normative, strategic, and operative reconciliations are conducted permanently. Budgetary (just as any other) decisions are taken on an ongoing basis according to the requirements of the actual situation. However, that does not mean that all budgetary issues have to or should be decided immediately when they arise. It only means that there will not be a formalised period that precisely defines at what point in time budgetary decisions have to be taken. Rather, the question of when the issue decisions are addressed is dealt with according to their timeliness. Urgent budgetary issues are attended to immediately; all others are taken according to their feasibility. Thus, there is no months-long process of °community° budget reconciliation anymore, but budgeting is based on a reflection of the current situation of °community° ('Totality^{SR}' and 'Capacity^{OR}', which includes the budgetary aspects); primary budgetary decisions ('Strategy^{SOR}' and 'Contract^{OR}') are taken only when the time has come. That means that different rhythms of decision making are allowed on the different logical levels. Instead of a joint resolution of 'Strategy^{SOR}', 'Contract^{OR}' once a year with a budget, multiple resolutions are possible at different times on each level. 'Strategy^{SOR}' decisions are taken whenever necessary, as are 'Contracts^{OR}'. The consequences of any decisions planned and taken will then immediately reflect in adequate representations of the °community° 'Totality^{SR}' and 'Capacity^{OR}'. Therefore, adequate methods and instruments are provided. The budget itself as a document still exists, but does not rely on the ongoing planning activities anymore. Rather, it is the instrument to communicate the financial accountability of the °community° to its residents and to the superordinated °county° and °state° layer authorities. Therefore, a reflection of 'Totality^{SR}', 'Capacity^{OR}' and 'Strategy^{SOR}', 'Contract^{OR}' is documented to provide an account of the ongoing activities and quality of °community° governance. Thus, the actors involved and affected are always able to gain an integrated understanding of the current situation. The following figure sketches a budget reconciliation that is being conducted continuously in time. Decisions are being taken on an ongoing basis according to their individual feasibility.

---

[713] It should be emphasized that the task and responsibility assignment as depicted in Figure 60 is only one possible setting. As in the systemic perspective, "who does what" is not decisive, but rather "what is being done and how". Therefore, many other systemic structures could be defined.

time

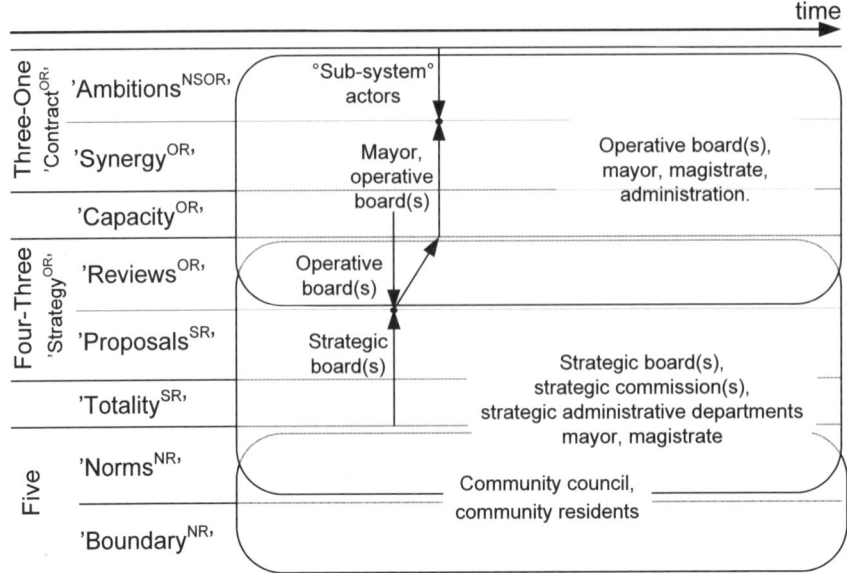

Figure 65. Suggested conduct of °community° planning

6.4 Excursus on Transduction

Transduction capacity is not addressed in this case study. However, a short example will demonstrate transduction issues in °community°. The grouping survey ("Gruppierungsübersicht") has been introduced as anticipatory for all requests regarding the overall sums of °communities'°' personnel expenditures and other cost types. Thus, for a councillor or a citizen to find out about (i.e. to receive 'Orientation[TR]' on) personnel expenditures, he may identify and consult the grouping survey.[714] Primarily, this requires him to know that this specific information is to be found in the grouping survey, which is part of the budget. Further, he needs to know under which specific group of personnel expenditures he will have to look, i.e. that personnel expenditures belong to the main group number four, etc. Thus, any special 'Queries[TR]' require in-depth knowledge of the bureaucratic conventions applied in Hessian °communities° to capture their 'Actuality[OR]'. 'Orientation[OR]' on such °community° matters is thus not easily achieved, especially for those °community° actors engaged on an honorary basis. Councillors regularly do not have much background knowledge of the legal and

---

[714] Or the summary certificates ("Sammelnachweise")

financial conventions used for describing and documenting °community° facts and issues. This makes it hard for them to acquire a sound, comprehensive understanding of the actual situation of their °community° and to maintain focus on the systemic °community° topics to be solved and on assessing alternative solutions. Therefore, it is not suprising that honorary councillors and community residents often feel overwhelmed in this situation.

6.5   eGovernance with eMedia

eMedia have been defined above as a sub-group of conventional media that provide a virtual space to create °system° structures (chapter 1.2, Figure 2). Hence, eMedia are a supplement that facilitates governing interactions. Through them, governing structures become tangible and can be formed according to specific °system° needs and requirements. If configured correctly, eMedia can increase conventional channel, change, and transduction capacities and thus enhance the social °systems° governing potential and viability. The following figure indicates which eMedia properties impact the capacity of °system° structures.

Hence, eMedia can supplement conventional °system° structures. As a consequence of their limitation in coping with the pragmatics of interaction, they are usually inadequate to replace conventional face-to-face encounters. Clearly, their most promising contribution is to integrate conventional structures and to bring them to their full potential, which in turn allows them to identify how existing governing structures can be

		Aspects of structure					
		Channel capacity		Change capacity		Transduction capacity	
		Tasks and responsibilities	Processes and sequences	Methods and instruments	Interfaces between methods	°System° and logical boundaries	Actor boundaries
Systemic interactions (Axioms of management)	Two / Two-One / Three / Three-One / Three-Two / Three*-One / Four / Four-Env / Four-Three / Five / Five-Four/ Three / Five-(Four-Three) / Five-One	1) Ubiquity of assessibility, 2) comprehensive actor involvement, 3) synchronicity of activities, 4) free graphical and pictorial illustration, 5) free design of process flows, 6) mass archivation and retrival of data.		1) Transformation of data according to defined algorithms, 2) Performing generalizations, distortions and specifying on representations, 3) Interlinking governing elements in representations.		1) Making explicit and addressable boundary judgments, 2) Clarifying logical levels of issues, and solutions, 3) Translating between actor languages, conventions, etc.	

Figure 66. Impact of eMedia on °system° structures

supplemented. eMedia can be understood as a toolkit for governing structures, which complements conventional face-to-face structures wherever
these are inadequate, too slow, unreliable, distant, unflexible, etc. Generally,
eMedia can support each of the structural aspects of interaction, thus helping
to implant optimum structural conditions. eMedia are a tool for establishing
and improving °system° structures and for eliminating structural deficiencies. The governance frame integrates conventional and eMedia perspectives on governance and thus provides the preconditions for an application and design of eMedia that is rooted in the specific governing needs of
the °community°. The following table shows what structural contributions
exemplary eMedia applications and services can provide to support the
governance of a social °system°.

Table 22. Structural contribution of common eMedia applications and services

eMedia application or service	Channel capacity		Change or transformation capacity		Transduction capacity	
	Tasks- and responsibilities	Processes and sequences	Methods and instruments	Interfaces between instruments	°System° and logical boundaries	Actor boundaries
Internet page	One-to-many, one-way traffic.		None. Do not engage in message transformation.		Functions of the user interface implemented in the web browsing application applied, e.g. change of script size, favourite pages memory, zoom, and scrolling functions, etc.	
Internet blog	Many-to-many, two-way traffic, asynchronous acitivity.					
Chat	Many-to-many, two-way traffic, synchronous activity.					
eMail	One-to-one / many, two-way traffic, asynchronous acitivity.				Functions of the user interface of eMail client, e.g. sort and search functions.	
Spreadsheet software	None. Does not engage in message transfer.		Calculations of all kinds, transformation of quantitative data into graphical illustrations.		Functions of the user interface, e.g. help function to support user defining adequate data transformations.	
Television	One-to-many, one-way traffic.		None. Do not engage in message transformation.		Usually none. Only some user interface functions, e.g. multiple languages for a film.	

Based on a systemic governance notion of social °systems°, eMedia can be applied and designed according to their structural condition. As soon as a systemic understanding of °community° structures has been captured based on a viability profile of °community° governance, it can be identified, which of the °community's° structural deficiencies are to be usefully addressed and eliminated through which eMedia tools. The criterion of viability is met when all characteristic interactions are established and provide requisite structural capacity in all three aspects. As soon as that is given, the actors involved can perform their °community° tasks continuously according to the timeliness of the issues at hand. For a °community° implementation, this may have the following consequences (looking at the structural aspects selected on in the case):

Channel capacity

Tasks and responsibilities

eMedia structures allow the designing of °community° interactions that make sure that the right actors attend to governing issues. It is no longer important where the actors involved are physically and how many there are. The minimum number of actors required to attend to a system topic can now be involved. Even large numbers of actors can theoretically participate synchronously or asynchronously to contribute and accommodate their knowledge and interests. Further, eMedia can ensure attendance to the systemic topics, independent of what their individual roles in boards, administrative departments or °sub-systems° are. Thus, eMedia allow for councillors, public servants, and community residents to be involved in determining actual °community° needs and developments ('Inquiry^{SR}') or in discussing the self-conception and identity of the °community° ('Boundary^{NR}'). Or even more advanced, community residents may be involved in the reconciliation of the °community° budget (i.e. 'Strategy^{SOR}', 'Contract^{OR}' reconciliation) as it has already been tested in some German °communities°.[715] Further, eMedia allow supporting the optimum assignment of °community° actors by their continuous reconciliation and commitment to their systemic tasks and responsibilities. By making explicit who is involved in what topics and responsible for which systemic decisions, individual roles are clarified and rooted in the °community° notion. From the perspective of °com-

---

[715] The project °community° budget with citizen involvement ("Kommunaler Bürgerhaushalt") of the German °state° of Nordrhein-Westfalen is an example. See State of Nordrhein-Westfalen and Bertelsmann Stiftung: Citizen involvement in budget reconciliation, Internetpage, 2007

munity°, it can thus be ensured that all systemic topics are being attended to. As has been suggested above, boards and formalised meetings will be defined according to their systemic contribution (thus, a strategic and an operative board might be established). With eMedia conventional face-to-face discussions will not be replaced, but most likely be conducted much more efficiently, effectively and to the point.

Processes and sequences

eMedia can also provide support so that the right actors can perform their actions at the right time. As it has been demonstrated above for the process of budget reconciliation, eMedia can facilitate a differentiated design of process flows between °community° actors and councils. Instead of formalised attendance to °community° in rather arbitrary intervals of one year, a viable °community° structure attends to governing issues concurrently. Issues are executed according to their specific priority and feasibility. Thus, °community° actors are enabled to engage in reconciling and revising plans concurrently, at any place and point of time. Instead of planning and decision making on a yearly basis, decisions will be taken with reference to the individual priorities and risks involved in the issue. However, the precondition for such a continuous engagement in planning and budgeting is that actors are aware of their systemic contribution. Further, they must be continuously informed on the °community's° 'Totality^{SR}' and 'Capacity^{OR}'. Therefore, eMedia will have to provide continuous consideration of these.

Change or transformation capacity

Methods and instruments

eMedia can provide applications that implement methods and instruments helping to conduct systemic topic solutions. All kinds of software tools allow specialised support for °community° governance. Actors are relieved from creating 'Records^{OR}' of °sub-system° implementation in regard to finanancial resource consumption, product quantities, quality measures, etc. summarizing past resource consumptions ('Reports^{OR}'), providing 'Orientation^{TR}' on remaining resources to °sub-system° responsibles, determining the 'Capacity^{OR}' of °community° to implement a 'Proposal^{SR}' suggested by a strategic board, elaborating a scenario anaylsis on possible future steps to be taken ('Totality^{SR}'), etc. Further, they support the formalisation and standardisation of all systemic topic reconciliations, e.g. by implementing a virtual product catalogue ('Any'). Therefore, eMedia can provide representations that interlink the governing elements of the community's activities, i.e. its 'images', 'instruments', 'actions' and 'actors' and their relations. 'Images' expressed as goals and products, quality measures, can be linked to financial resources ('instruments'), tasks ('actions'), and the persons responsible ('actors'). Thus, for each governing issue being addressed, the essential invariant governing aspects (governing elements) are clarified and can be referred to in whatever systemic topic is being addressed.

°System° boundaries and recursive layers

eMedia facilitate the delegation of tasks between recursive layers. It can be defined individually for every °community° to which degree it intends to autonomously implement activities and where it prefers to exploit synergies with other °communities° ('Super-Contract^{OR}' on °county° layer). Similarily, it may also look at how to exploit synergies between its °sub-systems° ('Contract^{OR}' on °community° layer). For instance, the registry office of a small °community° may not be able to perform all the administrative tasks required to implement a marriage due to its limited human resources. If the major 'instruments' being applied and 'actions' being taken were supported through eMedia, the administrative activities to accept the marriage could be split between the small °community° and a neighbouring °community° or executed by the superordinated authority on the °county° layer.

The following steps would be required for improving the governance of a °community° with eMedia:

1. Identify structural weaknesses in current implementation of the °community° notion using the viability profile (compare Figure 38 and Table 15).

2. Define structural requirements.

3. Identify potential of eMedia for improving existing structure.

4. Design supplementary structures based on eMedia.

Restart the procedure with step 1. If possible further provide facilitation support with eMedia.

7 Conclusion

Finally, in retrospect on the research questions and the objectives that were formulated (in chapter 1.2), the following remarks summarise the results of this research endeavor.

A holistic, integrated framework has been assembled based on cybernetic theory. Stafford Beer's managerial cybernetics and in particular his Viable System Model provided the primary essential contribution that facilitated the integrative perspective taken. The framework was then complemented and sharpened by various other system theories and was further inspired by the works of experts in Political Science, Governance, and New Public Management (for a complete list see chapter 1.3.2). It is only due to these theoretical predecessors that governance systemic foundation and framework have been possible.

As a constitutive element, the framework provides a constructivist *Weltanschauung* rooted in an autopoietic understanding of actors. Based on that understanding, an interactional perspective on governance has been taken, emphasising those constituent parts of interaction (intents, claims, preconditionings, representations) which reveal how structures lead actors to constitute "delimited contexts" among themselves, labelled °system° notions (compare "Inside view" in Figure 10). The understanding of how actors' link further deepened the conception of "system" itself and led to the recognition of a boundary as the constitutive logical limitation and legitimation of all °system° notions (compare chapter 2.3.1). Based on this, the concept of structure itself was rooted in interaction distinguishing three fundamental structural capacities (change, channel, and transduction capacity, see chapter 3.1.2 following) that set the pre-conditions for successful reconciliation between actors. During the process of developing an understanding of how actors create common 'delimited contexts' in interaction, the existence of an inside view on social °systems° was recognised and a logical anatomy of °system° notions identified (compare Figure 10 and Figure 24). Further, it was discovered that the initially broad contours of °system° anatomy do show invariant logical structures which can be revealed and described. These invariant logical structures were identified and characterised, subsequently formulating a set of logical and invariant systemic topics (compare chapter 4) that are to be resolved in all °system° notions. The recognition and conceptualisation of the invariances and interfaces between social °system° anatomy and its interactional structure as it is concentrated in the viability profile (compare Table 15) constitute the major insight, which enabled the empirical substantiation of the framework in the case study. It made clear that the properties of 'viability' and 'sustainability' as qualities of °system° governance depend on the interaction structures providing sufficient capacity for a reconciliation of the systemic topics. At this point, the conceptual tools for addressing governance from an interactional perspective were assembled. An integrated governance framework was formulated, which primarily meant that a meta-language was invented expressing °system° invariances in an interactional, second order perspective. With the concept of representation and its formalisation within the text, a way was found to embed the distinction between observer and object in the descriptive process. All of these steps were clearly not taken in succession but rather in a circular, recurrent yo-yo procedure. The details of the framework as they are described and summarised in chapter 4.8 represent the necessary and sufficient criteria required for governing structures to be viable and sustainable. Wherever these criteria are met, a dispersed °system° notion is merged into an integrated one (compare Figure 67).

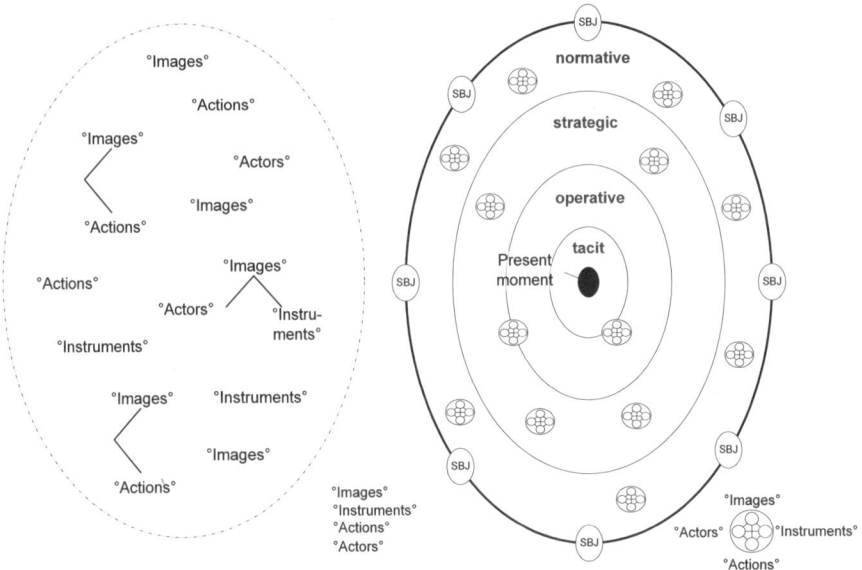

Figure 67. From a dispersed to an integrated °system° notion

In the final chapters the applicability and significance of the framework were demonstrated with a practical case study. It was shown how the language of the framework can be applied in the case of Hessian °communities°. Three aspects of system structure were chosen and empirical findings of these were described. Thus, the established °community° notions were diagnosed and suggestions for improving their structural design were formulated. Finally, it was shown that and how the framework integrates the eMedia perspective allowing its use as a supplement for designing new °system° structures as well as dissolving existing deficiencies.

Thus, looking at the governance framework, it becomes apparent that the conflict between the approaches chosen by the exponents of synthetic views on governance (see Table 1, chapter 1.1.3) is put into a different perspective. The authors cited focus either on structures or actors and choose individuals, organisations, and larger entities as the primary entities to build their theories. Now, the integrated framework shows that neither structures nor actors are primary; rather, both aspects merge in interaction and jointly evolve certain governing states. Whatever °system° notion actors engage, they create it through mutual reconciliation. The principle of recursion shows that neither an 'individual', 'organisation', nor any kind of 'social sector' are useful starting points for theory creation. Such distinction assumes that the entities are 'out there' and tangible for thorough examination and not created through actor engagement. With recursive layers being distinguished, it depends on the current °system° in focus, what context it is being looked at and what its underlying normatives are. Thus, higher °system° layers such as organisation, county, and/ or state become accessible to analysis but remain rooted in the logic of the individual actors at the same time. Ultimately, it is always the individual actors with whom ideas about systems, organisations, sectors, etc. originate, because it is only the individual that can produce and share concepts of how he perceives his world. This also makes clear that no 'organisation' or 'social system' can usefully be understood as an autopoietic entity, but only the cognitive and interactive processes of the individual actor.

Further, the research shows that 'politics' and 'administration' are limited categories for describing roles in governance contexts. Indeed, the distinction refers to the different °system° notions actors of each category tend to adopt as a consequence of their different deployment in °community° (compare table of typical boundary judgements, Table 10). However, this does not yet provide any useful indication of how they contribute to a °system° implementation. The systemic contributions of politicians as well as public servants or any other actor will vary largely depending on the contextual conditions of the °community° that is looked at and its embedment in a higher recursive layer °state°. Based on the developed framework, a fundamental suggestion can be made to recognise invariant system properties and consequently to build theories on these. Doing so will allow the shifting of the focus from the distinction of political and managerial rationalities to a governing rationality, which is rooted in the logical consequences of Ashby's law of requisite variety[716] and is anchored in the critically reflected normative frame of a °system° notion.

It follows from the findings that any theory building on social °systems° must recognise the fundamental invariances at the heart of how actors accommodate their common endeavors. Only based on these can comprehensive and applicable theories be created to support practice. Theories themselves have to reflect these invariances, which means primarily that they must make explicit where and why they assume invariances and when they simply describe variations of perceived ("real-world") phenomena. Ultimately, a sound theory of governance must be self-referential, i.e. it must explain the process and limitations which underly its own creation.[717] With the concept of representation and its formalisation within the text, a way has been found to embed the distinction between observer and the observed object in the descriptive process of the theory. This allows for self-referentiality, as the governance frame can now also be applied to the °system° notion set up for conducting research, i.e. the °research° notion (compare chapter 5.2). The self-referentiality of the theory allows to sharpen the use of the concept 'viability' as a property. Actors cannot appraise neutrally the viability of a °system° notion whether they are actively engaged in it or not. Their perspective is necessarily biased, evolving from their specific individual °system° notion (determined by their role, etc.). They cannot see it from a holistic independent perspective because they have only their individual transducers to apply (see chapter 3.4) and structural conditions under which they access the °system° notion. Therefore, the only way to legitimately assign the property 'viable' to a °system° notion is to establish a self-referential meta-structure that ensures continuously that the °system° structures are kept viable. A social °system° that establishes such a structure can then be referred to as "viable". Viability is nothing that can be designed once for all, rather it is something that must be triggered continuously by facilitating it.

---

[716] See chapter 2.2.4, footnote 97

[717] "Just as science develops through an interplay between theory and practice, so theory itself advances by a succession of intuitive and formal representations.", in Anderton, R.: (Formal development)

However, it has to be emphasised that the derived framework has not yet been completed or finalised. Rather, it should be understood as a foundation that invites further engagement in theory refinement and practical application. Although the theory sketched a holistic view on the governance of social °systems°, it is still a first step only, with further integrative potential. Therefore, additional fundamental principles may be consulted for theory assessment applying the yo-yo technique (chapter 1.3.2). One source might be Spencer Brown's "Laws of Form", which provide an extensive theory on how forms are created based on distinctions (every °system° is nothing but a shared form). Further potential for theory building can be expected in docking (and partly integrating) governance with a sound theory assisting in describing the dynamics of system pre-conditioning as they emerge from the interaction between actors. Such a theory would need to make understandable and analysable the dynamic changes taking place in the shared °system° notions between actors. Haken's Synergetics[718] provides a complete interdisciplinary science that explains the formation and self-organisation of structures in all kind of systems. It can obviously be applied to describe, explain, and analyse the dynamics of change in social °system° notions.

Based on the experiences of the case study and the theoretical implications identified, an outline can be provided for what kind of benefits an integrated approach to governance is likely to provide for °system° implementation:

1. °System° boundaries can be defined adequately to ensure that the beneficiaries of °system° implementation (i.e. the community residents or clients) are put in the focus in all °system° activities;

2. The contradiction between centralisation and decentralisation as well as local and global can be dissolved. The governance frame allows the development of a differentiated notion of subsidiarity and the derivation of the consequences for federalism;

3. All activities of the actors involved can be anchored in the °system° notion, i.e. in the purposes that are being aspired to. Tasks and responsibilities in actor assignments and meeting protocols can be defined to contribute optimally to resolving °system° issues. Thus, actors can focus on providing the systemic contribution that is expected from them;

---

[718] Haken, H.: (Synergetik)

4. Actor competences can be described systemically. Consequently, actors can be assigned to contribute according to their individual strength, without hierarchical limitations;

5. Governing methods and instruments can be configured to optimally serve the resolution of systemic topics. Interfaces can be designed to intertwine;

6. Facilitating reconciliations on governing issues by establishing a convention on how to address governing issues. What is achieved for the implementation of a °system° notion becomes visible and can be communicated through a common language. All kinds of governing issues and conflicts can be addressed precisely, which facilitates their solution.

This list is still incomplete. Further specific points become apparent when reflecting from a °community°, °health°, °company° perspective. However, the culmination of application will be the implantation of the governance frame in °system° structures. Therefore, facilitators and a facilitation procedure will have to be defined engaging in moderating and revising °community° structures, e.g. role definitions, council compositions, process flows, management directives, management terminologies, etc. A moderator has to be defined who is in charge of escorting community council, magistrate, and administration in their mutual reconciliations. That facilitation procedure will further require a sound monitoring of viability, enabling it to immediately identify the structural deficiencies that are emerging and engaging in moderating their solution.

Looking at the experience gained in the case study, we recognise that there is great need for application. Comprehensive frameworks for creating viable and sustainable °system° notions are not yet applied and not even known. With the ever increasing complexity, diversity, and dynamics in modern societies, it has become apparent that the viability and sustainability of °system° notions will often require support through eMedia. Rather than supporting or promoting the development of singular eMedia infrastructures and applications, the governance frame can enable °communities° to optimise their entire media and eMedia design in respect to supporting governance. Many actors can be involved in a form that corresponds both to their individual competences, requirements and interests and to °community° needs. However, for

> *"navigating by continuously perceiving the movements of the subsystems, and, dependent on these movements, adjusting the course"* [719]

close and real-time interactions are a pre-condition. If configured adequately, eMedia can provide such structures and promote the integration of their continuously growing, fragmented and diversified intentions and contexts in today's societies. The multiplicity of contexts must be made compatible, so that actors with a different *Weltanschauung* and varied interests find ways to get along and live together. May the ideas of the governance frame provide a fruitful contribution to the attainment of that goal.

---

[719] See respective citation, chapter 1.1.3, footnote 23

Bibliography

6, Perri (eGovernance): eGovernance: Weber's revenge?, in Dowding, K. M. and Margetts, H.: Challenges to Democracy: Ideas, Involvement and Institutions, Palgrave Macmillan, New York, 2003

6, Perri and others, (Holistic Governance): Towards Holistic Governance, Palgrave, New York, 2002

Adam, M., (Viability of social systems): Lebensfähigkeit sozialer Systeme. Stafford Beer's Viable System Model im Vergleich, Difo-Druck, Bamberg, 2001

Anderton, R. (Formal development): The need for formal development of the VSM, in Espejo, R. and Harnden, R.: The Viable Systems Model: Interpretations and Applications of Stafford Beer's VSM, Wiley, Chichester, 1989, p. 39-40

Arthur, Brian (Cognition): Cognition: The Black Box of Economics, in Colander, D.: The Complexity Vision and the Teaching of Economics, Edward Elgar Publishing, Northampton, Mass., 2000

Ashby, W. R., (Introduction): An Introduction to Cybernetics, Chapman & Hall, London, 1964

Ashby, W. R. and Conant, R. C., (Regulator): Every good regulator of a system must be a model of that system, in: International Journal of System Science, Volume 1/2, Issue 89, 1970, p. 97, http://pespmc1.vub.ac.be/EQKNOW.html

Baier, H., (Operative Planung): Operative Planung in Kommunen – Neukonzeption auf der Basis einer Kosten- und Leistungsrechnung, Josef Eul, Köln, 2002

Bandler, R., (Structure of magic II): The structure of magic – Volume II, Science and Behavior Books, 1980

Bandler, R. and Grinder, J., (Structure of Magic I): The Structure of Magic Volume I, Science and Behavior Books, Inc., Palo Alto, 1980

Barzelay, M., (How to argue NPM): How to argue about New Public Management, in: International Public Management Journal, Elsevier Science, Volume 2, Issue 2(A), 1999, p. 183-216

Bateson, G., (Ecology of mind): Steps to an ecology of mind, University of Chicago Press, 2000

Bateson, G., (Mind and Nature): Geist und Natur. Eine notwendige Einheit., Suhrkamp, Frankfurt/ Main, 1979

Beer, S (Beyond dispute): Governance or Government?, in Beer, S: Beyond dispute: the invention of team syntegrity, John Wiley & Sons, Chichester, 1994

Beer, S, (Cybernetics and Management): Cybernetics and Management, John Wiley, New York, 1959

Beer, S., (Diagnosing): Diagnosing the System for Organisations – Companion Volume to Brain of the Firm and The Heart of Enterprise, John Wiley & Sons, Chichester, 1985a

Beer, S., (Brain): Brain of the firm, John Wiley & Sons, Chichester, 1981

Beer, S., (Heart): The Heart of the Enterprise, John Wiley & Sons, Chichester, 1979

Beer, S., (Diagnosing): Diagnosing the System for Organizations – Companion Volume to Brain of the Firm and The Heart of Enterprise, John Wiley & Sons, Chichester, New York, Brisbane, Toronto, Singapore, 1985b

Beer, S. (How to run a country): National government: disseminated regulation in real time, or `How to run a country´, in Espejo, R. and Harnden, R.: The Viable System Model – Interpretations and Applications of Stafford Beer's VSM, John Wiley & Sons, Chichester, New York, Brisbane, Toronto, Singapore, 1989

Beer, S., (Dispute): Beyond Dispute: The Invention of Team Syntegrity, John Wiley & Sons, Chichester, 1994

Beer, S., (Decision): Decision and Control – The Meaning of Operational Research and Management Cybernetics, John Wiley & Sons, London, 1966

Beer, S. (How to run a country): National government: disseminated regulation in real time, or "How to run a country", in Espejo, R. and Harnden, R.: The Viable System Model – Interpretations and Applications of Stafford Beer's VSM, John Wiley & Sons, Chichester, New York, Brisbane, Toronto, Singapore, 1989

Beer, S., (Provenance): The Viable System Model: Its provenance, development, methodology and pathology, in: Journal of the Operational Research Society, Issue 35, 1984, p. 7-25

Ben-Eli, M. U. (Medical center): Strategic planning and management reorganization at an academic medical center: use of the VSM in guiding diagnosis and design, 1989, p. 299-332

Bertanalaffy, L. v., (General Systems Theory): General Systems Theory – A New Approach to the Unity of Science, in: Human Biology, Volume 23 / 1951, 1951, p. 302-361

Beyerle, M., (Staatstheorie und Autopoiesis): Staatstheorie und Autopoiesis – Über die Auflösung der modernen Staatsidee im nachmodernen Denken durch die Theorie autopoietischer Systeme und der Entwurf eines nachmodernen Staatskonzepts, Peter Lang, Frankfurt a.M., 1994

Bormann, M. and Stiezel, C., (Stadt und Gemeinde): Stadt und Gemeinde. Kommunalpolitik in den neuen Ländern, Bundeszentrale für politische Bildung, Bonn, 1993

Brühlmeier, D. and others, (Political planning): Politische Planung – Mittelfristige Steuerung in der wirkungsorientierten Verwaltungsführung, Haupt, Bern, Stuttgart, Wien, 2001

Bundeszentrale für politische Bildung, (Policy in community): Kommunalpolitik, Volume 242, 1998

Busch, P. and Dampney, C., (Tacit Knowledge Acquisition and Processing): Tacit Knowledge Acquisition and Processing within the Computing Domain: An Exploratory Study, Information Resources Management Association, Anchorage, 2000, p. 1014-1015

Bußmann, H., (Sprachwissenschaft): Lexikon der Sprachwissenschaft, Stuttgart, 1990

Checkland, P., (Information Systems): Information, Systems, Information Systems, Wiley, 1999

Checkland, P., (Systems Thinking Practice): Systems Thinking, Systems Practice, John Wiley, Chichester, 1999

City of Staufenberg, (Community documents): Overview on community documents, 1/5/2007, http://staufenberg.online-h.de/Archiv/aktenplan/index.html

Collins author's, (Dictionary): English Dictionary, Harpercollins, 2005

BGBl., Grundgesetz für die Bundesrepublik Deutschland, 28-8-2006

Druwe, U. (Rekonstruktion Autopoiese): Rekonstruktion der 'Theorie der Autopoiese' als Gesellschafts- und Steuerungsmodell, in Görlitz, A.: Politische Steuerung sozialer Systeme. Mediales Recht als politisches Steuerungskonzept., Centaurus, Pfaffenweiler, 1989, p. 35-58

Eco, U., (Semiotik und Philosophie): Semiotik und Philosophie der Sprache, Wilhelm Fink Verlag, München, 1985

Espejo, R. (Cybernetic method): A cybernetic method to study organizations, in Espejo, R. and Harden, R.: The Viable Systems Model – Interpretations and Applications of Stafford Beer's VSM, Wiley, Chichester, 1989

Espejo, R. (VSM revisited): The VSM revisited, in Espejo, R. and Harden, R.: The Viable System Model: Interpretations and Applications of Stafford Beer's VSM, John Wiley & Sons, Chichester, New York, Brisbane, Toronto, Singapore, 1989

Espejo, R. (Information Systems): Giving Requisite Variety to Strategy and Information Systems, in Stowell, F. A. and Howell, J. G.: Systems Science – Adressing Global Issues, New York, 1993

Espejo, R., (Requisite Variety): Giving Requisite Variety to Strategic and Implementation Processes: Theory and Practice, 2000

Espejo, R., (Systemic Thinking): What is Systemic Thinking?, in: System Dynamics Review, Volume June, 1994, p. 199-212

Espejo, R. and Gill, A., (VSM as a Framework): The Viable System Model as a Framework for Understanding Organizations, 1997, http://www.syncho.com/pages/pdf/Introduction%20to%20Viable%20System%20Model%20RETG.pdf

Espejo, R. and Harden, R., (Interpretations): The Viable System Model. Interpretations and Applications of Stafford Beer's VSM, John Wiley & Sons, Chichester, 1989

302 Bibliography

Espejo, R. and Harnden, R. (Conversation): The VSM: an ongoing conversation, in Espejo, R. and Harnden, R.: The Viable System Model. Interpretations and Applications of Stafford Beer's VSM, John Wiley & Sons, Chichester, 1989, p. 441-460

Espejo, R. and others, (Transformation and Learning): Organizational Transformation and Learning, A Cybernetic Approach to Management, Chichester, New York, Brisbane, Toronto, Singapore, 1996

Espejo, R. and Schwaninger, M., (Organizational Fitness): Organizational Fitness – Corporate Effectiveness through Management Cybernetics, Campus, Frankfurt a.M., 1993

Förster, Heinz von (Zukunft der Wahrnehmung): Zukunft der Wahrnehmung: Wahrnehmung der Zukunft, in Schmidt, S. J.: Wissen und Gewissen, Suhrkamp, Frankfurt am Main, 1974, p. 194-210

Frank, W. A., (Authority): Authority as Nurse of Freedom and the Common Good, in: Faith and Reason, Volume 4, 1990, p. 371-386, http://www.ewtn.com/library/THEOLOGY/FR90404.htm

Frisch, M. (Bildnis): Du sollst Dir kein Bildnis machen, in Frisch, M.: Tagebuch 1946-1949, Suhrkamp, Frankfurt a.M., 1949

Fuller, R. W., (Somebodies and nobodies): Somebodies and nobodies – overcoming the abuse of rank, New Society Publishers, Gabriola Island, 2003

Gälweiler, Aloys, (Corporate Strategy): Strategische Unternehmensführung, Campus, Frankfurt / Main, 2005

Gassmann, O., (Fallstudienforschung): Praxisnähe mit Fallstudienforschung, in: Wissenschaftsmanagement, Volume 6, Issue 3, 1999

Gershenson, C., (Contextuality): Contextuality: A Philosophical Paradigm, with Applications to Philosophy of Cognitive Science, Cognitive Science ePrint Archive, 8/2/2004, http://cogprints.ecs.soton.ac.uk/archive/00002621/01/PhilCogSci2-Contextuality.pdf

Glasersfeld, E. v., (Wissen, Sprache, Wirklichkeit): Wissen, Sprache und Wirklichkeit – Arbeiten zum radikalen Konstruktivismus, Vieweg, Wiesbaden, 1987

Gomez, P. and Zimmermann, T., (Unternehmensorganisation): Unternehmensorganisation – Profile, Dynamik, Methodik, Campus, Frankfurt a.M., 1997

Gordon, J. E., (Structures): Structures or, Why things don't fall down, Plenum Press, New York, 1978

Görlitz, A. and Burth, H. P., (Political control): Politische Steuerung – Ein Studienbuch, Leske & Budrich, Opladen, 1998

Griffin, E., (Communication Theory): A first look at Communication Theory, McGraw-Hill, New York, 1997

Grüning, G., (Theoretical basis of NPM): Origin and theoretical basis of New Public Management, in: International Public Management Journal, Elsevier, Volume 4, 2001, p. 1-25

Habermas, J., (Communicative action One): Theorie des kommunikativen Handelns, Volume 1, Suhrkamp, Frankfurt a.M., 1981

Habermas, J., (Communicative action Two): Theorie des kommunikativen Handelns, Volume 2, Suhrkamp, Frankfurt a.M., 1981

Haken, H., (Synergetik): Synergetik, Springer-Verlag, Berlin, 1982

Haken, H. and Schiepek, G., (Synergetik in der Psychologie): Synergetik in der Psychologie: Selbstorganisation verstehen und gestalten, Hogrefe Verlag, Göttingen, 2006

Haldemann, T. (New Public Budgeting): New Public Budgeting, in Schmid, H. and Slembeck, T.: Finanz- und Wirtschaftspolitik in Theorie und Praxis, Berne, 1997, p. 117-146

Hamel, G. and Prahalad, C. K., (Competing): Competing for the Future, Harvard Business School Press, Boston, 1994

Harnden, R. (Outside and then): Outside and then: an interpretative approach to the VSM, in Espejo, R. and Harden, R.: The Viable Systems Model – Interpretations and Applications of Stafford Beer's VSM, John Wiley & Sons, Chichester, 1989

Hayek, F. A. v., (Theorie komplexer Phänomene): Die Theorie komplexer Phänomene, Mohr, Tübingen, 1972

Hayek, F. A. v., (Law, legislation and liberty): Recht, Gesetzgebung und Freiheit: eine neue Darstellung der liberalen Prinzipien der Gerechtigkeit und politischen Ökonomie, Moderne Industrie, 1986

Herold, C., (Vorgehenskonzept): Ein Vorgehenskonzept zur Unternehmensstrukturierung: eine heuristische Anwendung des Modells Lebensfähiger Systeme, St. Gallen, Hochsch. fuer Wirtschafts-, Rechts- u. Sozialwiss., 1991

Gesetz und Verordnungsblatt für das Land Hessen (GVBl. I), Gemeindehaushaltsverordnung (GemHVO), 13-7-1973

Gesetz und Verordnungsblatt für das Land Hessen (GVBl. I), Hessische Gemeindeordnung (HGO), 1-4-2005

Hessischer Sädte- und Gemeindebund, (HSGB Webpage): Internetpräsenz, 2007, http://www.hsgb.de/

Hessisches Ministerium für Umwelt, ländlichen Raum und Verbraucherschutz, (Agenda21 Hessen): Implementation of Local Agenda21 in Hesse, 1/28/2007, http://www.hmulv.hessen.de/

Heylighen, F., (Formal expression): Advantages and limitations of formal expression, in: Foundations of Science, Volume 4, Issue 1, 1999, p. 25-56

Hill, W., Fehlbaum, R., and Ulrich, P., (Organisationslehre 1): Organisationslehre 1, Ziele, Instrumente und Bedingungen der Organisation sozialer Systeme, Paul Haupt, Bern-Stuttgart, 1994

Hoebeke, L., (Identity): Identity: the paradoxical nature of Organizational Closure, in: Kybernetes, Emerald, Volume Volume 35, Issue Number 1/2, 2006, p. 65-75

Husserl, E., (Erfahrung und Urteil): Erfahrung und Urteil. Untersuchungen zur Genealogie der Logik., Hamburg, 1948

Huxley, A., (Doors of perception): The Doors of Perception, Harper & Row, New York, 1954

Jackson, M. C. (Managerial significance): Evaluating the managerial significance of the VSM, in Espejo, R. and Harnden, R.: The Viable Systems Model: Interpretations and Applications of Stafford Beer's VSM, John Wiley, Chichester, 1989, p. 407-439

Jank, W. and Meyer, H., (Didaktische Modelle): Didaktische Modelle, Cornelsen, Berlin, 1991

Jann, W. (Wandel verwaltungspolitischer Leitbilder): Der Wandel verwaltungspolitischer Leitbilder: vom Management zu Governance?, in König, K.: Deutsche Verwaltung an der Wende zum 21.Jahrhundert, Nomos, Baden-Baden, 2002, p. 279-304

Kiesel, B., (Wirkungsorientierte Steuerung): Wirkungsorientierte Steuerung einer Landesverwaltung, Deutscher Universitätsverlag, Wiesbaden, 2005

Kikert, W. (Complexity, governance, dynamics): Complexity, governance and dynamics, in Kooiman, J.: Modern Governance, Sage, London, 1993, p. 191-204

Klaus, G., (Wörterbuch Kybernetik): Wörterbuch der Kybernetik, Berlin, 1968

Klönne, A. (Concept and reality of Community): Zum Begriff und zur Realität von politischer Gemeinde, in Ellwein, T. and Zoll, R.: Gemeinde als Alibi: Materialien zur politischen Soziologie der Gemeinde, München, 1972, p. 249-255

Knechtenhofer, B.: Der Einbezug von Beteiligungen in den jährlichen Abschluss der Gemeinde. Haupt, Bern, Stuttgart, Wien, 2003

Kommunale Gemeinschaftsstelle für Verwaltungsvereinfachung (KGSt), (Verwaltungsorganisation): Verwaltungsorganisation der Gemeinden, 1979

Kommunale Gemeinschaftsstelle für Verwaltungsvereinfachung (KGSt), (Produkte): Das Neue Steuerungsmodell. Definition und Beschreibung von Produkten, 8 / 1994, Köln, 1994

Kommunale Gemeinschaftsstelle für Verwaltungsvereinfachung (KGSt), (Verwaltungscontrolling): Verwaltungscontrolling im Neuen Steuerungsmodell, 15, Köln, 1994

Kommunale Gemeinschaftsstelle für Verwaltungsvereinfachung (KGSt), (Kontraktmanagement): Kontraktmanagement: Steuerung über Zielvereinbarungen, 4, Köln, 1998

König, R., (Gemeinde): Grundformen der Gesellschaft: Die Gemeinde, Hamburg, 1958

Kooiman, J., (Modern Governance): Modern Governance, Sage, London, 1993

Kooiman, J., (Governing as Governance): Governing as Governance, Sage, London, Thousand Oaks, New Delhi, 2003

Kooiman, J. and van Vliet, M., (Self-Governance): Self-Governance as a mode of Societal-Governance, in: Public Management, Routledge, 2000, p. 360-377

Krause, Detlef, (Luhmann-Lexikon): Luhmann-Lexikon, UTB Lucius&Lucius, Stuttgart, 2001

Kreisstadt Bad Hersfeld, (Budget of Bad Hersfeld): Haushaltsplan 2003, Administration of Bad Hersfeld, 12/13/2002

Lange, Stefan and Braun, Dietmar, (System und Akteur): Politische Steuerung zwischen System und Akteur, Leske und Budrich, Opladen, 2000

Leonard, A., (Momentum and Control): Between Momentum and Control, First Metaphorum Colloquium on Governance and Cybernetics, Sunderland, 2004

Leonard, D. and Sensiper, S., (Role of tacit knowledge): The role of tacit knowledge in group innovation, in: California Management Review, Berkeley, Issue Spring (electronic), 1998

Löhner, M., (Führung neu denken): Führung neu denken – Das Drei-Stufen-Konzept für erfolgreiche Manager und Unternehmen, Campus, Frankfurt a.M., 2005

Luehrs, R., Malsch, Th., and Voss, K. (Internet, Discourses and Democracy): Internet, Discours and Democracy, in Terano, T.: New Frontiers in Artificial Intelligence. Joint JSAI 2001 Workshop Post-Proceedings., Springer-Verlag, Heidelberg, 2002, p. 67-74

Luhmann, N., (Social Systems): Soziale Systeme. Grundriss einer allgemeinen Theorie., Suhrkamp, Frankfurt a.M., 1984

Luhmann, N., (Politische Steuerung): Politische Steuerung: Ein Diskussionsbeitrag, in: Politische Vierteljahresschrift, Volume 30, Issue 1, 1989, p. 4-9

Luhmann, N., (Politics of society): Die Politik der Gesellschaft, Suhrkamp, Frankfurt a.M., 2002

Luhmann, N., (Interpenetrationen): Interpenetrationen – Zum Verhältnis personaler und sozialer Systeme, in: Zeitschrift für Soziologie und Sozialpsychologie, Volume 6, 1977, p. 62-76

Luhmann, N., (Gesellschaft): Die Gesellschaft der Gesellschaft, Suhrkamp, Frankfurt, 1997

Luhmann, N., (Politische Planung): Politische Planung, Westdeutscher Verlag, Opladen, 1971

Malik, F. (Knowledge Organisation): Understanding a Knowledge Organisation as a Viable System, in Espejo, R. and Schwaninger, M.: Organizational Fitness, Corporate Effectiveness through Management Cybernetics, Campus, Frankfurt a.M., 1993, p. 93-115

Malik, F., (Complex Systems): Strategie des Managements komplexer Systeme – Ein Beitrag zur Management-Kybernetik evolutionärer Systeme, Haupt, Bern, Stuttgart, Wien, 2002

Mastronardi, P.: Konzeptionelle Erkenntnisse zur politischen Steuerung mit WoV, in: Lienhard, Andreas u.a. (Hrsg.), 10 Jahre New Public Management in der Schweiz. Bilanz, Irrtümer und Erfolgsfaktoren. Haupt, Bern, Stuttgart, Wien, 2005, p. 113-120.

Maturana, H. (Autopoiesis and society): Autopoiesis, Communication and Society, in Benseler, F., Hejl, P. M., and Köck, W.: Autopoiesis, Communication and Society: The Theory of Autopoietic System in the Social Sciences, Campus, Frankfurt a.M., New York, 1980

Maturana, H., Erkennen: Die Organisation und Verkörperung von Wirklichkeiten – Ausgewählte Arbeiten zur biologischen Epistemologie, Braunschweig, 1982

Maturana, H. (Everything said): Everything said is said by an observer, in Thompson, W.: Gaia: A way of knowing, Lindisfarne Press, Hudson, NY, 1987, p. 62-82

Maturana, H. and Varela, F., (Autopoiesis and Cognition): Autopoiesis and Cognition – The Realization of Living, Reidel Publishing, Dordrecht, London, Boston, 1973

Maturana, H. and Varela, F., (Tree of knowledge): El arbol del conocimiento: Las bases biológicas del conocimiento humano, Editorial Debate, Santiago, 1985

Maturana, H. and Verden-Zöller, G., (Liebe und Spiel): Liebe und Spiel – Die vergessenen Grundlagen des Menschseins, Carl-Auer, Heidelberg, 2005

Mayntz, R., (Soziale Dynamik): Soziale Dynamik und Politische Steuerung, Campus, Frankfurt & New York, 1997

Mayntz, R. (Funktionale Teilsysteme): Funktionale Teilsysteme in der Theorie sozialer Differenzierung, in Rosewitz, Bernd, Schimank, Uwe, and Stichweh, Rudolf: Differenzierung und Verselbständigung – Zur Entwicklung gesellschaftlicher Teilsysteme, Campus, Frankfurt a.M.; New York, 1988, p. 11-44

Mayntz, R. and Edelmann, B., (Soziale Prozesse): Eigendynamische Soziale Prozesse, in: Kölner Zeitschrift für Soziologie und Sozialpsychologie, Volume 39, Issue 4, 1987, p. 648-668

Mayntz, R. and Scharpf, F., (Gesellschaftliche Selbstregelung): Gesellschaftliche Selbstregelung und Politische Steuerung, Campus, Frankfurt & New York, 1995

McCoulloch, W. (Logical calculus): A logical calculus of the ideas immanent in nervous activity: Embodiments of mind, MIT-Press, Cambridge, 1943

McCoulloch, W. (What is a number): What is a number that a man may know it, and a man that he may know a number?: Embodiments of Mind, MIT-Press, Cambridge, 1961, p. 19-39

Merriam-Webster's authors, (Merriam-Webster): Article on 'Rationality', Merriam Webster, 2005

Merriam-Webster's authors, (Britannica): Article on 'Reason', 2005

Merriam-Webster's authors (Britannica): Online version of Merriam-Webster's Collegiate Dictionary: Encyclopædia Britannica 2005 Ultimate Reference Suite DVD, Encyclopædia Britannica Inc., 2005

Merriam-Webster's authors, (Merriam-Webster): Articles on 'coherence' and 'cohesion', Merriam Webster, 2005

Merriam-Webster's authors, (Merriam-Webster): Article on 'Culture', Merriam Webster, 2005

Miller, G. A., (Magical number seven): The Magical Number Seven, Plus or Minus Two: Some Limits on our Capacity for Processing Information, in: Psychological Review, Harvard University, Volume 63, 1956, p. 81-97

Morgan, G., (Images of Organization): Images of Organization – The executive edition, Berret-Koehler; Sage, San Francisco, 1998

Morgenstern, O. and Neumann, J. v., (Theory of Games): The Theory of Games and Economic Behavior, Princeton University Press, 1953

Ösze, Daniel, Managementinformationen im New Public Management: am Beispiel der Steuerverwaltung des Kantons Bern, Haupt, Bern, 2000

Piaget, J., (Wirklichkeit beim Kinde): Der Aufbau der Wirklichkeit beim Kinde, Klett-Cotta, Stuttgart, 1936

Piaget, J., (Biologie und Erkenntnis): Biologie und Erkenntnis, Fischer, Frankfurt, 1967

Piaget, J., (Genetische Epistemologie): Abriss der genetischen Epistemologie, Klett-Cotta, Stuttgart, 1970

Pierre, Jon and Peters, B. Guy, (Governance, Politics and the State): Governance, Politics and the State, St. Martin Press, New York, 2000

Polanyi, M., (Tacit dimension): The tacit dimension, Anchor Books, Garden City, N.Y., 1967

Proeller, I.: Auslagerung in der hoheitlichen Verwaltung. Haupt, Bern, 2002

Pylsyshyn, Z. (Analogue media): The imagery debate: Analogue media versus tacit knowledge, in Collins, A. and Smith, E.: Readings in Cognitive Science: A perspective from Psychology and Artificial Intelligence, San Mateo California, 1981, p. 600-661

Reif, K., (Haushaltsplan): Der Haushaltsplan – kein Buch mit sieben Siegeln. Die kommunalen Haushaltsgrundsätze, in: Die Gemeinde (BWGZ), Volume 16 / 2004, 2004, p. 600-629

Reinermann, H. and Lucke, J., (eGovernance): Speyerer Definition von eGovernance, Speyer, 2001, http://foev.dhv-speyer.de/ruvii/SP-EGvce.pdf

Remer, A., (Unternehmenspolitische Steuerung): Instrumente unternehmenspolitischer Steuerung: Unternehmensverfassung, formale Organisation und personale Gestaltung, de Gruyter, Berlin, New York, 1982

Rusch, G. (Kommunikation und Verstehen): Kommunikation und Verstehen, in Merten, K., Schmidt, S. J., and Weischenberg, S.: Die Wirklichkeit der Medien, Westdeutscher Verlag, 1994

Russell, B (Principles of Mathematics): The Contradiction: Principles of Mathematics, Cambridge University Press, Cambridge, 1903, p. 523-528, http://www. philoscience.unibe.ch/tools/digipdf/lehre/grundlagen/bertrand_russell.1992.pdf

Russell, B and Whitehead, A. N. (Theory of Logical Types): The Theory of Logical Types, in Russell, B and Whitehead, A. N.: Principia Mathematica, Cambridge University Press, Cambridge, 1927, p. 37-65, http://www.philoscience.unibe. ch/lehre/sommer03/typentheorie.pdf

Schaff, A. (Unscharfe Ausdrücke): Unscharfe Ausdrücke und die Grenzen ihrer Präzisierung, in Grassi, E.: Sprache und Erkenntnis und Essays über die Philosophie der Sprache, Rowohlt, Reinbeck, Hamburg, 1974

Scharpf, F., (Politische Steuerung und Institutionen): Politische Steuerung und politische Institutionen, in: Politische Vierteljahresschrift, Volume 30, Issue 1, 1989, p. 10-21

Schedler, K., (Performance Budget): Performance Budgeting in Switzerland – Implications for political control, 2/9/2007, http://www.inpuma.net/research/papers/sydney/kuno.html

Schedler, K.,: "... and politics?" Public Management Developments in the Light of two Rationalities, in: Public Management Review, 5(4), 2003, p. 533-550.

Schedler, K. and Proeller, I., (New Public Management): New Public Management, Haupt, Bern, 2000

Scherer, K. R. (Kommunikation): Kommunikation, in Scherer, K. R. and Wallbott, H. G.: Nonverbale Kommunikation: Forschungsberichte zum Interaktionsverhalten, Beltz, Weinheim; Basel, 1984, p. 14-24

Scherer, R. / Grabherr, D. / Walser, M.,: Selbstorganisation für eine nachhaltige Regionalentwicklung. Oder: Wohin steuert das Schiff – und wer steuert den Steuermann? Institut für öffentliche Dienstleistungen und Tourismus, St. Gallen, 2001

Scherer, R. / Schnell, K.-D.: Die Stärke schwacher Netze. Entwick-lung und aktuelle Situation der grenzübergreifenden Zusammenarbeit in der Region Bodensee, in: (Hrsg.), Jahrbuch für Föderalismus. Nomos, Baden-Baden, 2002

Schmidt, S. J. (Kopplung von Kommunikation und Kognition): Medien: Die Kopplung von Kommunikation und Kognition, in Krämer, S.: Medien, Computer, Realität: Wirklichkeitsvorstellungen in neuen Medien, Suhrkamp, Frankfurt a.M., 1998, p. 55-72

Schmidt, S. J. (18.Kamel): Medien, Kommunikation und das 18. Kamel, in Merten, K., Schmidt, S. J., and Weischenberg, S.: Funkkolleg Medien Kommunikation. Konstruktion von Wirklichkeit – Einführungsbrief, Deutsches Institut für Fernstudien an der Universität Tübingen, Winheim; Basel, 1990, p. 33-38

Schulz von Thun, F., (Miteinander Reden I): Miteinander Reden Band I, Rowohlt, 1981

Schwaninger, M., (Rückgekoppelte Exploration): Rückgekoppelte Exploration in der Forschung – Arbeitspapier 2.Fassung, IfB of St.Gallen, 1996

Schwaninger, M., (Conscious evolution): What can Cybernetics contribute to the conscious evolution of Organisations and Society?, in: Systems Research and Behavioural Science, John Wiley & Sons, Volume 21, Issue 5, 2003, p. 515-527

Schwaninger, M., (Managing complexity): Managing complexity: the path towards intelligent organizations., in: System Practise and Action Research, Plenum, New York, Volume 13, Issue 2, 2000, p. 207-241

Schwaninger, M., (Framework Intelligent Organisations): Intelligent Organizations: An Integrative Framework, in: Systems Research and Behavioural Science, John Wiley & Sons, Volume 18, Issue 2, 2001, p. 137-158

Schwaninger, M. (Intelligent Organizations): Intelligent Organizations – Powerful Models for Systemic Management, Springer, Heidelberg, 2006

Schwaninger, M., (Viable Systems Model): Das Modell Lebensfähiger Systeme – Ein Strukturmodell für organisationale Intelligenz, Lebensfähigkeit und Entwicklung, in: Diskussionsbeitrag des Instituts für Betriebswirtschaftslehre, IfB St.Gallen, Volume 20, 2000, http://www.ifb.unisg.ch/org/IfB/ifbweb.nsf/www-PubInhalteEng/IfB+Discussion+Papers

Schwaninger, M., (Corporate planning): Integrale Unternehmensplanung, Campus, Frankfurt a.M., New York, 1989

Schwaninger, M., (Structures): Structures for Intelligent Organizations, in: Diskussionsbeitrag des Instituts für Betriebswirtschaftslehre, IfB St.Gallen, Volume 20, 1996, http://www.ifb.unisg.ch/org/ifb/ifbweb.nsf/wwwPubInhalteGer/IfB+Diskussionsbeitraege?opendocument

Schwarting, G., (Effizienz Kommunalverwaltung): Effizienz in der Kommunalverwaltung, Teil I: Dezentrale VeranTwortung und Finanzsteuerung durch Budgetierung, Erich Schmidt Verlag, Berlin, 2004

Searle, J., (Intentionality): Intentionality: An Essay in the Philosophy of Mind., Cambridge University Press, New York, 1983

Spencer-Brown, G., (Laws of Form): Laws of Form, Allen and Unwin, London, 1969

Stake, R. E., (Art of Case Study): The Art of Case Study Research, Sage Publications, Thousand Oaks, 1995

Gesetz- und Verordnungsblatt für das Land Hessen (GVBl I), GemHVO on the Administrative and Capital Budget, no. 20, 13-7-1973

Gesetz- und Verordnungsblatt für das Land Hessen (GVBl I), Sample specifying Sec. 4 para 3 GemHVO General plan, no. 20, 13-7-1973

State of Nordrhein-Westfalen and Bertelsmann Stiftung, ((Kommunaler Bürgerhaushalt)): Citizen involvement in budget reconciliation, Ministery of interior, Nordrhein-Westfalen, 2007, http://www.buergerhaushalt.nrw.de/

Steiner, Reto, (NPM Swiss Municipalities): New Public Management in Swiss Municipalities, in: International Public Management Journal, Elsevier Science, Volume 3, 2000, p. 169-189

Susskind, L., McKearnan, S., and Thomas-Larmer, J., (Consensus Building): The Consensus Building Handbook, Sage, 1999

Türke, R. E., (Productive and sustainable forms of Governance): Towards productive and sustainable forms of interaction in Governance, in: Kybernetes, Emerald, Volume Volume 35, Issue Number 1/2, 2006, p. 164-181

Türke, R. E. (Building blocks): eGovernance. Building blocks for theory., in Suk-Kim, P. and Jho, W.: Building e-Governance: Challenges and Opportunities for Democracy, Administration and Law, International Institute for Administrative Science (IIAS/ IISA), Belgium; National Computerization Agency, Korea, Seoul, 2005

Türke, R. E., (Metaphorum): eGovernance – an integrated framework to promote Governance, in: Metaphorum Colloquium, University of Sunderland, April 30th and May 1st, United Kingdom, Volume Application of Cybernetics in Government, 2005

Türke, R. E. (Aspekte): eGovernance – Aspekte zur Steuerung sozialer Systeme, in Kahle, E. and Wilms, F. E. P.: Effektivität und Effizienz durch Netzwerke, Duncker & Humblot, Berlin, 2005

Türke, R. E., (Good Governance): Can eGovernance help to promote Good Governance?, in: hfp research publications, hfp Governance Consultants, Kelkheim, 2001

Türke, R. E., (Lisbon Conference): Research proposal on eGovernance, in: European Group for Public Administration Conference, Lisbon, Portugal 3-6 September, Volume Public Law and the Modernising State, Issue Research Workshop 2: Governance: What Do We Know?, 2003

Ulrich, G., (Staatliche Intervention): Politische Steuerung – Staatliche Intervention aus systemtheoretischer Sicht, Leske & Budrich, Opladen, 1994

Ulrich, H., (Unternehmung als produktives soziales System): Die Unternehmung als produktives soziales System, Paul Haupt, Bern; Stuttgart, 1970

Ulrich, H., (BWL als Sozialwissenschaft): Die Betriebswirtschaftslehre als anwendungsorientierte Sozialwissenschaft, 5, Haupt, Bern, Stuttgart, Wien, 2001

Ulrich, W., (Critique): A critique of pure cybernetic reason: The Chilean experience with cybernetics, in: Journal of Applied System Analysis, Volume 8, 1981, p. 33-59

Ulrich, W., (Critcal systems heuristics): Critical Heuristics of Social Planning: A New Approach to Practical Philosophy, Paul Haupt, Bern, 1983

Ulrich, W., (Reflective Practice): Reflective Practise in the Civil Society, in: Reflective Practice, Carfax Publishing / Taylor & Francis Ltd., Volume Volume 1, Issue Issue 2, 2000, p. 247-268

Ulrich, W., (Critical heuristics social systems): Critical heuristics of social systems design, in: European Journal of Operational Research, Elsevier Science, North-Holland, Volume 31, 1987, p. 276-283

Ulrich, W., (Quest for Competence): The Quest for Competence in Systemic Research and Practise, in: Systems Research and Behavioural Science, John Wiley, Volume 18, 2001, p. 3-28

UN Department of Economic and Social Affairs, (Agenda21): Agenda21 process, 1/28/2007, http://www.un.org/esa/sustdev/documents/agenda21/english/agenda-21toc.htm

Varela, F. (Self-Organisation): Two principles of Self-Organisation, in Ulrich, H. and Probst, G. J. B.: Self-Organisation and the Management of Social Systems, Springer, Berlin, 1984, p. 25-32

Vester, Frederic, (Kunst vernetzt zu denken): Die Kunst vernetzt zu denken – Ideen und Werkzeuge für einen neuen Umgang mit Komplexität, DVA, Stuttgart, 1999

Vickers, G, (Judgement): The Art of Judgement, Chapman and Hall, London, 1965

Waelchli, F. (VSM and Ashby's Law): The VSM and Ashby's Law as illuminants of historical management thought, in Espejo, R. and Harnden, R.: The Viable System Model: Interpretations and Applications of Stafford Beer's VSM, John Wiley, Chichester, 1989, p. 51-75

Watzlawick, P., Beavin, J. H., and Jackson, D. D., (Pragmatics of Human Communication): Pragmatics of Human Communication. A Study of Interactional Patterns, Pathologies, and Paradoxes <German>, Norton, New York, 1967

Watzlawick, P., Weakland, J. H., and Fisch, R., (Changing a system.): Changing a system. Change, Norton, New York, 1974

Wikipedia contributors, (Protocol): Definition of protocol, 2004, http://en.wikipedia.org/wiki/Protocol

Wikipedia contributors, (SWOT analysis): SWOT analysis, 2/1/2007, http://en.wikipedia.org/w/index.php?title=SWOT_analysis&oldid=104779048

Willemsen, Maarten Helmut, (Is Switzerland viable?): Die Schweizerische Eidgenossenschaft als lebensfähiges System, Universität St.Gallen, 1992

Willke, H., (Entzauberung): Entzauberung des Staates – Überlegungen zu einer gesellschaftlichen Steuerungstheorie, Athenäum, Königstein / Ts., 1983

Willke, H., (Ironie): Ironie des Staates, Suhrkamp, Frankfurt, 1992

Willke, H., (Steuerungstheorie): Systemtheorie III: Steuerungstheorie, Lucius&Lucius, Stuttgart, 2001

Willke, H., (Systems theory One): Systemtheorie I: Grundlagen, UTB Luci-us&Lucius, Stuttgart, 2000

Winograd, T. and Flores, F., (Understanding computers): Understanding computers and cognition: a new foundation for design, Addison-Wesley, Reading, Massachusetts, 1987

Winter, C., (Kontraktmanagement): Das Kontraktmanagement, Nomos, Baden-Baden, 1998

Wittgenstein, L., (Tractatus): Tractatus Logico-Philosophicus Philosophische Untersuchungen, 1, Suhrkamp, Frankfurt / M., 1988

World Bank: Sub-Saharan Africa: From Crisis to Sustainable Growth. World Bank, Washington DC, 1989

World Bank: Philippines Pilot E-Procurement System Retrieved 19.12.2003, verfügbar unter: http://www1.worldbank.org/publicsector/egov/philippines_eproc.htm

Yin, R., (Case study research): Case study research: Design and methods, CA: Sage, Thousand Oaks, 1989

Yolles, M., (VST and Logical Levels): Viable Systems Theory, Anticipation and Logical Levels of Management, London School of Economics, London, 9 / 2003, http://www.psych.lse.ac.uk/complexity/Conference/MauriceYollesPaper.pdf

Yolles, M., (Management Systems): Management Systems – a viable approach, Financial Times Management, London, 1999

Zack, M.H., (Codiefied knowledge): Managing codified knowledge, in: Sloan Management Review, Volume 40, Issue 4, 1999, p. 45-58

Zimmermann, C., Ehrensperger, M., Weber, K.: Erfahrungen und Praxisbeispiele, in: Bolz, Urs (Hrsg.), Public Private Partnership in der Schweiz. Grundlagenstudie – Ergebnis einer gemeinsamen Initiative von Wirtschaft und Verwaltung. Schulthess, Zürich, 2005, p. 297-385.

Summary

This research was inspired by the question of how sustainable development can be ensured for social systems. It attended the following questions in an explorative mode:

1. How can governance be captured in a holistic, integrated, and context-independent framework?

2. What system structures are required to establish a governance of social systems that is viable in terms of self-organisation, self-learning, and self-adaptation?

3. How can established system structures be designed to promote viability? Consequently, what can eMedia contribute to promote governance (eGovernance)?

Media theory inspired the conceptual underpinnings for the integrative perspective taken. Stafford Beers' managerial cybernetics and in particular his Viable System Model provided the theory of viability and sustainability. Further, this research was influenced by various other system theories and motivated by the works of experts in the fields of Political Science, Governance, and New Public Management.

To allow for an integrative conceptualisation of governance, a foundation was formulated indicating the *Weltanschauung* adopted and defining the primary concepts for integrative theory building. As a constitutive element, an interactional perspective on governance was taken based on autopoietic actors. Looking at how actors evolve their common contexts through continuous interaction, the constitutive elements of interaction have been recognised. Throughout the research process a logically invariant anatomy of system notions was revealed and designed to reflect the necessary and sufficient criteria for the *viability* and *sustainability* of social systems. It showed that the established interactions have to be rooted in the aspired purposes of the system notion. Therefore, underlying structures are required to continuously promote the reconciliation of characteristic invariant systemic topics. To make this assessable to empirical reflection, the developed framework formalised a meta-language that phrased the aspired system invariances from an interactional, second order perspective and allowed for a solid integration of the theories applied.

In parallel to the process of theory building, the applicability and significance of the framework was assessed in a practical case study. It was shown, how the framework can be applied for diagnosing the governing structures of Hessian communities and further, how these can be supported through eMedia supplementing the design of system structures and dissolving prevailing structural deficiencies. Based on the experiences made during the research process, major theoretical and practical implications were identified. On the theoretical side, taking an integrative perspective on governance based on first, logical principles was identified as key for building theory around the topic of governance and dissolving the major contradictions prevailing in contemporary approaches to governance. Here, the framework prepares the ground for further interdisciplinary theory building, some directions of which have been indicated. On the practical side, the applicability of the framework has been shown and the benefits identified. Now, the implementation of viable and sustainable governing structures is primarily a question of gaining practical experience and political support.

About the Author

Whether as consultant, trainer, or researcher, Ralf-Eckhard Türke supports social organizations in achieving their goals and implementing their purposes. His specific competence goes beyond conventional problem solving and lies in capacitating organizations to concentrate forces for a lasting, sustainable development. In addition to his expertise in professional fields he acquired substantial trans-disciplinary skills through the translation of innovative social theories into practical applications which has been supported by a multiplicity of international projects in private, public, and development aid contexts.

Graduated with a joint Masters Degree in Business Administration and Mechanical Engineering from the Technical University of Darmstadt, Germany, he ran through the doctoral program in International Business of the University of St.Gallen, Switzerland. The result of his research, i.e. a generic framework for the governance of social systems, is documented in this opus. Since 2008 the research on generic governance has been further advanced within the University of St. Gallen.

Besides these efforts, the author worked for organizations all over the world. In Buenos Aires, Argentina he supported the German-Argentinean Chamber of Commerce in conducting market and economic analyses for German investors (International Relations, Economic Development). In San Sebastián, Spain he prepared the re-location of an industrial plant proposing production and cost optimizations for a commodity supplier in the building industry (Business Re-engineering, Process cost analysis). At Havant, United Kingdom he led a process re-engineering project for the spare-parts management in a newly acquired plant of a leading consumer goods company (Supply Chain Management).

Over five years he supported a start-up consultancy firm at Kelkheim, Germany as a consultant and systems engineer for public and private organizations. Projects for various German state and city governments were carried out and public sector audits were conducted (Public Governance and Management, Public Finance, Performance Measurement, Management support systems).

Since 2005 he has been working for an internationally renown management centre in St.Gallen, Switzerland as a consultant and educator carrying out projects in private and public contexts including development aid (General Management, Organizational transformation and change, Strategy, Change Management, Public Institution Building).

Acknowledgements

There are many individuals who have significantly contributed to the completion of this research. I am forever indebted to Professor Stafford Beer, who profoundly influenced this work and the development of my own rigourous thinking. Regrettably, I have not been able to meet him personally; nevertheless, his profound thinking and character are only too vivid in his books and live on in his passionate followers all over the world. His ideas have had a profound and lasting influence on my thinking.

I am especially grateful to the mentors of this project, Professors Markus Schwaninger (chair) and Kuno Schedler (co-chair). Each of them brought a different intellectual viewpoint with his work and challenged my thinking throughout the research process. I particularly benefited from the exceptional openness of both towards my ideas and conceptual approach. With his teachings, Markus Schwaninger inspired the set-up of this research at its very origin. It was one of his writings I casually came across at the University of Mayence library which made a difference to everything else I had read before in my research on governance. I was fascinated, therefore contacted him to present my research ideas and was accepted. Throughout the research activity which followed, Markus Schwaninger pushed my interdisciplinary thinking and was constructively critical of my work, while always conveying his support. Kuno Schedler was the ideal co-chair for me. His work provided invaluable guidance both in my research and in my projects with public sector organisations. His insight into the public sector and deep understanding of its mechanisms and people instilled in me a continuing fascination with it. It was a breakthrough experience for me when he confirmed his support for my primary conceptual ideas after my presentation at the 2003 Lisbon conference of the European Group of Public Administration. Thanks to him I was able to follow my very specific and unconventional ideas and approach to conceptualising governance.

My deep gratitutde goes to Luc Hoebeke from Belgium, who is clearly one of the rare personifications of cybernetics. After we met in Sunderland in 2003, he accompanied this work and my own development as a researcher. I highly appreciate the tremendous amount of time and effort he dedicated to my study – he did not shy away from investing entire days and long travel times just to meet me midway between his home and mine. Lucs' presence, intellect, and scholarship have been and still are a constant source of inspiration.

Thomas Hauser and Kristian Furch played major roles in my formation as a researcher and consultant. Their great passion, enthusiasm, and mission to "change the world" combined with their strong impetus to truly implement their innovative ideas are highly contagious: I have definitely been infected. I have had the good fortune and privilege to be allowed to follow their path over several years. The experiences I gained in that time working with public organisations on state and community layers have been fundamental to this research.

Thanks to Professors Werner Ulrich and Peter Checkland, who chaired the Lugano Summer School of Systems Design in 2004 and gave me an intense introduction into the captivating facets of Soft Systems Methodology and Critical Systems Heuristics. Their rich bodies of thinking are still an invaluable source of reflection for me. The controversial discussions on soft and hard systems thinking have definitely fed my enthusiasm to look for a truly integrated path in my thinking.

Also, I would like to express my sincere thanks to Professor Fredmund Malik, who gave me the opportunity to continue my work in consulting and training applying and further advancing it in interesting projects. In the same line, thanks go to all my colleages at the Malik Management Centre St.Gallen who accompanied me there, especially to Frank Arnold, Nicole Bentivoglio, Kai Berendes, Felix Brunner, Philipp Christ, Heiko Eckert, Attila Färber, Klaus Galler, Christiane Gebhard, Gabriele Harrer, Ronald Herse, Max Hofer, Brigitte Kammerlander, Sebastian Marshall, Fabienne Mettler, Filippos Michalas, Marion Münnix, Jolanda Odiet, Karl-Heinz Oeller, Martin Pfiffner, Kai von Rappard, Martin Sammer, Anna Spitzmüller, Roger Sonderegger, Jörg Sauer, Maria Sourla, Peter Stadelmann, Peter Ungeheuer.

I would like to thank my friends and cybernetic colleagues from the Metaphorum group. Prof. Alfredo Moscardini and Annemaria Moscardini, who gave me such a warm welcome at their home in Sunderland, UK. Prof. Moscardini inspired me with some highly valuable links to the work of David Bohm, which stills feeds my thoughts. Roger Harnden from the

UK, who particularly inspired me with his writings at a very early stage in my research activity and gave his valuable comments at the Metaphorum conference in St.Gallen, Switzerland. John Clarke from Johannesburg, South Africa, whom I came to know at the Sunderland Metaphorum and met again at his home in Johannesburg. He gave me inspiring insights into his application of cybernetics in development work and in the fight against HIV-Aids in southern Africa. His passion for cybernetics is unmatched.

My deep gratitude goes to Almut Krechel, who spent a tremendous amount of time performing not only a language check of my research but a genuinely in-depth assessment of my logic and ideas – never superficial, always highly critical down to the last detail of each issue. For me she has become a dear soul mate with whom I hope to continue a lasting friendship of sharing our most recent inspirations and concerns. Many thanks also go to Almut's friend Dorothea Bartsch for so thoroughly proofreading my manuscript at the very last moment when time was of the essence.

Thanks to my dear friend Melanie Müller for being such an understanding flatmate during my time in Wiesbaden. Her presence gave me strength when I was digging in the depths of my research. Thanks also to Ilja Brezovac for his company and all the inspiring struggles we fought. You may have won the race for the PhD but I definitely won the one for the Nutella jar. And not to forget Ulf Lauer who introduced me to Melanie and with whom I share so many passions on Spain, Latin America and everything involved.

Thanks also to Kristian Landegren for accompanying me through some of the toughest month at the University of Mainz and particularly for taking me to Interlaken and showing me some essential steps beyond cybernetics. I know there are still some moves to be made. Further, thanks to Guido Fickenscher for being a brother in suffering at the University of Mainz, making my time most entertaining. I know you have been deep in the mud; I am so glad that you are on the mountaintop now. Thanks go also to Christoph Dengler for giving me a taste of how life can be composed beautifully into a rich mosaic of mutually re-inforcing poems, paintings, and melodies. Your approach is excellent for getting the most out of everything.

A big hug to Cristina-Ioana Crisan Tran, who was my closest research colleague at the chair of Professor Schwaninger also actively involved with Stafford Beers' work. Thanks so much for the good times in St.Gallen and at the conference in Maribor, Slowenia. And thanks of course for introducing me to Lena. How lucky I am for knowing Lena Martschenko. Together, we were able to find the most convenient and luxurious flat ever possible in

Zürich. It has provided such a great pleasure and comfort to us and continues to do so. Thanks so much, Lena, for your presence in the last years, you have made a time of great change and effort so much easier for me.

I would also like to thank all my dear friends who allowed me to be distracted from writing and who gave their support throughout this time. The following list is not meant to give the slightest indication of a hierarchy and it is certainly not complete: Hugs and kisses go to Ulrika Hinkel, who accompanied me for much of the way and gave me strength and confidence. You are in my heart; I will never forget you! Further, I have to mention Frank Pawlitschek, who has been one of my closest friends since schooltime. Although we have not spent nearly enough time together the last years, the depth of our friendship has given me strength ever since we met. Thank you so much for everything! In the same vein, special mention also goes to my dear friend Ilona Mücke, who probably knows me better than anybody, as we have shared so many life experiences. Special thanks go to Heike Gastl, who has been a dear friend since my schooldays and a companion throughout my research. Further to Mathias Baier, with whom I share some essential passions: music, cigars and nature. And last but not least to Jörg Bartels who has been a close mate in good times and in bad eversince Kindergarten.

There are no adequate words to express the gratitude that I owe to my family. My parents, Hildburg and Erhard Türke, to whom I dedicate this work, have always encouraged me to pursue my dreams. Their unconditional trust and support in every conceivable way have provided me with the strength to accomplish this task. My dear aunt Mechthild Schiersch always supported that strategy and saw me through the entire process. Repeatedly, she comforted me with exceptional all-inclusive escapes at her true paradise at the Zwischenahner Meer. Throughout that time, her daughters Claudia and Angelika Schiersch were my close companions and have become like sisters to me.

Zürich, June 2008   Ralf-Eckhard Türke
                                                    mail@ralf-eckhard.com

Printing: Krips bv, Meppel, The Netherlands
Binding: Stürtz, Würzburg, Germany